Luminos is the open access monograph publishing program from UC Press. Luminos provides a framework for preserving and reinvigorating monograph publishing for the future and increases the reach and visibility of important scholarly work. Titles published in the UC Press Luminos model are published with the same high standards for selection, peer review, production, and marketing as those in our traditional program. www.luminosoa.org

The publisher gratefully acknowledges the generous support of
the Philip E. Lilienthal Asian Studies Endowment Fund of the
University of California Press Foundation, which was established
by a major gift from Sally Lilienthal.

Hindu Pluralism

Democracy against Development: Lower Caste Politics and Political Modernity in Postcolonial India, by Jeffrey Witsoe (Chicago)

Into the Twilight of Sanskrit Poetry: The Sena Salon of Bengal and Beyond, by Jesse Ross Knutson (UC Press)

Voicing Subjects: Public Intimacy and Mediation in Kathmandu, by Laura Kunreuther (UC Press)

Writing Resistance: The Rhetorical Imagination of Hindi Dalit Literature, by Laura R. Brueck (Columbia)

Wombs in Labor: Transnational Commercial Surrogacy in India, by Amrita Pande (Columbia)

I Too Have Some Dreams: N. M. Rashed and Modernism in Urdu Poetry, by A. Sean Pue (UC Press)

The Place of Devotion: Siting and Experiencing Divinity in Bengal-Vaishnavism, by Sukanya Sarbadhikary (UC Press)

We Were Adivasis: Aspiration in an Indian Scheduled Tribe, by Megan Moodie (Chicago)

Writing Self, Writing Empire: Chandar Bhan Brahman and the Cultural World of the Indo-Persian State Secretary, by Rajeev Kinra (UC Press)

Landscapes of Accumulation: Real Estate and the Neoliberal Imagination in Contemporary India, by Llerena Searle (Chicago)

Polemics and Patronage in the City of Victory: Vyasatirtha, Hindu Sectarianism, and the Sixteenth-Century Vijayanagara Court, by Valerie Stoker (UC Press)

Hindu Pluralism: Religion and the Public Sphere in Early Modern South India, by Elaine M. Fisher (UC Press)

Hindu Pluralism

*Religion and the Public Sphere in
Early Modern South India*

Elaine M. Fisher

UNIVERSITY OF CALIFORNIA PRESS

University of California Press, one of the most distinguished university presses in the United States, enriches lives around the world by advancing scholarship in the humanities, social sciences, and natural sciences. Its activities are supported by the UC Press Foundation and by philanthropic contributions from individuals and institutions. For more information, visit www.ucpress.edu.

University of California Press
Oakland, California

Suggested citation: Fisher, Elaine. *Hindu Pluralism: Religion and the Public Sphere in Early Modern South India*. Oakland: University of California Press, 2017. doi: https://doi.org/10.1525/luminos.24

Library of Congress Cataloging-in-Publication Data

Names: Fisher, Elaine M., 1984- author.
    Title: Hindu pluralism : religion and the public sphere in early modern South
    India / Elaine M. Fisher.
Other titles: South Asia across the disciplines.
Description: Oakland, California : University of California Press, [2017] |
    Series: South Asia across the disciplines | Includes bibliographical
    references and index.
Identifiers: LCCN 2016046548 (print) | LCCN 2016048637 (ebook) | ISBN
    9780520293014 (pbk. : alk. paper) | ISBN 9780520966291 (e-edition)
Subjects: LCSH: Hinduism—India, South. | Religious pluralism—India, South.
    | India, South--Religion.
Classification: LCC BL1153.7.S68 F57 2017 (print) | LCC BL1153.7.S68 (ebook)
    | DDC 294.50954/8--dc23
LC record available at https://lccn.loc.gov/2016046548

CONTENTS

Acknowledgments ix

Introduction 1

1. Hindu Sectarianism: Difference in Unity 31

2. "Just Like Kālidāsa": The Making of the Smārta-Śaiva Community of South India 57

3. Public Philology: Constructing Sectarian Identities in Early Modern South India 99

4. The Language Games of Śiva: Mapping Text and Space in Public Religious Culture 137

Conclusion: A Prehistory of Hindu Pluralism 183

Appendix 195
Notes 203
Bibliography 251
Index 269

ACKNOWLEDGMENTS

As was common wisdom in the classical genres of Sanskrit textuality, a book simply cannot be undertaken without a preliminary homage of reverence to the sources of inspiration to whom we owe our existence as scholars and human beings. Words cannot do justice to my gratitude for the unwavering support and the depth of enthusiasm I have encountered from advisors, colleagues, and companions alike. The first iteration of this book originated as a doctoral dissertation at Columbia University written under the mentorship of Sheldon Pollock, who first opened my eyes to the potential of philology to envision possible pasts both inside and outside of the text. What this book has become today would have been inconceivable without his unwavering confidence both in the project itself and in the intellectual freedom to take risks on new archives and archaeologies. My gratitude goes out to the members of my dissertation committee, Jack Hawley, Sudipta Kaviraj, Rachel McDermott, and Indira Peterson, for their generous feedback and encouragement on every draft at each step of the journey. I owe my introduction to the textual canons of Śaivism and the world of digital philology to the generous mentorship of Somadeva Vasudeva during his time at Columbia.

The majority of the revisions to the manuscript were completed with the support of a Mellon Postdoctoral Fellowship at the University of Wisconsin-Madison from 2014 to 2016. Susan Friedman, director of the Institute for Research in the Humanities, deserves particular commendation for the remarkable collaborative community she fosters among fellows from diverse disciplinary backgrounds. My sincere thanks to Jessica Courtier, Megan Massino, and Sarah Guyer, and to my colleagues in the Mellon Fellowship program across three cohorts, Darien Lamen,

Daegan Miller, Amanda Rogers, Jolyon Thomas, Darryl Wilkinson, Anthony Fontes, Anja Jovic-Humphrey, Patrick William Kelley, and Golnar Nikpour, for their thoughtful consideration of countless drafts during our Mellon seminar meetings. I am grateful for the mentorship of Joseph Elder and, in particular, André Wink, who generously subjected himself to a review of the entire manuscript, and to the collegial feedback of faculty across disciplines at UW-Madison, including Florence Bernault, Jill Casid, Preeti Chopra, Bill Cronon, Bob Frykenberg, Viren Murthy, Ronald Radano, Mary Lou Roberts, Ellen Sapega, Sissel Schroeder, Mitra Sharafi, Sarah Thal, Luke Whitmore, and many others too numerous to count. I thank the faculty of the Center for Early Modern Studies and the Center for South Asia, particularly Lalita du Perron, for allowing me to share my research with the UW community. I would like to express my heartfelt appreciation to Laurie Patton, who took the time to travel to Madison to lead a seminar discussion of chapter 3, fostering an intellectually stimulating conversation on the conceptual issues underlying this work. My revisions were further facilitated by the thoughtful advice of Srilata Raman and by feedback I received at the American Institute of Indian Studies Dissertation-to-Book Workshop in 2014 from the directors, Brian Hatcher and Dan Gold, and the community of workshop participants.

The archival research and fieldwork that fueled this monograph were conducted in Pondicherry from 2010 to 2011 with the support of a Fulbright-Hays Doctoral Dissertation Abroad Fellowship. While in residence in Pondicherry, I was welcomed wholeheartedly by the faculty of the École française d'Extrême-Orient and the Institut français de Pondichéry owing to the generous institutional support of Dominic Goodall, Valérie Gillet, and Prerana Patel. Life in Pondicherry was abundant with opportunities to cultivate a multilingual research project, and I offer my sincere gratitude to the scholars in Pondicherry and beyond who shared their multilingual philological expertise, facilitating reconstruction of the discourses of early modern Sanskrit, Tamil, and Telugu, and for allowing me to secure my footing in the field of south Indian paleography, including Diwakar Acharya, H. N. Bhatt, Jean-Luc Chevillard, T. Ganesan, Dominic Goodall, Harunaga Isaacson, V. S. Rajam, H. V. Nagaraja Rao, Anjaneya Sarma, Sathyanarayana Sarma, Samuel Sudanandha, Sthaneshwar Timalsina, E. Vijaya Venugopal, and Eva Wilden. My knowledge of early Śaivism profited greatly from my association with the team of scholars I encountered during my travels: Alex Watson, Csaba Deszo, Csaba Kiss, Ginni Ishimatsu, Yuko Yokochi, Arlo Griffiths, and many others.

Logistically, my research would have been impossible to complete but for the generous assistance of archivists at manuscript libraries across south India, particularly the staff of the GOML and Adyar Libraries in Chennai; Dr. Perumal at the Tanjavur Maharaja Serfoji's Sarasvati Mahal Library; Siniruddha Dash at the New Catalogus Catalogorum Project at the University of Madras and the entirety of the NCC Project staff; P. L. Shaji at the Oriental Research Institute in Kariavottom,

Kerala, who secured reproductions of the crucial *Saubhāgyacandrātapa* manuscript in their collection; M. V. Raghavendra Varma at the Archaeological Survey of India; and the faculty and staff of the Roja Muthiah Research Library, the Kuppuswami Sastri Research Institute and the K. V. Sharma Research Institute in Chennai, the Sanskrit College in Tripunitthura, the University of Calicut, the Sri Chandresekhara Saraswathi Viswa Mahavidyalaya in Kanchipuram, and the Rashtriya Sanskrit Library and the Venkateshwara University Oriental Research Institute in Tirupati. Special thanks to Bharathy Laksmanaperumal, who facilitated my 2011 stay in Madurai for the performance of the Sacred Games of Śiva, to Giridhara Sastrigalu, who welcomed me with unhesitating hospitality during my stay in Sringeri, and most notably to the descendants of Nīlakaṇṭha Dīkṣita, whose enthusiastic support allowed me to witness the 2011 *ārādhanā* celebration of the seventeenth-century poet-theologian in their ancestral *agrahāra* in Palamadai.

I am particularly grateful for the painstaking assistance of Eric Schmidt, Maeve Cornell-Taylor, Bonita Hurd, and all of the staff at the University of California Press for bringing this project to fruition, for the enthusiastic support of Robert Goldman and the editorial board of South Asia across the Disciplines and the feedback of my anonymous reviewers at UC Press and SAAD. I am likewise grateful for the meticulous labors of Jay Ramesh, who reviewed the Sanskrit and Tamil diacritics in the manuscript before production.

Over the years, I have benefited deeply from the collaborative engagement and companionship of many colleagues at every stage of this project, in ways impossible to enumerate. My gratitude goes out to Crispin Branfoot, Yigal Bronner, Leah Comeau, Anthony Grafton, Chris Haskett, Barbara Holdrege, Larry McCrea, Christopher Minkowski, Polly O'Hanlon, Luther Obrock, Leslie Orr, Alexis Sanderson, Anna Seastrand, Davesh Soneji, Hamsa Stainton, Eric Steinschneider, Valerie Stoker, Audrey Truschke, Anand Venkatkrishnan, David Gordon White, Annette Wilke, Michael Williams, and every other voice I have engaged with along the journey. I owe an exceptional debt of gratitude to Sthaneshwar Timalsina for moral support during the writing of this dissertation, and to my entire extended family, especially Peggy Schwartz for writing support; Jason Schwartz for countless hours of feedback and encouragement, not to mention the depth of his confidence in my vision for the project; and Amelia for humoring me with her tolerance and patience.

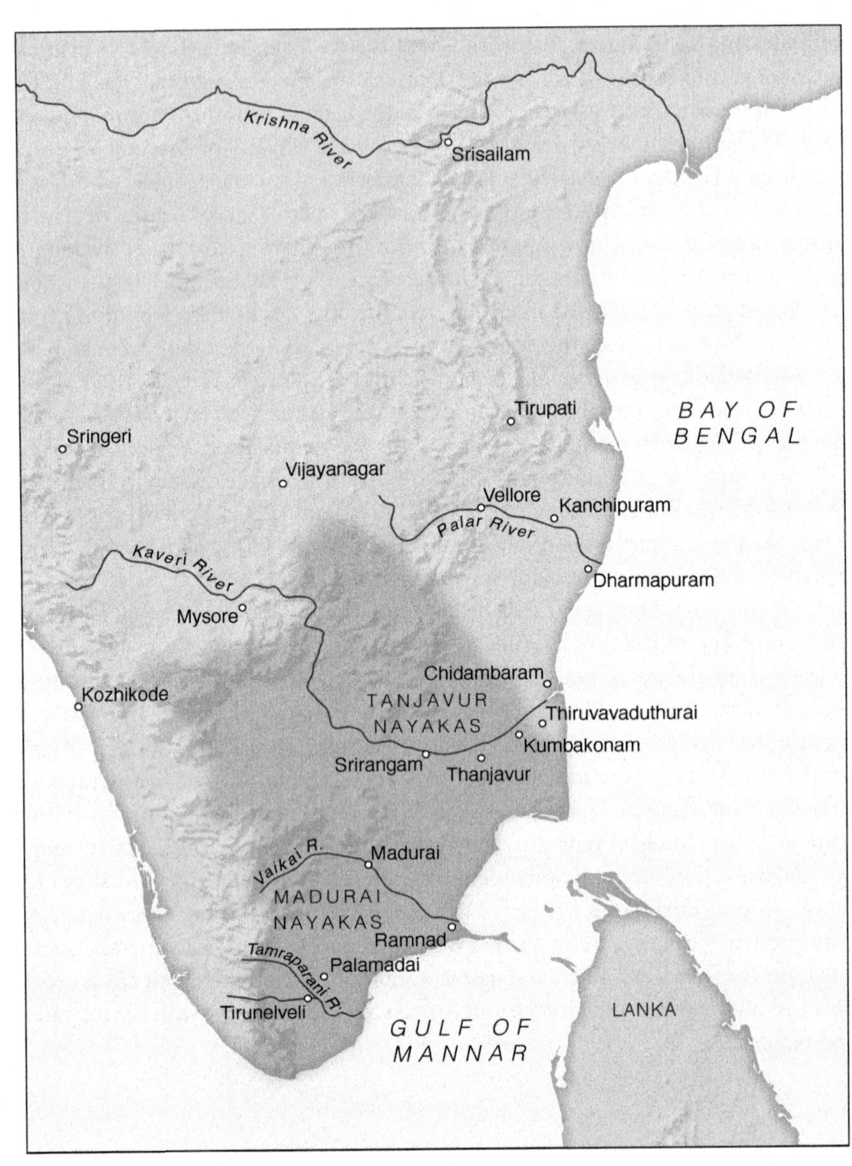

MAP 1. Map of South India: Madurai, Tamil Nadu, and surrounding area.

Introduction

SECTARIANISM AND PLURALISM

In the tranquility of a small Brahmin village on the outskirts of Tirunelveli in southern Tamil Nadu, past and present collide fortuitously for the twenty-first-century observer. This village, or *agrahāra,* granted by Madurai's chieftain Tirumalai Nāyaka to the illustrious poet-intellectual Nīlakaṇṭha Dīkṣita in the seventeenth century—or so the story goes—remains in the possession of the scholar's modern-day descendants. Still treasured as the true ancestral home of a family of Chennai businessmen and engineers, the village of Palamadai is repopulated annually for the calendrical celebrations of the life of Nīlakaṇṭha Dīkṣita: the anniversaries of his birth (*jayantī*) and death (*ārādhanā*). Although nearly four hundred years have elapsed since Nīlakaṇṭha himself graced the village's single street and worshipped the goddess Maṅgalanāyakī in its local temple, the past lives on through his descendants in more ways than one—not least of which are certain fundamental concepts about religion.

While engrossed in observing the Vedic recitation (*pārāyaṇa*) staged in honor of Nīlakaṇṭha's *ārādhanā* in January of 2011, I chanced to hear word from the family's elder, P. Subrahmanyan,[1] of a Western visitor who had received a particularly warm welcome during a previous season of festivities. This young researcher, I was told, was truly accepted as one of the family, and participated actively in all religious observances for the duration of his stay in the village—because, quite simply, this person was a Śaiva, a devotee of the Hindu god Śiva, and was wholeheartedly accepted as such by the community. Having received Śaiva *dīkṣā,* or "initiation," in his home country, he was able to recite without prompting the Lalitāsahasranāma, a hymn popular among the family, and fluently navigated the codes of conduct a

FIGURE 1. The Śaṅkarācārya Maṭha in Palamadai, outside of Tirunelveli, Tamil Nadu. This branch monastery of the Sringeri Śaṅkarācārya lineage was commissioned in the 1990s by descendants of Nīlakaṇṭha Dīkṣita. Jagadguru Bhāratī Tīrtha personally visited the village to perform the installation of the *maṭha*. The family proudly displays photos of the Jagadguru visiting the house Nīlakaṇṭha himself is believed to have inhabited in Palamadai.

Śaiva initiate would be expected to observe. Curious to learn more, I inquired of Dr. Subrahmanyan, "Then, do you believe this person has become a Hindu?" "Oh no," cautioned the elderly Brahmin. "There is no need for someone from the West to become a Hindu. Our teacher, Jagadguru Bhāratī Tīrtha, has shown that everyone must practice the religion they have learned in their home country. They can remain Christian and still follow the same path as we Hindus do."

Implicit in this seemingly self-contradictory message we can perceive a confluence of two distinct systems of categorization. Beneath the translucent veil of Hindu universalism accumulated in recent centuries, an older model of religious identity remains equally definitive of social interactions for present-day inhabitants of Palamadai. To be a Hindu, Dr. Subrahmanyan suggests, requires Indian heritage and birth in a Hindu family, an assumption as old as V. D. Savarkar's nationalist envisioning of Hindutva—a state of being that inheres in its members and cannot be extrinsically cultivated. And yet, to be a Śaiva is something else altogether. A Śaiva, one may glean, is an individual who has adopted a particular set of ritual practices, beliefs, and cultural values suitable for participation in a Śaiva religious community. Becoming a Śaiva, however, is by no means categorically dependent on one's identity as a Hindu, according to this model. Rather, the stark juxtaposition of these two terms, *Hindu* and *Śaiva,* calls attention to the categorical drift that the centuries have witnessed within the religion that we—contemporary scholars as well as practitioners—now call Hinduism.

Much has been written in recent years about the historical origins of the category of Hinduism. The Hindu religion itself has been postulated both as a construct of the colonial enterprise and as an organic whole that emerged gradually from within the Indic cultural system through systematic reflection and encounter with dialogical Others. Advocates of the first position have argued that the very idea of Hinduism was fabricated in the service of foreign interests, whether by European Orientalists or the British colonial regime.[2] On the other hand, critics of this constructionist argument have sought to locate a moment of juncture before colonial intervention at which the very idea of a unitary religion crystallized in the Indian cultural *imaginaire*.[3] The birth story of Hinduism, in other words, has been told and retold in scholarly literature of the past decades. What all accounts share, however, is the postulate that by some means or other Hinduism has been transformed into a unitary religion, in which any diversity is necessarily eclipsed by the internal cohesion of the concept itself. By attempting to narrate a genealogy of the present, however, scholarship has perhaps gone too far in erasing the variegated textures of the Indic religious landscape, layers of difference that persist unabated to this day beneath the guise of Hindu unity.

Indeed, among the definitions of Hinduism proffered by practitioners themselves, the most celebrated today are those that elevate unity over diversity—quintessentially, perhaps, and most notoriously, the definition put forth by V. D. Savarkar in his monograph *Hindutva*, first published in 1923. In Savarkar's vision, Hinduism, as a unified religion, is coterminous with the geographical boundaries of the emerging nation-state that would soon become India, the cultural unity of the concept of Hindutva thus prefiguring the anticipated political unity of the Indian nation-state. Fewer are aware, however, of a competing definition of the Hindu religion offered by Savarkar's contemporary and compatriot in the struggle for Indian independence, Balagangadhar "Lokamanya" Tilak, publicized during a speech at the 1892 Gaṇapati Festival in Pune. In the form of a memorable Sanskrit verse, Tilak defines Hinduism as follows:

> Acceptance of the ultimate validity of the Vedas, multiplicity of ways
> of worship
> And lack of restriction on the divinity that one may worship:
> This is the definition of the [Hindu] religion.[4]

A mere three decades, it seems, made a substantive impact on the self-reflexive definition of Hinduism articulated from within the tradition. What stands out in Tilak's definition, for those who read Savarkar's Hindutva as an inevitable prologue to the rise of an exclusivist Hindu fundamentalism, is the apparent diversity that Tilak locates in what many twentieth-century and contemporary Hindus experience as a unified religion. Our attention is drawn to the phrases "multiplicity" and "lack of restriction," as Tilak underscores the seemingly obvious fact that under the umbrella of Hinduism lies the coexistence of a diverse array of communities, each with its own chosen deity and mode of worship. What are we to make of Tilak's emphasis not on the unity but on the diversity of Hinduism? In fact, when we consult the historical archive of precolonial Indian religion, we find a great deal of precedent for Tilak's claim that the unity of Hinduism must be predicated upon its internal diversity. Over the centuries immediately preceding the rise of British colonialism, early modern south India, for instance, witnessed the crystallization of a number of discrete Hindu lineages and devotional communities. The boundaries between these communities, indeed, were deliberately circumscribed through the efforts of public theologians, each of whom was committed to defending the authenticity of his sectarian lineage as the pinnacle of an overarching Hindu orthodoxy.

With this book, I set out to complicate just what it means for us to speak of the unity of Hinduism—and, specifically, what it meant to be a Hindu on the eve of British colonialism. At whatever stage a unitary concept of Hinduism may be said to have emerged—and this subject has generated no small amount of controversy— the diverse religious communities we describe collectively as Hinduism have each preserved a fundamental independence. This independence comes to light, historically, both in the social institutions that govern their practice and in the religious identities embodied through participation in these traditions. In short, Hinduism has historically exhibited a marked tendency toward pluralism—and plurality—a trend that did *not* reverse in the centuries before colonialism but, rather, accelerated through the development of precolonial Indic early modernity. This is not to say, obviously, that diversity is absent in other world religions; nor is it to invalidate the usage of *Hinduism* by practitioners and observers, past and present, to describe genuine commonalities in doctrine and practice. And yet, to be a Śaiva or Vaiṣṇava in early modern India, to be a Mādhva, Smārta, Gauḍīya, or a member of any other such community, constituted the core of one's religious identity with a nuance that inclusivist categories such as *āstika* (orthodox) or Vaidika (Vedic) failed to capture. Even today, when a unified Hinduism is experienced as a living reality, Hindus such as the residents of Palamadai maintain a deliberate awareness of their simultaneous identity as Śaivas—and more specifically, Smārta-Śaivas affiliated with the lineage of the Sringeri Śaṅkarācāryas, devotees of the current Jagadguru Bhāratī Tīrtha Svāmigaḷ.

Nevertheless, the bare fact of Hinduism's plurality before British intervention and the nationalist movement takes us only so far in understanding how Hindu identities were experienced, performed, and re-created in the religious ecosystem of early modern South Asia, a region in the midst of rapid social and economic transformation largely unattributable to the beneficence of the European world system. In our received scholarly narrative, succinctly, Hindu difference has been read though the lens of the term *sectarianism*. In the academic study of Hinduism, *sectarianism*, by and large, signifies nothing more than "Śaivism and Vaiṣṇavism"—the worship of so-called sectarian deities. And yet, to participate in Śaiva or Vaiṣṇava religiosity, in this reading, militates against the unity of a presumed Brahminical hegemony. This metanarrative resonates with the popular use of *sectarianism* to connote deviance from the mainstream, thus, in the context of Hinduism, translating devotion as dissent, and community as a potential precursor to communalism. One of my primary aims in this book, in this light, is to excavate the emic genealogy of Hindu sectarianism—a mode of religious engagement, I contend, that did not fragment a primordial whole but was the primary vehicle for the earliest expressions of Hinduism as a unified religion. One could not be a Hindu in late-medieval or early modern India without first and foremost being something else, without participating in a community governed by the religious institutions and networks that formed the backbone of a broader religious public.

Hindu sectarianism, as we will see, is by no means equivalent to Śaivism and Vaiṣṇavism writ large on India's historical stage. Not all of Śaivism was equally sectarian, nor was all of Śaivism's history equally Hindu. By the middle of the first millennium of the Common Era, Śaivism had crystallized as a functionally distinct religion⁵—perhaps even, as Alexis Sanderson has argued, the dominant religion of the greater Sanskrit Cosmopolis. It was only by the late-medieval period that Śaivism began to represent itself as a "sect" of a larger orthodoxy we might call Hinduism. Regarding this period, we can begin to speak, with a certain trepidation, of such a phenomenon as Hindu sectarianism, as the very phrase presumes the preexistence of a larger whole—namely, Hinduism itself. Historically speaking, emic categories such as *āstika* (believers) and Vaidika (Vedic), terms that isolate a purported orthodoxy from heterodox religious movements, achieved a newfound popularity concurrently with terms for individual sectarian communities, such as *sampradāya*. Certainly, taxonomies of "orthodox" (*āstika*) and "heterodox" (*nāstika*) sects came to occupy the theologians of medieval and early modern India, whose doxographical treatises may suggest a similar conceptual understanding of the relationship between sect and religion, as Andrew Nicholson has argued in his 2010 monograph, *Unifying Hinduism*. And yet the seeming unity that late-medieval theologians located in Hindu scripture—Vedas, Upaniṣads, Purāṇas, and the six *darśana*s, or schools of philosophy—is thoroughly permeated by difference. Purāṇas, for instance, were understood as intrinsically sectarian—Śaiva or Vaiṣṇava—and were interpreted in light of the Āgamas and sectarian Dharmaśāstras, scriptures accepted only by particular sectarian traditions.

Indeed, within the emerging *āstika*, or "orthodox," fold, not all Hindu *darśana*s were accorded equal authority. By the sixteenth century, the regnant discipline of Hindu theology was without question Vedānta, the traditional exegesis of the

Upaniṣads as modeled after the Brahmasūtras of Gauḍapāda. Formerly a philosophical tradition relegated to the margin of Indian intellectual life, Vedānta experienced a dramatic renaissance in south India during the late-medieval and early modern periods, but entered the public domain as a discourse not of consensus but of contention. In fact, sectarian theologians from disparate Śaiva and Vaiṣṇava communities differentiated themselves primarily by way of their trademarked exegetical interpretation of the Brahmasūtras, demarcating their identity on the basis of ontological doctrine, whether "dualist," "nondualist," or some variation thereof. Indeed, a novel commentary on the Brahmasūtras had become the ticket to competing in the marketplace of emerging Hindu sectarian communities. Nevertheless, there was no such thing as an unequivocally Hindu Vedānta: the discipline was fragmented at the core along sectarian lines, divisions that simultaneously correlated philosophical ontology with religious identity.

The story this book tells, then, is not only one of theology and doctrine but also one of communities and publics: the story of how a particular Hindu sectarian community—namely, the Smārta-Śaivas of the Tamil country—acquired its distinctive religious culture. More broadly speaking, however, to delineate what constitutes a sectarian community in early modern south India requires a theorization of how new religious identities come to be shared and remembered across time and space: in other words a theory of south India's early modern publics. Such publics, indeed—and religious publics no less—were invariably multiple, overlaid with one another in the urban space of thriving temple towns and connected with each other across space by networks of patronage and pilgrimage. Religious publics crystallized, by and large, around the charismatic authority of renunciant preceptors, pontiffs of monastic lineages with branch communities spanning the southern half of the subcontinent and often beyond. And yet the modes of religious identity cultivated by their devotees were promulgated, first and foremost, by a discourse we can aptly describe as public theology, circulated through the writings of major sectarian intellectuals who sought both to cultivate common bonds of devotion and to foster shared modes of public engagement that visibly demarcated the boundaries between distinct sectarian communities. As a result, fashioned through reciprocal dialogue and polemic, sectarian communities functioned as independent public spheres, cultivating, in other words, a pluralistic religious landscape that mediated conflict through independent coexistence.

HINDU SECTARIANISM: A EUROPEAN INVENTION?

Sectarianism is a term that has been firmly ingrained in Western scholarly literature on Hinduism for more than a century—and with a definition that, at best, may seem peculiarly idiosyncratic and, at worst, dangerously misleading. In contemporary parlance outside the discipline, *sectarianism* most often connotes violence and aggression, leading many sociologists and twentieth-century historians to treat *sectarianism* as a self-evident synonym for *communalism*. Historians of religion, upon mention of the term *sect,* may gravitate toward an invocation of the work of Ernst Troeltsch, who, drawing on Max Weber, proposed the distinction between *church* and *sect* foundational to our use of the latter term in the Western context.[6] According to Troeltsch, a church, the institutional foundation of a parent religion, represents the conservative establishment of a particular religion, imbricated with deep-rooted ties to political power and an elite social constituency. A sect, on the other hand, Troeltsch defines as a breakaway fragment of a parent religion, a small-scale movement designed as a reformation or a protest of social stagnancy in the religious mainstream, often catering to the needs of socially disadvantaged or marginalized populations. Such a definition of *sect* may prove appealing to scholars of bhakti, or devotional Hinduism, who narrate bhakti unproblematically as a religious movement that fostered populist resistance against the so-called Brahminical mainstream, as saints of all social backgrounds were revered for their charismatic authority.[7] The majority of scholarship on Hinduism, however, makes use of the term *sectarianism* in a much more restricted, and indeed peculiar, vein—quite simply, as a stand-in for the compound "Śaivism and Vaiṣṇavism," a form of Hinduism that grounds itself in the worship of a particular deity.

How can we account for such an omnipresence of the term *sectarianism* in this idiosyncratic usage, to which scholars adhere unfailingly despite the connotations of violence and incivility that its popular meanings may inspire? The very classification of the core divisions of Hinduism as sects, according to this definition, runs afoul of an insoluble historical problem: namely, the assumption that a unified Brahminical Hindu "church" has always existed, under the shadow of which protest movements, from early Buddhism to the anticaste protests of medieval Maharashtra,[8] strove to assert their independence. Indeed, a perusal of the archive of Orientalist scholarship on Indian religions confirms that Hindu sectarianism, as a scholarly category, was born from the well-documented alliance of European philology and the colonial state apparatus, filtered in the process through Christian theological categories. This very usage of Hindu sectarianism seems to have been first articulated by Sir Monier Monier-Williams, Oxford's Boden Professor of Sanskrit, in his monograph *Brahmanism and Hinduism* (1891), with negligible variation from its contemporary manifestation. As Monier-Williams writes, "What then is the present idea implied by Hindu Sectarianism? It is clear from what has been already stated that every Hindu creed ought to be regarded as unorthodox which exalts favorite personal deities to the position of the one eternal, self-existing Spirit (Ātman or Brahma), in contravention of the dogma that even the highest divine personalities are finite beings destined ultimately to be absorbed into that one finite Spirit. Of course it must be understood that when Śaivism and Vaiṣṇavism deny this dogma they offend against orthodoxy."[9]

What, then, is the problem with the worship of Viṣṇu or Śiva as the cornerstone of a Hindu's religious identity? Hindu sectarianism, in Monier-Williams's estimation, constitutes a seditious—or even malignant—threat to a primordial unity of a religion he calls "Brāhmanism": "Hindu sectarianism is something more than the mere exclusive worship of a personal god. It implies more or less direct opposition to the orthodox philosophy of Brāhmanism." Rife with the rhetoric of a neo-Vedānta that would privilege a monistic reading of the Upaniṣads as the unchanging essence of Indian religion, Monier-Williams's model foregrounds unity over diversity, reducing in the process the rich variation in Hindu religious identity to a discordant threat to the legacy of India's golden age. Moreover, that Monier-William's usage was consonant with the Christian theology of his day, intriguingly enough, is surreptitiously revealed in the very same monograph. In Calcutta in 1883, Monier-Williams tells us, the Indian Christian convert Keshab Chandar Sen publicly disseminated a decree of the Bishop of Exeter, his 1881 New Dispensation, which included the following pointed claim: "Thus saith the Lord—Sectarianism is an abomination onto Me, and unbrotherliness I will not tolerate."

Our usage of the term *sectarianism*, it would appear, in effect not only reproduces the rationale of Orientalist polemic but also encodes a theological worldview distinctly foreign to Śaivism and Vaiṣṇavism in their lived reality. It is perhaps no surprise that, at a moment when the very concept of world religions itself was just beginning to crystallize in the Western cultural imaginary,[10] Orientalist philology embarked on a quest to recover the historical unity of an unadulterated Brahmanism. Indeed, over the preceding two centuries, European missionaries and observers in south India, as William Sweetman (2003) has demonstrated, were utterly unaware of such a concept as a unified Hinduism, identifying Śaivism and Vaiṣṇavism as distinct religious communities. Roberto de Nobili and Bartholomäus Ziegenbalg, in effect observing an India considerably less conditioned by European categories, arrived quite naturally at a crucial insight that escaped even the painstaking philology of Sir Monier Monier-Williams: namely, that Śaivism and Vaiṣṇavism, since at least the early second millennium, had been by no means socially marginal forces, subaltern shadows of a Brahminical mainstream. Indeed, writing in the seventeenth- and eighteenth-century Tamil country, de Nobili, Ziegenbalg, and their contemporaries would have to have been willfully blind not to observe that public life in early modern south India had been functionally segmented along the lines of distinct religious communities.

From within Hindu sectarian institutions themselves, likewise, our inscriptional record reveals that by the sixteenth century, Hindu religiosity was fundamentally mediated by the boundaries of sectarian identity. In 1533, for instance, in the course of renewing his endowments to the major religious sites of south India, Acyutadevarāya of Vijayanagara set forth an explicit proclamation that imperial grants to two of Kanchipuram's most important temple complexes ought to be equalized. The direct intervention of the emperor of Vijayanagara, one might surmise, ought to have resolved this patronage dispute in no uncertain terms. Nevertheless, his vassal, Sāḷuva Nāyaka, taking advantage of his own administrative control over temple donations in the region, reapportioned a greater percentage of the endowment to the temple of his choice. When this misappropriation of funds was brought to light, Acyutadevarāya attempted to remove any ambiguity in his stance by inscribing his decree in stone on the temple walls as a visible reminder to all temple officiants and onlookers.[11] The conflict, as it turns out, stemmed directly from the polarized sectarian affiliations of the temples in question: dedicated to Varadarāja, in one case, and Ekāmranātha, in the other—regional strongholds of Vaiṣṇava and Śaiva devotionalism, neighbors and chief rivals in one of south India's most active and diverse temple towns.

These traces of competition for material resources and royal sanction indicate a deeper and more pervasive fault line underlying both the social and the intellectual dynamics of early modern south India—that is, sectarian competition, particularly between Śaiva and Vaiṣṇava adherents of prominent monastic lineages. During Cōḷa rule some centuries earlier, the Tamil South had already adapted to an economic structure in which the temple served as a primary node of economic distribution and a focal point for political authority. This pattern of social organization attained a new prominence under Vijayanagara and Nāyaka rule, as temples developed into megatemples, and monastic institutions began to hold a larger share of both the economic and the symbolic capital circulated by temple complexes. Monastic lineages that enjoyed heightened prestige during this period included regional "vernacular" traditions such as the Tamil Śaiva Siddhānta as well as multiregional Sanskritic traditions, such as the Mādhvas and Śrīvaiṣṇavas, whose branch outposts in Kanchipuram, Kumbakonam, and other Tamil temple towns were connected to broader networks spanning the southern half of the subcontinent. Often we find that these lineages staked their claims to authority in major temple complexes quite visibly by enshrining the spiritual and philosophical accomplishments of their most renowned adepts directly on temple walls.

At the same time, the systemwide centrality of these monastic lineages accompanied, and exacerbated, a marked increase in intersectarian debate in the intellectual sphere. Leading intellectual figures of the period began not only to define themselves explicitly by their sectarian identity but also to actively contribute to the demarcation of community boundaries, thus exerting a tangible influence on the extratextual shape of south Indian society. One of the best-known examples on the Śaiva side, for instance, is Appayya Dīkṣita (ca. 1520–1592), renowned for tireless efforts to propagate a Vedānta strictly for Śaivas—specifically, the Śaiva Advaita philosophy of Śrīkaṇṭha's commentary on the Brahmasūtras. In fact, Appayya was sufficiently motivated to promulgate his own interpretation of Śaiva Advaita philosophy that he founded an academy in his home village of

Adaiyappalam for that express purpose and composed numerous didactic *stotras* to circulate among his pupils.[12] Visitors to Adaiyappalam today will find that Appayya immortalized his own desire to propagate the Śaiva Advaita doctrine on the walls of the Kālakaṇṭheśvara Temple, a temple he commissioned as a setting for such instruction:

> Raṅgarāja Makhin, the instructor to the learned, performer of the
>   Viśvajit sacrifice,
> And son of a performer of the great Sarvatomukha sacrifice,
> Had a son renowned as Appayya Dīkṣita, devotee of the Moon-
>   crested Lord [Śiva].
>
> On account of him the fame of the illustrious king Cinnabomma,
>   breaker of the power of kings, was undefeated [*avyāhata*].
> He excavated Śrīkaṇṭha's commentary to establish the doctrine of
>   Paramaśiva.
> He, Lord Appayya Dīkṣita, son of the illustrious Raṅgarāja, has
>   created
> This most lofty and sublime abode of the Lord of Kālakaṇṭha,
>   resplendent like the white mountain.[13]

This opening pair of Sanskrit *praśasti* verses frames Appayya Dīkṣita's life and scholarship in explicitly sectarian terms. Ostensibly author of a hundred works, many of them groundbreaking treatises in Mīmāṃsā (Vedic exegesis) and poetics, including the "best-selling" textbook on rhetoric, the *Kuvalayānanda*, Appayya is remembered by his community almost exclusively for his Śaiva theology—a reputation he himself appears to have fostered through this auto-eulogistic *praśasti*. Rather than literary theorist, or even "polymath" (*sarvatantrasvatantra*), Appayya's public persona is that of reviver of the doctrine of Śrīkaṇṭha, foremost among the devotees of Śiva. This Sanskrit verse, likewise, is followed by a donative inscription in Maṇipravāḷam documenting that Cinnabomma had agreed to sponsor five hundred scholars to study Appayya's theology at the Kālakaṇṭheśvara Temple in Adaiyappalam and another five hundred in Vellore, thus financing Appayya's project of disseminating Śaiva Advaita philosophy to the extended Śaiva scholastic community:

Hail! Beginning in the Śaka year 1504 [i.e., 1582 c.e.], in the Citrabhānu year, having composed the *Sivārkamaṇidīpikā* so that the *Śrīkaṇṭhabhāṣya* may be taught to five hundred scholars in the temple of Kālakaṇṭheśvara, and after having received an unction of gold from the hand of Cinnabomma Nāyaka, having acquired gold and *agrāhāras* from the hand of Cinnabomma Nāyaka so that the *Sivārkamaṇidīpikā* also may be taught to five hundred scholars in Vellore—may this abode of Śiva, the creation of Appayya Dīkṣita, who composed one hundred works, beginning with the *Nyāyarakṣāmaṇi* and the *Kalpataruparimala*, be auspicious.[14]

With such an institutional setting in place for propagating his theological vision, it is no wonder that Appayya's primary epithets (*birudas*) in academic discourse were Śrīkaṇṭhamata-sthāpanācārya[15]—"the establishing preceptor of Śrīkaṇṭha's doctrine"—and Advaita-sthāpanācārya, "the establishing preceptor of nondualism." Appayya's grandnephew Nīlakaṇṭha—whose exploits guide much of the analysis of this book—remembered his illustrious ancestor primarily for his contribution to Śaiva theology, particularly his *Śivārkamaṇidīpikā*, which some have argued represents a truly unprecedented maneuver to authenticate a Śaiva Advaita interpretation of the Brahmasūtras. That Nīlakaṇṭha considered Appayya an authority on Śaiva ritual practice as well as theology is made clear in the *Saubhāgyacandrātapa*, Nīlakaṇṭha's unpublished esoteric ritual manual, which I discuss in chapter 2, in which Nīlakaṇṭha repeatedly refers to Appayya's *Śivārcanacandrikā* as a primary authority.[16] Even within public literary circles, Nīlakaṇṭha commemorated his uncle first and foremost not for his literary theoretical advances or his poetic commentaries, but for his composition of the *Śivārkamaṇidīpikā*, a feat for which his patron, Cinnabomma, literally showered him in gold (*kanakābhiṣeka*).[17]

On the side of his antagonists, leading Vaiṣṇava theologians of the period were all too well acquainted with Appayya's theological project in the *Śivārkamaṇidīpikā*, taking special note of their own preceptors' attempts to refute his arguments and minimize his influence. For instance, the Śrīvaiṣṇava hagiographer Anantācārya recalls the particular rivalry between Appayya Dīkṣita and a scholar of his own lineage, Pañcamatabhañjana Tātācārya, so named for ostensibly "demolishing five doctrines":

> Best of those learned in Śaiva theology, the illustrious Appayya Dīkṣita
> Of great fame, who had defeated his enemies, shone at Cidambaram.
> Appayya Dīkṣita composed the text titled the *Śivārkamaṇidīpikā*,
> Always devoted to the Śaiva religion, hostile to the Lord [Viṣṇu].[18]

> Tātayācārya, having set forth the "Demolishing of Five Doctrines,"
> The *Pañcamatabhañjanam*,
> Protected the undefeated [*avyāhata*] doctrine of the illustrious
>   Rāmānuja.
> He, the great teacher, of great splendor, having made the *Caṇḍamāruta*,
> Protected that undefeated doctrine of that best of ascetics.[19]

As Anantācārya tells us, Pañcamatabhañjana Tātācārya composed the *Caṇḍamāruta* in direct response to Appayya's *Śivārkamaṇidīpikā*. And through his efforts, the Śrīvaiṣṇava doctrine of Rāmānuja remained "undefeated" (*avyāhata*), at least according to the hagiography of his lineage. On the Śaiva side, we meet with this same term, *avyāhata*, in the Adaiyappalam inscription as royal imagery for the alliance of Cinnabomma and Appayya Dīkṣita, the crest-jewel of Śaiva theologians who adorned his court. Evidently, being theologically "undefeated" was a goal that persistently preoccupied the intellectual discourse of the sixteenth and seventeenth centuries in south India. Although the Sanskrit intellectual circles of the Nāyaka courts fostered an impressive display of erudition in all fields of *śāstric* learning, no discipline so preoccupied public discourse as did theology, whether Śaiva or Vaiṣṇava. To be undefeated, then, in such a competitive marketplace of ideas was no small matter, and yet the honor seems to have been claimed equally by all participants.

In short, intellectual life in early modern south India—and indeed public religious life in general—had become polarized to the extreme, on both the institutional and the philosophical planes. Sectarian theology, employed strategically in debates between rival sects, became a defining structural pillar of the region's intellectual sphere in the sixteenth and seventeenth centuries, to an even greater degree than was true in preceding centuries. In some cases, conversation became heated, judging by the titles of sectarian pamphlets, ranging from Appayya Dīkṣita's *Madhvatantramukhamardana* (Crushing the face of Madhva's doctrine) to the possibly even more graphic insults of Benares pandits in subsequent generations as tensions became still more elevated: *Durjanamukhacapeṭikā* (A slap in the face of the wicked), *Durjanamukhamahācapeṭikā* (A *great* slap in the face of the wicked), *Durjanamukhapadmapādukā* (A boot to the lotus mouth of the wicked), and so forth.[20] To better understand these rising sectarian tensions—in terms of both their theological influence and their social significance—requires a closer look at the origin and development of these debates and the textual strategies through which these debates were conducted.

While the religious networks of south India most readily point to the role of sectarianism in the Hindu religious landscape—since monasteries and megatemples visibly demarcate the terrain of rival Śaiva and Vaiṣṇava communities—Hindu sectarianism was by no means a phenomenon restricted to the South. In fact, we witness a veritable explosion of distinct Hindu communities in the domain of north India beginning around the fifteenth and sixteenth centuries, demarcated in emic terms through the authority of lineage, or *sampradāya*.[21] Mirroring closely the social dynamic of the South, Vaiṣṇava devotional *sampradāyas* vied to establish themselves through Rājput and Mughal patronage, setting down institutional roots in the Vaiṣṇava heartland of Braj and its greater cultural ambit across Rajasthan. In fact, the groundbreaking work of John Stratton Hawley (2015) has situated the bhakti movement as such as the foundation of sectarian identity in Hindu north India, and as a phenomenon of the Mughal period (1526–1707) rather than of Indian antiquity. Mughal rule, some would argue, fostered in a literal sense a sectarian marketplace—as the spread of sectarian networks was heavily facilitated by the Mughal support of fiscal exchange across the northern half of the subcontinent.[22] And over the following century, much of the Vaiṣṇava heartland witnessed a thoroughgoing state-sponsored sectarianization, as Sawai Jai Singh II set out to homologize the public religious culture of eighteenth-century Jaipur—a domain in which orthodoxy was described not as *Hindu* but as *Vaiṣṇava*.[23]

Speaking constructively about sectarianism, then—in a manner that seeks to denude the term of its Orientalist overtones—requires us to resituate Hindu communities in their social and cultural context. Indeed, only a decontextualized doctrinal mélange, arguably, could have prompted Monier-Williams to read the religiosity of Śaivism and Vaiṣṇavism as belligerent dissent from a unified Brahminical church—a mysterious institution, to be sure, that will be found nowhere in our inscriptional record. To be a Śaiva or a Vaiṣṇava in early modern south India, was, to the contrary, not simply to believe in the supremacy of Śiva or Viṣṇu but to belong to a socially embedded community and to mark one's religious identity as a member of a particular religious public. Sectarian communities are not Venn diagrams of people and doctrines, demarcated by drawing artificial boundaries; they are dynamic social systems composed of networks of religious actors, institutions—temples, monasteries, lineages—and the religious meanings they engender. In the words of Niklas Luhmann, for instance, by which he defines a social system, we might describe a sectarian community as a "meaning-constituting system,"[24] an operationally closed set of social institutions that maintains—and in fact reconstitutes—its own boundaries internally through the structures of meaning it generates. That is to say, Hindu sects function autonomously from one another as meaning-constituting systems, each individually reproducing the religious institutions that endow participation in that community with sectarian-inflected religious identity.

Thus, while making an appeal, on the grounds of Vedāntic exegesis, to an umbrella religion we may call Hinduism, sectarian communities maintained an internal coherence and mutual independence comparable to the discrete social systems of modern society, such as the political or legal systems, which Luhmann analogizes to the independent but permeable interactions of discrete biological systems. In south India, for instance, major sectarian communities such as the Śrīvaiṣṇava and Mādhva Vaiṣṇava lineages, and the Tamil Śaiva Siddhānta, attained virtually complete autonomy on a social as well as a doctrinal level by becoming major economic shareholders in the networks of exchange centered at major temple complexes and monasteries. This is not to say, naturally, that interactions between sectarian communities did not occur on a regular basis. In fact, it is just such interactions—whether polemical exchanges, competition for resources, or theological influence and reaction—that allow each sect to maintain its distinctive identity in the face of changing circumstances. A Hindu sectarian community, in short, mirrors closely what Luhmann describes as an autopoietic system, creating and maintaining its doctrines, ritual practices, and modes of religious expression from within its own boundaries.

A self-constituting religious tradition, in other words, generates its own meaning-creating institutions—monasteries, lineages (*paramparā*), temple complexes, sites of performance, and so on. These institutions in turn produce artifacts of religious meaning—doctrine, canon, hagiography, ritual practice, sectarian dress, and other semiotic signals—as the intellectual property, if you will, of those sectarian institutions, effectively erecting conceptual boundaries between competing traditions. When viewed macroscopically, the aggregate of such mutually independent systems facilitates the balance of an entire ecosystem—or, in our case, a religion inflected to its core by pluralism.

RELIGION IN EARLY MODERN SOUTH INDIA

Much like Europe, India in the seventeenth century was in the midst of a transition, a substantial rethinking of religious boundaries on both the institutional and the philosophical levels. The Indic religious landscape was brimming with iconoclasts, luminaries, and reformers, each with a vision of how to navigate the complexities of an increasingly divisive and sectarian social order. And, much as in the European case, many were keen to raise awareness of their opponents' shortcomings, critiquing the excesses they perceived in the religious institutions around them.

Take, for instance, Nīlakaṇṭha Dīkṣita, seventeenth-century poet laureate of Madurai in southern Tamil Nadu. Let's refer to Nīlakaṇṭha, for the time being, as the "Indian Voltaire"—an ironically incongruous comparison that we will have a chance to revisit shortly. Best known in academic circles for his incisive satirical wit, our poet rivals Voltaire in his willingness to publicly lambaste the moral degenerates of his day who occupied positions of clerical or political authority, and he did so to great comedic effect. In his work the *Kaliviḍambana* (A travesty of time), Nīlakaṇṭha exposes the shortcomings of the scholars and priests in his company:

> If you want to triumph in learned societies, do not be afraid, do not pay attention, do not listen to the opponent's arguments—just immediately contradict them! Unflappability, shamelessness, contempt for the adversary, derision, and praise of the king: these are the five grounds of victory. . . . If the arbitrator is not learned, one wins by shouting. If he is learned one has only to insinuate bias: "Greed" is the premise, "money" is the probandum, "the priest" is the example, "personal advance" is the result: such is the correct syllogistic procedure.[25]

Nīlakaṇṭha continues at great length to deride all manner of religious officiants and charismatic authorities, from astrologers to mantra-sorcerers and ascetics. Each of them, in Nīlakaṇṭha's satirical portrait, fails dramatically to live up to the principles of his profession, exhibiting instead a thoroughgoing deceitfulness and opportunism. In such rhetoric, it is tempting to hear the ringing echo of Voltaire's own cry "Ecrasez l'infame!"—"Crush the infamous!"—referring most likely to the clergy he found so burdensome in the Europe of his generation. Given this portrait, it may come as no surprise that scholars have located a semblance of secularism in the textual culture of early modern India, whether manifesting as social critique or as public adjudication of religious disputes. And thus, Nīlakaṇṭha himself enters into academic literature in the West the very image of the secular public intellectual.

And yet, a closer look at Nīlakaṇṭha's writings reveals an entirely different picture. When he was not penning satirical diatribes, Nīlakaṇṭha was composing some of the most heartfelt devotional poetry ever written in the Sanskrit language—a case could even be made to include him in the canon of Indian devotional, or bhakti, poetry, a category typically reserved for vernacular lyric composition. Likewise, Nīlakaṇṭha's philosophical prose includes a commentarial essay on a popular Sanskrit hymn, the *Śivatattvarahasya* (The secret of the principle of Śiva). The introduction to this essay doubles as a theological counterpolemic, as Nīlakaṇṭha defends his own religious tradition, Śaivism, against the scathing critiques of his rivals from Vaiṣṇava communities. But perhaps the most intriguing of Nīlakaṇṭha's works, and certainly the most unexpected based on our assumptions, is a manual for esoteric ritual practice, the *Saubhāgyacandrātapa* (Moonlight of auspiciousness). Entirely unknown to Indological scholarship to date, the "Moonlight" provides us with an insider's account of the esoteric Śrīvidyā tradition of Śākta, or goddess-oriented Tantric ritual, a tradition of which Nīlakaṇṭha himself was an avid practitioner. This would be tantamount to discovering, in the European sphere, that the French Voltaire, outspoken critic of theological excess, had spent his spare hours practicing Rosicrucian ritual or angelic magic.

When we attend to the texts, Nīlakaṇṭha emerges as a man of profound religious commitments, both in his personal practice and in his public theological agenda. One may rightly wonder, in fact, whether the term *secular* could possibly do justice to the complexity of his life's work. And yet, academic literature on early modern India has scarcely noted the theological investments of scholars such as Nīlakaṇṭha; recent studies consistently depict such intellectuals purely as poets, logicians, and social theorists, implicitly secular in their public outlook. Most notably, over the course of the previous decade, Sheldon Pollock's Sanskrit Knowledge Systems Project has considerably advanced our knowledge of early modern thought in India. In doing so, this team of scholars has uncovered discursive patterns that invite direct comparison with the European Renaissance and early modernity, including a return to the classics of Sanskrit thought—an Indic neoclassicism—and a fascination with the idea of "newness," giving unprecedented sanction to intellectual innovation. Others have located a mounting historical consciousness in the writings of early modern intellectuals and literati, revealed not through historiography as a discrete textual genre but through narrative "textures" that evoke an awareness of historical change (Narayana Rao et al. 2003). It is in such features that recent scholarship has sought to locate a distinctively Indic "modernity."

Such strictly textual scholarship on Indian early modernity builds on the rich terrain of extratextual work that has excavated a pervasive transformation in the economic, political, and social dynamics of early modern Indian polities. We need not, of course, assume intellectual changes to be derivative of socioeconomic change—invoking in the process the much maligned base-superstructure dichotomy. Ample evidence exists, however, that a model of modernity characterized in part by shifts in capital flow had found a home in early modern India. The work of Sanjay Subrahmanyam (2001), for instance, complicates the traditional narrative, inherited from the economic imperialism brought on by colonial intervention, that early modern India had been stultified by a homegrown epidemic of economic stagnation. Instead, Subrahmanyam proposes a revised model for mapping modernity as a transregional phenomenon fabricated through global exchange between multiple regions of the globe, with South Asia itself playing an integral role in this multidimensional web of exchange. This "conjunctural" model of multiple modernities essentially challenges Immanuel Wallerstein's (1976) traditional explanation of early modernity's onset as a virus borne by the vector of capitalism spreading from the European center to peripheries around the globe.

In short, recent research into seventeenth-century India has ambitiously sought to reveal a distinctively Indic early modernity, one that developed in dialogue with its Western counterpart rather than being exported in toto owing to the beneficence of a European "civilizing" power. With such a project in mind, the temptation to compare looms high on the horizons, with all the promises and limitations that comparison typically invokes. As historian of religions Jonathan Z. Smith has taught us, comparison often operates through a sort of sympathetic magic, creating a semblance of similarity through a process of contact or contagion. Wary of the consequences of unduly hasty comparison, Smith further invites us in his book *Drudgery Divine* to engage in a comparison not of similarity but of difference—to compare so that the unique features of each standard of comparison appear all the more salient. It is in the spirit of Smith's dictum that I have invoked the image of Nīlakaṇṭha Dīkṣita as the Indian Voltaire. The comparison rings true at first glance; and yet the role of anticlerical iconoclast does a remarkably poor job of explaining what motivated Nīlakaṇṭha to compose his works, and an even poorer one of clarifying how his ideas influenced seventeenth-century south Indian society. Seeing the limitations of this comparison, one would scarcely believe that not a single scholar to date has remarked on the theological agenda of Nīlakaṇṭha Dīkṣita. Likewise, scholarship has barely scratched the surface of the actual theology of Nīlakaṇṭha's granduncle Appayya Dīkṣita, who has been credited with reinventing south Indian Śaivism and its accompanying philosophical discourses a century before.[26]

And yet the influence of Nīlakaṇṭha's theology is by no means marginal. Remembered by their descendants as the equivalent of living saints, both Nīlakaṇṭha and his granduncle Appayya were instrumental in rethinking the theological boundaries between the sectarian Hindu communities of south India, Śaiva and Vaiṣṇava alike. Between the two, Appayya and Nīlakaṇṭha contributed significantly to the articulation of the fundamental pillars of Smārta-Śaivism—in matters of theology, devotion, ritual practice, and even the constitution of its religious public. Evidently, "secularism"—or the critique of religion—is the last thing we should expect to uncover in the writings of early modern south India. In fact, the evidence points in the opposite direction. In the early centuries of the Common Era, philosophers across religious boundaries—Hindu, Buddhist, Jain, and even atheist (Carvāka)—found common ground for intellectual debate through formal epistemology, or *pramāṇa* theory, a framework that, by foregrounding common means of ascertaining shared knowledge such as perception and inference, allowed partisans to engage in dialogue while bracketing religious presuppositions entirely. In contrast to the European case, then, early modern intellectuals in south India instigated a radical theologization of public discourse, such that even the very tools of their intellectual work—approaches to text criticism and the interpretation of scripture (e.g., Mīmāṃsā, Nyāya), previously founded on a shared epistemology— were claimed as the exclusive property of particular Hindu sectarian communities. In short, not until the sixteenth century did religion became the constitutive language of public intellectual exchange in south India.

In the European context, historians remain rightfully skeptical of the extent to which Enlightenment Europe had denuded its intellectual discourse of theological concerns—although exceptions do exist, and the movement to revitalize secularization as the telos of modernity is alive and well even today.[27] Nevertheless, it is difficult to underestimate the centrality occupied in the sociological study of religion by the metanarrative that modernity, as such, is necessarily heralded by a concomitant decline in religiosity. From Max Weber to Peter Berger, theorists have adamantly described secularism as an intrinsic feature of modernity itself, many presupposing that religion would inevitably die out or become obsolete in the course of time. Even in recent years, as the resurgence of fundamentalism around the globe has disabused many sociologists of religion of their faith in the teleology of secularism, theorists, such as Charles Taylor (2007), present us with claims that secularism remains intrinsic to the very experience of modernity. Within the substantial literature on secularization theory, Taylor identifies two primary subsets of definitions given for the concept of secularism. On one hand, secularism can be an attribute of belief, suggesting that individuals in modernized societies are far less likely to profess belief in a higher power or the doctrines of organized religion. On the other hand, *secularization* can refer exclusively to the removal of religious content from public space and civil society without reference to personal belief or private religious practice. Taylor, for his part, chooses to adopt elements of both approaches as constitutive of what he calls the "secular age."

Early modern India, to the contrary, exhibited neither of these tendencies that Taylor believes encapsulate the range of theories of secularization.[28] With regard to religious belief, we can locate no major thinkers of the precolonial period who personally disavow the very idea of religion—not even vociferous iconoclasts such as Kabir, whose critiques of Hindu and Muslim dogmatism are matched by enraptured descriptions of subtle-body experiences and fervent adherence to the power of the divine Name.[29] This is, to put it mildly, a striking counterexample to the European narrative and cannot be overemphasized. Even though India at the beginning of the Common Era was home to a number of flourishing atheist schools of philosophy, in the early modern centuries, atheism, or even skepticism, played virtually no role in public discourse. Perhaps it should come as no surprise, indeed, that India fails to conform to an ostensive gold standard upheld as the harbinger of modernity in western Europe. Not only has it become a matter of common sense to question the European teleology of modernity, implicating civilizations around the globe in the march of progress, but also theorists have gone so far as to locate a genuinely theological project within the Western concept of secularism, proper to the religious terrain of post-Reformation Europe. Such a theme is perhaps most interestingly theorized in the 2013 work of Giorgio Agamben undertaking an archaeology of the theological concepts that underlie such mainstays of Enlightenment rationality as sovereignty, law, and the very concept of economy.

What then, was the place of religion in early modern India, if we can even be so bold as to imply with this question the possibility of an answer in the singular? In speaking of a *theologization* of public discourse—or in speaking of Nīlakaṇṭha Dīkṣita as public theologian—care must be taken, first and foremost, to steer clear, on one hand, of the European metanarrative of secularization and, on the other hand, of its implied opposite, or the failure of India to secularize. To date, theorists of the early modern in South Asia have scrupulously avoided mentioning religion—whether its presence or decline—as an intrinsic feature of Indic early modernity. To point out the obvious—namely, that religion in precolonial India showed no signs of rational interrogation, let alone evacuation from the public sphere—would be to tread dangerously close to painting precolonial India as the irrational, mystical Other that missionaries and British Orientalists envisioned: in other words, as an India that simply failed to modernize. Rather than endorsing a theology underlying Western modernity as unproblematically universal, we are better served by returning to the archive to excavate the theology of India's early modern publics, acknowledging that India's early modernity will be permeated by a distinctive theological vision.

The alternative to adopting such metanarratives, perhaps, is to bracket the diachronic itself for some time: historiography, as Hayden White (1975) has taught us, cannot avoid implicating itself in the art of emplotment. Speaking synchronically of Nīlakaṇṭha Dīkṣita as a public theologian demands instead a delineation of what precisely constitutes the public in the intellectual discourse of his contemporaries in post-Vijayanagara south India. To map the concept of the public—to say nothing of the omnipresent "public sphere"—directly onto Indian society, however, could result in more than a few historical anachronisms. We would be remiss not to question implications of an Indian public sphere, particularly before the overt Western influence of the colonial encounter. One has to take care, naturally, to avoid privileging Eurocentric concepts and teleologies in the study of the non-Western world. Over the past decades, however, the notion of an extra-European public, varying by degree from its presumed European model, in and of itself has ceased to be a conceptual problem. We can speak equally of a public sphere in early modern England or in Safavid Iran (Rahimi 2011) without an overt fear of unwarranted parochialism. Such a public, however, must be contextualized within its South Asian context, particularly as it relates to the place of religion in early modernity. Because the very idea of the public, in certain formulations, implicates a rationalist critique of religiosity as such, a South Asian analogue of the public sphere must above all make room for the existence of religiously inflected publics—that is, for public spaces and channels of discourse that are rooted in the lifeworlds and religious cultures of particular sectarian communities.

PUBLIC THEOLOGY: OR, THE CONSTRUCTION OF INDIA'S SECTARIAN PUBLICS

The very idea of a religious public, read through the prescriptive lens of liberal political theory and the precedent of a Western model of civil society, may strike the contemporary reader as a sheer contradiction in terms. A brief thought experiment, however, may clarify why such a concept never came under fire in Indian intellectual circles. It is no surprise that, after Europe witnessed the ravaging destruction of the Wars of Religion, educated minds across the continent would seek to limit the influence of religion in the domains of politics and civil society. In India, on the contrary, history unfolded differently, and the relationship between religion, society, and violence took on another form altogether. In 1598, to name a single example, a group of Vaiṣṇava clergy in Tamil Nadu sought royal sanction to install a prominent temple image of Viṣṇu for worship at the temple of Cidambaram, one of the most staunchly Śaiva sacred centers of the Indian subcontinent. In retaliation, the Śaiva priests threatened to commit mass suicide to prevent the image of Viṣṇu from being installed, and twenty priests ended up jumping to their deaths from the temple tower. So far as our historical records can detect, this was the face of religious violence in early modern south India. Where religious violence did erupt in premodern India, it did not take the shape of large-scale militarized clashes on the scale of the European Wars of Religion,[30] which might have imprinted a memory of cultural trauma on the popular imagination—as, for instance, was undoubtedly the case in the aftermath of independence and partition in twentieth-century South Asia. And while no culture is immune to the everyday violence of inequity and coercion, much of which is inflected with religious concerns, such everyday violence can rarely suffice to shift public opinion toward instigating a renunciation of religion as such. No one, to our knowledge, took another life specifically over a competing interpretation of the Brahmasūtras.

Quite simply, there were no Wars of Religion in India to prompt a critical response from Indian intelligentsia. Organized religion never experienced substantial backlash from intellectual circles, as social conditions never warranted a move toward limiting religion in public space. In fact, far from moving toward a secularization of public discourse, early modern thought in India became radically theologized in its outward expression. Classical knowledge systems that had previously eschewed any mention of divinity rapidly adopted the vocabulary of devotionalism and sectarian piety.[31] It is with this *theologization* of public discourse in mind that I add the second of our two terms to the word *public*—and that term is *theology*. By identifying in early modern south India the rise of a distinctively new public theology, I wish to argue that theological discourse was by no means incidental to the intellectual history of the period, nor was it a stultified relic of premodern Indic civilization. To the contrary, sectarian theology was crucial to the social and cultural constitution of south India by the sixteenth century, leaving an enduring impression on the religious landscape of the region today. Religious identity and community formation have taken the shape they have today largely because of the influence of the theologization of discourse and the discourse of theology.

The term *public theology,* as employed in the study of contemporary American religious discourse, was first coined by Martin E. Marty in an influential 1974 article on the extratextual ambitions of the renowned American theologian Reinhold Niebuhr, whose eloquent words frequently influenced the deliberations of policy makers and worked their way into the speeches of presidents. Public theologians, according to Marty's model, do not merely operate in the abstract, ruminating about the nature of divinity; they also, in a particularized and concrete fashion, engage with the beliefs and conduct of the religious at large. Broadly speaking, public theologians are those "various figures who have interpreted the nation's religious experience, practice and behavior in light of some transcendent reference" (Marty 1974, 332). Seventeenth-century south India, naturally, was no nation-state in the modern sense, and we cannot speak meaningfully at this point in history of a South Asian civil society, deemed necessary by some analysts as the purview of public theology. Nevertheless, in their theologically inflected writings, Nīlakaṇṭha and his contemporaries addressed—and indeed spoke on behalf of—a religious public unconstrained by the walls of a monastery, the vows of asceticism, the hierarchies of lineage (*paramparā*), or the boundaries of any single religious institution. They spoke on behalf of a public that spanned a multiplicity of social locations, hailing from a number of distinct caste, regional, and linguistic communities, all of which had come to participate in the networks of an overarching Śaiva public culture.

This phrase *public theology* contains two key words that I believe are fundamental to understanding both the motivations behind intellectual discourse in seventeenth-century south India and this discourse's effects on subsequent generations. The first of these is the term *public*. The most widely known theory of the public (or of publicness, Publicität) is naturally Habermas's concept of the public sphere. In its original formulation, Habermas's "public sphere" was intended to describe a unique structural transformation in European society, contemporaneous with or somewhat postdating Nīlakaṇṭha's floruit of the mid-seventeenth century. In Habermas's model, late seventeenth-century Europe witnessed the emergence of a public domain, housed in the coffee shops and salons of an educated bourgeois society, in which public opinion was crafted through the process of rational debate. This "bourgeois public sphere" coincided temporally—and indeed causally, for Habermas—with the rise of political liberalism and early capitalist social orders, forming a necessary foundation for constitutional democracy as we understand it today.

Coffee shops, one may presume, were not commonplace in the urban metropolis of early modern south India,[32] although the literary salon (*sabhā*), a South Asian institution of considerable antiquity, is another question entirely. Nevertheless, early modern India shared with Europe a flourishing network of scholars who began to gather in publicly demarcated spaces to debate issues of timely social interest. In north India, for example, the renowned scholars of Benares, one of the intellectual capitals of the subcontinent, petitioned to rebuild one of the city's legendary temples, the Viśveśvara Temple. In the temple's new incarnation, they constructed a pavilion known as the Mukti Maṇḍapa, the "Liberation Pavilion," designed as a public meeting hall in which scholars applied their scriptural expertise toward solving vexing social problems of their day.[33] In south India as well, poets and theologians traveled great distances to attend seasonal temple festivals, where performances of Sanskrit dramas served as conventions of regionwide literary society. Similarly, in written discourse, social debate flourished as representatives from rival religious sects put forth pamphlet after pamphlet defending their social and theological agendas. Our manuscript archives show a dramatic upsurge in debate through these "pamphlet wars" as sectarian tracts circulated widely across the region during the seventeenth century.

Of course, the most notable shortcoming of Habermas's model when applied to early modern India is, broadly speaking, the issue of religion. Although Habermas, at least in his early work, does not address the issue, the bourgeois liberal discourse that constituted his public sphere most certainly *was* concerned with religion. More precisely, it was concerned with the *limitation* of religion in public space and discourse and, as a result, has often been implicated in the Western metanarrative of secularization. What, then, do we mean by the phrase *religious publics*? As numerous critics of Habermas have pointed out since the publication of his work in English in 1989, such a concept of the public sphere is by definition fundamentally antithetical to religion, founded as it is upon Enlightenment norms of rational discourse. That is, publicity, in Habermas's estimation, centers on a neo-Kantian notion of communicative rationality, mapping onto a civil society that has deliberately evacuated religious concerns from the content of public discourse. In this context Hindu public theology stands out as the precondition for a rather different sort of public, fabricated by a mode of discourse that, while by no means nonrational, was fundamentally religious in its guiding concerns. The theologization of discourse, succinctly, is the process of Hindu theology's *going public*—leaving the confines of the monastery or temple complex to cultivate the public ethos of a particular sectarian community, in the process demarcating it conceptually from its competitors.

In India, succinctly, sectarian tensions prompted an embrace rather than a rejection of religion in public space. No one religious sect was in a position to advocate universal orthodoxy for its doctrines; but rather, sectarian lineages cultivated separate and parallel public domains, each of which was suffused with the religious signifiers of that sect. Even today, visitors to India observe that religious signs and symbols permeate the landscape; and yet, no singular orthodoxy emerges from their conjunction, as each set of symbols belongs to a separate community with its own lineage, history, and devotional practice. And theologically speaking, the defense of this parallel sectarianism can be traced directly to the religious discourse of Indian early modernity. The theological debates of early modern India cultivated a heightened public awareness of sectarian identity that prompted relatively little violence or outright antagonism but greatly accelerated the formation of distinct religious communities across most of the subcontinent. It is precisely to describe the doctrinal dimensions of sectarian community formation during this period that I propose to locate a newly emerging public theology in the discourse of early modern south India. Public theology, in other words, served as the conceptual architecture for a parallel religious sectarianism that remains to this day the defining feature of the Hindu religion or, potentially, even of religious identity across the Indian subcontinent.

One of the central theoretical aims of this book, then, is to make the case for the early modern Indian public: one that, unlike its European counterpart, remained thoroughly and unapologetically inflected by religious concerns—specifically, the religiosity of distinct sectarian publics. Unlike the European case, then, we are obliged to speak not of a public sphere in the singular but of *publics*, as theologians of each sectarian community took initiative in reshaping the rules that governed public engagement of devotees and their interactions with those outside the tradition. The very idea of publics as multiple, naturally, comes as no surprise in the wake of numerous critiques of Habermas, as Nancy Fraser (1990), Michael Warner (2002), and others have aimed to decenter the normativity of the bourgeois public sphere by documenting the fragmentation of public discourse along lines of gender, class, or sexuality. These counterpublics, as Fraser describes them, by very definition run counter to a singular, hegemonic social order, in contradistinction to which they provide a social space for the cultivation of identities that conflict with the dominant cultural order. We have already seen, however, in the context of Hinduism, that the narrative of a singular hegemonic Brahminism against which sectarian identities are defined runs afoul of numerous historical incoherencies. Sectarian publics, as a result, are not Fraser's counterpublics, nor are they spaces of resistance. Rather, sectarian publics exist parallel to one another, often colliding with networks of institutions occupying the same geographical and urban space. Sectarian publics are defined dialectically against one another rather than as subaltern shadows of a singular bourgeois Hinduism—which, when situated in the seventeenth century, is quite simply an anachronism.

This does not preclude, naturally, the possibility of such counterpublics existing elsewhere in premodern India. While publics can indeed generate a powerful setting for social critique, India's scholarship, as with that of Europe, was produced and consumed largely by a restricted class of educated elite—indeed, this is precisely the class of people who participated in Habermas's public sphere. Likewise, the sectarian religious publics of early modern south India, while constituted in part by the Sanskritic discourse of theological speculation, extended well beyond the boundaries of intellectual circles to include those of diverse social backgrounds who interface with sectarian institutions. As our historical archive bears out, the architecture of the sectarian public was indubitably founded upon a sort of rationality, couched in the language of Sanskrit *śāstra*—systematic philosophical discourse—or its equivalents in the numerous vernaculars of south India. Sectarian theologians were by and large elite social agents, whether Brahmins by class or members of groups with a significant economic power base in south India, such as the Vēḷāḷas of the Tamil country. The constituency of such a public, as a result, cannot possibly evoke the universal connotations of the twentieth-century usage—*the public* as an umbrella term for all individuals—which Habermas himself highlights as antithetical to his own vision of the public sphere. Nevertheless, *the sectarian public* is by no means an exhaustive descriptor, and by no means excludes the potential explanatory force of other overlaying public domains. Nor does the *Hindu* in "Hindu sectarian publics" imply that there were no publics composed of Muslims, Christians, Jains, or adherents of any other religious community. Rather, by the "Hindu sectarian publics of south India," what is intended is simply an empirical description of one of the most salient sources for the construction of personal identity and belonging across the Hindu religious ecology of south India's early modernity.

As in the European case, furthermore, Indian intellectual debates held wide-ranging consequences that changed the face of popular culture and society well beyond the confines of intellectual circles. For this reason, when I use the term *public* in *public theology,* I refer to the educated public of which Habermas speaks, but also to the resonances of public discourse across diverse sectors of society, what we might describe as another sort of "public" in modern parlance. This "other" sort of public—the domain of popular culture, if you will—is as fundamental an object of inquiry as the manuscripts of elite philosophical treatises. It is perhaps just this sort of public that is best captured by the work of Christian Novetzke (2016), who locates a public sphere in thirteenth-century Maharashtra that by virtue of its modes of discourse is not necessarily rational nor even necessarily literate. In India, these two publics were by no means the disparate phenomena one might imagine, and I would hazard to guess this holds true across cultures and continents. The question, methodologically speaking, is how to trace the influence that the "bourgeois public" exerted on a wider public culture, which Arjun Appadurai and Carol Breckenridge (1995), most notably, have described as "public culture." When studying preprint and premedia religious cultures, the task requires careful attention to patterns of discourse and religious practice.

Take, for example, Nīlakaṇṭha Dīkṣita's engagement with the popular mythology of the city of Madurai, which I treat in greater detail in chapter 4. One of Nīlakaṇṭha's literary and devotional interests was a cycle of myths known as the "Sacred Games of Śiva," a set of sixty-four narratives depicting the divine interventions of the god Śiva in Madurai, where Nīlakaṇṭha himself lived in the seventeenth century. Through his religious literature and devotional hymns, Nīlakaṇṭha contributed actively to circulating and popularizing the "Sacred Games" among Śaivas of all social backgrounds, well beyond the Madurai region. As a result, the "Sacred Games" attained such heights of popularity in the city of Madurai that festival performances of several of the narratives were added to the calendrical rituals of the city's central temple, and they are still performed to this day. In short, Nīlakaṇṭha's influence reached well beyond the circles of Śaiva Brahmins to shape the popular religious culture of Śaivas across south India. The study of sectarian publics, in short, does not restrict us to the analysis of discrete, provincial worldviews—to the contrary, it is the intersection between such publics and the wider population at large that marks perhaps our most fruitful point of inquiry for understanding the shifts in religious identity and values that govern the *longue durée* of the history of Hinduism.

PLURALISM AND PUBLIC SPACE

By reframing the practice of Hinduism in light of its early modern precursors, this book aims to resituate Hindu sectarianism as a precolonial, and distinctively non-Western, form of religious pluralism. In the annals of both colonial and contemporary historiography, as we have seen, Hindu sectarianism translates nearly uniformly as divisive dissent, virtually bordering on violent hostility. Such rhetoric, in effect, reduces the myriad of Hindu communities that deviate from the monism of neo-Hindu universalism to inconsequential noise at best and to heresy at worst. Historically speaking, however, it also dissuades us from inquiring into the socioreligious foundation of their precolonial coexistence: just how did Śaiva and Vaiṣṇava practitioners relate to each other in the public space of early modern south India? Moving beyond the impact of specific public theologians as this rhetoric was translated and transposed into a range of discursive arenas, how more generally can we understand the very relationship between religion and publicity precipitated by a religious landscape in which sectarian institutions emerged as regional power brokers, polarizing the movement of individuals in public space and the embodiment of religious identity? Our evidence, in short, allows for a reformulation of the very criteria for a non-Western pluralism, founded not on the prescriptive model of a Western civil society but on the historically descriptive account of the role of religion in public space and public discourse. In the present day as well, much of this precolonial pluralism has survived the superimposition of Hindu universalism and structures the spatial experience of religion in urban locales across the Indian subcontinent.

On a number of occasions, I have framed undergraduate seminars with the following question: "How would you feel if you walked out of this building and discovered a crowd venerating a shrine of the Virgin Mary on the first street corner, a group engaged in Islamic prayer across the street, and several individuals sitting in meditation in front of a *śivaliṅga* on the next block?" Anecdotal and counterintuitive as this statement may be, the perplexity that registers on the students' faces reveals just how poorly the Western model of civil society can account for the spatial experience of religion common in urban centers across India. The prescription, for instance, that religious dialogue be fostered in intercommunal "civic centers" makes little sense in a landscape in which street shrines are more normative than anomalous and the majority of businesses in middle-class neighborhoods bear outward signs of religious affiliation.[34] In Triplicane, Chennai, in 2017, one cannot walk down a major street without visibly encountering two distinct religious networks, with individuals dressed in either Muslim or Hindu garb, their foreheads bare or marked with ash and a *bindu* of *kuṃkum*, patronizing entirely distinct restaurants and shops that happen to be located a few feet from one another. While visibly distinguished by their embodiment of religious identity, these communities move in the same public space, and the street belongs to neither. Such urban pluralism has found a receptive audience in recent years among scholars of the global cityscape, uniting the experience of religious pluralism in contemporary India with the cultural and economic fragmentation of late capitalism. William Elison (2014), for instance, has addressed the particular phenomenon of *darśan* as public recognition, resituating the worship of Sai Baba in Mumbai within the framework of recent theories of space and visual culture.

But is such "disjuncture and difference," in the words of Arjun Appadurai (1990), the distinctive property of global postcapitalism, a fragmentation produced by the schizophrenia of a modernist mass culture as Jean Baudrillard (1995) or Fredric Jameson (1991) would have it? A multicentric cultural landscape, at least within the Indian context, has premodern precedents; the urban pluralism of contemporary India owes as much to its early modern antecedents as to the hegemony of economic globalization. And yet, returning once again to seventeenth-century south India, we can find no better example than the invention of Madurai's Cittirai Festival, which I explore in more detail in chapter 4. The festival, celebrated annually in April/May in Madurai's Mīnākṣī-Sundareśvara Temple, and which has become the city's most iconic public celebration, owes its distinctive shape to the active negotiation, some three hundred years ago, of religious diversity in public space. Before undergoing a strategic rebranding during Nīlakaṇṭha's own watch, the Cittirai Festival was a strictly Vaiṣṇava observance, commemorating Viṣṇu's journey to the Vaikai River in the center of the city to liberate the sage Maṇḍūka from the bondage of his past sins. In the early seventeenth century, the marriage of Śiva and Mīnākṣī was rescheduled to coincide with the Vaiṣṇava Cittirai Festival, essentially fusing Madurai's best-loved Śaiva and Vaiṣṇava holidays into a single citywide celebration.

Indeed, situating Viṣṇu's journey at precisely this moment must have appealed to connoisseurs of the *Tiruviḷaiyāṭal Purāṇam,* the "Sacred Games of Śiva," which by the seventeenth century had come to describe Viṣṇu himself as officiating at Śiva's marriage in the Mīnākṣī-Sundareśvara Temple. And yet Viṣṇu never reaches the marriage ceremony in the city center, turning back after reaching the Vaikai to his home in the Aḻakar Temple on the outskirts of town. Over time, popular narrative tradition evolved to account for this lapse in consistency.[35] Viṣṇu, according to this anecdote, reaches the Vaikai only to learn that he is late for the wedding, and that the event has already taken place in his absence; at this point, the infuriated deity reverses his course, pausing on his journey home to make select stops for his personal enjoyment.

What this reconstruction of Madurai's Cittirai Festival illustrates is not simply the management of tensions between religious communities—an obligatory cornerstone of any model of pluralism—but the mapping of spatial geographies of religiosity that were evolving in seventeenth-century Madurai. The twin processions of the sacred couple and Viṣṇu map onto the religious networks of Śaiva and Vaiṣṇava Hindus, patronized and performed throughout much of the twentieth century by entirely distinct castes and lineages that owed their allegiance to Śiva or Viṣṇu, respectively. In the seventeenth century, these communities seized the festival occasion for the exchange of honors from the Nāyaka rulers of Madurai, allowing individuals to navigate the symbolic economy centered on the temple complex. The festival served as a venue for public performance of works of devotional literature—Parañcōti's *Tiruviḷaiyāṭal Purāṇam* being just one example—which consolidated popular religious identity around new sites of memory as the legends came to be performed as part of the temple's seasonal calendar.

A sectarian community, in short, was not a subset of civil society, an aggregate of individuals who met privately to partake of a commonly shared religious sentiment. Sectarian communities were lived and performed in public space, with geographies that often seamlessly overlaid one another without necessitating communal conflict. Institutionally established in the religious landscape by temples and monasteries—sites that occasioned the embodiment of a shared religious identity—sectarian communities were visibly marked as public religious communities, fostering the readily legible performance of sectarian identity in public space. This is not to say, obviously, that conflicts never occurred between these parallel public domains; indeed, as we have seen, moments of tension were fundamental to the formulation of the boundaries between sectarian communities and the publics they cultivated. Pluralism, however, can be most accurately described not as the absence of conflict but as its effective resolution—a process that in Hindu early modernity was facilitated not by the removal of religion in public but by its active publicization, by the shared performance of plural religiosities.

THE MAKING OF A SECTARIAN COMMUNITY: PUBLIC THEOLOGY IN ACTION

As a case study of this larger socioreligious dynamic, this book examines the sectarianization of Hinduism in microcosm by telling the story of a particular Hindu sect in the process of coming into being. This community, the Smārta-Śaiva tradition of south India—otherwise known as Tamil Brahminism[36]—ranks among a handful of independent Hindu lineages that, when viewed in toto, palpably dominates the public religious life of south India today. And yet little scholarship to date has inquired into its contemporary religious culture, let alone the historical conditions of possibility that led to its emergence.[37] The renunciant branch of modern Smārta-Śaivism, the Śaṅkarācārya order of ascetics, has garnered significant attention as a pan-Indian monastic lineage rooted in four (or five) *maṭha*s at the corners of the Indian subcontinent and as a primary vehicle for the dissemination of Advaita Vedānta philosophy. Before the early modern centuries, however, Vedānta was the exclusive purview of such ascetic orders, as the theological canon expressly forbade its practice by all but Brahmin renunciants. Smārta-Śaivism, however, as a sectarian community, incorporated the charisma of the Śaṅkarācārya Jagadgurus into the consolidation of an extensive lay populace, many of whom began to cultivate a relationship of personal devotion with these iconic figures. Many of these lay theologians, in turn, crafted the systems of meaning that gave birth to the religious culture of Smārta-Śaivism as such. As a result, it is in their writings—their doctrine, polemic, ritual procedures, and devotional poetry—that this project's inquiry is grounded.

The public theology of the Smārta-Śaiva community in and of itself is a discourse still in need of excavation. I draw primarily from the theologically inflected writings of major sectarian theologians—whether philosophical speculation or overt sectarian polemic. The first task at hand, then, has been both to reconstitute the discourse of public theology and to allow it to tell its story to contemporary audiences. Only when read as an active field of discourse can Śaiva public theology speak to the lived reality beyond the text, in which theology is enacted through public ritual and socioreligious institutions. I bring the pamphlets of virtual unknowns in dialogue with the polished treatises of iconic Śaiva and Vaiṣṇava theologians. As a historical archive, necessarily constrained by the happenstance of manuscript collection and preservation, this source material provides a representative sampling of the theological discourse that shaped the boundaries of the nascent sectarian communities of sixteenth- and seventeenth-century south India. As a result, the vast majority of sources cited are either unpublished manuscripts or published editions rarely accessible in readable condition.

The textual culture of early modern south India, moreover, is fundamentally polyglot in its linguistic composition. Products of a hybrid Tamil-Telugu regional culture, Smārta Brahmins, educated in the classical Sanskritic knowledge systems, rubbed shoulders with court poets and theologians writing exclusively in the Tamil and Telugu vernaculars. Indeed, the educated publics they addressed likely overlapped to a significant degree. A responsible inquiry into this discursive field, then, must necessarily take a multilingual approach to the textual archive, particularly when the object of study is not simply the text itself but simultaneously the context—the extratextual sectarian community shaped by that same multilingual discourse. Śaiva theology, to name but one example, was written in Sanskrit, Tamil, Telugu, and Kannada—and Sanskrit-educated theologians were by no means ignorant of their vernacular counterparts.

Chapter 1 begins by setting the scene for the emergence of an autonomous Smārta-Śaiva sectarian community. I first contextualize the salient features of early modern Smārta-Śaivism through their genealogical development from earlier pan-Indian Śaiva Tantric traditions. Śaivism, as we will see, in its earliest instantiations required no reference to an overarching religious identity that we might call Hinduism; as a result, *Śaiva* and *sectarian* are by no means synonyms but rather a dyad in need of historical disambiguation. Moving forward in history, then, I situate the earliest stages of the community's manifestation within the milieu of early sectarianization in south India. I conclude this chapter by introducing the major players in the sectarianization of Smārta-Śaivism in the sixteenth and seventeenth centuries, particularly Nīlakaṇṭha Dīkṣita, poet laureate of the Nāyaka kingdom of Madurai, whose theology may be viewed as representative of the generation of intellectuals who played midwife to the emergent Smārta-Śaiva community.

Chapter 2 captures the moment of crystallization of the major structural features of Smārta-Śaivism at around the turn of the seventeenth century. Specifically, this moment marks the juncture at which the south Indian Śaṅkarācārya lineages, centered institutionally at Sringeri and Kanchipuram, came to function as the doctrinal and institutional hubs of a public sectarian network that extended far beyond the walls of the monastic lineages themselves. Although certain monasteries had been incorporated as religious institutions some centuries before, particularly the Sringeri *matha* in western Karnataka, and had even entered into relationships of ideological exchange with ruling powers,[38] the seventeenth century witnessed a marked transformation in the religious public that came to define itself in relationship to these monastic lineages. This chapter focuses on the case of the Śaṅkarācārya networks of Tamil Nadu, which, in the process of ensconcing themselves institutionally in the vicinity of Kanchipuram, forged an alliance with the intellectual elite of Sanskritic Śaiva circles. As a result, Nīlakaṇṭha Dīkṣita and a number of his close associates entered into devotional relationships with Śaṅkarācārya preceptors and publicly professed their allegiance to the esoteric ritual tradition associated with the Śaṅkarācārya lineages, the Śrīvidyā school of Śākta Tantrism. We witness the emergence, in the space of a generation, of a completely unprecedented socioreligious network, one that has proved foundational to the present-day constitution of south Indian Smārta-Śaivism.

In chapter 3, I examine the doctrinal constitution of "orthodox" Smārta-Śaivism from the outside in—that is, by way of polemical encounter with rival sectarian traditions, such as the Mādhva and Śrīvaiṣṇava communities, both major shareholders in the transregional south Indian networks of monasteries and temple complexes. Beginning in the mid-sixteenth century, sectarian polemic suddenly irrupts in popularity as a distinct textual genre, as major theologians launch a discoursewide, interdisciplinary inquiry into the canonical status of scriptures affiliated exclusively with particular sectarian traditions, such as the Śaiva and Vaiṣṇava Purāṇas. Debate soon overflows the confines of strictly philosophical contention, as polemicists circulate pamphlet after pamphlet with the express aim of discrediting, on text-critical grounds, the scriptural foundations of rival lineages. We observe, as a result, a heightened philological sensitivity emerging at all levels of public discourse, which, in the process of cementing the text-critical foundations of both Śaiva and Vaiṣṇava claims to orthodoxy, provides a conceptual language for differentiating sectarian communities as autonomous social systems.

In chapter 4, I explore the influence of sectarian theology on the wider public religious culture of the Tamil region by reconstructing the emergence of the Sthalapurāṇa of Madurai as a living canon of Śaiva religious experience. First entextualized in the thirteenth century, the *Tiruviḷaiyāṭal Purāṇam*—a cycle of narratives depicting Śiva's sixty-four sacred games in the city of Madurai—emerged out of the domain of elite literary practice and went on to transform the public face of local Śaiva religiosity, in no small part owing to the intervention of Madurai's Śaiva public theologians. The "Sacred Games" attained the status of a public site of memory over the course of mere decades owing to the cross-pollination of the Tamil region's diverse, multilingual literary cultures—Tamil, Telugu, and Sanskrit—later venturing into the territories of Marathi and Kannada as well. As a result of their dramatic upsurge in literary popularity, several of Śiva's "Sacred Games" were woven into the texture of Śaiva temple ritual, publicly enacted to this day as annual processional festivals. In short, by interfacing with a multilingual domain of public culture, theologians such as Nīlakaṇṭha exerted an influence well beyond the circles of Śaiva Brahmins and shaped the popular religiosity of Śaivas across south India. Public theology, in the case of the *Tiruviḷaiyāṭal Purāṇam*, began with the poetry of celebrated Sanskrit and Tamil literati only to leave an indelible impression on public religiosity of the region, as the "Sacred Games" are today inextricable from the experience of being a Śaiva in the city of Madurai.

My archive is primarily textual, but always thoroughly contextualized. I analyze religious discourse with a view of text not merely as a world unto itself but as a medium for communication, for the production and dissemination of systems of meaning that constitute sectarian systems as lived religious communities. In fact, it is the very project of public theology that gives rise to the structures of meaning that perpetuate religious communities such as the sectarian traditions of early modern south India. I aim to illustrate, through the study of intellectual history in microcosm, how public theological discourse both constructs and maintains the cultural artifacts—from monasteries to ritual performance to soteriological belief—that endow each religious community with its autonomous sectarian identity. I aim to document the sectarianization of Hinduism not in its aftermath, then, but in its very process of coming into being.

Hindu Sectarianism

Difference in Unity

He, the Lord [Śiva], is my God—I remember no other even by name.
—NĪLAKAṆṬHA DĪKṢITA, *ŚIVOTKARṢAMAÑJARĪ*

VAIDIKA AND ŚAIVA

Hinduism, in its own words, is a religion thoroughly permeated by difference. Even on the eve of V. D. Savarkar's coining of the term *Hindutva*—the specter of a unified and hegemonic Hindu nation underlying the Hindu nationalist movement— many of Hinduism's own spokesmen prided their religion for what they saw as an innate propensity for internal pluralism.

And yet, whereas Balagangadhar "Lokamanya" Tilak, as we have seen, centers his definition of Hinduism explicitly on its "multiplicity of ways of worship / and lack of restriction on the divinity that one may worship," nineteenth-century Orientalist scholarship advocated a different model of Hindu difference, one that threatened to fragment the ostensive original unity of India's golden age. It was this fractious and divisive form of Hinduism that Oxford's own Sir Monier Monier-Williams described, perhaps for the first time, as Hindu sectarianism—that is, the worship of Śiva or Viṣṇu as supreme deity.

Scholarship on Hinduism to this day has exponentially expanded our corpus of knowledge on the history of Vaiṣṇavism and Śaivism but, perhaps not unpredictably, has left Monier-Williams's definition virtually intact. Indeed, the word *sectarian*, in the vast majority of monographs, serves as a virtual stand-in for the conjunction of "Śaivism and Vaiṣṇavism." Our historical archive, however, tells a very different story: sectarianism, as it emerged in the late-medieval and early modern period, was not a fragmentation of original unity but a synthesis of originally discrete religions that gradually came to be situated under the umbrella of a unified Hindu religion in the early second millennium. To be a Hindu, at the earliest moments of the religion's internal coherence, was by definition to be a "sectarian"—that is, to be a Śaiva or Vaiṣṇava adherent of a particular lineage and community. Indeed, at those very moments in history when the shadow of a unified Hinduism can be glimpsed in the writings of pioneering intellectuals, Hindu religious communities on the ground took great pains to signal their fundamental independence from one another. Take the following verse, for instance, extracted from a hymn of praise, inscribed in 1380 C.E. on the walls of the Cenna Keśava Temple, a Vaiṣṇava center of worship in Belur, Karnataka:

> The one whom Śaivas worship as "Śiva," Vedāntins as "brahman,"
> The Buddhists, skilled in the means of valid knowledge, as "Buddha,"
>   the Logicians as "Creator,"
> Those with a mind for the Jaina teachings as "Arhat," Mīmāṃsakas
>   as "Ritual"—
> May he, Śrī Keśava, always grant you the results you desire.[1]

Although we may not know its exact circumstances of composition, this verse captures a pervasive motif of Hindu religious thought: one particular God, revered by a community of devotees, encapsulates in his—or her—very being the entire scope of divinity. Although in situ the inscription also served the purpose of *praśasti*, or "royal encomium," of a local ruler by the name of Keśava, this verse circulated widely, accruing variants here and there, as a fixture of devotional liturgy across communities. Nevertheless, the standard of comparison (the *viṣṇupakṣa* of the *śleṣa*) of the pun sends an unambiguous message: in the eyes of his fourteenth-century Vaiṣṇava worshippers, it was Śrī Keśava who came to subsume the deities of competing traditions, both those that were generally understood as heterodox, or *nāstika*—Buddhists and Jains—and those we would consider "Hindu," or *āstika*—such as Śaivas or Vedāntins. Implicit in this verse is an argument not for irenic tolerance or universalist pantheism, nor for the essential unity of all Hindu traditions, but for, literally, the supremacy of Vaiṣṇavism and of the god Viṣṇu as the telos of all religious practice.

This phenomenon is of course not unique to Vaiṣṇava theology. In fact, we find its mirror image in one of the most celebrated of Śaiva hymns, which to this day remains a cornerstone of Śaiva liturgy across the subcontinent, the *Śivamahimnaḥ Stotram*.[2] In this case, the *Śivamahimnaḥ* enshrines Śiva himself as the ultimate goal, objectively speaking, of practitioners of all religious systems, irrespective of the personal sentiments of the devotees who follow those diverse paths. From the mouth of its ostensible author, Puṣpadanta, a *gandharva* seeking to regain favor with Śiva, we hear the following:

> The Vedas, Sāṅkhya, Yoga, the Pāśupata doctrine, and the Vaiṣṇava:
> Where authorities are divided, one says, "This is highest," another,
>   "That is beneficial,"

> Due to such variegation of the tastes of men, who enjoy straight or
>   crooked paths.
> *You alone* are the destination, as the ocean is the destination of the
>   waters.[3]

By describing Śiva *alone* as the destination of all religious practitioners, the *Śivamahimnaḥ* elevates the deity of one "sectarian" tradition—that of the Śaivas—above the otherwise level playing field that encompasses all other branches of what we typically categorize within Vaidika "Hinduism." The very category of "Hinduism," however, when applied indiscriminately to Puṣpadanta's proclamation, allows the most obvious import of the above verse to escape our grasp. Certainly, followers of all the traditions mentioned by name in this verse have habitually been circumscribed within the overarching category of Hinduism, on the grounds that each one of them, to some degree, subordinates itself to the canonical authority of an overarching Brahminical religion.[4] Such an argument has been phrased perhaps most eloquently by Brian K. Smith, in his *Reflections on Resemblance, Ritual and Religion* (1989). Adopting the Vedas themselves as the iconic authority to which all of Hinduism must adhere, even if only in name, Smith proposes the following definition for Hinduism as a unitary religion: "Having reviewed the analytically separable (but in actuality usually conflated) types of definitions Indologists have constructed for the construct called Hinduism—the inchoate, the thematic, and the social and/or canonical—I now wish to offer my own working definition, locating myself firmly within the camp of the canonical authority as constitutive of the religion: *Hinduism is the religion of those humans who create, perpetuate, and transform traditions with legitimizing reference to the authority of the Veda.*"[5]

On the basis of Smith's definition, one would be hard pressed to defend the case that the Śaivism espoused by the *Śivamahimnaḥ* is, strictly speaking, a branch of Hinduism. To argue, as Smith does, that Hinduism consists primarily of those traditions that invoke the authority of the Vedas suggests that individual Hindu communities, or philosophical schools, subordinate themselves to a set of Vaidika values, which serves as a linchpin for theological legitimacy, or at least seek to legitimate themselves through seeking out a Vaidika semiotic stamp of approval. And yet the *Śivamahimnaḥ* reverses this polarity entirely, subordinating the Vedas themselves (*trayī*) to yet another overarching category, a canonical authority in and of itself—the category of Śaivism. Much of what survives of early Śaiva literature corroborates Puṣpadanta's declaration that Śiva—and Śaivism—transcend the Vedas themselves, rather than falling within their purview. Sociologically speaking, in fact, this is no hollow rhetorical gesture. By the middle of the first millennium of the Common Era, Śaivism, rather than Hinduism or Brahminism, could justifiably be described as the dominant religion of the Indian subcontinent.

Such is the case that has been made by Alexis Sanderson in his monograph-length study, "*The Śaiva Age*" (2009). Sanderson argues, in essence, that during the medieval period—roughly from the fifth century to the thirteenth century—Tantric Śaiva knowledge systems both replaced their Brahminical counterparts as the primary ritual technology of ruling kings and served as the model par excellence for religious practice in public temple worship and in elite soteriological paths. Other major religious communities, such as the Buddhists and Pāñcarātrika Vaiṣṇavas, began to make bids for royal patronage through a wholesale adoption of Śaiva models of ritual and textuality, thus becoming colonized, so to speak, by the cultural idiom of Tantric Śaivism. Śaiva theologians, as a result, approached the traditional knowledge systems of Vaidika Brahminism with a thoroughgoing skepticism, either rejecting outright the validity of the Vedas or relegating Vaidika theology to the status of a stepping-stone for reaching the higher truths of Śaivism.

It is the latter group of Śaivas, naturally—those who creatively co-opted the models of Brahminical religious practice in service of a transcendent Śaiva religion—who attained the highest visibility, not to mention political clout, within the social order of medieval South Asia. In the domain of ritual in particular, Brahminical models were often recycled wholesale, laminated with a Śaiva inflection that marked them as belonging to the new soteriological systems of Śaivism. Śrāddha rituals, or oblations for the deceased ancestors, for instance, remained a standard observance for Śaiva initiates, and Śaiva ascetics adopted many of the daily protocols of their Brahminical counterparts, down to the minutiae of prescriptions for brushing one's teeth.[6] Likewise, in the domain of theology, Śaiva exegetes regularly subordinated entire Vaidika philosophical traditions to their commentarial agendas. One has only to consider the example of the Śaiva *tattva* systems, the hierarchical mapping of "levels of reality" known best from the Sāṅkhya and Yoga schools of Brahminical theology. Śaiva theologians, quite simply, recycled the entire paradigm of the twenty-five Sāṅkhya *tattvas*, adding an additional, superior, set of eleven *tattvas* by a process of philosophical agglutination.

And yet we would lose something fundamental to our knowledge of the history of South Asian religion were we to simply reduce the early period of Śaivism to a theme and variation on early Brahminical religion. Despite their careful co-option of the classical Indic past, Śaiva exegetes rarely lost sight of the fundamental paradigm shift they perceived as separating themselves from their Brahminical predecessors. Our earliest extant Śaiva literature exhibits a remarkably ambivalent stance toward Vedic revelation, paying outward respect to the institutions of Vedic learning while elevating the Śaiva community to a hierarchical plane above the baseline of the Brahminical tradition. In essence, in these early strata of Śaiva textual culture, Śaivism was something fundamentally distinct from, and ultimately superior to, Vaidika "orthodoxy." It was Śaivism that subsumed Vedicism under its overarching umbrella of authority, rather than Vedicism subsuming Śaivism as one "sect" within an ostensive "Hindu" whole.

Take, for instance, the Śivadharma,[7] our earliest surviving example of Śaiva Dharmaśāstra literature. While its generic conventions are modeled on the classical tradition of Brahminical Dharmaśāstra, the Śivadharma lays out a code of conduct distinctive to Śaiva initiates, and great pains have been taken to emphasize the vast gulf separating Śaiva religious practice from analogous Vaidika observances:

> Therefore, a hundred times the merit is accrued from giving a clay
> vessel to Śiva
> Than would be accrued from giving a gold vessel to one who has
> mastered the Vedas.
>
> Fire oblations, the Vedas, sacrifices, and abundant gifts to the
> teacher:
> All of these, even by the crore, are not equivalent to the worship of
> the *śivaliṅga*.[8]

In the minds of its exegetes, then, early Śaivism condoned Vedicism while superseding its confines by orders of magnitude. In very much the same manner, an existing Vaidika ritual technology became thoroughly subordinated to Śaivism over the course of this paradigm shift that Sanderson has called the Śaiva Age. Such can be observed, for instance, in one of our earliest accounts of Śaiva-specific ritual procedures: the installation of the *liṅga,* or the *liṅgapratiṣṭhānavidhi.* Our textual exemplars for this procedure date back to the earliest surviving Śaiva Siddhānta scriptural corpus—specifically, the Niśvāsaguyhasūtra.[9] In this account, much of the process of installing and consecrating a *śivaliṅga* is pervaded by a self-conscious Vedicization. Specific Vedic mantras are prescribed for Ṛgveda, Yajurveda, Sāmaveda, and Atharvaveda priests, each of which is conceptually equated with one of the four directions. And yet we must not lose sight of the fact that the very goal of this procedure is, after all, the installation of a *śivaliṅga,* an aniconic representation of the god Śiva, without whom the ritual would be meaningless.

Other passages, in contrast, exhibit an even more hostile stance toward Vedicism, completely rejecting the authority of the Vedas themselves, let alone Śrauta ritual and its auxiliaries. The more ostensibly antinomian traditions, inhabiting the fringes of the Śaiva cosmopolis, were particularly likely to incorporate an outwardly anti-Vedic rhetoric. Among scriptures of the Kaula Mārga, the Kulasāra (c. seventh century C.E.), for instance, essentially classifies those learned in the Vedas as *nāstikas,* equal to Jains and Buddhists in their fundamental inability to grasp the true state of affairs.[10] In other instances, Śaiva partisans have been known to advocate the wholesale abandonment of the Vaidika cultural heritage.

The following passage from the circa-seventh-century Śivadharmottara illustrates with characteristic vehemence just how pointed the anti-Vaidika strains within the Śaiva fold had become: "Purāṇa, the Mahābhārata, the Veda, and the great *śāstras*: all of these, expansive tomes meager in dharma, surely waste one's life."[11]

The Śaivism of the Śaiva Age, in short, defies any attempts to classify it as a sect of Hinduism or Brahminism. Indeed, the most wildly influential Śaiva traditions—those of the Śaiva Mantramārga, or Āgamic Śaivism, generally speaking—diverged so thoroughly from the Brahminical past in theology, ritual, and scriptural canon that whatever one may describe as the substantively "religious" building blocks of the new Śaiva world order were for all intents and purposes transformed beyond recognition. To cite a singularly poignant example, the traditions we refer to broadly as Tantric Śaivism—or the Śaiva Mantramārga, in the words of Alexis Sanderson—structured their soteriology around a single provocative claim: Śaiva initiation (*dīkṣā*) is the effective cause of liberation. And the implications of this assertion—that a mere *ritual,* in and of itself, possesses the means to sever the bonds that tie the individual soul to transmigratory existence—radically recast the sociological implications of elite Indic religion. In fact, Śaiva initiation in many traditions offered the promise of completely eradicating one's intrinsic caste identity, transforming all initiates into Brahmins without the need for renunciation. As a result, even the more socially normative branches of early Śaivism effectively circumvented the strictures of *varṇāśramadharma*, providing both kings and Śūdras with access to liberation. The following rhetoric, for instance, reappears frequently in early Śaiva literature, subordinating caste difference to the inclusivity of Śaiva initiation, a theme that would emerge centuries later as a cornerstone of bhakti religiosity, best known for its appearance in the Bhāgavata Purāṇa:

> I am not partial to either a Caturvedī or a Dog-cooker, if he is my
> devotee.
> One may give to him and take from him; he should be worshiped as
> I myself.[12]

That such caste-blindness was enforced in practice in Śaiva circles, moreover, is expressed eloquently in the following passage from the Svacchanda Tantra, modeled after an earlier exemplar from the Niśvāsa corpus. Here, Śaiva initiates are said to accrue impurity not from mixing castes, as the strictures of *varṇāśramadharma* would suggest, but rather for failing to be caste-blind—that is, for importing Brahminical normativity where it does not belong:

> Those who have been initiated by this very procedure, O Beautiful-
> Faced One,
>
> Brahmins, Kṣatriyas, Vaiśyas, Śūdras, and others likewise, O Dear
> One,

All of these have the same dharma—they have been enjoined in the
    dharma of Śiva.

They are all said to bear matted locks, their bodies smeared with ash.
All Samayins should eat in one line, O Beautiful-Faced One.

There should be one [line] for Putrakas, one for Sādhakas likewise,
And one for Cumbakas—not according to one's prior caste.

They are remembered in the *smṛtis* as having only one caste: that of
    Bhairava, imperishable and pure.
Having had recourse to this Tantra, one should not mention some-
    one's previous caste.

Should a man mention the prior caste of a Putraka, Sādhaka,
Or of a Samayin, he would require expiation, O Goddess.

He burns in hell for three of Rudra's days, five of Keśava's days,
And a fortnight of Brahmā's days.

Therefore, one must not discriminate, if he wishes to obtain the
    supreme goal.[13]

Speaking of the soteriological as well as the social, Śaiva religious practice was
no mere translation of Brahminism, preserving the religious paradigm of an earlier age under the auspices of an alternative social order. After all, Śaiva initiates kept no sacred fires in their homes, rarely pursuing training in Śrauta ritual
officiation—in short, entirely spurning the ritual duties incumbent on elite members of Brahminical society. The Vedas themselves faded into the background, as
Śaiva extracted their essence in the form of the Śatarudrīya, the hymn to Rudra
found in the Taittirīya Saṃhitā of the Kṛṣṇa Yajurveda, and the Gāyatrī mantra,
abandoning large-scale Vedic recitation as such. In its place, a new ritual technology emerged with the Śaiva Mantramārga, irreducible to its historical antecedents
in the Brahminical period, that fundamentally transformed the face of elite religious practice across religious boundaries. An entirely new corpus of scriptures
emerged over the centuries, establishing new canons for public temple worship
as well as the individual soteriological practice of householders and ascetics. The
individual practitioner, for instance, adopted elaborate disciplines of the body,
ritually purifying the constituents of his being (*ātmaśuddhi* and *bhūtaśuddhi*) and
investing his hands—the instruments of ritual—and the remainder of his body
with elements of the divine in the form of mantras (*sakalīkaraṇa, nyāsa*).[14] The
goal of such bodily disciplines is, quite simply, to achieve liberation or supernor-
mal powers by transforming the initiate into Śiva himself. It is this soteriological
goal—the transformation of the adept into Śiva, a Śiva on earth, or his deity of

choice, through Tantric ritual practice—that most definitively shifted the paradigms of Indic religious practice and theology for centuries to come.[15]

Early Śaivas, in essence, (1) rejected the authority of Vedic scripture, (2) disregarded the social hierarchies of *varṇāśramadharma,* often dismissing them as mere "custom" with no divine sanction, and (3) engaged in core religious practices that bore minimal resemblance to Brahminical custom. As a result, the Śaivism of the Śaiva Age can scarcely be described as a sect of Brahminism. Nor can the Vaiṣṇava or Buddhist communities that rapidly conformed to the fashions of the Śaiva Mantramārga. Śaivism, during this formative period, was functionally independent from any parent religion we may wish to describe as "Hinduism," charting its own course in defiance of the religious norms that preceded it. It was the centuries following the Śaiva Age, however, that witnessed the incorporation of Śaiva traditions under the umbrella of a new Vaidika orthodoxy, which, arguably, we may for the first time describe as Hinduism, as Śaiva theologians hastened to justify their long-standing traditions according to the standards of Vedic normativity.

THE SECTARIANIZATION OF HINDUISM: ŚAIVISM AND BRAHMINICAL ORTHODOXY

In spite of the wide-ranging transformations of the Śaiva Age, Hinduism as we know it did in fact emerge, and a number of scholars have argued that it emerged quite a bit earlier than previously suspected, independent of the meddling gaze of European colonial regimes. For instance, in his book *Unifying Hinduism,* Andrew Nicholson marks the years between the twelfth and sixteenth centuries as the interstitial period in which the notion of Hinduism as a unitary religion began to crystallize in the minds of Indian thinkers. During these centuries, Nicholson argues, scholars begin to compose doxographical compendia that, by virtue of their very scope, implicitly assert the unity of the *āstika* or Vaidika discourses they group together. Only after these centuries, which Nicholson refers to as the late-medieval period, did the unity of Hinduism become irrevocably naturalized in Indic theological discourse. Perhaps it is no coincidence, in fact, that this late-medieval period followed immediately on the tail end of the Śaiva Age, suggesting another system-wide shift in the paradigms of religious practice, stretching well beyond the boundaries of doxographical treatises.

Within Śaiva circles as well, the unimpeded independence of Śaivism began to give way to a circumspect deference to Vaidika normativity as the Śaiva Age drew to a close. In fact, the Śaivism of the late-medieval period began to position itself less as an independent religious system than as an orthodox exemplar—or, one might even say, a *sect*—of Brahminical Hinduism. In south India, for instance, theologians of the Sanskritic Śaiva Siddhānta tradition launched a truly unprecedented campaign to align the social constituency of the Śaiva fold with the norms of *varṇāśramadharma,* violating centuries of precedent that excluded Śaiva initiates from caste regulations. Such a position was advocated, for instance, by the twelfth-century Śaiva Siddhānta theologian Trilocanaśiva in his *Prāyaścittasamuccaya,*[16] a handbook on the expiation of sins for Śaiva initiates who have lapsed in their observance of Brahminical purity codes:

> When eating, one must always avoid forming a single line with
>   members of different castes.
>
> Should a Brahmin eat in such a way out of ignorance, with
>   Kṣatriyas, Vaiśyas, or Śūdras,
> Having realized it in the midst [of eating], he must stop, and then,
>   having sipped water many times,
>
> He should recite [the Aghora mantra] ten times, twenty times, or
>   thirty times, respectively,
> [Or, likewise,] should he realize it at the end of the meal, one, two,
>   or three hundred times, respectively.
>
> Having eaten in a line with members of unknown castes, he should
>   repeat it three hundred times.
> Or with others who may not form a line, unknowns, or others born
>   against the grain. . . .
>
> Having eaten something that was touched by the leavings of Śūdras
>   and the others, or by Antyajas,
>
> Having eaten something that is by nature impure, or made impure
>   by touch or action,
> He should bathe, going without food, and should also drink the five
>   cow substances.[17]

Judging from the *Prāyaścittasamuccaya,* scant difference can be discerned between the Śaiva and Brahminical views on intercaste purity rules. Had Trilocanaśiva not ceaselessly advocated use of the Aghora mantra, one of the five *aṅga* mantras of the Śaiva Siddhānta, as a virtual cure-all for expiable sins,[18] one would scarcely realize that the above passage belonged to a Śaiva-specific handbook rather than a treatise on Brahminical Dharmaśāstra. In fact, in Trilocanaśiva's stance, we find a mirror image of the early Śaiva rejection of caste difference, which had elevated one's status as a Śaiva initiate above any markers of social standing, which were considered extrinsic to one's true identity. Instead, by Trilocanaśiva's day in the twelfth century, Śaivas defended the orthodoxy of their lineages not on strictly Śaiva theological grounds but rather by citing their conformity to the social mores of the classical Vaidika tradition. In terms of social conduct, Śaiva Saiddhāntikas, for Trilocanaśiva, were by definition Vaidika Hindus.

In the domain of theology as well, Trilocanaśiva's contemporaries and successors adopted a surprisingly accommodationist strategy with regard to currents of Vaidika theology that were soaring in popularity in the early centuries of the second millennium—most notably among these, Advaita Vedānta. Historically, the Śaiva Siddhānta tradition had maintained a staunchly dualist cosmology, asserting the immutable difference between Śiva and his creation, and between individual souls, or *jīvas*, who maintained their discrete identities even after liberation. Such a theology blends poorly, on strictly logical grounds, with the nondualist precepts of Advaita Vedānta philosophy. Nevertheless, by the fifteenth and sixteenth centuries, Saiddhāntika exegetes had so thoroughly assimilated the conventions of an Advaita-inflected theology that Saiddhāntika treatises in both Sanskrit and Tamil—and even redactions of Saiddhāntika scriptures[19]—were habitually sprinkled with the idioms of Vedānta. Scholars spared no opportunity, moreover, to genuflect to the authority of the Vedic corpus, defending Śaiva-specific scriptures and practice on the grounds of their ostensibly Vaidika pedigree.

One particularly striking example of this trend is the commentary of a certain Kumārasvāmin (circa fifteenth century) on the *Tattvaprakāśa* of Bhojadeva,[20] a succinct encapsulation on Śaiva Siddhānta theology. Unlike previous commentators, such as Aghoraśiva, who scrupulously adhere to the canon of Saiddhāntika doctrine, Kumārasvāmin repeatedly launches into extended digressions about the Vedic roots of the Śaiva Āgamas and Tantras, never hesitating to intersperse his discourses with references to Mīmāṃsā categories of ritual, even going so far as to assert that Śiva himself consists of the Vedas. He writes, "'He is victorious' means that he exists on a level above everything else. Why? Because his body, unlike other bodies, lacks the qualities of arising and destruction, and so forth. And that is because he consists of the Vedas, because the Vedas are eternal [*nitya*]."[21] Having thoroughly accepted the Mīmāṃsaka principle of the *apauruṣeyatva*—the authorless eternality—of Vedic scripture, Kumārasvāmin apparently felt it natural to equate Śiva, being similarly eternal, with the very substance of Vedic revelation. The remainder of Kumārasvāmin's commentary, in fact, proceeds in a similar vein, never straying far from his veritable obsession with the Vedas themselves.

To illustrate just how far Kumārasvāmin's exegetical agenda has wandered away from the mainstream of his own tradition, we can contrast the tenor of his commentary with that of an earlier commentator, the twelfth-century theologian Aghoraśiva, one of the most celebrated theologians of the south Indian Śaiva Siddhānta, head of the southern branch of the Āmardaka Maṭha at Cidambaram.[22] Aghoraśiva, quite logically, approaches the *Tattvaprakāśa* as a primer on the foundational theological concepts of Śaiva Siddhānta, highlighting the disagreements of his own system with those of his philosophical rivals. Take, for instance, Aghoraśiva's analysis of the first verse of the *Tattvaprakāśa*, a *maṅgala* verse in praise of Śiva:

> The one mass of consciousness, pervasive, eternal, always liberated,
> powerful, tranquil—
> He, Śambhu, excels all, the one seed syllable of the world, who
> grants everyone his grace.[23]

Unpacking the theological significance of each of these seemingly inconsequential adjectives, Aghoraśiva elaborates on this verse in the following commentarial passage. The prototypically Śaiva terminology that inflects his prose has been italicized for emphasis below:

> Here, the teacher, for the sake of completing the work he has begun without obstacles, with this first verse in the Ārya meter, praises Paramaśiva, who is *without kalās, transcending all of the tattvas,* who is the efficient cause of the undertaking of the treatises of the Siddhānta: "The one mass of consciousness," and so forth. Here, by the word "consciousness," *the powers of knowledge and action* are intended. As it is stated in the *Śrīman Mṛgendra Āgama: "Consciousness consists of the [goddesses] Dṛk and Kriyā."* The compound "a mass of consciousness" means he of whom the body is an aggregate of consciousness alone. It is not the case that he is inert, as held by those who believe Īśvara to consist of time, action, and so forth, because it would be impossible for something that is not conscious to undertake action without the support of something conscious. Nor is it reasonable that he is facilitated by a *body consisting of bindu,* because that would entail the consequence that he would not be the Lord, and, because he himself would then require another creator, one would arrive at an infinite regress with regard to his having another creator or having himself as a creator. . . .
>
> "Pervasive" means that he exists everywhere; he is not confined by a body, as the Jains and others believe, nor does he have the property of expansion and contraction, because such a one would necessarily be flawed with properties such as nonsentience and impermanence. "Eternal" means that he lacks any beginning or end; he is not momentary, as Buddhists and others believe, because, being destroyed at the very moment of his coming into existence, he could not possibly be the creator of the world. Now, if one says that the liberated souls as well have just such characteristics, he says, *"Always liberated." He is eternally liberated; it is not that he, like the liberated souls, is liberated by the grace of another Lord,* because this would result in infinite regress. . . .
>
> "Grants everyone his grace": grace, here, is a subsidiary property to creation and the others. And thus, he bestows enjoyment and liberation to all souls by means of the *five acts: creation, preservation, destruction, concealment, and grace.*[24]

Here, Aghoraśiva adheres faithfully to the canonical theological models of the Śaiva Siddhānta, seizing the opportunity to compile the classic refutations of non-Śaiva explanations for the creation of the world. His proof texts, likewise, are drawn exclusively from the Saiddhāntika Āgamas, such as the Mṛgendra Āgama and the Mataṅgapārameśvara. Throughout, his commentary is sprinkled with technical terminology that virtually never appears in non-Śaiva Brahminical the-ology, such as his reference to Dṛk and Kriyā as the two powers (*śaktis*) of Śiva, a stock trope that preceded the more familiar three *śakti* model—*jñāna, icchā,* and *kriyā*. Perhaps best known is the category of the five acts of Śiva—*sṛṣṭi* (cre-ation), *sthiti* (preservation), *saṃhāra* (destruction), *tirobhāva* (concealment), and *anugraha* (grace)—the latter of which, the grace that uplifts individual souls from bondage, provides Aghoraśiva with the most natural, and certainly the historically correct, explanation for the term *sarvānugrāhaka,* "granting everyone his grace," in the root text.

Kumārasvāmin, for his part, takes little interest in the obvious explanation for *sarvānugrāhaka,* preferring to import a model for how Śiva liberates individual souls that is entirely foreign to classical Śaiva theology, one that instead suspi-ciously resembles the core theology of Advaita Vedānta:

> For, unmediated [*aparokṣabhūta*] knowledge [*jñāna*], in fact, is the cause of su-preme beatitude [*apavarga*]. And its unmediated quality arises when the traces [*saṃskāra*] of ignorance [*avidyā*] have been concealed through intensive meditation [*nididhyāsana*]. And intensive meditation becomes possible when the knowledge of Śiva arises through listening to scripture [*śravaṇa*] and contemplation [*manana*]. And those arise because of the purification of the inner organ [*antaḥkaraṇa*]. That [purification] occurs through the practice of daily [*nitya*] and occasional [*naimi-ttika*] ritual observance, with the abandoning of the forbidden volitional [*kāmya*] rituals. Volitional scriptures, resulting in worldly fruits, such as: "One who desires animals should sacrifice with Citrā sacrifice" [Taittirīya Saṃhitā 2.4.6.1], have come forth to cause Brahmins whose minds are preoccupied with worldly results to set forth on the Vedic path; those that result in heaven, [likewise, do so for] those who are eager for heaven; and scriptures such as the Śyena, which prescribe the procedure for ritual murder, to cause those who are eager to destroy their enemies to proceed on the Vedic path.
>
> Thus, in sequence, through practicing daily and occasional rituals, from main-taining the sacred fires, from performing the Agnihotra oblation, and so forth, and through practicing those rituals that destroy sin, such as the enjoined bathing pro-cedure, when the purification of the mind becomes possible, when one turns away from volitional activity, when the purification of the inner organ arises, which takes the form of the desire to know the self [*ātman*] through the practice of daily and oc-casional rituals, when the knowledge of Śiva has arisen through listening to scripture and contemplation, after the destruction of ignorance and its traces through repeat-ed practice at intensive meditation, when unmediated knowledge of the essence of Śiva arises, liberation [*mokṣa*] occurs. Such is stated in the Mokṣadharma and other scriptures: "Dharma is enjoined everywhere; heaven is the arising of its true fruit. The ritual practice of dharma, which has many doors, is indeed not fruitless here." In this passage, those who engage in ritual prescribed by Śruti and Smṛti, as enjoined by Maheśvara, are liberated; those who do not do so continue to transmigrate.[25]

The textual register of Kumārasvāmin's commentary could scarcely be more directly opposed to that of his predecessor. The neo-Brahminical exegete not only imported the entirety of his philosophical apparatus from the most quintessentially orthodox of the Brahminical darśanas—namely, Vedānta and Mīmāṃsā—but also effectively subordinated the goals of Śaiva religious practice to an Advaitin soteriology. In place of the Saiddhāntika Āgamas, Kumārasvāmin quotes the Vedas, the Upaniṣads, and the Mahābhārata in support of his unconventional claims. Most strikingly, the knowledge of Śiva, for Kumārasvāmin, bears no relationship to Śaiva initiation, ritual practice, or Śiva's grace-bestowing power, but arises strictly as a result of constant meditation on the truths of Upaniṣadic scripture, serving as the direct cause of liberation, here referred to as *mokṣa*. By equating Śiva himself with the goal of Vedāntic contemplation, Kumārasvāmin overturned a centuries-long precedent of not merely indifference but active hostility to the philosophical precepts of the Vedānta school of thought. Śaivas, in fact, had traditionally expressed a thoroughgoing disdain for the term *mokṣa* for the Vedāntin assumptions it imported into discussions of liberation. Such a sentiment was perhaps best captured by the lion's roar of the Saiddhāntika theologian Bhaṭṭa Rāmakaṇṭha II in his provocatively titled *Paramokṣanirāsakārikā* (Stanzas on the refutation of the mokṣa doctrines of others), and his autocommentary (*Vṛtti*) on these aphorisms.[26] As Rāmakaṇṭha opines, scathingly: "To aim for the annihilation of the self is the ultimate in foolishness: 'The greatest heavyweights among the fools are those for whom the Self is destroyed [in liberation].'"[27]

Writing from Kashmir in the tenth century, Rāmakaṇṭha II spared no effort in demolishing the edifice of Vedāntin soteriology, approaching the tradition with hostility equal to the scorn which he showed other *āstika* and *nāstika* perspectives. And yet the vehemence of his arguments was lost on his successors in the south, who—beginning around the twelfth century or thirteenth century with our earliest Śaiva commentaries on the Brahmasūtras, Śrīkaṇṭha's *Brahmasūtrabhāṣya* and Śrīpati's *Śrīkarabhāṣya*—began to approach the Vedānta tradition not merely as a cogent analytical system, worthy of incorporation within the Śaiva fold, but as a fundamental cornerstone of Śaiva sectarianism. In other words, for Śrīkaṇṭha and Śrīpati, it was Vedānta that secured the status of Śaivism as a full-fledged representative of Vaidika, or Hindu orthodoxy. Our earliest known examples of a Vedānta-inflected Śaivism,[28] which include the *Śrīkaṇṭhabhāṣya*, *Śrīkarabhāṣya*, and Haradatta's *Śrutisūktimālā*, proved enormously influential first on the fledgling Sanskritic Vīraśaiva lineages of the greater Vijayanagara region—which had gradually incorporated local communities of Kālāmukhas and reformed Pāśupatas, who appear to have been particularly amenable to Śaiva Advaita theology. Śaiva Saiddhāntikas from both Tamil and Sanskrit lineages were increasingly swayed by the popularity of Advaita across the region, increasingly abandoning their commitment to a philosophical dualism. Subsequently, the Smārta-Śaiva community of the Tamil country generated an enormous output of Advaita Vedānta speculation, particularly following the community's introduction to Śrīkaṇṭha's *Bhāṣya* through the pioneering efforts of Appayya Dīkṣita, who allegedly "reinvented" Śrīkaṇṭha's philosophy in the Tamil South.[29]

Indeed, by the time of Appayya Dīkṣita in the sixteenth century, south Indian Śaivism had so thoroughly assimilated itself to the demands of a monistic Advaita Vedānta that Appayya himself, much like Kumārasvāmin, found it natural to equate knowledge of Śiva with the central mysteries of Advaita Vedānta. In a particularly telling interlude at the outset of his *Śivārkamaṇidīpikā*, his commentary on Śrīkaṇṭha's *Brahmasūtrabhāṣya*, Appayya narrates Śrīkaṇṭha's fondness for the *daharākāśavidyā*, the Upaniṣadic meditation on the subtle void at the center of the heart,[30] which, for Śaivas, had become the dwelling place of Śiva himself. Seamlessly integrating Śaiva and Vaidika worldviews, Appayya aims to dispel all doubts in the minds of his readers that the *ātman*, or Self, revealed in the Upaniṣads is none other than Śiva himself:

> This Teacher is devoted to the *daharavidyā*. For precisely this reason, to give it form, he will repeatedly gloss the passage "the supreme brahman, the divine law, the truth" throughout his commentary, owing to his inordinate respect. And because he himself is particularly fond of the *daharavidyā*, he will explain in the Kāmādhikaraṇa that the *daharavidyā* is the highest among all the other *vidyā*s. Thus, he indicates the reference he intends to offer by the word "to the supreme Self," which indicates a qualified noun, referring specifically to the *daharavidyā* as received in his own *śākhā*. For, it is revealed in the Taittirīya Upaniṣad: "In the middle of that top knot is established the supreme Self."
>
> Some people, saying that the supreme Self is different from Śiva, delude others. As a result, with the intention that virtuous people might not go astray, he qualifies [the supreme Self] as follows: "to Śiva." The Teacher will quite skillfully prove in the Śarīrādhikaraṇa that the supreme Self is, quite simply, Śiva himself.[31]

For the Śaivas of early modern south India, then, Śiva was none other than the *ātman*, or brahman, the highest truth of Vedic revelation, and consequently, Śaivism was none other than the epitome of Hinduism. Unlike the Śaivism of the Śaiva Age, Appayya Dīkṣita's Śaivism could no longer stand alone, outside the purview of a preestablished Hindu orthodoxy. What defines early modern Śaivism unmistakably as a sectarian community, a unit within a larger whole, is at once its deference to the norms and canonical beliefs of a Hinduism grounded in Vedic revelation, and its stubborn insistence that Śaivism itself—the traditions of interpretation set forth by worshippers of Śiva—constituted the whole, and indeed the very essence, of the Vedas themselves. The following aphorism, which circulated freely among Appayya's generation, encapsulates this contention:

> Among the disciplines of knowledge, Scripture is best; within Scripture, the Śrīrudram;
> Within that, the five-syllable mantra; and within that, the two syllables: *Śiva*.[32]

HINDUISM IN THE SECTARIAN AGE: POLEMICS, PHILOSOPHY, AND THE STRUGGLE FOR ORTHODOXY

By the time that Appayya Dīkṣita composed his magnum opus—his commentary on the Śrīkaṇṭha Bhāṣya, the *Śivārkamaṇidīpikā*—the Śaiva Age had come and gone in south India. Indeed, over the preceding centuries, the religious landscape of south India had already shifted dramatically under the rising pressures of sectarian rivalry. Mādhvas, Śrīvaiṣṇavas, and other religious communities rubbed elbows in search of patronage, jostling together in a socioreligious space that was being rapidly parceled out to competing sectarian lineages. And while many of south India's prominent Śaiva and Vaiṣṇava lineages trace their origin to pioneering theologians of the late-medieval period (the twelfth or thirteenth century), by the sixteenth and seventeenth centuries Hindu sectarianism had become not only a doctrinal but also an institutional cornerstone of the south Indian religious landscape. Monasteries and megatemples emerged as regional power centers in their own right, their pontiffs negotiating alliances with kings and emperors and disseminating the values of their community through transregional monastic networks.[33] Early modern Śaivas, in short, were not the only community to appoint themselves as the pinnacle of Hinduism—or to secure the social and political clout necessarily to make a case for their exclusive claim to orthodoxy.

To compete in the marketplace of proliferating sectarian identities, an emerging community required, first and foremost, a "Hindu theology"—that is, a doctrinal justification of Śiva or Viṣṇu as supreme deity based strictly upon a shared canon of Hindu sources. It is no accident that Śaiva theologians, as we have seen, undertook a self-conscious rapprochement between the Śaiva Āgamas and Vaidika custom and philosophy, most notably with the philosophical exegesis of the Upaniṣads promulgated as Śaṅkara's Advaita Vedānta. Succinctly, sectarian communities on the cusp of early modernity sectarian communities in south India—both Śaiva and Vaiṣṇava—structured their theology as a matter of course around competing interpretations of the Brahmasūtras, resulting in the proliferation of Vedāntas in the plural, a philosophical phenomenon that Lawrence McCrea and Ajay Rao have referred to as the "Age of Vedānta."[34] As a result, sectarian communities in south India were now forced to speak a common conceptual language and to affiliate themselves with one particular branch of Vedāntic exegesis. Śrīvaiṣṇavism, for instance, became increasingly synonymous with Viśiṣṭādvaita, nondualism of the "qualified" absolute; to be a Mādhva, by and large, implied affiliation with Dvaita, or dualist, Vedānta. And over the course of the early modern centuries, Śaivas in south India gradually cemented an alliance with the nondualist Advaita Vedānta, both in the form of faithful reproductions of Śaṅkara's Advaita and in the form of the Śaiva-Advaita synthesis that Appayya had adopted from his Vīraśaiva predecessors. In other words, a community's stance on Vedāntic ontology—the nature of the world according to the Upaniṣads—became the philosophical foundation of intersectarian polemic.

While Vedāntic speculation was largely practiced in the formalized idiom of Sanskrit systematic or *śāstric* thought, early sectarian commentators on the Brahmasūtras regularly dabbled in a genre that more closely resembled polemics than philosophy. Indeed, the very project of Śaivism and Vaiṣṇavism's becoming Hindu necessitated the emergence of a creative hermeneutics,[35] as theologians across sectarian lines sought to locate the distinctiveness of their devotional practice in the very text of the Vedas and Upaniṣads. The best known among these influential reinventions of tradition, perhaps, was undertaken by Madhva, a thirteenth-century Vaiṣṇava theologian and progenitor of the Mādhva sectarian community, which to this day attracts a substantial following across Karnataka and beyond. While Madhva achieved notoriety among subsequent generations of Śaivas and Vaiṣṇavas alike for allegedly inventing Vedic scriptures that none of his competitors could access, it was his Vedic exegesis that more directly contributed to the consolidation of Vaiṣṇava sectarianism in south India. That is, Madhva staked the Vaidika pedigree of his teachings on what philologians would most likely describe as creative misreadings, insisting, for instance, on reading the well-known "great statement," or *mahāvākya,* of the Chāndogya Upaniṣad *tat tvam asi*—"thou art that"—as *a-tat tvam asi,* "thou art *not* that," thus sanctioning his Dvaita, or dualist, interpretation of the Brahmasūtras, the ultimate incommensurability of the individual soul and universal godhead.

But above all, Vaiṣṇavas from distinct sectarian communities during these pivotal centuries took particular care to scour the Vedic and Upaniṣaic corpus for explicit mentions of Viṣṇu himself. After all, to claim that Mādhva Vaiṣṇavism or Śrīvaiṣṇavism, as the case may be, spoke for the true veracity of Vedic speech required that the Vedas distinctly and unambiguously affirm that Viṣṇu alone is the supreme God. Rāmānuja, for instance, and other theologian giants of the Śrīvaiṣṇava tradition, spilled a substantial volume of ink in the hopes of establishing that the very mention of the word *Śiva* or *Rudra* in Vedic revelation must be construed adjectivally—the word *Śiva* literally meaning "auspicious"—and not as a reference to a particular Hindu God. Acyuta, on the contrary, a well-known name of Viṣṇu that literally translates as "unwavering" or "imperishable," could under no circumstances be read as an adjective modifying another deity such as Śiva. Many of these hermeneutic maneuvers would have a lasting impact on theological practice for centuries to come—as the proliferation of sectarian polemic prompted a critical revisioning of acceptable reading practices for Hindu scripture, a phenomenon I return to in chapter 3. But perhaps the most fertile ground for sectarian polemic proved to be the corpus of sectarian Purāṇas. Although Purāṇa itself was universally accepted among Hindu sectarian communities as a legitimate textual authority, the vast majority of these Purāṇas were originally written to invoke the sole authority of Śiva, Viṣṇu, or some other particular deity. As a result, certain criteria had to be derived to adjudicate on the grounds of relative authority between Purāṇas that seemed to support competing sectarian communities.

Take, for instance, Rāmānuja's (twelfth-century) seminal statement on the sectarian Purāṇas, found in his *Vedārthasaṅgraha* (Compendium on the meaning of the Vedas), a trope that would surface repeatedly in the polemical writings of theologians for generations:

> Some ages of Brahmā were mixed, some were predominated by Sattva, others predominated by Rajas, and others predominated by Tamas. Brahmā, having articulated this division of eons, described the greatness of their essences, articulated in various Purāṇas, insofar as he consisted of the *guṇas* Sattva and so forth, respectively. As is stated in the Matsya Purāṇa:
>
>> That Purāṇa which was stated long ago by Brahmā in each eon,
>> Its greatness is described according to its own form.
>
> And furthermore, in particular:
>
>> The greatness of Agni and Śiva is praised in the Tāmasa [Eons]
>> In the Rājasa [Eons], they know the highest greatness of Brahmā.
>> And in the Sāttvika Eons, Hari has the highest greatness.[36]

In Rāmānuja's understanding, then, the Vaiṣṇava Purāṇas could be accorded a higher degree of veracity than the remainder of the Purāṇic corpus owing to the authoritative status of their speaker: because Brahmā had not been intoxicated by the adverse affects of the *guṇas* (qualities) of *rajas* (passion) and *tamas* (torpor), the two less desirable ontological substrates of Sāṅkhya cosmology, he was able to articulate the Vaiṣṇava Purāṇas with full cognizance of the ultimate truth they contain. Tropes such as this marked the battleground between sectarian traditions in both north and south India—indeed, Rāmānuja's linking of sectarian Purāṇas with the Sāṅkhya *guṇas* would soon be repeated well outside his institutional home in the far South of the subcontinent. Perhaps the most intriguing example, in fact, is the sixteenth-century Bhedābhedin philosopher Vijñānabhikṣu, himself an avowed Vaiṣṇava, who strategically replicates Rāmānuja's paradigm in the process of commenting on a scripture that was unmistakable to all readers of his generation as a Pāśupata Śaiva work: the Īśvara Gītā (The Lord's song). Here we find Vijñānabhikṣu evoking the tried and true argument that Śiva's scriptures are *tāmasa śāstra*, delusory because they were composed under the influence of ontological degradation. The very text of the Īśvara Gītā, he contends, can be trusted as authoritative scripture only because Viṣṇu himself had enjoined Śiva—face to face—to speak only the truth.[37]

It is ironic that in his more overtly sectarian moments, Vijñānabhikṣu himself—whom Andrew Nicholson represents as spokesman for the *unification* of Hinduism—advocates the genuine incommensurability of Śaiva and Vaiṣṇava revelation. Certainly, an overarching concept of unity does exist in Vijñānabhikṣu's practice of doxography, as Nicholson has argued, given that theologies are grouped together in a system only for a particular exegetic purpose. But that purpose, more often than not, is founded more securely on difference—that is, on the hierarchy of forms of knowledge—than on unity. In fact, upon comparing doxographic compendia by rival authors, we find that, by and large, doxographies are composed by theologians who have an overt sectarian agenda and a sectarian identity that informs the core of the author's own devotional practice. Madhusūdana Sarasvatī, for instance, author of the *Prasthānabheda*, made his life's work the synthesis between the philosophical apparatus of Advaita Vedānta and the devotional world of Kṛṣṇa bhakti. Evidently, for Madhusūdana, the unity of Hinduism was predicated upon a particular interpretation of its theology and practice—one rooted securely in Vaiṣṇavism. Vijñānabhikṣu, for his part as well, belies in his own words the very unity of Hinduism that his doxography would purportedly establish: elsewhere in commenting on the Īśvara Gītā, Vijñānabhikṣu declares decidedly that Advaita Vedāntins, or *māyāvādins*—card-carrying members of the six orthodox "Hindu" schools of philosophy (*ṣaḍdarśanas*)—are in essence not Hindus at all but heretics (*pākhaṇḍa*s): "Many heretical *śāstras*, from the Purāṇas through Advaita Vedānta, are known to have been composed by Śiva. But, it is not at all natural that Viṣṇu intentionally composed such heretical *śāstras*; rather, Keśava composed the delusory *śāstras* at the behest of Śiva alone."[38]

For early modern Hindu theologians of south India and beyond, then, Hinduism was a unity qualified at its core by plurality. While recognizing their rivals, ostensibly, as coreligionists engaging in polemical dialogue under the assumption of a shared scriptural canon and philosophical language, sectarian theologians from the late-medieval period onward were thoroughly preoccupied not with unity but with difference—with advocating the truth of one Hindu community above all others. Indeed, Vijñānabhikṣu himself astutely recognized that the Advaita Vedānta of the sixteenth century was no neutral philosophical undertaking but, rather, a project that in many cases served to consciously underwrite the authority of Brahminical Śaivism. It is this Sectarian Age that is the starting point of the present inquiry into the Hindu religious landscape of the early modern Tamil country—and, more specifically, what precisely it meant to be a Hindu in early modern south India. In turn, what we learn about Hindu identity at the cusp of early modernity tells a story of a Hindu pluralism that not only survived the colonial encounter but also continues to be evoked by many who call themselves Hindu across the Indian subcontinent and the diaspora to this day.

SMĀRTA-ŚAIVISM IN CONTEXT: THE PUBLIC
THEOLOGIANS OF EARLY MODERN SOUTH INDIA

Hindu sectarian communities, crystallizing in the late-medieval or early modern centuries, invoked the legacy of the past while promulgating radically new modes of religious identity. This was the south India in which the Smārta-Śaiva tradition as we know it first began to come into view and began to distinguish itself from contemporary communities of Śaivas and Vaiṣṇavas alike. Also known today as Tamil Brahminism, the Smārta-Śaiva community of the modern age has recently featured in the work of C. J. Fuller and Haripriya Narasimhan, who investigate the sociality of being Brahmin in twentieth-century Tamil Nadu; and its contemporary religious lifeworld has best been captured by Douglas Renfrew Brooks, particularly its seamless intertwining of Śaiva orthodoxy and Śrīvidyā Śākta esotericism. The history of its origins, or of how Smārta-Śaiva theologians came to speak for an emerging religious community, is a story that remains to be told. Smārta-Śaivism, it turns out, first acquired its distinctive religious culture during the generation of Appayya Dīkṣita's grandnephew, a poet-intellectual of no small repute: Nīlakaṇṭha Dīkṣita, court poet and minister to Tirumalai Nāyaka of Madurai, devout Śaiva and ardent devotee of the goddess Mīnākṣī, and one of history's first Smārta-Śaiva theologians.

Nīlakaṇṭha Dīkṣita is best known as one of early modern India's most gifted poets, famed for his incisive wit and the graceful simplicity of his verse, which contrasts markedly with the heavily ornamentalist style popular in post-Vijayanagara south India. And yet, despite his considerable gifts as a poet, Nīlakaṇṭha left his lasting mark on south Indian society not as a poet but as a theologian. We know that Nīlakaṇṭha had established himself at the Madurai court during Tirumalai Nāyaka's reign, with terms of employment that may have included both literary and sacerdotal activities.[39] On the literary side, he composed a number of works of courtly poetry, or *kāvya*, ranging from epic poems to hymns of praise venerating his chosen deities, Śiva and Mīnākṣī, the local goddess of Madurai.[40] He authored fewer works of systematic thought (*śāstra*), which include a commentary (*Prakāśa*) on Kaiyaṭa's *Mahābhāṣyapradīpa*,[41] as well as two works of theology: the *Śivatattvarahasya* (The secret of the principle of Śiva), a discursive commentary on the popular Śaiva hymn the *Śivāṣṭottarasahasranāmastotra* (The thousand and eight names of Śiva); and the *Saubhāgyacandrātapa* (The moonlight of auspiciousness), a *paddhati*, or ritual manual of the Śrīvidyā Śākta Tantric tradition, in which Nīlakaṇṭha was initiated by the Śaṅkarācārya ascetic he names as his guru, a certain Gīrvāṇendra Sarasvatī.[42] Indeed, a number of anecdotes handed down among Nīlakaṇṭha's descendants have preserved memory of his Śākta leanings, including the belief that Appayya Dīkṣita bequeathed to him his personal copy of the Devīmāhātmya.

Perhaps most noteworthy, however, is a legend that circulates freely among Nīlakaṇṭha's descendants, purported to explain the passion that moved him to compose his hymn to the goddess Mīnākṣī, the *Ānandasāgarastava* (Hymn to the ocean of bliss). Nīlakaṇṭha, rumor has it, was employed to oversee the construction of Tirumalai Nāyaka's New Hall, the Putu Maṇṭapam, directly outside the Mīnākṣī-Sundareśvara Temple in the center of Madurai in honor of the city's new and revised celebration of the divine couple's sacred marriage—a curious set of circumstances we will have the opportunity explore further in chapter 4. Among the statues commissioned to grace the pillars of the New Hall was a true-to-life figure of Tirumalai Nāyaka's chief queen.[43] When artisans had nearly completed chiseling the final lifelike features of Madurai's queen, a stone chanced to fall suddenly upon the statue, leaving a noticeable indentation upon the statue's thigh. Nīlakaṇṭha, out of reverence for the divine plan of Śiva and Mīnākṣī, instructed the artisans not to correct the indentation, with full faith that such an occurrence was not possible save for Śiva's grace, which allowed the queen to be represented as she truly was, down to the last detail. When Tirumalai Nāyaka learned of Nīlakaṇṭha's decree, he exploded with rage at the thought that Nīlakaṇṭha could have possessed intimate knowledge of the queen's body, as a birthmark in fact graced the queen's upper thigh at precisely the place where the stone fell. As a result, he promptly sent his soldiers to have his minister blinded for the offense. Engrossed in meditation on the goddess at the time, Nīlakaṇṭha foresaw his fate and, in a fit of despair, seized two coals from his ritual fire and fearlessly gouged out his own eyes. Mīnākṣī, pleased with Nīlakaṇṭha's unwavering devotion, immediately restored his sight, and Nīlakaṇṭha responded by spontaneously composing the *Ānandasāgarastava* in heartfelt gratitude for the goddess's grace.

Nīlakaṇṭha's memory, then—the legacy he left among his nineteenth- and twentieth-century descendants—centered not on his poetic prowess and famed satirical wit but on his unparalleled devotion for the goddess. But what about his own contemporaries? Was he best known in his immediate circles as poet and grammarian or as public theologian? As a member of the Dīkṣita family, early modern south India's most noteworthy clan of scholars, Nīlakaṇṭha was situated directly at the center of textual circulation across the southern half of the subcontinent. Beyond the South, Nīlakaṇṭha maintained direct contact with outspoken representatives of the *paṇḍit* communities of Varanasi,[44] possibly India's most vibrant outpost of intellectual activity during the early modern period. Perhaps it is no surprise, then, that Nīlakaṇṭha was in a position to speak more directly than any other Smārta-Śaiva of his generation to the theological disputes that irrupted in south Indian religious discourse during his lifetime and the preceding century.

On one hand, local memory preserved a keen awareness of Nīlakaṇṭha's centrality to the intellectual networks of the period. In works of poetry authored shortly after Nīlakaṇṭha's lifetime, we discover allusions to his influence on subsequent

generations appended to transcripts of his students' and grand-students' compositions. Take, for instance, the following verse recorded in a manuscript of a commentary (*vyākhyā*), written by one Veṅkaṭeśvara Kavi, on the *Patañjalicaritra* of
Rāmabhadra Dīkṣita:

> In which [commentary] he, Veṅkaṭeśvara Kavi, his qualified student,
>   textualized the glory
> Of Rāmabhadra Makhin, whom he describes as the Indra of the
>   earth,
> Whom Nīlakaṇṭha Makhin instructed to compose the
>   *Rāmabāṇastava,*
> Who, in turn, the sage Śrī Cokkanāthādhvarin made to write the
>   great commentary.[45]

What is particularly noteworthy about this verse, among numerous others like
it that refer directly to Nīlakaṇṭha and his contemporaries, is the awareness it preserves of the process of intellectual influence. Nīlakaṇṭha, as Veṅkaṭeśvara tells us,
was made to compose the "great commentary" by one of his instructors in *śāstra,*[46]
the grammarian Cokkanātha Makhin; and Nīlakaṇṭha himself in turn exerted a
direct influence on the poetry of his own pupil, Rāmabhadra Dīkṣita, who, as we
will see, shared many of Nīlakaṇṭha's own religious predilections, an ideal representative of the Smārta-Śaivas of the seventeenth century.[47] It is by no means
difficult, when studying early modern India, to underestimate the immediacy of
the intellectual exchange taking place between scholars, comrades and antagonists
alike. And yet we have ample evidence to indicate that exchange among scholars of
the period had begun to take place with unprecedented rapidity; theologians setting forth provocative works of polemic, for instance, could expect a vituperative
reply from an opponent within a mere handful of years. This puts us, as scholars,
in a particularly advantageous position to understand just how concretely intellectual dialogue—theology being no exception—influenced the shape of extratextual
society, even in the absence of the types of documentary data historians typically
employ. The context, quite often, is visible in the texts themselves.

We do, on the other hand, have access to one particularly fruitful body of
material evidence that speaks to the idea of Nīlakaṇṭha as an active scholar, as
a portion of Nīlakaṇṭha's personal library has in fact been preserved among the
collections of the Tanjavur Maharaja Serfoji's Sarasvati Mahal Library. These six
manuscripts were certainly owned by Nīlakaṇṭha himself, as each bears what may
very well be the original signature of the seventeenth-century scholar: the phrase
"Nīlakaṇṭhadīkṣitasya" or "Nīlakaṇṭhadīkṣitasya prakṛti" (the copy of Nīlakaṇṭha
Dīkṣita) inscribed in identical handwriting in Grantha script. On those manuscripts that were evidently handed down to Nīlakaṇṭha's sons, we find that distinct
Grantha hands have inscribed "Āccā Dīkṣitasya" or "Gīrvāṇendra Dīkṣitasya" on

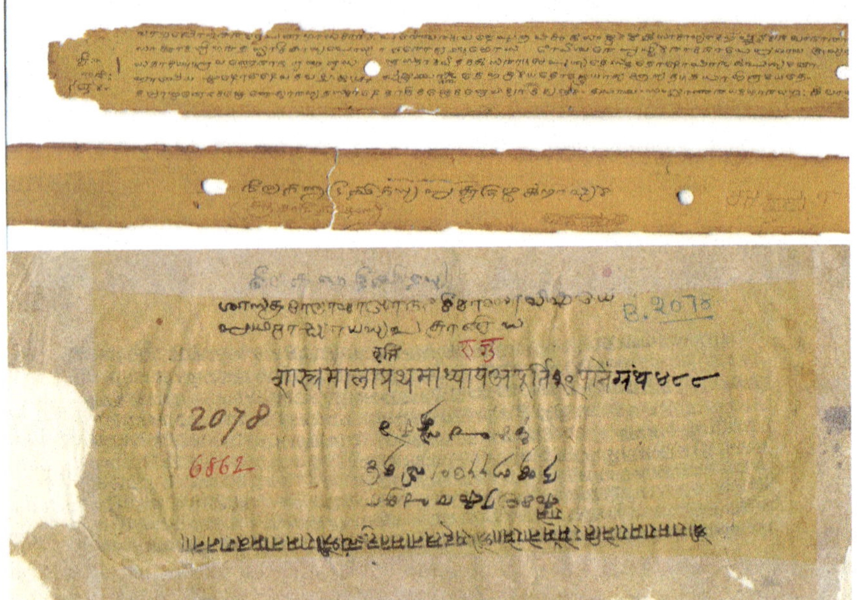

FIGURE 2. Reproductions of two manuscripts bearing what appears to be the signature of
Nīlakaṇṭha Dīkṣita, currently held at the Tanjavur Maharaja Serfoji's Sarasvati Mahal Library.
First manuscript: Palm-leaf cover of a *Ṛgbhāṣya* manuscript in Nīlakaṇṭha's possession
(D 6924). On the left we see in Grantha script the inked inscription "Nīlakaṇṭhadīkṣitasya
prakṛti ṛkbhāṣyam," and below it the uninked "āccādīkṣitasya," suggesting that this manuscript was passed down into the possession of Nīlakaṇṭha's eldest son, Āccān Dīkṣita. The
uninked "āccā," to the right, may be the handwriting of Āccān Dīkṣita. Second manuscript:
From the *Śāstramālāvyākhyāna* sent to Nīlakaṇṭha Dīkṣita by its author, Ananta Bhaṭṭa (D
6862). Nīlakaṇṭha's name is written in Grantha at the bottom in the same hand as in the first
manuscript. In the center, in Grantha script, we read, "kamalākaraputrānantabhaṭṭapreṣitam
idaṃ pustakam," or "This book was sent by Kamalākara's son Ananta Bhaṭṭa."

the very same cover folios. By far the most noteworthy of the six, however, are two
Devanāgarī paper manuscripts evidently copied by scribes in north India during
the seventeenth century, both the products of leading Varanasi intellectuals: select
chapters of the *Dinakarabhaṭṭīya,* or the *Śāstradīpikāvyākhyā,* of Dinakara Bhaṭṭa
and the *Śāstramālāvyākhyāna,* a work of Mīmāṃsā, of Ananta Bhaṭṭa.[48] On the
latter, the *Śāstramālāvyākhyāna,* is written the following remarkable memoran-
dum in yet another Grantha hand: "Kamalākaraputrānantabhaṭṭapreṣitam idaṃ
pustakam." (This book was sent by Ananta Bhaṭṭa, son of Kamalākara Bhaṭṭa.)
In short, we have physical evidence to document the direct intellectual exchange
between Nīlakaṇṭha and his contemporaries in Varanasi, who appear to have sent
him offprints of their Mīmāṃsā works in progress for review.

Our evidence, succinctly, provides us with ample opportunity for resituating Nīlakaṇṭha in time and space, as a theologian with active networks both in his immediate locale in Madurai and across the Indian subcontinent. Historically speaking, however, our archive presents us with certain challenges in ascertaining the precise terms of Nīlakaṇṭha's courtly employment.[49] Intriguingly, some scholars, such as A. V. Jeyechandrun, have put forth the bold assertion that Nīlakaṇṭha himself was directly involved in the ritual and logistical implementation of affairs in the Mīnākṣī-Sundareśvara Temple, including the "Sacred Games of Śiva"—entextualized in his own Sanskrit epic, the *Śivalīlārṇava* (The ocean of the games of Śiva). Jeyechandrun justifies this hypothesis on the basis of the excerpt from the *Stānikarvaralāṟu,* a Tamil record of the temple's priestly families, in which we learn that a certain Ayya Dīkṣita provided direct counsel to Tirumalai Nāyaka regarding the establishment of these festivals: "Lord Tirumalai Nāyaka . . . established an endowment under the arbitration of Ayya Dīkṣita, instructing that the Sacred Games be conducted in the manner established by the Purāṇas." Unfortunately, a careful reading of this passage in context renders Jeyechandrun's conclusion unlikely, as the Ayya Dīkṣita in question most likely refers to a certain Keśava Dīkṣita, mentioned explicitly in the paragraphs immediately preceding and following this passage, whom Tirumalai Nāyaka accepted as *kulaguru* and assigned to the post of *maṭhādhipatya* in the Mīnākṣī-Sundareśvara Temple.[50] Leaving aside the issue of this particular passage, however, evidence suggests that Nīlakaṇṭha's jurisdiction did extend far enough to include adjudicating sectarian affairs outside of the strictly literary sphere. For instance, a direct reference to Nīlakaṇṭha's role in moderating public intellectual debate has come down to us through Vādīndra Tīrtha, the disciple of the Mādhva preceptor Rāghavendra Tīrtha,[51] whose *Guruguṇastava* informs us that Nīlakaṇṭha granted an official accolade to Rāghavendra's treatise on Bhaṭṭa Mīmāṃsā by mounting it on an elephant and processing it publicly around the city:

> Just as when your treatise on the Bhaṭṭa system was mounted on an
> elephant
> To honor you by the jewel among sacrificers [Makhin] Nīlakaṇṭha,
> whose doctrine was his wealth,
> Your fame, O Rāghavendra, jewel among discriminating ascetics,
> desirous of mounting the eight elephants of the directions, has
> indeed of its own accord
> Sped away suddenly to the end of the directions with unprecedented
> speed.[52]

A further record somewhat indirectly lends credence to Jeyechandrun's hypothesis, confirming that during the reign of Tirumalai Nāyaka, Vaidika Brahmins were authorized to arbitrate temple disputes on the basis of their scriptural expertise.

This Tamil document, preserved and translated by William Taylor in this *Oriental Historical Manuscripts,* records an incident in which Śaiva and Vaiṣṇava arbitrators, "Appa Dīkṣita" and "Ayya Dīkṣita," respectively, were assigned to present opposing viewpoints regarding the scriptural sanctions for temple iconography:

> Having thus arranged the plan, the whole was begun to be carried into execution at once, in the tenth day of *Vyasi* month of *Acheya* year, during the increase of the moon. From that time forwards, as the master [Tirumalai Nāyaka] came daily to inspect the work, it was carried on with great care. As they were proceeding first in excavating the *Terpa-kulam,* they dug up from the middle a *Ganapathi,* (or image of Ganesa,) and caused the same to be condensed to dwell in a temple built for the purpose. As they were placing the sculptured pillars of the *Vasanta-Mandabam,* and were about to fix the one which bore the representation of *Yega-patha-murti* [Ekapādamūrti] (or the one-legged deity), they were opposed by the *Vaishnavas.* Hence a dispute arose between them and the *Saivas,* which lasted during six months, and was carried on in the presence of the sovereign. Two arbitrators were appointed, *Appa-tidshadar* on the part of the *Saivas,* and *Ayya-tidshader-ayyen* on the part of the *Vaishnavas:* these consulted Sanscrit authorities, and made the *Sastras* agree; after which the pillar of *Yega-patha-murti* was fixed in place.[53]

The remainder of this passage provides no further clues as to the identities of either of the state-sanctioned arbitrators, referred to here only by honorifics commonly employed to address Vaidika Brahmins, "Ayya" and "Appa."[54] Historically grounded anecdotes such as these, however, provide us with invaluable information concerning the roles that court-sponsored Brahmin intellectuals such as Nīlakaṇṭha Dīkṣita were appointed to fulfill under the rule of Tirumalai Nāyaka. Much of the secondary literature somewhat uncritically proposes potential titles of employment for Nīlakaṇṭha—ranging from the English "chief minister" or "prime minister" to the Sanskrit *rājaguru*—without considering that such positions may not have been operative in the seventeenth-century Nāyaka states or may not have been typically assigned to Brahmin scholar-poets. While some neighboring regimes in the seventeenth-century permitted enterprising Brahmins to rise to high positions in public administration and statecraft,[55] many of these states had adopted Persianate models of governance that had made minimal inroads to the far south of the subcontinent even by the seventeenth century. Unfortunately, no evidence exists to confirm the appointment of a Brahmin minister under a title such as *mantrin* in the Madurai Nāyaka kingdom; the nearest equivalent, the post of *pradhāni,* was typically granted to members of the Mutaliyār caste rather than Vaidika Brahmins. Similarly, the strictly sacerdotal functions of a *rājaguru* seem to have remained in the hands of distinct lineages; the nearest equivalents under the reign of Tirumalai Nāyaka appear to have been Keśava Dīkṣita, belonging to a Brahmin family traditionally responsible for conducting the ritual affairs of the Mīnākṣī-Sundareśvara Temple, and a Śaiva lineage based in Tiruvanaikkal near

Srirangam known as the Ākāśavāsīs,[56] whom numerous inscriptions describe as having received direct patronage from Tirumalai Nāyaka, and with whom the Nāyaka is alleged to have maintained a personal devotional relationship.

Strictly speaking, our textual archive remembers Nīlakaṇṭha as engaging with the world outside of the court and *agrahāra* through primarily intellectual means. Contemporary references confirm unambiguously that Nīlakaṇṭha presided over the city's literary society, which sponsored the public performance of Sanskrit dramas at major regional festivals,[57] and that he was granted the authority to award official recognition to scholarly works he deemed worthy of approval, such as Rāghavendra Tīrtha's work on Bhāṭṭa Mīmāṃsā. The precedent of the anonymous Appa Dīkṣita would suggest that Nīlakaṇṭha, as with other Smārta Brahmins under royal patronage, may well have exercised his extensive command of the Śaiva textual canon in the service of temple arbitration. In fact, citations from his *Saubhāgyacandrātapa* and *Śivatattvarahasya* indicate that Nīlakaṇṭha was uncommonly well acquainted with scriptures such as the Kāmika Āgama and Kāraṇa Āgama, principal authorities for south Indian Saiddhāntika temple ritual, and the Vātulaśuddhottara Āgama, one of the chief sourcebooks for Saiddhāntika temple iconography. While Nīlakaṇṭha may also have been regularly or occasionally commissioned to perform Vedic sacrifices, and although his intimate knowledge of Śrīvidyā was likely prized by Tirumalai Nāyaka owing to its centrality in the royal esoteric cult of south Indian kingship at the time,[58] little evidence survives to confirm these possibilities.

And yet, other mentions of Nīlakaṇṭha during his own lifetime aimed to articulate not his intellectual standing but his spiritual authority, representing him as no less than an incarnation of Śiva himself. For instance, Nīlakaṇṭha's younger brother, Atirātra Yajvan, whom we will have occasion to meet again shortly, offers an homage to his brother's public influence in Madurai that is less an homage to his intellectual talents than a veritable deification, as "the beloved of Dākṣāyaṇī manifest before our eyes" (*sākṣād dākṣāyaṇīvallabhaḥ*). It is no wonder that, within the tradition, Smārta-Śaiva theologians such as Appayya Dīkṣita and Nīlakaṇṭha Dīkṣita are recognized in the work of Appayya's descendant Śivānanda in his *Lives of Indian Saints* as living divinities and honored in their villages of residents with *samādhi* shrines—typically the burial places of liberated saints. Such memory is echoed by many of Nīlakaṇṭha's latter-day descendants as well, who remember the pioneering theological duo of Appayya and Nīlakaṇṭha as incarnations of Śiva and the goddess, respectively.[59] When visiting the ancestral *agrahāra* of Nīlakaṇṭha's family, Palamadai, which was said to have been granted to him by Tirumalai Nāyaka himself, a member of Nīlakaṇṭha's family, P. Subrahmanyam, stated the following:

We are descendants of the great sage Bharadvāja. In his dynasty was born Appayya Dīkṣita, who is called the Kalpataru of Learning. He was one of the greatest men who lived in the seventeenth-century *[sic]*, so more than three hundred years ago. And he is claimed by great people as an *aṃśāvatāra* [partial incarnation] of Lord Śiva himself. And then Nīlakaṇṭha Dīkṣita was his brother's grandson—brother's son's son. And he is also one of the greatest people who lived later in the seventeenth century. And he's acclaimed to be an *aṃśāvatāra* of Parāśakti. So we have descended from these great people.[60]

While we need not make any affirmations of Nīlakaṇṭha's divine origin, history bears out the memory of his descendants that Nīlakaṇṭha was intimately involved in laying the groundwork of an emerging religious community, and that he became one of the first to embody a distinctively Smārta-Śaiva religious identity. As a result, I narrate the social and conceptual origins of the Smārta-Śaiva community largely through the perspective of Nīlakaṇṭha and his close acquaintances, who wrote from the focal point of an emerging sectarian community. Although Nīlakaṇṭha is remembered primarily in the Western academy as a secular poet, modern-day Smārtas in Tamil Nadu remember an altogether different Nīlakaṇṭha, one whose primary contribution to Sanskrit textual history was as a Śaiva theologian. To cite a final example, when I first discussed my research with the scholars at the Kuppuswami Sastri Research Institute in Chennai, I had scarcely mentioned Nīlakaṇṭha Dīkṣita's name when I was met with a resounding chorus of the refrain from one of Nīlakaṇṭha's Śaiva hymns, the *Śivotkarṣamañjarī* (Bouquet of the supremacy of Śiva): "He, the Lord, is my God—I remember no other even by name."[61] Nīlakaṇṭha, as they informed me, was no less than Sanskrit literary history's most iconic and eloquent Śaiva devotee.

2

"Just Like Kālidāsa"

The Making of the Smārta-Śaiva Community of South India

Every May in the city of Madurai, devotees from across south India gather to celebrate the wedding of the god Śiva and the goddess Mīnākṣī in Madurai's annual Cittirai Festival. The god and goddess leave the temple to greet the public in the city square as the streets become inundated with crowds, music, and impromptu dancing. In the seventeenth century, not far from the city center, one could also witness the performance of Sanskrit dramas, newly composed for the occasion and staged by south India's most talented poets in honor of the festivities.[1] In May of 1650, just such a play, called the *Marriage of Kuśa and Kumudvatī*, was debuted in a temple pavilion by court poet Atirātra Yajvan. For literati across the region, this was an occasion both for devotional pilgrimage and for the convention of a regionwide literary society, over which his elder brother, Nīlakaṇṭha Dīkṣita himself, Atirātra tells us, presided as "master of ceremonies" (*sabhāpati*). While traditionally Sanskrit dramas opened by praising a patron and offering stage directions, Atirātra chose instead to present his audience with a remarkable autobiographical declaration: "This poet, being himself a devotee of the goddess—just like Kālidāsa—does not even take a breath without her command, much less compose such a literary work."[2]

In light of the fervent sincerity of Atirātra's confession, we might expect the *Marriage of Kuśa and Kumudvatī* to read as a tale charged with theological import, perhaps carrying resonances of the mythology and worship of the goddess who is at the center of this festival occasion. In reality, however, despite its considerable aesthetic charms, the narrative of the work is an entirely conventional—one might even say secular—account of love, loss, and reconciliation. But if the great goddess herself is apparently far from germane to the occasion at hand, how are we to make sense of Atirātra Yajvan's earnest confession that his heartfelt devotion not only is foundational to his experience of the world but also forms the cornerstone of his work as a poet and scholar? And why does Atirātra compare himself to Kālidāsa, the most renowned Sanskrit poet of literary antiquity, whose writings scarcely contain the slightest trace of goddess devotion?

Kālidāsa, a fourth-century poet who dwelt in the Gupta and Vākāṭaka courts of central India, is remembered by scholarship and the Indian poetic tradition alike as the greatest celebrity of Sanskrit literary history, famed for his graceful command of the Sanskrit language. In Kālidāsa's world, literature was an elite courtly enterprise segregated from the religious experiences of those who composed it. Like the majority of poets of Sanskrit classical antiquity, Kālidāsa participated in the erudite idiom of what Sheldon Pollock has called the Sanskrit Cosmopolis, a literary aesthetic that served the needs of royal power rather than those of the temple or monastery. Indeed, as Pollock has argued, the defining feature of classical Sanskrit literary culture was precisely its elision of particularities, whether in reference to place, time, or the personal devotional commitments of individual composers. For this reason, subsequent poets writing not only in Sanskrit but also in Telugu, Marathi, and other vernacular languages could be hailed by their contemporaries as Abhinava-Kālidāsa—the *new* Kālidāsa—simply by virtue of their literary virtuosity. To be just like Kālidāsa, for most of Indian history, had little to do with devotion and everything to do with laying claim to credentials that transcended time, space, and sectarian identity.

In the present context, however, Atirātra Yajvan's confession is far from timeless. To the contrary, Atirātra released his statement into the public space of Madurai's most cherished public festival at a crucial moment in the history of Hindu sectarian communities in south India, at a moment in which Kālidāsa was being reinvented as not only a scholastic but also a spiritual figurehead of the emerging Smārta-Śaiva community. Known today in popular parlance as "Tamil Brahminism"—although by no means are all Brahmins in Tamil Nadu either Smārta or Śaiva—the Smārta-Śaiva community itself was only in the process of being imagined in the early seventeenth century as a self-contained social entity. While the very idea of a community being imagined into existence may evoke the legacy of Benedict Anderson and the origins of nationalism, nations and sectarian communities do have one thing in common: both must rest upon an imagined collectivity founded upon shared features of identity, from language to devotional practice to the imagined legacy of a sacred past. Just as history is reinvented in the service of nation-building, a nascent sectarian community, though unattested in past centuries, requires a hagiography with an illustrious patrimony of the likes of Kālidāsa, widely celebrated as the greatest poet of Sanskrit literary history.

Self-consciously crafting the identity of their emerging community, the Smārta-Śaivas lay claim to the legacy of Kālidāsa as well as that of Śaṅkārācarya, India's most iconic philosopher, as the exclusive intellectual property of the Smārta-Śaiva community. At first glance, such a claim appears superficially plausible: the community produces elegant works of Sanskrit poetry and rigorous philosophical tracts founded on Śaṅkara's Advaita philosophy. But recall again the words of Atirātra Yajvan: when he tells us he is just like Kālidāsa, his intent is not simply to express that he has composed timeless poetry. Indeed, the comparison he draws is founded on an altogether different commonality: namely, that both he and his illustrious predecessor do not draw a single breath that is not inspired by the goddess's grace. By crafting a new hagiography for history's greatest Sanskrit poet, Atirātra Yajvan and his community reinscribed the Sanskrit literary tradition with new and unprecedented meanings scarcely imaginable within the classical past.

Atirātra Yajvan, in fact, is not the only poet to forge a conceptual alliance between the Sanskrit intellectual enterprise and the devotional worship of the goddess. Rather, his confession exemplifies a pervasive transformation of the religious ecology of the early modern Tamil country, one that began to crystallize perhaps a number of decades before the *Kuśakumudvatīyanāṭaka* was first performed in Madurai. Among the noteworthy intellectuals employed in the seventeenth-century Nāyaka courts of Madurai and Tanjavur, a remarkable number were affiliated not merely by familial ties but also by a shared participation in sectarian religious networks.[3] Indeed, on the Śaiva side, within the space of a single generation, Atirātra, Nīlakaṇṭha, and their colleagues across the Tamil country began to evoke their personal sectarian identities through remarkably similar textual and devotional practices. South Indian Vaiṣṇavism, for instance, whether Mādhva, Śrīvaiṣṇava, or otherwise, already had a history by the seventeenth century—a history that had been entextualized by poets and theologians and instituted in practice through religious centers such as temple complexes and monasteries. It was only in the early seventeenth century, in contrast, that Smārta-Śaivism first laid claim to a shared hagiography, began to profess devotional relationships with ecclesiastical authorities, and perhaps most strikingly, began to cultivate a shared esoteric ritual practice.

Indeed, for the Smārta-Śaiva theologians of seventeenth-century Madurai, the goddess in question was not simply Mīnākṣī, juridical figurehead of the Nāyaka state and divine embodiment of the Madurai region, whose sacred marriage the city was commemorating in a public festival at the very moment Atirātra compared himself to the great Kālidāsa. His allusion, to the contrary, was intended to invoke the worship of Lalitā Tripurasundarī, the lineage deity of the Śrīvidyā school of Śākta Tantrism. Śrīvidyā is a goddess-centered (Śākta) esoteric ritual tradition that, while guarded carefully in the initiatory lineage, has become something of an open secret in Tamil Brahmin society, forming a cornerstone of the collective culture of Smārta-Śaiva religiosity. Śrīvidyā, in its mature form, first flourished on the opposite side of the subcontinent some centuries earlier, in early second-millennium Kashmir,[4] where it acquired the unmistakable stamp of the region's sophisticated Śaiva and Śākta philosophical and ritual idiom. That Śrīvidyā was exported to the far South soon after its initial zenith in Kashmir is revealed unmistakably in the *Tirumantiram*,[5] a work of the Tamil Śaiva canon heavily inflected with Śrīvidyā imagery. Its systematic ritual practice is best known to contemporary scholars and practitioners alike through the works of Bhāskararāya, an eighteenth-century resident of the Maratha court of Tanjavur, whose pathbreaking works have yet to be definitively situated in cultural context.[6] And yet, that an entire generation of seventeenth-century literati professes to have actively engaged with the Śrīvidyā tradition puts us in a position to reconstruct a crucial moment in its efflorescence the Tamil South—and, more importantly, its role in shaping the contours of Smārta-Śaiva religious culture.

Indeed, Śrīvidyā initiation began to spread like wildfire, virtually without precedent, through the intellectual circles of Nāyaka south India in the early seventeenth century, and with it came the institutional apparatus of the preceptors who provided this initiation: the Śaṅkarācārya lineages of south India.[7] The renunciants of the Śaṅkarācārya, or Daśanāmī, order trace their heritage through their hagiographies to the eighth-century theologian Śaṅkarācārya, who wrote the pioneering Advaita, or nondual commentary on the Brahmasūtras, the core scripture of Advaita Vedānta philosophy. So named for their hagiographical forebear, the "Śaṅkarācāryas," or Jagadgurus—literally "world teachers"—of these lineages serve in succession as the abbots, or preceptors, of independent regional monasteries, each of which maintains branch outposts across the Indian subcontinent. Two of the five principal Śaṅkarācārya monasteries, or *maṭhas*, that exist today speak to the Smārta-Śaiva constituents of south India—one in Sringeri, on the western coast of Karnataka, and one in Kanchipuram, in northern Tamil Nadu. Beginning in the late sixteenth century, the charismatic saints of the Śaṅkarācārya tradition began to attract a substantial lay following across the Tamil region. Included in their ranks were many of the most influential theologians and intellectuals who belonged to the first generation of the emergent Smārta-Śaiva community.

Cementing their ties to their new institutional homes, the Śaṅkarācārya Jagadgurus of the Tamil country initiated leading Smārta-Śaiva theologians as their disciples[8] and, at the same time, into the esoteric ritual practice of Śrīvidyā, which remains the personal cult of the Śaṅkarācāryas of Sringeri and Kanchipuram to this day.[9] In fact, despite the purportedly covert nature of Śrīvidyā ritual, a substantial body of textual evidence survives in which various intellectuals acknowledge firsthand their devotional relationships with Śaṅkarācārya preceptors and attempt to negotiate a place for Śrīvidyā practice within a wider Śaiva orthodox culture. It is this master-disciple relationship that secured a connection between the Śaṅkarācārya monasteries themselves and the wider lay population, who came to participate in what I refer to as the Smārta-Śaiva community. Thus for the first time in South Asian history—in the late sixteenth and early seventeenth centuries—we encounter lay householders professing devotion for a Śaṅkarācārya preceptor and receiving from that preceptor an initiation that would formally grant them access to a community of devotees. In contrast, Appayya Dīkṣita himself, despite his systematic engagement with Vedānta philosophy, mentions the name of no Śaṅkarācārya preceptor in his entire oeuvre. In essence, rather than fragmentary accounts of personal devotional practice, we discover an active discursive network—and one that had begun to radically alter the social fabric of sectarian identity in early modern south India.

Addressing a substantively different social context, the original Śaṅkarācārya, we may recall, went so far as to expressly forbid the study and practice of Vedānta among nonrenunciants. As a role model, then, Śaṅkarācārya fits somewhat ambiguously with the social and religious values of seventeenth-century south Indian intellectuals. As a result, it may come as no surprise that Smārta-Śaiva theologians of the seventeenth-century promulgated a radically revised hagiography of the original (Ādi) Śaṅkara. While the eighth-century philosopher himself was an avowed Vaiṣṇava and adamant critic of both Śaiva and Vaiṣṇava Tantric practice, the Śaṅkarācārya of seventeenth-century hagiography emerged—just like Kālidāsa—as a Śākta devotional poet and pioneer of Śrīvidyā esoteric ritual, whose life culminated in pilgrimage to the seat of the goddess Kāmākṣī in Kanchipuram and rapture with the vision of the god and goddess as Kāmeśvara and Kāmeśvarī, the sixteen-year-old divine couple in sexual union.

Likewise, the Smārta-Śaivas of the seventeenth century envisioned a radically different Kālidāsa, one who scarcely resembled his historical namesake of the fourth or fifth century. Inspired perhaps by a creative misconstrual of the meaning of the poet's name, as the *dāsa,* or "servant," of the goddess Kālī, they recast him as an ardent devotee of the goddess whose literary craft was the direct expression of divine grace. In fact, the identities of these two hagiographical figureheads of Smārta-Śaivism were often deliberately blurred, which produced a single—or at least monochrome—ecclesiastical history of the Smārta-Śaiva community. The theologian Lakṣmīdhara, for instance, in commenting on the *Saundaryalaharī,* or "Waves of Beauty," a devotional goddess hymn anachronistically attributed to Śaṅkara, extols the virtues of Kālidāsa in terms that had previously been reserved solely for the eighth-century Advaita philosopher: the "Blessed Feet [Bhagavatpāda]" of Kālidāsa. And then, in violation of our expectations, he tells a story that explains why Kālidāsa has been granted this lofty status, attributing Kālidāsa's poetic genius solely to the divine intervention of the goddess in his life: "The Blessed Feet of Kālidāsa, being deaf and dumb, spoke the pair of hymns, the *Laghustotra* and *Carcāstotra,* through the power of the contact of [the goddess's] hand with his forehead. By that power, the goddess placed the water used for bathing Her lotus feet in his mouth."[10] The Kālidāsa of the Smārta-Śaiva community, then, was born not only without poetic talent but also without the capacity for speech; the goddess, by her grace, saw fit to elevate his status by placing in his mouth the water used to bathe her feet, a widespread symbol in Hindu traditions for the grace-bestowing power of a particular deity or saint. More specifically, in the Tantric discourses where the trope originated, this substance is equated with an alchemical nectar that flows in the subtle body of a human being. Transmuted through the practices of Kuṇḍalinī yoga, this nectar divinizes the body of the adept. Dripped into the mouth of the young Kālidāsa, it transformed an impotent voice into the most sublime vehicle of poetic speech known to Indian history. Emulating the transformation they accorded to the young Kālidāsa, Smārta-Śaiva theologians, then, represented their worldly profession as an externalization of their inner devotional experiences. For many of these poets, Śākta devotionalism and literary genius were fundamentally inextricable from each other.

By tracing this newfound prominence of Śaṅkarācārya and Kālidāsa in Smārta-Śaiva religious culture, I aim, in this chapter, to tell the story of the emergence of Smārta-Śaivism as a distinct sectarian community. As a fledgling sect of Hinduism competing for social prestige and patronage with the better established institutions of the Śrīvaiṣṇava, Mādhva, and Tamil Śaiva Siddhānta lineages, Smārta-Śaivism, like its rivals, was founded first and foremost on networks of religious agents. In this case, we can trace the coalescence of Smārta-Śaivism as a religious community to the first inroads of the Śaṅkarācārya lineages in the Tamil country, which soon began to build connections with the lay populace and, in particular, with local theologians who gave voice to the devotional commitments, doctrines, and values of the community at large. Through these foundational forays into shaping a public religious culture for the Smārta-Śaiva community, theologians such as Nīlakaṇṭha Dīkṣita, Atirātra Yajvan, and many of their contemporaries first made room for the practice and embodiment of a new sectarian identity. Whether produced in the guise of devotional poetry, commentarial treatises, or ritual manuals, these works served, succinctly, to consolidate the religious culture of Smārta-Śaivism. Circulating strictly within the confines of a delimited religious public, their compositions readily evoked the authors' shared commitment to Śrīvidyā ritual and devotion to Śaṅkarācārya preceptors, an omnipresent feature of this sphere of intellectual production and circulation. These writings, in other words, formed a field of discourse that actively consolidated the networks of temples, monasteries, and religious publics that came to constitute the Smārta-Śaiva community.

ŚAṄKARĀCĀRYAS AND SMĀRTA BRAHMINS

Let us rejoin the scene at Madurai's Cittirai Festival at the debut of Atirātra Yajvan's Sanskrit drama. Among the author's relatives and colleagues likely in attendance that day, a number were responsible for poetic, didactic, and devotional compositions in Sanskrit that refer directly, in no uncertain terms, to their personal relationships with Śaṅkarācārya preceptors and their knowledge of esoteric Śākta ritual and theology. Take, for instance, the celebrated poet Nīlakaṇṭha Dīkṣita himself, honored on that day by his younger brother as master of the court's elite literary society, who opens his Sanskrit *mahākāvya*, the *Śivalīlārṇava*, with the following benedictory verse:

> What good is Śiva, proud that the Daughter of the Mountain is half
>   his body?
> I worship him who in his entire being consists of the Daughter of
>   the Mountain—Gīrvāṇa, the best of *yogins*.[11]

Here, Nīlakaṇṭha includes in his traditional set of benedictory verses an homage to the preceptor he elsewhere acknowledges as guru, Gīrvāṇendra Sarasvatī—who is superior even to Śiva himself, Nīlakaṇṭha opines with a trope of rhetorical censure, as Śiva's traditional iconography (Ardhanārīśvara) depicts Pārvatī as half of his body, while his own is in essence a full incarnation of the goddess herself. Very little, unfortunately, is known about Gīrvāṇendra Sarasvatī as a historical figure, best known for his single surviving composition, the *Prapañcasārasaṅgraha*, an extensive textbook of practical mantra applications modeled directly on the *Prapañcasāra* attributed to Śaṅkara, with a number of chapters devoted to Śrīvidyā. As for the history of his lineage, Gīrvāṇendra himself, by way of conclusion to the *Prapañcasārasaṅgraha*, acknowledges the three previous preceptors of his tradition: he is a disciple of one Viśveśvara, disciple of Amarendra or Amareśvara,[12] disciple in turn of a previous Gīrvāṇendra.[13] Given his occasional invocations of Malayalam vocabulary, or "Keralabhāṣā," in addition to the local Tamil vernacular, it is plausible that Gīrvāṇendra himself relocated his lineage to Kanchipuram from Kerala in the late sixteenth century.

While little is known about these predecessors, his successors, on the other hand, include a number of the most noteworthy scholars of Advaita Vedānta of the late sixteenth and early seventeenth centuries.[14] Among these noteworthy disciples, the most widely recognized is Nṛsiṃhāśramin, a prolific and respected scholar of Advaita.[15] Family history remembers him as a close friend and advisor to Appayya Dīkṣita, Nīlakaṇṭha's granduncle, and he is reputed to have directly influenced Appayya's works of Advaita.[16] At the outset of his *Advaitadīpikā*, Nṛsiṃhāśramin refers to Gīrvāṇendra Sarasvatī by name, even declaring that it was at his behest that he undertook to compose the work.[17] Svayamprakāśayati, another of the period's leading Advaita scholars, also accepted Gīrvāṇendra as his preceptor. But perhaps more intriguing still, yet another of Gīrvāṇendra's noteworthy students was one Bodhendra Sarasvatī, understood by tradition to be the same individual revered as the fifty-ninth Jagadguru of the Kāñcī Kāmakoṭi Pīṭha, Bhagavannāma Bodhendra Sarasvatī. Whatever his actual monastic affiliation may have been, Bodhendra Sarasvatī recognizes Gīrvāṇendra Sarasvatī as his guru in his *Hariharādvaitabhūṣaṇa,* as well as in his *Ātmabodhaṭīkā,* in which he describes him as follows:

> The preceptor installed at the seat of the Advaita lineage
>   [*advaitapīṭhasthita*], his inner form luminous with the delightful
>   knowledge of the Self,
> I worship him always inside my heart, Gīrvāṇendra, the best of
>   *yogin*s, pure of heart.[18]

In addition to his esteem for his guru, Bodhendra conveys to us that Gīrvāṇendra was considered the head of a certain lineage by his use of the phrase *advaitapīṭha,* suggesting an established monastery or institutional center for the propagation of Advaita thought. Beyond the association with Advaita, we are given no further information as to this lineage's self-portrayal or the location of its center of operation. Nevertheless, the memory of Bodhendra Sarasvatī as equivalent to one of the pontiffs of the Kanchipuram Śaṅkarācārya lineage is highly suggestive, particularly in light of the rather distinctive initiatory title borne by nearly all of Gīrvāṇendra Sarasvatī's gurus and disciples: "-Indra Sarasvatī," an appellation attested only among the preceptors of two Kanchipuram orders, that of the Kāmakoṭi Pīṭha Śaṅkarācāryas and the lineage of Rāmacandrendra Sarasvatī, better known as Upaniṣad Brahmendra, a late seventeenth-century ascetic so named for his feat of commenting on 108 Upaniṣads. In short, Gīrvāṇendra Sarasvatī was a highly celebrated and influential figure among renunciant scholars of Advaita and most likely the pontiff of a monastic order centered in Kanchipuram, one that bears some historical relationship to the lineages now most commonly associated with the city.[19]

On the other hand, Gīrvāṇendra Sarasvatī's importance extended beyond the confines of the monastery walls, attracting the attention of a number of court intellectuals, including Nīlakaṇṭha Dīkṣita—who went so far as to name his son, Gīrvāṇendra Dīkṣita, after his preceptor. Nīlakaṇṭha's sentiment is best captured from his own words, expressed eloquently in one of his versified hymns, the *Gurutattvamālikā,*[20] a garland of twenty-eight stanzas (*nakṣatramālā*) devoted entirely to his guru and rich with devotional sentiment:

> A few people, here and there, have been saved by ancient gurus,
>   through the
> Purification of all six Śaiva *adhvan*s—*tattva, sthāna, kalā, pada,
>   akṣara,* and *mantra.*[21]
> But, with the single *mantra adhvan,* made manifest in his work the
> *Sārasaṅgraha,* Gīrvāṇendra Guru unchains the entire world, from
>   the proudest to the humblest.

My thirst to accept the water of your feet and smear their purifying
  dust,
To bear on my forehead at length those feet resembling two golden
  lotuses,
O master, even a hundred lifetimes cannot fulfill! And yet,
You will never obtain even a single rebirth, except in the minds of
  your devotees.

Pointing the way to austerities [*kṛcchra*], it removes all hardships
  [*kṛcchra*] of its own accord;
It swallows our karma by the roots, bringing our actions [karma] to
  fulfillment;
Bestowing liberation to all who hear it, may this four-syllable mantra,
Gīr-vā-ṇe-ndra, be my comfort so long as I draw breath.

If the descent of power [*śaktipāta*] is certainly the fruit of fortune
  from an
Array of meritorious action conditioning this lifetime, amassed
  through the bondage of endless mortal bodies,
It is still conveyed through contact with the compassionate glance of
  the preceptor.
Thus, proclaim, you who are freed from error, that there is no reality
  [*tattva*] higher than the Guru![22]

Nīlakaṇṭha makes it abundantly clear over the course of the hymn that the
preceptor he honors is none other than the author of the *Prapañcasārasaṅgraha*,
a composition "adept at manifesting the heart of the great sayings of Śaṅkara."[23]
He proceeds to honor Gīrvāṇendra Sarasvatī variously as *kulaguru*—preceptor of
one's family, clan, or lineage—or as "mantra guru," the bestower of a sectarian
or esoteric initiation by means of the revelation of a mantra, which Nīlakaṇṭha
implicitly claims to have received through the process of *śaktipāta*, the descent of
power or grace at the hand of the initiatory guru, affirmed to be the sole source of
liberation in many schools of Śaiva thought.[24] Such initiation also carried with it
ritual obligations designed to cultivate a devotional experience directly linking the
devotee with his chosen preceptor; indeed, the visualized worship of the preceptor
was an essential part of the daily enactment of Smārta-Śaiva liturgy. As with all
Śaiva traditions from the middle of the first millennium, in fact, the initiating guru
or teacher was equated for all intents and purposes with the god Śiva himself. The
preceptor, as a result, was seen as possessing the capacity to bestow the liberating
power of Śiva's grace through ritual initiation, severing the bonds that tied the
individual soul to the cycle of transmigration. An initiate, therefore, who wished
to attain liberation himself, could cultivate a devotional bond with his personal

teacher, which, when inculcated through a regimen of ritual practice, facilitated the union of the disciple with Śiva himself.

Taken as a whole, the evidence strongly suggests that it is this Girvāṇendra Sarasvatī who provided Nīlakaṇṭha with the initiation required to pursue knowledge of Śrīvidyā ritual, the procedure for which the renowned poet-theologian sets forth at length in his unpublished ritual manual, a previously unknown work (*paddhati*), the *Saubhāgyacandrātapa* (Moonlight of auspiciousness). In the context of adjudicating ritual procedure, Nīlakaṇṭha cites the *Prapañcasārasaṅgraha* on a number of occasions, referring to its author by the honorific *asmadārādhyacaraṇāḥ*, "the one whose feet are fit to be worshipped by me." Interestingly enough, Nīlakaṇṭha is not the only one of his immediate circle to refer in such laudatory terms to Girvāṇendra Sarasvatī. In fact, a similar claim is made by another of the most prominent intellectuals of his day, Rājacūḍāmaṇi Dīkṣita, best known as the author of the *Kāvyadarpaṇa*, one of the most celebrated treatises of aesthetic theory written in later centuries. For our present purposes, however, Rājacūḍāmaṇi was also the author of a highly refined narrative chronicle of the life of Śaṅkara titled the *Śaṅkarābhyudaya* (The ascension of Śaṅkara),²⁵ a reworking of the traditional "universal conquest" narrative that concludes with Śaṅkara ending his life in Kanchipuram and establishing the Śrīcakra, the Śrīvidyā icon or ritual diagram at the heart of the Kāmākṣī Temple.

Rājacūḍāmaṇi prefaces his work, in addition to an impressive resume of his academic achievements, with a number of benedictory verses addressed to Girvāṇendra Sarasvatī, in which he confides that this same preceptor came to him in a dream and instructed him to write the *Śaṅkarābhyudaya*. Rājacūḍāmaṇi refers to his preceptor as "a veritable Śaṅkarācārya, situated at the far shore of speech, the creator of the compilation on the essence of the Prapañcasāra."²⁶ The term "a veritable Śaṅkarācārya" (*paryāyaśaṅkarācārya*) prompts close attention but leaves us with more questions than answers. Does Rājacūḍāmaṇi mean to say that he considers Girvāṇendra to be an incarnation of the original Śaṅkarācārya, or that he was one among a lineage of successive preceptors who adopted the title Śaṅkarācārya, as do the present-day lineages of Jagadgurus? The text of the *Śaṅkarābhyudaya* leaves no doubt, however, that Rājacūḍāmaṇi Dīkṣita himself envisioned an intimate connection between Śaṅkarācārya and Kanchipuram, best exemplified by the work's seventh chapter, in which Śaṅkara completes his pilgrimage and his life by establishing in Kanchipuram (rather than Kashmir) the Sarvajñapīṭha, the "Seat of the Omniscient" and the heart of the Śaṅkarācārya lineages—a claim supported today, quite naturally, only by the Kanchipuram Śaṅkarācārya lineage.

Given the testimony of Nīlakaṇṭha Dīkṣita and Rājacūḍāmaṇi Dīkṣita, two of seventeenth-century south India's most prominent intellectual figures, Girvāṇendra Sarasvatī's fame seems to have circulated well beyond his immediate lineage, serving as a pivotal link in the nascent social alliance between Smārta

Brahmins and the lineages of Śaṅkarācārya preceptors. Before the generation of Nīlakaṇṭha and Rājacūḍāmaṇi, not a single nonrenunciant Sanskrit intellectual professed a personal or family allegiance to a Śaṅkarācārya order. Even Appayya Dīkṣita, Nīlakaṇṭha's granduncle, who devoted much of his intellectual energy to reviving the Śaiva Advaita philosophy of Śrīkaṇṭha and transmitting it liberally to his students, to our knowledge makes no such claim.[27] That Gīrvāṇendra Sarasvatī was not an isolated charismatic figure but a participant in a larger social configuration becomes clear in the following generation: among Nīlakaṇṭha's pupils, Rāmabhadra Dīkṣita,[28] one of the leading lights among the first generation of scholars at the Maratha court of Tanjavur, adopted a similar relationship with the ascetic and scholar of Advaita Kṛṣṇānanda Sarasvatī. In fact, Rāmabhadra honors his own preceptor and lineage with a unique hymn, one reminiscent of Nīlakaṇṭha's *Gurutattvamālikā*, titled the *Ācāryastavarājabhūṣaṇa*, commemorating (and even addressing in the vocative!) a similar devotional hymn written by Brahmānanda Sarasvatī in honor of their mutual preceptor, Kṛṣṇānanda, the *Ācāryastavarāja*.[29]

> Your birth from Brahmānanda himself, your brilliant golden form,
> The three worlds made subject to you, your familiarity with all the
>   sciences;
> The insightful praise refuge to you, which even for a moment gives
>   birth to happiness,
> *Ācāryastavarāja!* What poet would be bold enough to praise your
>   virtues?
>
> Surely the feet of Kṛṣṇānanda, on occasions of worship bearing a
>   double multitude
> Of tender blooming lotuses, with heaps of buds, strewn by assem-
>   blies of learned men,
> Become even more radiant when you are attached to them. And yet,
> I declare that it is you who are indeed the most charming,
>   *Ācāryastavarāja.*
>
> The elixir of life of the entire world, a cloud serves mostly to please
>   the young *cātaka* bird;[30]
> Bringing joy to all, the moon awakens at will for the pleasure of the
>   night-blooming lotus.
> *Ācāryastavarāja,* you bring bliss to the learned of the world, and
>   now,
> You bedeck yourself most particularly for the delight of
>   Rāmabhadra's heart.[31]

In addition to Rāmabhadra's evident devotion to his lineage—manifested in his celebration of its textual incarnation in the form of the *Ācāryastavarāja*—his mode of address, compelling all learned scholars to take delight in his composition, makes it unambiguously clear that Rāmabhadra intended his hymn not for the confines of a monastery but for a more public consumption among connoisseurs of sophisticated Sanskrit verse. Moreover, that the audience he invokes is at once impeccably educated in Sanskrit poetics and philosophy and sympathetic toward Rāmabhadra's devotion to his chosen lineage suggests that, by the late seventeenth century, affiliation with Śaṅkarācārya preceptors had become an unproblematic, or even commonplace, feature of Smārta Brahmin identity.

Such an implication, in fact, is fully supported by the sheer evidence of numbers: a staggering number of south Indian intellectuals, beginning around the seventeenth century, came to be involved one way or another with Śaṅkarācāryas, Śāktism, Advaita philosophy, and if we extrapolate from the emerging pattern, most likely all three at once. Reference might be made to Kālahasti Kavi, an acquaintance of Nīlakaṇṭha, who composed the *Bhedadhikkāravivṛti*, a commentary on Nṛsiṃhāśramin's treatise. One might mention a certain resident of Kanchipuram who referred to himself as "Kāmākṣīdāsa" (servant of the goddess Kāmākṣī) and, by his own admission, received Śaiva *dīkṣā* at the hand of Appayya Dīkṣita himself. Or, one might take the case of Rāmabhadra's pupil Nalla Adhvarin, who refers to himself in his *Advaitarasamañjarī* as a disciple of Sadāśiva Brahmendra, the latter himself the author of a popular compendium, the *Siddhāntakalpavallī*, based on Appayya's *Siddhāntaleśasaṅgraha*. Taken together, these figures exemplify the emergence of a network of theologians, who over the course of several decades, participated actively in the reimagination of the institutional boundaries and the religious culture of the Smārta-Śaiva sectarian community.

As it turns out, the most intriguing works of the this formative period of Smārta-Śaiva religious culture have yet to be studied, remaining untranslated and largely inaccessible to academics and modern-day practitioners alike. Perhaps the most revelatory of these documents is the *Saubhāgyacandrātapa* of Nīlakaṇṭha Dīkṣita. A manual for the daily ritual obligations of the Śrīvidyā initiates, the *Saubhāgyacandrātapa* is a far cry from the insipid cookbook-like procedural manuals that often go by the name *paddhati*. After all, Nīlakaṇṭha was one of the greatest stylists of the Sanskrit language in the precolonial period, in his prose as well as his poetry. What we discover, instead, is an instructive (to us as well as his pupils) intertwining of ritual and social commentary, through which Nīlakaṇṭha actively negotiates a place for Śrīvidyā ritual practitioners (*upāsakas*) within the broader orthodox climate of south Indian Śaiva Siddhānta.[32]

The second work to be addressed is a little-known commentary on a Sanskrit hymn popular in south India, the Ambāstava, attributed at the time to Kālidāsa.[33] The author of the *Ambāstavavyākhyā*, Ardhanārīśvara Dīkṣita, was the elder brother of Rājacūḍāmaṇi Dīkṣita and, like his brother, was extensively well-read in the classics of Śrīvidyā scripture. As a didactic treatment of what was likely a popular work of poetry in his day, Ardhanārīśvara's commentary consistently strives to establish a canon for the interpretation of Śākta verse, ranging from the earliest-known Śrīvidyā scriptures to the personalities construed by his contemporaries as the archetypal Śākta devotees: Śaṅkara and Kālidāsa. In doing so, this commentary casts Śaṅkara and Kālidāsa as the forerunners and champions of a sanitized model of Śrīvidyā *upāsanā* suited to the social demands of orthodox Smārta Brahmins.

The final work under discussion is the aforementioned *Śaṅkarābhyudaya* of Rājacūḍāmaṇi Dīkṣita, by far the most aesthetically refined example of the Śaṅkaradigvijaya genre and, perhaps for that reason, one of the least studied.[34] One of the few such narratives to situate the final destination of Śaṅkara's journey in Kanchipuram, the *Śaṅkarābhyudaya* forges an intrinsic connection between the lineage of Śaṅkarācārya, Kanchipuram, its resident goddess Kāmākṣī, and Śrīvidyā ritual practice. In particular, the final two cantos of the work contain an array of astoundingly precise references to the esoteric vocabulary of Śrīvidyā, including a sixteen-verse hymn to Kāmākṣī that embeds each of the syllables of the Śrīvidyā mantra, leaving the reader with no doubt that the author was intimately familiar with Śrīvidyā ritual and viewed this practice as inextricably connected to the lineage of Śaṅkara.

To be clear about what is at stake in these rhetorical strategies, Nīlakaṇṭha and his colleagues did not promulgate Śākta ritual and theology purely through their own social capital. Rather, they substantiated the authority of their lineage by invoking two of Indian history's most celebrated cultural figures: Kālidāsa, the most celebrated poet of Sanskrit literary history (or perhaps of any Indian literary tradition), and Śaṅkarācārya, the figurehead of the Advaita school of Vedānta philosophy, which had become the language of intersectarian debate in south India for much of the second millennium. Through this process, Śrīvidyā came to be understood unequivocally by seventeenth-century Smārta Brahmins as the teachings of Śaṅkara and Kālidāsa themselves. Within the Western tradition this phenomenon evokes the Renaissance European defense of the Hermetic tradition, in which the walls of the Vatican immortalized portraits of Hermes Trismegistus, who was understood by prominent intellectuals to have disseminated the esoteric truth of the Christian doctrine many centuries before Christ. For Nīlakaṇṭha Dīkṣita to cite Śaṅkarācārya as the forefather of Śrīvidyā *upāsanā* is strikingly reminiscent of the claim of a poet-intellectual in the court of Queen Elizabeth, Sir Philip Sidney, stating that

> Mercurius Trismegestius, who (if the bookes which are fathered vppon him bee his in déede, as in trueth they bee very aunciient) is the founder of them all, teacheth eueyywhere, That there is but one God: That one is the roote of all things, and that without that one, nothing hath bene of all things that are: That the same one is called the onely good and the goodnesse it selfe, which hath vniuersall power of creating all things. . . . That vnto him alone belongeth the name of Father and of Good.[35]

Śrīvidyā, for Nīlakaṇṭha and his contemporaries, was not a novel fashion in Smārta-Śaiva circles but the central insight of India's greatest intellectual luminaries. In recasting the hagiographies of Śaṅkarācārya and Kālidāsa, then, the Smārta-Śaiva theologians of seventeenth-century south India aimed, not only to rewrite the "ecclesiastical history" of the Śaṅkarācārya monastic lineages, but also to provide a model for religious belonging in their own day and age. Their ecstatic devotion, couched in the garb of the sophisticated poet and intellectual, was no abstract ideal but, rather, served as a model for the self-fashioning of the Smārta-Śaiva theologian. Spared the rigors of an ascetic lifestyle of renunciation, these householder theologians found themselves saddled with the unique obligation of constructing a new religious public, one that cohered around a unified religious culture and shared sites of public memory. When the Smārta-Śaiva theologian spoke of his sectarian identity, he was, simply, *just like Kālidāsa,* the consummate literary genius who received his talents through the grace of the goddess herself, whom he held dearer than his own life breath. Just like Kālidāsa, these theologians portrayed themselves in their poetry and scholastic ventures as the paragons of the poetic talent of their generation and the ideal devotees of Śaṅkarācārya and of the goddess.[36]

ŚRĪVIDYĀ AND SOCIETY IN NĪLAKAṆṬHA DĪKṢITA'S *SAUBHĀGYACANDRĀTAPA*

Nīlakaṇṭha Dīkṣita—poet, satirist, iconoclast, and one of early-modern India's sharpest literary minds—is well-known and celebrated by connoisseurs of Sanskrit verse even today for his uniquely bold personality and incisive satirical wit.[37] Many Indian and Western scholars alike are well-acquainted with his *mahākāvyas* (epics), *stotras* (hymns), *śatakas* (centuries), and other works, including his piercing *Kaliviḍambana* (A travesty of time), which lambastes with equal facility the many degenerate characters frequenting the royal courts of his day, from poets to priests and mantra-sorcerers. His views on literary theory are conservative in the extreme, calling for artists to rein in their obsessions with puns and linguistic feats and return to the straightforward beauty of the Sanskrit language. Given this picture, perhaps it is no wonder at all that few scholars in the Indian or Western academy are aware that this same Nīlakaṇṭha Dīkṣita composed a rather different sort of work as well: a ritual manual for the Tantric worship of the goddess Lalitā Tripurasundarī: the *Saubhāgyacandrātapa,* or "The Moonlight of Auspiciousness."[38]

To our knowledge, the *Saubhāgyacandrātapa* survives only in a single Grantha-script palm-leaf manuscript, now housed at the Oriental Research Institute at the University of Kerala, Kariavattom. The manuscript itself is incomplete: only the first two chapters (*paricchedas*) survive from a work that most likely comprised at least five chapters.[39] Although it is always a tragedy to lose access to a fragment of intellectual history, what does survive of this work provides a wealth of information concerning Nīlakaṇṭha Dīkṣita's authorship of the work, his canon of textual sources, and even allusions to the interactions and tensions between sectarian communities. The colophon included at the end of the first *pariccheda* includes the same formulas adopted regularly by the Dīkṣita family in self-description,[40] suggesting that the manuscript was transmitted within the family. Still more convincing is the internal evidence of citation: on matters of ritual procedure, Nīlakaṇṭha often acknowledges the authority of the *Śivārcanacandrikā* of Appayya,[41] whom he describes as "our grandfather" (*asmatpitāmahacaraṇāḥ*) or, somewhat eccentrically, with the proud but affectionate "Our Dīkṣita" (*asmaddīkṣitaḥ*). In addition, the *Saubhāgyacandrātapa* is referred to by name in yet another Śrīvidyā manual composed by his younger brother Atirātra Yajvan, whom we have already encountered as the featured playwright of Madurai's Cittirai Festival. This work, titled the *Śrīpadārthadīpikā* or *Śrīpadārthavyavasthā*, may now be entirely lost, but had been recovered before 1942 by P. P. S. Sastri, who managed to reproduce the following excerpt:

> This is examined at great length by our venerable grandfather in the *Śivānandalaharī*, thus there is no need to expound it here. . . . The adjudication is described according to the *Saubhāgyacandrātapa*, a text difficult to fathom by numerous techniques of exegesis, written for the upliftment of students by our elder brother, the honorable Nīlakaṇṭha Dīkṣita, the polymath capable of summarizing all systems of thought, an incarnation of our central deity.[42]

In fact, it would appear that the authorship of Śrīvidyā manuals became something of a family tradition in Nīlakaṇṭha's generation, as he further discloses in his own *paddhati* that *his* elder brother, Āccān Dīkṣita, also authored such a text: "This position was articulated by our venerable grandfather in the *Śivārcanacandrikā*, and our venerable elder brother accepted the very same position in the *Saubhāgyapaddhati*."[43] No trace has yet been located of this *Saubhāgyapaddhati*, but the combined evidence does call for a revision of the narrative put forth by the descendants of the Dīkṣitas,[44] which states that Nīlakaṇṭha himself acted independently, and somewhat eccentrically, in pursuing initiation under Gīrvāṇendra Sarasvatī. Rather, at least three of five brothers were intimately familiar with the Śrīvidyā system and composed interreferential treatises on the subject—far less a coincidence than what one would call a sectarian tradition. No reference seems available to suggest definitively that earlier generations of the family were involved in any form of Śākta ritual practice; and yet in his devotional hymn to the goddess Mīnākṣī, the *Ānandasāgarastava*, Nīlakaṇṭha provides us with an intriguing but ambiguous biographical anecdote concerning his granduncle:

> It was Appayya Dīkṣita himself who first offered to you his very self,
>   dedicating to you his entire family.

> Who are you, great goddess, to overlook me, your ancestral servant?
> And who am I to fail to worship you, my family deity?[45]

Here, Nīlakaṇṭha appears to offer a plaintive reminder to Mīnākṣī, the resident goddess of Madurai, that Appayya Dīkṣita had brought the family into a contractual relationship of sorts with her, their *kuladevatā* (family deity). While Appayya himself is silent on the issue, Nīlakaṇṭha appears to endorse the veracity of this event; and in fact Nīlakaṇṭha's descendants today continue to revere Mīnākṣī as their *kuladevatā*.[46] On the other hand, the deity addressed in the *Ānandasāgarastava* is not Mīnākṣī as such but rather the local goddess understood as a manifestation of the transregional goddess Lalitā Tripurasundarī, the deity of the Śrīvidyā tradition, a fact that Nīlakaṇṭha reveals to the careful reader by embedding her traditional visualization in the hymn, rather than that of Mīnākṣī. Specifically, Nīlakaṇṭha describes the deity as holding in her four hands the noose, goad, sugarcane bow, and arrows, and describes her row of teeth as consisting of the *vidyā* (*vidyātmanaḥ*)—in other words, each tooth corresponds to a syllable of the Śrīvidyā mantra.[47]

Although publicly Appayya was the devout Śaiva par excellence, was he secretly a worshipper of the goddess? Sadly, we have no evidence to confirm or refute Nīlakaṇṭha's audacious claim beyond a reasonable doubt. And yet the theological proclivities Nīlakaṇṭha did inherit from his granduncle inflect his Śrīvidyā-centric writings with a flavor unattested elsewhere in the textual history of Śrīvidyā. Specifically, the *Saubhāgyacandrātapa* undertakes the project of bridging the gap between the Śrīvidyā textual canon and the orthodox Śaiva perspectives of the Sanskritic Śaiva Siddhānta tradition, a school of thought far removed from Śrīvidyā's earlier ritual and philosophical influences. As the Śrīvidyā exegetical tradition grew to maturity in Kashmir between the eleventh and thirteenth centuries, its earliest engagement with philosophically rigorous models of ontology and cosmology took place in the context of the Śākta-Śaiva traditions of the Kashmiri renaissance.[48] As a result, early Śrīvidyā shows the marked influence of a number of nondual Śākta-Śaiva Tantric traditions—the Trika and Pratyabhijñā schools in particular—popular in Kashmir at the time. It was only significantly later that Śrīvidyā came to play a foundational role in the Smārta religious culture of the Tamil South. Today Śrīvidyā in south India is practiced primarily in accordance with the writings of Bhāskararāya, resident scholar at the eighteenth-century Maratha court of Tanjavur, who eschewed engagement with traditional Śaiva schools of thought in favor of a more modernizing, Vedicizing agenda.[49] The interstitial period, to which Nīlakaṇṭha belongs, is largely uncharted territory.

What we discover in Nīlakaṇṭha's work is a deliberate alliance between Śrīvidyā Śāktism and south Indian Śaiva Siddhānta. At first glance, this alliance of disparate perspectives may seem implausible. Originally a pan-Indian tradition of the

Śaiva Mantramārga dating back as early as the fifth century of the Common Era,[50] Śaiva Siddhānta maintained a staunchly dualist cosmology for the majority of its history,[51] showing only minor or negligible engagement with Śākta-centric theologies. Beginning in the mid-seventh century, Śaiva Siddhānta had become the royal cult of the south Indian Pallava and Cōḷa dynasties, providing the liturgy and protocol for nearly all major Śaiva temples in the region. By the early second millennium, the Sanskrit-based Śaiva Siddhānta became the dominant Śaiva sect in the Tamil region, alongside of which developed a distinctively Tamil Śaiva Siddhānta school with its own lineage and Tamil language scriptures. And from Nīlakaṇṭha's vantage point in the mid-seventeenth century, south Indian Śaiva Siddhānta had undergone yet another phase change over the previous century, in which the orthodox currents of Śaiva Siddhānta had increasingly accommodated nondualist influences. Examples of such hybrid works include the *Śaivaparibhāṣā* of Śivāgrayogin and, of course, the numerous Śaiva works of Appayya Dīkṣita, who inherited the doctrinal stance he calls "Śivādvaita" from the Sanskritic Vīraśaivas of the fifteenth and sixteenth centuries in the vicinity of Srisailam in northern Andhra Pradesh.[52]

It was this emergent nondualist Śaiva Siddhānta climate that fostered Nīlakaṇṭha's Śrīvidyā-Siddhānta synthesis, a model for the thoroughgoing compatibility he perceived between the "Vaidika" orthodoxy of the Śaiva Siddhānta and its esoteric counterpart, Śrīvidyā. Nowhere does Nīlakaṇṭha acknowledge the authority of any particular Saiddhāntika lineage or preceptor, and in fact he refers only sparingly to the works of known human authors, aside from those of Gīrvāṇendra Sarasvatī and his granduncle Appayya, preferring to engage directly with a wide range of Śaiva and Śākta scriptures. However, his knowledge of the Āgamas,[53] classical Saiddhāntika scripture, is encyclopedic, as citations are sprinkled liberally throughout the *Saubhāgyacandrātapa*, as well as in his *Śivatattvarahasya*, an erudite commentary on the popular *Śivāṣṭottarasahasranāmastotra* (The thousand and eight names of Śiva) clearly intended for an educated but exoteric audience. Nevertheless, that Nīlakaṇṭha viewed Śrīvidyā and Saiddhāntika orthodoxy as intertwined is made explicit in the *Śivatattvarahasya* as well. For instance, on one occasion he maintains that a form of Śiva prevalent in Śrīvidyā, Kāmeśvara, is in fact a "highly esoteric" (*atirahasya*) manifestation of the Saiddhāntika Maheśvara—an ontologically subordinate, qualified (*saguṇa*) form of Śiva—whose visualization can only be learned directly from the mouth of one's initiatory preceptor.[54]

As eccentric and creative as Nīlakaṇṭha's synthesis may seem to an outside observer, Nīlakaṇṭha himself goes to great lengths to demonstrate not only that his views are entirely orthodox and grounded in the Vedas but also that the esoteric teachings of Śrīvidyā are no less than the entire purport (*tātparya*) of the Vedic corpus. Take, for instance, the structure of Nīlakaṇṭha's first chapter (*pariccheda*), a conceptual introduction to the ritual material treated thereafter. He begins from a foundation agreeable to members of any Vaidika sect, stating that the highest aim of human existence is liberation from the cycle of rebirth, and that the means to achieving this is to be found in the scriptures, primarily the Upaniṣads. Nīlakaṇṭha adduces a number of Upaniṣadic passages and, with some creative exegesis and grammatical maneuvering, arrives at the desired conclusion:[55] "Thus, that the knowledge of Śiva, qualified by Cicchakti as so described, is the means of achieving liberation is ascertained to be the purport of all scriptures, having come forth from the same mouth."[56]

Here, Nīlakaṇṭha's strategy is at once eminently traditional (the idea of the *tātparya,* or "purport," being a mainstay of the Mīmāṃsā tradition of Vedic hermeneutics) and iconoclastic, in that he manages to superimpose on the authority of the Vedas an entire cosmological system foreign to their original context. "Cit-śakti," as Nīlakaṇṭha refers to her here, is a conceptual model of the female divinity as the "power of consciousness," herself the means by which her consort Śiva acts in the world and, in fact, the material cause of the world itself; this concept is best known from the Pratyabhijñā school of Kashmiri Śaivism, later fundamental to much of Śrīvidyā thought as well. As Nīlakaṇṭha himself puts it, "Thus so far has been established: that Śiva is not a material cause, and that Śakti is the material cause of the universe, consists of consciousness, and is nondifferent from Śiva."[57] In essence, tracing the core cosmological and soteriological precepts of his lineage of practice to the secure foundations of the Vedas, Nīlakaṇṭha sets the tone for his approach to problems of ritual legitimacy as well. Never deviating from the orthodoxy of Vaidika culture or from the precepts of Śrīvidyā practice, his adjudication of socially sensitive issues is at once entirely "Smārta" and entirely "Tāntrika." To do any less would be to fall short of the demands of scripture, "because," as he tells us, "the Tantras themselves explicitly teach a combination of the Vaidika and Tāntrika systems."[58]

This being the case, if one accepts that the knowledge of Śiva qualified by Cicchakti is conducive to liberation, then how exactly does one go about achieving such knowledge? First, Nīlakaṇṭha replies, we must understand what does *not* work: the method typically recommended by Advaita Vedānta—that is, the study and contemplation of Upaniṣadic teachings. The alternative he reaches for, however, is more subtle than it appears at first glance. What is called for is the path of devotion, or bhakti—but with a twist that sets Nīlakaṇṭha's argument distinctly apart from what the word *bhakti* typically calls to mind: *bhakti,* he tells us, is a synonym of *upāsanā,* the esoteric ritual worship of a particular deity. As a result, devotional sentiment alone does not suffice but must be accompanied by the ritual techniques prescribed by the Āgamas—that is, the scriptures of particular sectarian traditions—which Nīlakaṇṭha declares unambiguously to be equally as authoritative as the Vedas on matters of ritual procedure:

The word *devotion* signifies a form of votive worship that is synonymous with "internal worship" [*upāsanā*] in so far as it evokes a particular mode of being—the words *upāsanā, meditation,* and *contemplation* [*nididhyāsana*] being synonyms. One who is intent on that achieves liberation in a single lifetime. Such is revealed by the exemplified statement. Nevertheless, ritual practice, although not revealed in scripture, is established to be a necessary component of *upāsanā* on the maxim "How much more?"[59] . . .

One might argue, given the revelation of the Āgamas as nonauthoritative: how can one learn from them the procedure of worship? No—this statement does not mean that the general class of Āgamas is nonauthoritative, . . . because, since it is adjudicated in the Mahābhārata itself that the Āgamas of the Pāśupatas, etcetera, are authoritative,[60] they are also equivalent to the Vedas in matters associated with modes of offering that are dependent on Vaidika worship. But, those [texts] among them that teach left-handed practice opposed to the Vedas are nonauthoritative.[61]

In essence, Nīlakaṇṭha has subsumed the entire soteriological function of *nididhyāsana*—and with it, the entire injunctive apparatus of Vedānta—under the umbrella of Śrīvidyā ritual worship, or *upāsanā*. The very term *upāsanā*, in Nīlakaṇṭha's creative exegesis, provides a particularly apt locus for the fusing of key concepts in Advaita Vedānta and Śrīvidyā. Etymologically translating as "service," the concept of *upāsanā* has a rich history in the theology of Advaita Vedānta; the term is often equated specifically with *nididhyāsana* not simply as "repeated concentration" but as a ritualized series of *dhāraṇās*, or meditative procedures, intended to facilitate direct awareness of the absolute brahman. These *dhāraṇās* are traditionally known in the corpus of Advaita Vedānta philosophy as the Brahmavidyās, which modern commentators have enumerated in a fixed list of thirty-two.[62] While the compound *brahmavidyā* in the singular may translate literally as "the knowledge of brahman," the plural form generally alludes to an esoteric meditative regimen rarely discussed in its full systematicity. Among early modern Smārta-Śaivas, the most popular of the Brahmavidyās was unquestionably the Daharākāśavidyā,[63] the meditation on brahman in the cave of the heart, to which Appayya himself accorded pride of place in the Śivādvaita of Śrīkaṇṭha. Nīlakaṇṭha, for his part, reveals his acquaintance with the Brahmavidyās through an allusion in his hymn of lament, the *Śāntivilāsa:*

> From boyhood, that skill that I amassed having established myself
> In the Brahmavidyās through obedience to the feet my guru,
> Now has somehow been transformed into a means for entertaining
> Kings who listen nightly to my stories as a means of falling asleep.[64]

It is unfortunate, though not surprising, that Nīlakaṇṭha never fully elaborates on his understanding of the Brahmavidyās of Advaita Vedānta. He does return to the subject, however, at regular intervals throughout his second *pariccheda,* to emphasize that certain ritual preparations, such as applying the Śaiva *tilaka,* the *tripuṇḍra,* and smearing the body with ash, must regularly be done as a subsidiary component of Brahmavidyā practice. The only *vidyā* referred to by name, unsurprisingly, is the

Daharavidyā, frequently favored by the Śivādvaita philosophical tradition in particular,[65] even before the work of Nīlakaṇṭha's granduncle Appayya.

By equating their practice, however—under the term *nididhyāsana*—with *upāsanā*, Nīlakaṇṭha's claim evokes a double entendre that rhetorically equates Advaita Vedānta with Śrīvidyā itself. Some care should be taken to distinguish between the term *upāsana* in the neuter,[66] employed by Śaṅkarācārya to denote meditative practice ancillary and subordinate to the realization of *brahmajñāna*, and the feminine *upāsanā* that Nīlakaṇṭha invokes. In south India Śrīvidyā, *upāsanā* is not merely meditative visualization but is also the term of choice for referring to the entire Śrīvidyā ritual system; a practitioner of Śrīvidyā is generally known as a Śrīvidyā *upāsaka*. Through this maneuver, Nīlakaṇṭha not only gives Śrīvidyā a Vedic stamp of approval but also argues, via creative exegesis, that the injunction to perform Śrīvidyā ritual is sanctioned by the Vedas—and in fact is the essential purport, or *tātparya,* of the entire Vedic corpus.

Having established the validity of his sources and the conceptual foundation of his mode of practice, Nīlakaṇṭha proceeds with his treatment of the daily ritual duties of the Śrīvidyā practitioner on the basis of the Āgamic prescriptions—of both Śaiva and Śākta origin. Although all sectarian Āgamas, ostensibly, partake of equal veridicality, the procedure (*itikartavyatā*) for the worship of Mahātripurasundarī, the central deity of the Śrīvidyā tradition, ought to be procured both from the Śaiva Siddhānta Āgamas—to which he refers as the "Divyāgamas" and the "Kāmikāgama and other Śaiva Tantras"[67]—and from the Śākta Tantras such as the "Vāmakeśvarītantra," widely accepted as the foremost scripture of Śrīvidyā. On the other hand, the same Saiddhāntika Āgamas Nīlakaṇṭha invokes as authorities for esoteric Śākta practice had a much broader currency in the religious economy of seventeenth-century Tamil Nadu, being at once the purview of Siddhānta monastic lineages and the repository of procedural guidelines for nearly all of Śaiva temple worship in the Tamil region. Given the context, the approach of citing purely Śaiva scriptures to justify procedural injunctions on Śākta worship strikes the reader as less pragmatic than socially expedient, anchoring the practice of a socially marginal lineage in the broader culture of Śaiva orthodoxy.

This is not to say, of course, that Nīlakaṇṭha is not completely sincere in claiming that Śrīvidyā is at the heart of both Vedic and Śaiva orthodoxy. Nor is his adoption of Śaiva orthodoxy in any way artificial; Nīlakaṇṭha's own *Śivatattvarahasya* and Appayya's *Śivārcanacandrikā* demonstrate beyond doubt that the family's practice and cultural self-understanding was thoroughly grounded in the heritage of south Indian Śaivism. Nevertheless, the synthesis between these two modes of self-understanding, on one hand, and pragmatic codes of ritual and social action, on the other, had evidently become a conceptual problematic for Nīlakaṇṭha that required a careful and deliberate negotiation. Take, for instance, Nīlakaṇṭha's extended discussion of daily (*āhnika*) ritual duties and life-cycle rituals (*saṃskāra*) prescribed separately in the Vaidika Dharmaśāstras and in the Tantras: are practitioners of a particular sectarian *upāsanā,* who are also Smārta Brahmins, required to undergo Tantric *saṃskāras* as well as the Vaidika *saṃskāras*? Nīlakaṇṭha concludes, with the support of his elder brother, Appayya, and Gīrvāṇendra Sarasvatī that Tāntrika *saṃskāras* are intended only for Śūdras, whereas additional daily rituals may need to be adopted according to the variety of *upāsanā* in question. This issue, contemplated at length by Nīlakaṇṭha's contemporaries as well,[68] held significant consequences for the social constitution of Śaiva communities across the subcontinent: the position advocated here by Nīlakaṇṭha permitted Vaidika intellectuals to constitute sectarian Tantric practice as integral to their immediate social network while maintaining the social signifiers of inclusion in a transregional elite Brahminical orthodoxy.

The same may be said of other, more visible issues of sectarian comportment, such as the marking of one's sectarian identity through embodied insignia such as the *tilaka,* a sectarian marker borne on the forehead. Nīlakaṇṭha interrupts his discussion, interspersed with ostensibly esoteric ritual matters, to adjudicate the public comportment of Śrīvidyā initiates. Taking issue with the Śākta-centric practice of more transgressive, or Kaula, lineages in the region, he maintains that Śrīvidyā initiates ought to display only the Śaiva sectarian *tilaka,* the tripuṇḍra, thus representing themselves not simply as Śrīvidyā practitioners but as members of the broader Smārta-Śaiva public.[69] In short, Nīlakaṇṭha situates his *Saubhāgyacandrātapa* at the forefront of a sectarian community at a key moment of transition. Engaging systematically with external players from the mainstream Śaiva Siddhānta to the more transgressive south Indian Kaula Śāktas,[70] Nīlakaṇṭha's intellectual work negotiates the boundaries of the early modern south Indian Smārta community. By introducing into this discursive sphere a sustained and detailed treatment of Śrīvidyā ritual practice, Nīlakaṇṭha's voice directly contributed to the fact that Śrīvidyā ritual and theology constitute a cultural pillar of Smārta practice to this day.

WHEN TANTRA BECOMES ORTHODOXY: ARDHANĀRĪŚVARA DĪKṢITA AND THE BIRTH OF SAMAYIN ŚRĪVIDYĀ

Among the various compositions attributed to Śaṅkarācārya over the years, by far the most numerous are his assortment of *stotras,* or hymns, widely recognized and recited today by Smārta Brahmins in all regions of India. For many, Śaṅkara's corpus of hymns includes a set of *stotras* to the goddess known as the *Pañcastavī* (Five hymns), which in the seventeenth century were attributed instead to the genius of Kālidāsa, understood then as now as one of the fountainheads of the Sanskrit literary tradition. Śaṅkara's most widely recognized Śākta hymn, however, is the *Saundaryalaharī,* or "Waves of Beauty," a work of high *kāvya* popular enough to have accrued over the centuries several commentaries and an abundance of variant readings. Among such attested variants, one in particular caught the eye of early modern Smārta readers and is preserved today in the commentary on a hymn of the *Pañcastavī:* the *Ambāstava* (Hymn to the mother)[71] by Ardhanārīśvara Dīkṣita,[72] brother of the celebrated literary theorist Rājacūḍāmaṇi Dīkṣita of the court of Tanjavur, and son of Ratnakheṭa Dīkṣita of the court of the Cenji Nāyakas.

In his critical edition of the *Saundaryalaharī,* Norman Brown reconstructs verse 102 as follows:

> Your chest bearing the weighty breasts arisen from it, your gentle
>   smile,
> The love in your sidelong glance, figure resplendent like the blos-
>   somed kadamba flower:
> Intoxicating Cupid has created [*janayām āsa madano*] an impres-
>   sion of you in the mind of Śiva.
> Such is the highest fulfillment, O Umā, of those who are your
>   devotees.[73]

Ardhanārīśvara Dīkṣita's rendering, on the other hand, preserves a crucial variant in the second half of this verse, one that has proven foundational to a certain school of interpretation, not only of the *Saundaryalaharī* itself, but also of Śaṅkarācārya's oeuvre as a cohesive theological enterprise:

> *Samayins meditate in the mind* [*janayantaḥ samayino*] on your
>   deception of Śiva.
> Such is the highest fulfillment, O Umā, of those who are your
>   devotees.[74]

Although this variant may result in a rather less plausible or aesthetically satisfying verse, it provides our commentator with an ideal textual foundation for his exegetical project: a defense of a particular subschool of south Indian Śrīvidyā exegesis typically referred to as the "Samaya" school, of which the locus classicus is the sixteenth-century *Saundaryalaharī* commentary of Lolla Lakṣmīdhara.[75] A term that defies succinct English translation, *samaya* most literally denotes a mode of conventional behavior or a contractual agreement, from which usage it came to signify a set of social conventions adopted by initiates in many Śaiva traditions.[76] In Lakṣmīdhara's idiosyncratic appropriation, however, the term becomes meaningful only when paired with its antithesis, *Kaula:* whereas Kaula Śrīvidyā, in theory, accepts without reservation the use of objectionable ritual elements such as the notorious *pañcamakāras,* or five impure substances,[77] Samaya Śrīvidyā constrains its ritual observances in accordance with the strictures of Vaidika orthodoxy. In fact, Lakṣmīdhara even suggests that ideal Samayins must eschew any external ritual worship altogether in favor of strictly mental observance. Hence, the reading "Samayins visualize in the mind."

Although one might expect Lakṣmīdhara's Samaya school to have attracted a fair following among the ranks of Brahminical orthodoxy, to date scholarship has discovered negligible textual attestation that such a "school" in fact ever arose in response to his programmatic essay. In fact, the Samaya doctrine is often depicted as confined exclusively to Lakṣmīdhara's *Saundaryalaharī* commentary itself. South Indian Śrīvidyā today leans heavily in favor of a reformed version of the Kaula *mata* as expounded by Bhāskararāya, whose popularity among contemporary initiates has all but eclipsed Lakṣmīdhara's legacy. In this light, Ardhanārīśvara Dīkṣita's *Ambāstavavyākhyā* is a particularly intriguing textual artifact, one of the few surviving texts known to systematically advocate the Samaya position.[78] And yet, not only does Ardhanārīśvara accept the category of Samaya as expounded by Lakṣmīdhara, but he also stages his commentary as an explicit defense of the Samaya doctrine, signaled with little ambiguity in the title chosen for his commentarial essay: "Enlivening the Doctrine of the Samayins" (*Samayimatajīvana*). Evidently for Ardhanārīśvara, the Samaya doctrine was indeed a real entity and one of imminent relevance to his contemporaries, thus calling for a certain commentarial "enlivening."

By enlivening the school promulgated by his predecessor Lakṣmīdhara, who himself "enlivened" the sixteenth-century court of Vijayanagara, Ardhanārīśvara is not engaged in a mere scholastic mimesis of a forgotten work of scholarship. His *Samayimatajīvana* does, in fact, deliberately invoke Lakṣmīdhara's Samayācāra commentary, down to the very details of commentarial mechanics. It is the gap *between* Ardhanārīśvara's work and its prototype, however, that reveals the hidden seams of the sectarian community that Ardhanārīśvara and his contemporaries were in the process of constituting. In the intervening generation or two, we observe a vast gulf in the self-constitution of Samaya Śrīvidyā both through a conscious redaction of its scriptural corpus and through its public image as an esoteric wing of orthodox Smārta-Śaivism. As we have seen, Ardhanārīśvara's generation witnessed the emergence of an unprecedented alliance between Smārta intellectuals and ascetics of the Śaṅkarācārya monastic orders, a trend in which his family is known to have participated. Lakṣmīdhara's Samaya doctrine, then, initiates an equally unprecedented doxographical revisioning of the lineage's purported founder, Śaṅkarācārya, here understood as the original exponent of a domesticated, Vedicized form of esoteric Śākta ritual practice. At the same time, by attributing the Ambāstava itself to Kālidāsa, Ardhanārīśvara advances this project a step further, claiming Kālidāsa, as well, as a foundational figurehead in the emerging hagiography of Smārta-Śaivism. In essence, the *Ambāstavavyākhyā* lays an intellectual foundation for the self-understanding of Smārta Śrīvidyā initiates as active participants in the ongoing legacy of both Śaṅkarācārya and Kālidāsa, a sectarian community at once entirely Vaidika and entirely Śākta.

First, let us consider the evidence that Ardhanārīśvara's *Samayimatajīvana* does indeed systematically recapitulate the doctrinal position of Lakṣmīdhara. Not once during his commentary does Ardhanārīśvara quote Lakṣmīdhara or refer to him or his work by name. And yet, from the nuts and bolts of commentarial practice to the social values, doctrines, and works cited, the *Samayimatajīvana* is unmistakably a direct imitation of Lakṣmīdhara. Take, for instance, his commentarial mechanics: Ardhanārīśvara co-opts piece by piece the structure of Lakṣmīdhara's verse analysis, beginning with a painstakingly literal gloss of each word (for example, the rather rudimentary gloss *amba! mātaḥ!* occurs often in both), and ending with a prose restructuring of the word order (both authors introduce this section with the phrase *atra itthaṃ padayojanā* rather than with a more common term such as *anvaya*) and a brief diagnosis of literary ornaments in the verse.[79] Stylistics aside, however, the most striking point of comparison is the authors' shared canon of textual sources. Ardhanārīśvara, for his part, makes no secret of the authority underlying his work. After showcasing his family credentials with the traditional benedictory verses, he declares that two Śrīvidyā treatises in particular constitute the doctrinal foundation of his commentary:

> Having reflected again and again, with discrimination, on the two
>   treatises written by Śaṅkarācārya,
> Known as the *Saubhāgyavidyā* and *Subhagodaya*, may I compose
>   this text according to their path.[80]

In this succinct encapsulation of his tradition's theological heritage, Ardhanārīśvara confidently attributes to Śaṅkarācārya himself a pair of Śākta theological tracts claimed to defend the reformed Vaidika Śrīvidyā popular among seventeenth-century Smārta intellectuals. No manuscripts have yet been located matching the description of the *Saubhāgyavidyā* or *Subhagodaya*,[81] although both Ardhanārīśvara and Lakṣmīdhara provide substantial quotations, suggesting that the pair of works were readily accessible in the seventeenth century. That these two Śrīvidyā treatises had come to be routinely acknowledged as the works of Śaṅkarācārya is confirmed by Rājacūḍāmaṇi Dīkṣita in his *Śaṅkarābhyudaya*. While depicting Śaṅkarācārya's completion of his education, he provides a resume of the young prodigy's scholastic endeavors, including the two works in question:

> At the command of Guru Govindapāda, who was a treasury of
>   virtue,
> He first set forth the commentary on the thousand names of Viṣṇu.
>
> Having churned the great ocean of Mantra and Āgama with the
>   churning stick of his intellect,
> He extracted the nectar that was the treatises beginning with the
>   *Prapañcasāra*.

He measured out the *Saubhāgyavidyā* as well as the ritual handbook,
   the *Subhagodaya:*
Two jewel boxes for depositing the meaning of the science of
   mantra.

To those of lesser eligibility, singularly attached to awareness of
   brahman with qualities,
He granted favor, bestowing hymns to Hari and Hara.

He granted treatises based on the nondual nature of the self,
As well as hundreds of further hymns, foremost being the
   Saundaryalaharī.

He drew out the commentary on the Upaniṣads, which, arrayed
   with recurring floods of virtues,
Made manifest the nondual truth of the Self in the palm of one's
   hand dispelling primordial, infinite delusion. . . .

At the age of twelve, having reflected there upon the essence of the
   scriptures with the Brahminical sages absorbed in meditation,
He effortlessly composed the auspicious commentary, deep and mel-
   lifluous, on the collection of *sūtras* of Śrī Vyāsa, crest jewel among
   preceptors.[82]

While these two works, the *Saubhāgyavidyā* and *Subhagodaya,* do not typically
figure in hagiographies or popular memory of Śaṅkara's legacy, the *Subhagodaya* in
particular is the foremost authority cited by Lakṣmīdhara and Ardhanārīśvara in
defense of the very notion of a Samaya school of Śrīvidyā. Indeed, for Lakṣmīdhara,
the Samayamata is no less than the central theological project of Śaṅkarācārya,
"the knower of the truth of the Samaya doctrine" (*samayamatatattvavedinaḥ*),
who, he claims,[83] crafted the entire *Saundaryalaharī* as a covert but systematic
exposition of the doctrine. Thus, it is unsurprising that both commentators accept his attributed theological works as a central pillar of their analysis, including the *Saundaryalaharī,* the *Saubhāgyavidyā* and *Subhagodaya,* and even the
Saubhāgyacintāmaṇi, a third Śrīvidyā treatise attributed by Ardhanārīśvara to the
pen of Śaṅkara.[84]

In addition to Śaṅkara's Śrīvidyā oeuvre, Lakṣmīdhara invokes a second group
of source texts as a mainstay of his exegetical project, one that Ardhanārīśvara in
turn implements enthusiastically in service of the Samaya doctrine. Known collectively as the Śubhāgamapañcaka (The five pure scriptures), these five Śrīvidyā
"Saṃhitās"—undoubtedly referred to as such to evoke a Vedic resonance—bear
the names of the mythological Vedic sages to whom their authorship is attributed: Vasiṣṭha, Sanaka, Śuka, Sanandana, and Sanatkumāra.[85] According to
Lakṣmīdhara, Śākta *upāsaka*s have often strayed from the Vedic fold by accepting

the more transgressive Tantras without proper reservation, failing to discriminate between those intended for orthodox Vaidikas and those appropriate only for Śūdras.[86] After providing a systematic inventory of the sixty-four Tantras listed in the Vāmakeśvarīmata, delimiting those eligible to adopt their teachings, he concludes that with few exceptions, Vaidika practitioners of Śrīvidyā should restrict themselves to the precepts of the Śubhāgamapañcaka, which he considers the foundational scriptural authority for Samaya practice:

> In the Śubhāgamapañcaka, the array of ritual practices is examined in accordance with the Vedic path alone. This path, examined by the Śubhāgamapañcaka, was set forth by the five sages Vasiṣṭha, Sanaka, Śuka, Sanandana, and Sanatkumāra. This alone is what is conventionally referred to as "Samaya conduct." In just the same way, I also have composed this commentary according to the views of Śaṅkara Bhagavatpāda precisely by taking the support of the Samaya doctrine in accordance with the Śubhāgamapañcaka.[87]

In this extended digression, Lakṣmīdhara constructs an impeccable claim to Vedic orthodoxy, one that offered a considerable appeal to a new generation of Śākta intellectuals who held a vested interest in maintaining the orthodox reputation of their families and literary societies.[88] Breaking from the textual sources of the earlier Kashmiri Śrīvidyā tradition, he promotes in its place an entirely Vedicized scriptural canon that seems to have gained little currency in south India before his influence. Decentering the Kashmiri exegetes and all early Śākta Tantras aside from the Vāmakeśvarīmata, he supplements his core canon with liberal citations from the Ṛgveda, texts of the Taittirīya Śākhā of the Kṛṣṇayajurveda, early Upaniṣads, the classics of Sanskrit court literature from the *Mālatīmādhava* to the *Naiṣadhīyacarita,* and, of course, the Śākta hymns attributed to Kālidāsa. Ardhanārīśvara Dīkṣita, in turn, follows closely in Lakṣmīdhara's footsteps, adopting as his core canon the *Saubhāgyavidyā, Subhagodaya, Saundaryalaharī, Śubhāgamapañcaka,* the hymns of Kālidāsa, and the Vāmakeśvarīmata, interspersed with the best sellers of courtly literary theory such as the *Kāvyādarśa, Kāvyaprakāśa, Alaṅkārasarvasva,* and *Candrāloka.*

In short, Ardhanārīśvara Dīkṣita's *Ambāstavavyākhyā* not only mimetically replicates the textual practices of Lakṣmīdhara's commentary but also expands upon its larger project of repackaging Śrīvidyā *upāsanā* to suit the needs of a more Vedicized and Vedicizing audience.[89] When it comes to the doctrinal innovations of the Samaya school, however, Ardhanārīśvara proves himself an even more meticulous advocate of its principles than Lakṣmīdhara himself. Where Lakṣmīdhara makes bold and seemingly unfounded assertions about Samaya doctrine, Ardhanārīśvara painstakingly documents the textual support underlying Lakṣmīdhara's claims, demonstrating their fidelity to the position taken by Śaṅkarācārya in the *Subhagodaya.* After all, for Ardhanārīśvara, the Samaya school is by no means the invention of Lakṣmīdhara, seeing as he nowhere credits him as the source on which his commentary was modeled. Rather, his ambition is to communicate unambiguously that the Samaya is nothing less than the central teaching of Śaṅkarācārya—through the words of Śaṅkarācārya himself.

Take, for instance, the two central contentions of the Samaya doctrine: first, that Samayins ought to perform worship of the Śrīcakra through interior visualization rather than with external implements; and second, that whereas Kaulas typically perform such worship by concentrating on the lower two *cakras*, or subtle yogic centers, of the body, Samayins worship only in the *brahmarandhra* at the crown of the head. Both of these points are fervently championed by Lakṣmīdhara, who is able to inform us—with remarkable clarity on the material culture of Śākta worship—that Kaula practitioners of Śrīvidyā worship a Śrīcakra inscribed on birch bark, cloth, gold, silver, or some similar surface.[90] Nevertheless, during his extended digression on the Samaya-Kaula division, which spans several pages of the printed edition, nowhere does he adduce a single piece of unambiguous evidence in support of his views from the works of Śaṅkara. In fact, his lack of evidence often leads him to a precarious position. In one instance, instead of supporting his own argument, he remarkably selects a verse from the *Subhagodaya* that seems to state precisely the opposite, necessitating a series of replies to his anticipated objections:

> As it is stated in the *Subhagodaya*: "The qualified adept should meditate on the goddess Tripurasundarī, seated in the middle of the orb of the sun, bearing in her hands the noose, goad, bow, and arrows. He may quickly infatuate the three worlds, along with flocks of the best of women." . . .
>
> Now, some may argue that because external worship is prohibited to Samayins, it is prohibited to worship [the goddess] as seated in the orb of the sun. That is not correct.[91]

Rather than convincingly establishing the intended thesis, the remainder of the passage takes on something of an apologetic tone, engendering a sharp divide between scripture and commentary. The tenor of the verse he cites bears no particular resemblance to the literary aesthetic or values of the sixteenth-century Samaya school, evoking instead the archaic language of early Śrīvidyā scripture, such as the Vāmakeśvarīmata, which contains numerous such references to the efficacy of Śrīvidyā as essentially a sex-magic technology ("He may quickly infatuate the three worlds, along with flocks of the best of women"). Lakṣmīdhara seems, moreover, to have intentionally misread the phrase "the orb of the sun" (*sūryamaṇḍala*) in his *Subhagodaya* citation, as the phrase more often refers to a location in the subtle body around the region of the navel—a sense that would certainly do no service to his argument. It is no wonder that, throughout the argument, he prefers to cite one of his own works, a certain *Karṇāvataṃsastuti* (Hymn to the earrings [of the goddess]),[92] which proves much more amenable to his desired conclusion.[93] Succinctly, on the basis of his thoroughgoing hesitancy, one is tempted to suspect that Lakṣmīdhara did not have access to a citation that would unambiguously ground the Samaya doctrine in the words of Śankara; his only clear evidence for the connection of the Samaya to Śankarācārya is his creative exegesis of the *Saundaryalaharī* itself.

Ardhanārīśvara, on the other hand, suffers from no lack of textual exempla. Unlike Lakṣmīdhara in his abortive attempt to attribute his thesis to Śankara, Ardhanārīśvara assembles a number of lengthy and detailed passages from the *Subhagodaya* that bear an astounding, and in fact rather suspicious, resemblance to the core doctrines of the Samaya school:

> Because external worship is prohibited to Samayins, they are to perform worship only internally. . . . As is stated in the *Subhagodaya*, in the chapter on the instruction of Kaulas:
>
>> Some heretics, chiefly Kaulas and Kāpālikas, devoted to external worship,
>> Are scorned by the Vedas, because their precepts are not supported by scripture.
>> My doctrine is that they are fallen due to practicing what is prohibited.
>> Therefore, the worship of the throne [*pīṭha*] and so forth does not apply to Vaidikas.
>> The sages Vasiṣṭha, Sanaka and others, being devoted to internal worship,
>> Obtained their desired attainment. Thus, internal worship is superior.
>> Now, if one objects that rituals for ground preparation, installation of deities,
>> And so forth, as described by the Āgamas and Atharvaṇas, would be prohibited—
>> This is true. Those are stated in accordance with individual eligibility.
>> Those desiring liberation have no eligibility for such worship.
>> Thus, Samayins perform worship and so forth only in the inner *cakras*.[94]

Intriguingly, Ardhanārīśvara's *Subhagodaya* seems to say precisely what a Samayin intellectual would like to hear. By the time of Ardhanārīśvara's *Ambāstavavyākhyā*, the ambiguity of source material and argument we witness in Lakṣmīdhara's commentary has given way to perfect symmetry between source text and conventional theological wisdom. Further still, Ardhanārīśvara's *Subhagodaya* establishes its own authority by appealing to the Śubhāgamapañcaka by describing the sages Vasiṣṭha, Sanaka, and the others as the prototypical practitioners of Samaya Śrīvidyā. Had Lakṣmīdhara inherited a version of the *Subhagodaya* so faithful to his own views, it seems highly unlikely that he would have resisted supplying the citations. The fact that he did not—and that Ardhanārīśvara had access to such passages in abundance—strongly suggests that in the intervening decades, the *Subhagodaya* itself was heavily redacted to conform to newly emerging understandings of the social role of Śrīvidyā and of Śankarācārya's legacy.[95]

In short, Ardhanārīśvara's generation had witnessed, in a surprisingly short time frame, a thorough redaction of the core scriptures of Samaya Śrīvidyā—suggesting not only a shift in religious values but also, more importantly, a community of initiates responsible for the redaction. It was during the decades between Lakṣmīdhara and Ardhanārīśvara, then, that the foundation was laid for the acceptance of Samaya Śrīvidyā as a cornerstone of Smārta-Śaiva religiosity.

Indeed, Ardhanārīśvara introduces two substantial modifications to our previous knowledge of the Samaya school, as attested by Lakṣmīdhara's work alone, both of which illustrate the diffusion of Samaya values across a wider community of Smārta Brahmin practitioners. First, Ardhanārīśvara expands Lakṣmīdhara's efforts to categorize the religious ecology of Śrīvidyā practitioners in south India. Where Lakṣmīdhara adopts an analytic distinction between "Former" and "Latter" Kaulas[96] in order to reconcile the apparent doctrinal inconsistencies between two verses of the *Saundaryalaharī*,[97] Ardhanārīśvara proposes an expanded typology of three types of "former" and four types of "Latter" Kaulas, along with a delineation of multiple categories of Samayin initiates. And yet, that Ardhanārīśvara is able to produce a precise and definitive list of seven types of Kaulas illustrates a process of conceptual reification, whereby Lakṣmīdhara's speculation has been elevated to the level of a scripturally authenticated model for navigating the sectarian landscape of seventeenth-century south India. In fact, the non-Samayin Śāktas he enumerates—worshippers of the transgressive and ferocious goddesses Mātaṅgī, Vārāhī, Bagalamukhī, and Bhairavī—were genuine participants in the religious economy of Ardhanārīśvara's day, from whom Samayin Smārta Brahmins wished to strictly demarcate themselves.

Second, and by no means less consequential, is the Vedicization of types of worship previously forbidden to Smārta Brahmins under Lakṣmīdhara's strictures.

> Samayins, for their part, are fourfold: (1) those intent on worship according to Vedic procedures of external images of the Śrīcakra fashioned out of gold, etc., (2) those intent on both internal and external worship, (3) those intent on external worship only, and (4) those lacking in any worship. Among these, those adepts who have not acquired experience in yoga worship the goddess in images of the Śrīcakra according to Vedic precepts. Those who have become somewhat established in yoga worship externally and internally, those who are established in yoga worship the goddess only internally, and as for those who have obtained purity of mind, their manner of worship has been expounded previously.[98]

While Lakṣmīdhara forbids the external worship of any Śrīcakra image to Samayins, Ardhanārīśvara clearly accepts the worship of gold Śrīcakra icons as socially normative within Smārta religious culture. Based on historical evidence, in fact, Ardhanārīśvara's pronouncement appears to accurately capture the devotional practice of seventeenth-century Samayins: Nīlakaṇṭha Dīkṣita's lineage descendants, most notably, proudly display in his *samādhi* shrine an image of the Śrīcakra they believe to have been his personal object of worship.[99]

But while speaking volumes about ritual practice and scriptural redaction among Śrīvidyā initiates, Ardhanārīśvara's work, by virtue of its commentarial project, joins that of Atirātra and his contemporaries, who crafted a hagiographical past for the Smārta-Śaiva community. By selecting Lakṣmīdhara's template as the structural principle for an entirely different commentary, Ardhanārīśvara

FIGURE 3. The three *pūjā* images pictured in fig. 2 have been handed down in Nīlakaṇṭha's family and are believed to have been worshipped personally by Nīlakaṇṭha Dīkṣita. As the Tamil caption clarifies, the image on the right is Nīlakaṇṭha's personal *śrīcakra*, the Śrīvidyā *yantra*. This black-and-white photograph is mounted in Nīlakaṇṭha Dīkṣita's *samādhi* shrine in Palamadai, near Tirunelveli in southern Tamil Nadu. All three *pūjā* images are now in the possession of Jagadguru Bhāratī Tīrtha Svāmigaḷ of Sringeri. I have personally seen two of them on his public *pūjā*; unfortunately, the Jagadguru's attendants deny any knowledge of the *śrīcakra*'s location.

transposes the authority behind the Samaya doctrine from the purported author of the *Saundaryalaharī*, Śaṅkarācārya, to the perceived author of the *Ambāstava*, Kālidāsa. Echoing the sentiment of Atirātra Yajvan expressed at Madurai's Cittirai Festival, Ardhanārīśvara reshapes Kālidāsa's identity into a fusion of celebrated *mahākavi* and loyal servant of the goddess Kālī ("Kālī-dāsa"),[100] merging both of these attributes in the author of the *Ambāstava*, an orthodox Samayin's expression of personal devotion. With no less a figure than Kālidāsa representing the power of orthodox Śāktism, it is little surprise that Śrīvidyā offered seventeenth-century Smārta intellectuals a meaningful paradigm for integrating various facets of their ideal personas: Smārta Brahmin, devotee of the Śaṅkarācārya lineage, and not least, poet-celebrity. Śākta devotionalism and literary genius were, for many of these poets, causally interrelated and functionally inextricable from each other. This is expressed perhaps most eloquently by Nīlakaṇṭha Dīkṣita himself in the benediction to his *Śivalīlārṇava* (The sacred games of Śiva), evoking a pair of commonly cited legends linking the poetic aptitude of two south Indian poets—the Tamil bhakti saint Ñānacampantar and the Sanskrit poet Mūkakavi—to their unmediated contact with the goddess's grace. In his own words:

> One became a poet through the breast milk of the Mother, another
> through her *tāmbūla* spittle.
> Desiring to achieve even greater elevation [*unnati*], I served the
> more elevated [*unnata*] corner of Her eyes.[101]

ŚAṄKARĀCĀRYA WORSHIPS THE GODDESS: ŚRĪVIDYĀ'S NEW SACRED GEOGRAPHY

"Just like Kālidāsa," the Śaṅkarācārya of seventeenth-century south India was not only a devout worshipper of the goddess but also a consummate poet, fusing ecstatic devotion and literary virtuosity in impromptu hymns of praise. While Ardhanārīśvara's project reframed Kālidāsa as the prototypical cosmopolitan poet and Śākta devotee, another Smārta theologian—who happened to be his own younger brother—crafted a similar identity for Śaṅkarācārya through his daring and innovative biographical account of the eighth-century Advaita Vedāntin. The *Śaṅkarābhyudaya* (The ascension of Śaṅkara) of Rājacūḍāmaṇi Dīkṣita, a work of refined courtly poetry (*kāvya*), is counted among several works in the genre of Śaṅkaradigvijaya (Śaṅkara's conquest of the directions) chronicles, hagiographies that recount the traditional narrative exploits in the life of Śaṅkara, from boyhood to liberation.

Rājacūḍāmaṇi's treatment of the material, however, differs significantly from the standard conventions of the genre in two crucial respects, both of which are rarely observed in the extensive body of secondary literature on the Śaṅkara hagiographical tradition. As we have seen, Śaṅkara's early childhood and renunciation was, for Rājacūḍāmaṇi, the zenith of his textual production, conspicuous for the authorship attributed to him of the two Samayin Śrīvidyā treatises, the *Saubhāgyavidyā* and *Subhagodaya*. It is the end of Śaṅkara's life, however, that occupies the entire latter half of Rājacūḍāmaṇi's work: these chapters consist entirely of a poetic travelogue of Śaṅkara's final pilgrimage, culminating in his beatific vision of Kāmākṣī in the Kanchipuram Temple. In the process, the *Śaṅkarābhyudaya* situates itself securely within the orbit of devotional poetry, evoking this legacy through a series of ornate and impassioned lyric hymns placed directly in the mouth of Śaṅkara himself. But perhaps more strikingly, Śaṅkara's poetic craft, for Rājacūḍāmaṇi, is unabashedly esoteric in its imagery, directly embedding the fifteen-syllable Śrīvidyā mantra in its verse and providing an extended ritual visualization of the Śrīcakra and the abode of the goddess and her attendants. In short, no other Śaṅkaradigvijaya chronicle colorfully ascribes to Śaṅkara an intimate acquaintance with the intricacies of Śrīvidyā *upāsanā*. By fusing this celebration of the esoteric with courtly literary practice, Rājacūḍāmaṇi crafts Śaṅkara—just like Kālidāsa—as a literary genius whose verse flowed spontaneously from his devotion to the goddess, homologizing in the process the social roles of poet and *tāntrika* in the Smārta religious imaginary.

Despite its unique features, however, the *Śaṅkarābhyudaya* has garnered less attention than competing hagiographies, largely owing to the institutional politics of the Śaṅkarācārya monastic lineages. According to the narrative most commonly accepted by Smārtas today across the subcontinent, Śaṅkara bequeathed the legacy of Advaita philosophy to subsequent generations by establishing four monasteries in each of the four cardinal directions—the southern direction being accounted for by Sringeri in western Karnataka—and culminated his life of pilgrimage and adventure by defeating his rivals and ascending to the Sarvajñapīṭha ("the Seat of the Omniscient") located in Kashmir. Rājacūḍāmaṇi's *Śaṅkarābhyudaya* is one of a few such narratives that redirect the course of Śaṅkara's journey toward the South, situating Śaṅkara's final ascent and liberation in the Tamil city of Kanchipuram rather than Kashmir. This shift is widely interpreted by the Tamil Smārta community to indicate that Śaṅkara in fact established five monasteries, the four traditional monasteries being branches of a single overarching institution, the Kāñcī Kāmakoṭi Pīṭha of Kanchipuram. As a result, scholarly considerations of Śaṅkara's life story are often overshadowed by polemic, and supporters of the Sringeri lineage are often eager to discredit the authenticity and manuscript transmission of any text associating Śaṅkara with Kanchipuram.

Among other commonly circulating Śaṅkaradigvijaya narratives, two such works, Anantānandagiri's *Śaṅkaravijaya* and Cidvilāsa's *Śaṅkaravijayavilāsa*, both name Kanchipuram as the site of Śaṅkara's final ascent. Likewise, both chronicles bear the outward signifiers of affiliation with a lineage of Śrīvidyā practice, as both conclude that Śaṅkara's chief accomplishment in Kanchipuram was to establish the Śrīcakra that currently lies at the heart of the Kāmākṣī Temple. In fact, the recurrent patterns of citation and phrasing in the two chronicles suggest strongly that both emerge from roughly the same cultural milieu. We possess no reliable indications of their dates or places of composition, save that both must have existed before the *terminus ante quem* of the Mādhavīya *Śaṅkaravijaya* in the mid-eighteenth century, as this somewhat notorious narration of Śaṅkara's life story borrows liberally from all previously extant versions.[102] Given their emphasis on Kanchipuram, one expects that both texts originated in the South; and indeed, a close reading of their Śrīvidyā allusions reveals that both place themselves within the cultural orbit of the Lalitopākhyāna, a narrative and liturgical excerpt from the Brahmāṇḍa Purāṇa that has remained a constitutive part of the south Indian Śrīvidyā heritage for centuries—so prototypically Tamil in its rhetoric, in fact, that it frames itself around Agastya, the southern sage, and his journey south toward the abode of Kāmākṣī in Kanchipuram.[103]

As a result, dubious voices are in no short supply, claiming either that Rājacūḍāmaṇi Dīkṣita, the celebrated court poet of seventeenth-century Tanjavur, did not write the text we have received as the *Śaṅkarābhyudaya,* or that the crucial chapters—the seventh and eighth *sarga*s, in which Śaṅkara arrives in Kanchipuram and worships Kāmākṣī with Śrīvidyā-inflected hymns and meditation—were interpolated directly by representatives of the Kāmakoṭi Pīṭha. Such a position was advanced by, for instance, one R. Krishnaswami Aiyer in his critique of the Kāmakoṭi Pīṭha and its claims to historical antiquity, in which he paints the *Śaṅkarābhyudaya* as a modern forgery: "It is quite patent that this Kavya was published years after the Madhaviya just to discredit the authenticity of the latter."[104] Aiyer is correct about the limited discussion of manuscript evidence in the published editions. Two editions have been published to date, one in the Sanskrit serial journal *Sahṛdaya* in 1914–1915, and the second in 1986 by S. V. Radhakrishna Sastri. Both include all eight *sarga*s of the work, with a number of variants in the somewhat fragmentary eighth *sarga* to suggest either independent transcriptions of a common manuscript or distinct manuscript sources for this chapter. Unfortunately, neither editor is forthcoming about the manuscripts used to compile the edition or the editorial practices involved.

Among several manuscripts available in libraries across the subcontinent, most are duplicates of a paper transcript of the first six *sarga*s, transmitted in either Grantha or Devanāgarī script, accompanied by the commentary of a certain Rāmakṛṣṇa Sūri.[105] I have also located a distinct transcript of the entire eight chapters (*sarga*s) at the K. V. Sharma Research Institute in Chennai with no commentary, which shows minor variants from both published editions. Two further manuscripts appear to be housed at the library of the Śāradā Pīṭha in Sringeri and at the Punjab University Library in Lahore, neither of which I have been able to access.[106] Based on manuscript evidence alone, given that the six-*sarga* version circulates exclusively with the commentary of Rāmakṛṣṇa Sūri, the original was most likely abridged by the commentator himself, who may have been affiliated with a competing monastic lineage that did not consider the ending of the text acceptable to orthodox wisdom—either for its emphasis on Kanchipuram or its elaborate visualization of the divine union of Kāmeśvara and Kāmeśvarī.[107]

Stylistic evidence, on the other hand, demonstrates beyond a reasonable doubt that the entire eight chapters were authored by Rājacūḍāmaṇi himself. The fourth through seventh *sarga*s of the *Śaṅkarābhyudaya* are framed around Śaṅkara's tour of the prominent pilgrimage centers of south India, progressing in tenor by the fifth chapter to a garland of successive hymns to the presiding deities written in highly ornate verse, comparable in literary style to Rājacūḍāmaṇi's other works of courtly poetry. Providing a direct continuation of the pilgrimage narrative, the seventh chapter emerges seamlessly from the end of the preceding narrative, contributing to a sense of intensification as the poetic register of Śaṅkara's hymns heightens with heavier meters and richer phonic textures. Throughout the hymns, the distinctive features of Nāyaka-period south Indian verse are unmistakable: with techniques ranging from rich alliteration to *yamaka* (paronomasia) and Dravidian front rhyme (the rhyming of the first syllables of each foot of a verse), the poet executes the baroque aesthetic of the period with a skill paralleled by few of his contemporaries. Similarly, our author delights in interspersing more obscure grammatical forms among the verses at regular intervals, showing a particular preference for the *-tāt* form of the imperative (e.g., *bhavatāt*) and feminine perfect participles. Take, for instance, the following verses from the hymn to Kāmākṣī in the seventh *sarga,* which aptly exemplify the idealized aesthetic of the age:

> kanaka-kanattanuvallī-janaka-samacchāyatuṅgavakṣojā |
> sanaka-sanandadhyeyā ghanakabarī bhātu śailarājasutā ||

> May daughter of the mountain shine, with her cloud-black braid,
>   contemplated by the Sages Sanaka and Sananda,
> The peaks of whose breast cast a shadow like to that of the father of
>   the creeper-figured girl glistening like gold.

> lavatām aghaṃ nayantī nava-tāmarasaśriyā dṛśā bhajatām |
> bhava-vāmatanur mama sā bhava-tāpavimuktaye bhavatāt ||

> Leading sin to minuteness with her eyes equal in splendor to fresh
>   lotuses,
> May she, who is the left half of Śiva's body, release me from the
>   agony of existence.[108]

In short, to successfully forge a missing seventh *sarga* of the *Śaṅkarābhyudaya* would have proven exceptionally challenging for the leading poets of the seventeenth century, let alone for modern polemicists.[109] In register and phonic texture, then, Rājacūḍāmaṇi's hagiography of Śaṅkara diverges sharply from the versions promulgated by his near contemporaries, even those affiliated with the Śaṅkarācārya lineages of the Kanchipuram region. Undoubtedly, all Śaṅkara chronicles whose narratives culminate in Kanchipuram participated in promulgating a new religious imaginary, forging a connection between Śaṅkarācārya, Kanchipuram, and Śrīvidyā esotericism. And yet on a theological level as well, Rājacūḍāmaṇi proves himself an innovative iconoclast, sprinkling his narrative and devotional verse with esoteric allusions rarely found in cosmopolitan courtly literature.

Take, for instance, the case of Anantānandagiri, who describes Śaṅkara's installation briefly, with no salient ritual detail and only a cursory allusion to the philosophical significance of the Śrīcakra:

> Because the Śrīcakra is the very form of the unity of Śiva and Śakti, its unity with the *vidyā* [i.e., the Śrīvidyā mantra] and the self is consequentially established because of their complete nondifference. Thus the indication is that the worship of the Śrīcakra

is to be performed by all who desire liberation. Therefore, the Śrīcakra was installed by your honor so that the fruit of liberation might be obtained merely by seeing it.[110]

The author then proceeds to quote a somewhat extended passage, without attributing any source, concerning the physical characteristics of the Śrīcakra. Interestingly enough, the same passage occurs in the Cidvilāsīya *Śaṅkaravijaya* as well, with minor variants in transmission, but merged seamlessly into the text so as to betray no hint that the passage was interpolated from an outside source:

> The triangle, octagon, and the pairs of decagons likewise,
> And the fourteen-sided *cakra:* these are the five Śakti *cakras.*
> The seed, the eight-petaled and likewise sixteen-petaled lotus,
> The square, and the four gates: these are the Śiva *cakras,* in order. . . .
> He who knows the invariable connection of the Śaiva
> And also Śākta *cakras,* respectively, is a knower of the *cakras.*[111]

This is the extent of Śaṅkara's installation of the Śrīcakra in Anantānandagiri's account. Although neither of our authors acknowledges its source, we are fortunate that Bhāskararāya, writing from eighteenth-century Tanjavur, quotes this same passage in his Lalitāsahasranāma commentary, crediting it to the Brahmāṇḍa Purāṇa and thus situating it unmistakably within the Lalitopākhyāna tradition.[112] In short, we can fairly definitively contextualize both the Anantānandagiri and Cidvilāsīya chronicles within the same south Indian Śrīvidyā tradition, one with a center of gravity in Kanchipuram and the Kāmākṣī Temple, taking the Lalitopākhyāna as a primary pillar of its scriptural canon. That Śaṅkara's association with Kanchipuram had been deeply integrated into cultural memory by the late seventeenth century is confirmed as well by the *Patañjalicaritra* of Rāmabhadra Dīkṣita, pupil of Nīlakaṇṭha Dīkṣita, whose brief summary of the Śaṅkara narrative includes as a matter of course a mention of Kanchipuram as Śaṅkara's final destination: "Having served his preceptor Govinda at length with devotion, when his [Govinda's] own greatness was established through liberation beyond the body, having fashioned the Advaita commentary, having conquered the directions, the noble Śaṅkara took up residence in Kanchipuram."[113]

Narratologically speaking, Rājacūḍāmaṇi's *Śaṅkarābhyudaya* outlines a trajectory remarkably similar to that of the final chapter of Śaṅkara's earthly life. And yet its textual register could hardly be more divergent. While all three texts emerge from the same extended cultural sphere, the Anantānandagiri *Śaṅkaravijaya,* as can be seen from the above quotations, is rather rudimentary in prose style and in the specificity of its content. Cidvilāsa's treatment of the same event, while presented at greater length in a more polished *anuṣṭubh* verse, differs little in content, even incorporating the exact same passage from the Lalitopākhyāna as his competitor, Anantānandagiri. Both authors are also familiar with Kanchipuram, referring by name to its Śaiva and Vaiṣṇava resident deities, Ekāmranātha and

Varadarāja. No further esoteric content, however, appears in either chronicle. In fact, we meet with quite the opposite later on in Cidvilāsa's *Śaṅkaravijayavilāsa*. Although the Śrīcakra is typically closely associated with the initiatory tradition of Śrīvidyā and its more esoteric regimen of ritual practice, this need not always be the case, particularly in the Tamil country, where the Śrīcakra is regularly installed in major Śaiva temples across the region at the base of the image of Śiva's consort, even in the absence of any Śrīvidyā-based liturgical worship.[114] It need not come as a great surprise, then, when, a few chapters after Śaṅkara's installation of the Śrīcakra, Cidvilāsa describes him vehemently denouncing the heresy of a group of Śrīvidyā *upāsakas* he encounters during his travels:

> The all-knowing preceptor, Śaṅkarācārya, beheld them.
> He asked them as if unworthy of respect, seemingly impassioned:
> "Having abandoned the *tripuṇḍra* on your forehead, why do you
>   bear *kuṃkum?*
> Why have you cast off your white clothing and put on red
>   garments? . . .
> Indeed, you have met with such bad acts as a result of your sin."
> When the best of preceptors had spoken, the ones who had under-
>   taken the Śākta path [replied]:
> "O sage, what are you saying today? This arises from ignorance of
>   our doctrine. . . .
> Certainly, the supreme Śakti of Śiva is united with the manifest
>   goddess herself.
> She is the cause of the world, her essence beyond the [three]
>   qualities.
> By the power of that Śakti, the great truth in its entirety was
>   created. . . .
> Thus, it is service to her lotus feet that bestows liberation.
> It is purely with delight that we bear her symbols, the *kuṃkum* and all.
> Thus we bear her sandal always on our arms and even on our throats.
> From this we Śrīvidyā *upāsakas* are eternally liberated in this
>   lifetime."[115]

As one might expect, Śaṅkara responds by refuting their heresy, instructing them in the philosophical orthodoxy of Advaita Vedānta. In short, we can discern in Cidvilāsa's treatment of this event a desire to distance himself from the more esoteric content of Śrīvidyā ritual practice, or from lineages of Śāktas he viewed as too transgressive to take part in normative Śaiva society. After all, the Śāktas he describes had taken steps to visibly demarcate themselves from orthodox Brahmins, abandoning the Śaiva *tripuṇḍra,* wearing red clothing and *kuṃkum*—a color with long-standing Śākta resonances—and even branding themselves with the Devī's sandals on their arms and throat. Intriguingly, as we will see in the next chapter,

Cidvilāsa's opinion on the subject is closely in line with that of Nīlakaṇṭha Dīkṣita concerning the necessity of orthodox Śaivas wearing the *tripuṇḍra* rather than Śākta sectarian insignia.

Rājacūḍāmaṇi, on the other hand, makes no effort to conceal his detailed and intimate acquaintance with the intricacies of Śrīvidyā *upāsanā*. To the contrary, the seventh and eighth chapters of the *Śaṅkarābhyudaya* contain an astonishing number of references to particular elements of Śrīvidyā practice. These esoteric elements, far from being obscure allusions discernible only by a handful of initiates, provide the primary structuring device for the climax of the work, mediating the narration of Śaṅkara's beatific vision of Kāmākṣī's abode and his ascension to the state of enlightenment. As Śaṅkarācārya approaches Kanchipuram in the middle of the seventh *sarga,* he enters the temple of Kāmākṣī and summarily dismisses a host of opponents, ascending to the Seat of the Omniscient, which Rājacūḍāmaṇi here refers to as the *vidyābhadrāsana* ("the throne of wisdom"). While Śaṅkara's philosophical battles with heretical sects form the backbone of most Śaṅkaradigvijaya chronicles, the *Śaṅkarābhyudaya* addresses the matter with a handful of verses, leaving behind Śaṅkara's propagation of Advaita philosophy in favor of a more fundamental task: his worship of Kāmākṣī, the goddess who wears the Vedānta as her girdle belt. As he sings, bursting into a spontaneous hymn of praise, he recites a series of fifteen verses that spell out, through the first syllable of each verse, the fifteen-syllable Śrīvidyā initiatory mantra:

> KA-ruṇārasasārasudhāvaruṇālayaviharamāṇadṛkkoṇam |
> aruṇādharam avalambe taruṇāruṇakānti kim api tāruṇyam ||

> I take support in that indescribable youthfulness with red lower lip,
> radiant like the fresh sunrise,
> The corner of whose eyes conveys an ocean of nectar that is the
> essence of compassion.

> E-ṇīdṛśam aiśānīṃ śoṇīkṛtadaśadiśaṃ śarīrarucā |
> vāṇīmadhuripuramaṇīveṇīkusumāṅghrinakharuciṃ vande ||

> I bow to the doelike northeastern direction, which reddens the ten
> directions with the splendor of her body,
> Whose toenails have the luster of the flowers in the braids of the
> beloved of Madhu's enemy, Lakṣmī, and Sarasvatī.

> Ī-ḍāmahe maheśīṃ cuḍāvinyāsabhūṣitasudhāṃśum |
> vrīḍānurāgaśabalakrīḍāvīkṣāvaśaṃvadamaheśām ||

> I worship the great goddess, whose array of tresses is ornamented by
> the moon,
> Whose numerous bashfully impassioned games and glances have
> made Śiva subservient.

LA-valīlatāmatallīnavalīlāgandhilalitatanuyaṣṭau |
bhava līlābhṛti ca mano lavalīḍhajapāruṇimni taruṇimni ||

May my mind always rest on that youthfulness, which has licked a
  portion of the
Redness of the *japā* flower, the stalk of whose body is made lovely by
  a charm and fragrance like that of the best of Lavalī creepers.[116]

The hymn continues, over its fifteen verses, to commence each verse with a
syllable of the Śrīvidyā root mantra (*mūlamantra*): "ka e ī la hrīṃ—ha sa ka ha
la hrīṃ—sa ka la hrīṃ."[117] And just in case any of his readers fail to notice this
structuring devise, he calls attention to it explicitly at the conclusion of the hymn,
ensuring that his "esoteric" reference will not go unnoticed: "Thus propitiating
Kāmākṣī, who dwells on the bank of the Kampā River, established in her external
abode, in verse with syllables laid out in sequence according to the fifteen-syllable
mantra, moving to bow down into the familiar interior of the cave, he praised
Bhagavatī Śyāmalā, who was seated at the entry."[118]

And so Śaṅkara proceeds to sing a similar hymn of praise to Śyāmalā, understood in the Lalitopākhyāna tradition as the *mantriṇī* (chief minister) of Lalitā,
here seen guarding the entryway to the cave on the bank of the Kampā River traditionally believed to be the true abode of Kāmākṣī. True to form, Rājacūḍāmaṇi
embeds his six-verse hymn to Śyāmalā as well with mantric syllables, comprising
the two subordinate mantras "aiṃ hrīṃ śrīṃ" and "aiṃ klīṃ sauḥ."[119] At this point,
following the hymn to Śyāmalā, the narrative reaches its climax: seemingly pleased
with his richly ornamented *stotra*s, Kāmākṣī grants Śaṅkara a visionary experience
of her true abode, the city of Śrīpura on the central peak of Mount Meru, which
Rājacūḍāmaṇi documents in painstaking detail through the 111 verses of the eighth
sarga:

Thus having praised her, the mother of the universe, entering inside
  [the cave]
On the bank of the Kampā River, favored by rows of groves of wish-
  fulfilling trees,
He rejoiced, seeing before him, immediately, in an instant, a certain
  mountain peak,
Leader of the clan of golden mountains, purified by the lotus feet of
  Kāmākṣī.[120]

If anything, the linguistic register and imagery of the eighth *sarga* present us
with an even more intriguing fusion. Shifting from high *kāvya* meters to a steady
anuṣṭubh throughout the entire chapter, Rājacūḍāmaṇi evokes the rhythm and
cadence of liturgical recitation even while retaining the rich phonetic texture and
ornaments of language (*śabdālaṅkāra*) so characteristic of his style: "I meditate on

a certain [*kāñcana*] city of Kāmākṣī, known as Śrīpura, with nīpa palm, mango, and ebony [*kāñcanāra*] trees with golden [*kāñcana*] sap."[121] And yet the emphasis in this chapter shifts from poetics to the particulars of the visualization, as the author spares no opportunity to match the imagery of his verse to the scripturally sanctioned map of Śrīpura, down to the proper lists of attendant deities in every enclosure of the city. As with Anantānandagiri and Cidvilāsa, Rājacūḍāmaṇi's source for the geography of Kāmākṣī's abode is the Lalitopākhyāna, which appends to the core narrative of the slaying of Bhaṇḍāsura an iconographically elaborate description of Śrīpura, including its eight outer enclosures with walls made of various metals, and its seventeen nested palaces composed of different gemstones, inside of which exists the Cintāmaṇigṛha, the home of the Śrīcakra. Rājacūḍāmaṇi describes each of these levels with precision, continuing up the mountain peak, where the various geometric enclosures (*āvaraṇa*) of the Śrīcakra lead inward toward the central *bindu*, the abode of the esoteric forms of the divine couple, Kāmeśvara and Kāmeśvarī.

A sample of Śaṅkara's extended visualization, compared with its source material in the Lalitopākhyāna, will suffice to illuminate both the elegance and phonetic texture of Rājacūḍāmaṇi's verses and the precision with which he seeks to capture the authentic iconography of Śrīpura and the Śrīcakra, even embracing descriptors that might offend the sensibilities of the more conservative voices in Smārta Brahmin society:

From the *Śaṅkarābhyudaya:*

I visualize here Mahākāla, radiant like the sun [*kapiśābham*],
Ardently attached to liquor [*kapiśāyana*], eagerly embracing the
    neck of Mahākālī.

May his seat, known as the Kālacakra, with the radiant *bindu*, tri-
    angle, and pentagon,
And eight- and sixteen-petaled lotuses, confer upon me long life.[122]

From the Lalitopākhyāna:

Mahākālī and Mahākāla, proceeding at the command of Lalitā,
Create the entire universe, dwelling on the first path.
The Kālacakra has become the seat of him, Mataṅga,
Surrounded by four enclosures, delightful with the *bindu* in the
    center.
The triangle and pentagon, the sixteen-petaled lotus,
And also the eight-petaled lotus. Mahākāla is in the center.[123]

Such parallels are numerous and, taken as a whole, leave little doubt that Rājacūḍāmaṇi has reworked what he believes to be the salient elements from the Lalitopākhyāna into a smoothly polished sequence. Further up the mountain, describing the nine enclosures of the Śrīcakra, Rājacūḍāmaṇi exercises similar care to refer by name to the particular attendant *śakti*s residing at each level, details that may seem insignificant from a narrative or even aesthetic point of view but which would be integral to a systematic visualization or installation (*nyāsa*) of the respective enclosures in the context of ritual practice:

From the *Śaṅkarābhyudaya:*

May the Śakti of the Triple City protect me, surrounded by those
    known as Prakaṭā,
Superintending over the triple *cakra,* the Deluder of the Three
    Worlds [Trailokyamohana].

And above, may those shining Śaktis, in rows on the golden seat,
Beginning with Kāmākarṣiṇikā be our wish-fulfilling cows.[124]

From the Lalitopākhyāna:

And inside is that triple *cakra,* the Deluder of the Three Worlds.
In this are the Śaktis, among whom are those known as Prakaṭā.[125]

From the *Śaṅkarābhyudaya:*

The goddess of the triple city, Samayā dwells, holding a rosary,
In the Cakra that Fulfills All Desires [Sarvāśāpūraka], with the
    Guptayoginīs in order.

We worship the goddesses beginning with Anaṅgakusumā,
Situated above that, on the lines of the golden seat.[126]

From the Lalitopākhyāna:

These are the Guptayoginīs, and Tripureśī is the mistress of the *cakra,*
The superintendent deity of the *cakra* is known as Sarvāśāpūrikā.[127]

After ascending to the peak of the Śrīcakra, Śaṅkara embarks on an extended panegyric of the esoteric form of divinity he witnesses there, Kāmeśvara and Kāmeśvarī, Śiva and his consort in the form of a sixteen-year-old amorous couple. And it was through these elaborate hymns of praise to Kāmeśvara and Kāmeśvarī, Rājacūḍāmaṇi tells us, rather than through contemplation or philosophical insight, that Śaṅkara reached the end of his journey and attained direct knowledge of brahman, the formless absolute: "In this manner, he bowed with humility to the great *yantra* of the imperishable Kāma with garlands of language. . . . Silently worshipping Kāmeśvarī, who dwells on the bank of the Kampā River, Śaṅkara, the refuge of the triple worlds, realized the bliss of brahman."[128]

For Rājacūḍāmaṇi, evidently, Śaṅkara was not only a member of the Sanskrit literary elite but also a passionate, well-trained adept in what he considered the highest mysteries of the Śrīvidyā tradition. Writing from a cultural milieu that regarded the *Saundaryalaharī* as an authentic work of the eighth-century Vedāntin, Rājacūḍāmaṇi and his contemporaries venerated Śaṅkara as a Śākta poet of high Sanskrit verse as well as an ardent personal devotee of Kāmākṣī, two identities that were intimately intertwined both for Śaṅkara himself and the seventeenth-century poet-theologians who adopted this image as a model for their own self-fashioning. It is no accident that fully half of the *Śaṅkarābhyudaya* consists of these devotional "garlands of language," culminating in a series of esoteric hymns showcasing some of the more ornate and sophisticated poetic devices on offer by the Sanskrit language. Evidently, for Rājacūḍāmaṇi, much as for his brother, to be a cultured, orthodox Śākta is by definition to be a first-class poet as well—and Śaṅkara, just like Kālidāsa, was a Śākta poet par excellence. Indeed, in Rājacūḍāmaṇi's vision, it is as a poet, rather than as a philosopher, that Śaṅkara ascended to the throne of wisdom in Kanchipuram. The following verse, in particular, alludes to Śaṅkara's poetic conquest in the language of *śṛṅgāra rasa*—the erotic sentiment—evoking the divine lovemaking of Kāmeśvara and Kāmeśvarī:

> "Alas, don't force me so suddenly, without having defeated me
> On the path of poetry, dripping with erotic sentiment."
> It was as if Brahmā himself, having conquered Sarasvatī,
> Who had spoken thus, ascended to the throne of wisdom.[129]

ŚAṄKARĀCĀRYA, ŚRĪVIDYĀ, AND THE MAKING OF A SECTARIAN COMMUNITY

Just like Kālidāsa—the historical Kālidāsa as well as his seventeenth-century counterpart—the Smārta-Śaiva theologians of early modern south India were accomplished wordsmiths, crafting their public personae as well as their personal devotionalism in Sanskrit verse. But how do hymns of praise or ritual manuals manufacture a community, a sectarian tradition unprecedented in Indian history?

Niklas Luhmann, as we have seen, defines a social system, such as a sectarian community, as a "meaning-constituting system,"[130] an operationally closed set of social institutions that maintains—and in fact reconstitutes—its own boundaries internally through the structures of meaning it generates. That is to say, Hindu sects function autonomously from one another as meaning-constituting systems, each individually reproducing the religious institutions that endow participation in that community with sectarian-inflected religious identity. Luhmann illustrates the functional independence of such systems through analogical appeal to the models of biology, on both a microscopic and a macroscopic level. An individual cell, for instance, exhibits metabolic functions that both perpetuate the cell itself and maintain the boundary that separates it from its immediate environment. That is, although cell walls are permeable, a cell functions as an organism unto itself, maintaining itself independently from its immediate neighbors. To extend this analogy to the study of religion, a self-constituting sectarian community generates its own meaning-creating institutions—monasteries, lineages (*paramparā*), temple complexes, sites of performance, and so on. When viewed macroscopically, the aggregate of such mutually independent systems, whether sects or cells, facilitates the balance of an entire ecosystem—or, as the case may be, an entire society.

Sectarian social systems, within the larger religious ecosystem that is Hinduism, we find, maintain an internal coherence and mutual independence comparable to those of discrete biological systems, or of the functional social systems that Luhmann describes as comprising modern society, such as the political or legal systems. We can describe early modern Hinduism as a Sectarian Age in that discrete sectarian communities came to thrive in remarkable social and doctrinal independence from one other. In south India, for instance, major sectarian communities such as the Śrīvaiṣṇava or Mādhva Vaiṣṇava lineages, or the Tamil Śaiva Siddhānta, attain virtually complete autonomy on a social as well as doctrinal level by becoming major economic shareholders in the networks of exchange centered at major temple complexes and monasteries. This is not to say, naturally, that interactions between sectarian communities do not occur on a regular basis. In fact, it is just such interactions—whether polemical exchanges, competition for resources, or theological influence and reaction—that allow each sect to maintain its distinctive identity in the face of changing circumstances.

3

Public Philology

Constructing Sectarian Identities in
Early Modern South India

THEOLOGY BEYOND THE TEXT

The very idea of theology, in early modern India no less than in Europe, generally connotes a strictly textual enterprise. And yet the written word, in published print or palm-leaf manuscript, when circulated within an extensive community of readers or deployed strategically for political ends, often leaves an indelible impression on the world outside of the text. In the European context, one would scarcely doubt that the manifestos of Martin Luther, although consisting of nothing but the written word, occasioned a seismic shift in the religious landscape of Europe when nailed to the church door.

In much the same way, the theology of early-generation Smārta theologians sought to transcend the scope of its textual medium, intervening in religious disputes that had lasting implications for the embodied and lived religious identities of Śaivas across caste and language communities. The majority of the works discussed in the preceding chapter—ranging from Tantric ritual manuals to devotional poetry charged with esoteric significance—were intended for the eyes and ears of a select group of initiates. When Smārta-Śaiva theologians revealed their personal engagement with Śrīvidyā Śākta Tantrism, they aimed to cultivate—and explicate to their coreligionists—interior modes of religiosity that were transmitted within relatively delimited social boundaries, consolidating the internal dynamics of the fledgling Smārta-Śaiva community. Nīlakaṇṭha Dīkṣita, most notably, renowned in professional circles for his satirical wit and literary genius, documents in his Śrīvidyā-inflected writings his devotional relationship with his guru, Gīrvāṇendra Sarasvatī, and his authoritative command of the intricacies of Tantric ritual worship. One might expect, then, that when Nīlakaṇṭha spoke as

99

public theologian, addressing the Śaiva community of his day, his public agenda would arise organically from his inner convictions. In fact, quite the opposite turns out to be the case: Nīlakaṇṭha's exoteric theology was designed to cultivate a public religious culture that diverged markedly from his own private devotion.

To place this public theological enterprise in context, Nīlakaṇṭha and his contemporaries were faced with navigating the radical sectarianization of south India's Hindu religious landscape, which in the early seventeenth century was still in the process of unfolding. In the wake of the decline of the Vijayanagara empire, individual sectarian communities, including not only the Smārta-Śaivas but their Vaiṣṇava rivals as well, vied for control of regionwide megatemples. They instituted competing networks of monasteries with vast landholdings that became primary shareholders in the agricultural production and economic circulation at the foundation of south Indian polities. Succinctly, for Smārta-Śaiva theologians, much was at stake in representing themselves as orthodox Hindus with a convincing interpretation of Hindu scripture. Their continuing patronage, on one hand, and their appeal to the broader lay population, on the other, depended to a substantial degree on how suitably they represented themselves as constituting the pinnacle of a unified Hindu religion encompassing the Vedas, Purāṇic mythology, and popular ritual practice such as temple *pūjā*.

As a result, Smārta-Śaivas pursued their public theology with the same intensity they invested in their esoteric worship. Instead of circulating their devotional poetry to a wider public, Smārta-Śaiva theologians engaged in a project we can describe as "public philology"—text criticism that serves as public theology. On one hand, they established normative standards for the interpretation of exoteric Śaiva classics of mythology and liturgy; Nīlakaṇṭha Dīkṣita, for instance, composed a commentary on a popular Śaiva hymn, "The Thousand and Eight Names of Śiva," one that, for perhaps the first time, systematically identifies for a wider lay public the mythological tropes in a hymn they recited on a daily basis. Other public theological ventures were thinly veiled attacks on the scriptural canons of a rival sectarian community, designed to discredit that community's claim to scriptural orthodoxy. A particularly appealing target, for instance, was the corpus of sectarian—that is, Śaiva or Vaiṣṇava—Purāṇas, mythology sacred to the Śaivas or Vaiṣṇavas, respectively; because of their prolixity and informal style of composition, Purāṇas were often riddled with internal inconsistencies, making them easy marks for textual critique. In fact, Nīlakaṇṭha appended an entire polemical prologue to his *Śivatattvarahasya*—"The Secret of the Principles of Śiva," ostensibly a commentary on a popular Śaiva hymn—to ward off philological polemic that would undermine the ritual sanctity of the hymn in question.

One may note, in Nīlakaṇṭha's hasty defense of Śaiva orthodoxy, that his method is neither strictly philosophical nor polemical, appealing to a priori rationality or impassioned politics of identity. His method, rather, is text critical: he enters the arena of sectarian debate armed only with the technology of scriptural exegesis.

Indeed, philological reasoning and text criticism appear to have taken on an unprecedented centrality in the intersectarian debate of early modern south India. In the place of doctrinal and philosophical critique, scholars frequently challenged rival schools on the grounds of textual instabilities in the primary scriptures of their tradition.[1] The result of these ongoing critiques was an increasing fascination with the hermeneutics of textual interpretation and even the etymology of key terms of sectarian importance—all in the service of demarcating the jurisdiction of one sectarian tradition from another. Partisans of sectarian communities, even across caste and linguistic boundaries,[2] began to approach the very idea of scriptural meaning, and even of textual signification in general, with fresh eyes.

In this light, the early modern centuries provide ample evidence to make the case for a philological turn in Hindu sectarian theology, which, far from representing the reprobate degeneracy of Brahminical elitism, played a central role in the construction, dissemination, and embodiment of religious identities in the world outside of the text. Actively delimiting the boundaries between Hindu sectarian communities, public philology, I argue, constitutes not only an intriguing chapter in the intellectual history of the subcontinent but also a crucial factor in the rapid sectarianization of the Hindu religious landscape during the early modern centuries. In turn, the philological disputes that emerge, through their legislation of religious embodiment of sectarian identities, speak directly to shifts in the nature of religious publicity—indeed, the very idea of the religious public in early modern south India.

Nīlakaṇṭha Dīkṣita concludes the lengthy polemical interlude in his *Śivatattvarahasya* with the exasperated declaration "Enough with swatting at flies!"[3] And yet this "swatting at flies," as he considered it, was genuine intellectual work, such that it captivated the attention of the majority of scholars of his day. Thus, it is the process of intellectual fly-swatting that concerns us—an ongoing endeavor that proved fundamental to the scholarly activity of the seventeenth century and remained constitutive of sectarian community boundaries for centuries. Nīlakaṇṭha Dīkṣita, for example, interrogates a seemingly self-evident category of prolixity (*ativistṛtatva*) as follows:

> For, what indeed is it that we call "prolixity"? Is it simply the fact of containing a large number of verses? Or is it being found to contain a greater number of verses than the preconceived number? If it is the first, you cannot prove your case, because this kind of prolixity applies to all Purāṇas. The second, however, is not established. For, one should ask the very person who censures by saying, "The expected number of verses in their entirety are not found, thus the text has lost its original recension," how could it be possible to maintain prolixity as having those very stated characteristics? [That is, how can a text be overly condensed and prolix simultaneously?][4] Or, let prolixity consist of something else—then, whatever that may be, would it not occur in all manners in the Vaiṣṇava Purāṇas as well? Thus, are you bent on deluding others with your useless ablatives ["because's"]? Enough of this.[5]

It is one thing to refer to prolixity in common idiom—"Enough of this pro-lixity!" (*alam ativistareṇa*)—and quite another thing to pause to interrogate the category, asking, What indeed is it that constitutes this property we call "prolixity" (*kim ativistṛtatvaṃ nāma*)? And it is another thing still to apply such philological acumen to text problematics that threatened the standing of one's religious com-munity: namely, are the Śaiva Purāṇas, mythology sacred to the god Śiva, noth-ing but textual forgeries that replaced a previously lost manuscript tradition? It is this sort of philological reasoning, and its social and discursive dimensions, that rose to the forefront of theological dialogue in sixteenth- and seventeenth-century south India.

PHILOLOGY AND PUBLIC RELIGIOUS CULTURE

Public philology, unlike the literature on Śrīvidyā devotionalism, was no internal Smārta-Śaiva affair. Under the pressure of elevated competition for material re-sources, brought on by the fragmentation of Vijayanagara into the Nāyaka king-doms, sectarian leaders of all stripes—both proponents of Smārta-Śaivism, such as Appayya and his grandnephew Nīlakaṇṭha Dīkṣita, and quite a number of influ-ential scholars of Vaiṣṇava lineages such as the Mādhvas and Śrīvaiṣṇavas—turned to text criticism to mobilize their own communities through parallel currents of polemical sectarian argumentation. This wide-ranging fascination with philolog-ical reasoning can also be witnessed through a discursive survey of the genres and themes that rose to an unprecedented popularity, and which now clutter the manuscript libraries of south India with numerous revisions and reproductions. Among the popular themes of these polemical treatises, we find both abstract con-siderations of textual meanings, such as analyses of the *tātparya*, or "general pur-port," of the Mahābhārata, Rāmāyaṇa, Bhāgavata Purāṇa, and other texts popular across sectarian lines, as well as adjudications of the fine points of etymology and hermeneutics. Through ongoing cycles of debate, for example, numerous indi-vidual tracts were composed to formulate and refute theories as to why the name *Nārāyaṇa* contains a retroflex *ṇ* in its final syllable—and what implications this retroflex *ṇ* may hold with regard to the singularity of Vaiṣṇava orthodoxy.[6]

Such pyrotechnics with phonetics may strike the observer as radically discon-nected from the embodied practice of south Indian Hinduism. What part could the retroflex *ṇ* in *Nārāyaṇa* possibly play in the devotional relationship cultivated by Vaiṣṇava practitioners with their chosen deity? Inquiring into the theology of text criticism—no less than a study of texts studying texts—would appear anathema to what theorists have described as the "materialist turn" in the study of religion. In recent years, the attention in the discipline has turned—and rightly so—away from what Vasquez (2010) describes as its Protestant roots in "suffocating textual-ism" toward a salutary emphasis on the material aspects of religious practice, from the production and circulation of religious goods and material culture to networks of human relationships (Orsi 2006) and translocal flows (Tweed 2008). And yet, in the case of the textual practices of south Indian early modernity, philology was intimately intertwined with the material practices of religion, providing not an escape but an authoritative underpinning for the object-centered, bodily, or spatial religious practices across Hindu sectarian communities. Paradoxically, as we shall see, a study of texts studying texts tells a great deal about the embodied religious identity of the early modern subcontinent.

Strictly speaking, to locate philology—most commonly recognized as a European textual science that flourished in the nineteenth century—in the textual practices of seventeenth-century India presents us with a number of historical and theoretical ambiguities. How precisely do we define the term *philology* in this context, and can such a term possibly correlate with anything in the emic conceptual map of a seventeenth-century south Indian pandit? In his programmatic essay defending the discipline of philology and its future prospects, Sheldon Pollock (2009) defines philology, broadly speaking, as "the discipline of making sense of texts[,] . . . the theory of textuality as well as the history of textualized meaning."[7] By way of this transhistorical definition, Pollock makes the case for philology as a global phenomenon, a critical reflexivity toward textual meaning that surfaces at various occasions and in numerous textual cultures, irrespective of language and location. As such, there is nothing intrinsically European or modern (or even early modern) in this model of philology, a concept that can be applied fruitfully to any number of historical scenarios.

Nevertheless, our historical narratives often portray philology, in its regnant role as queen of the sciences, as a prototypically early modern invention, allied as it was with the Renaissance rediscovery of the Western world's classical past and, in turn, with the rise of Orientalism as colonial-period scholars reconstructed a parallel golden age of India's pre-Islamic antiquity. In social and historical context, a genuine case could be made that Renaissance Europe revolutionized the practice of philology, as exegetes expanded the extant corpus of classical works, moving in a rapidly urbanizing world in which printed books not only were readily available but also circulated fluidly as a commodity of trade. Renaissance humanists, Anthony Grafton (2015) has argued, prefigured the institutionalized philology of eighteenth- and nineteenth-century universities by developing an arsenal of new text-critical techniques—attention to the individuality of an author's voice, for instance—to build on the foundations of the classical and scholastic past. In the domain of early modern India, then, did the philology of Hindu sectarian theologians merely echo or expand the techniques of textual interpretation developed by philosophers and linguists over the preceding two millennia?

When applied to the entire historical field of Indic textuality, the very idea of philology may seem to suffer from a troubling overextension (or *ativyāpti,* as

Sanskrit scholars would call it). Simply put, making sense of texts, or even language, is perhaps the single fundamental building block of Indian systematic thought. Such was argued, for instance, by Frits Staal (1965) in his well-known essay "Euclid and Panini," in which he maintains that the grammatical systematicity of Pāṇini's approach to the Sanskrit language played a crucial structural role in the history of Sanskritic discourse, much as geometrical reasoning proved foundational to philosophy in the Western world. One is not hard pressed to think of examples of both Sanskrit and vernacular discourse that would qualify as philology, ranging from Kumārila's source-critical evaluation of Smṛti literature, Purāṇas, and the Āgamic corpus,[8] to the Marathi poet-saint Eknāth's critical edition of the *Jñāneśvarī*.[9] Although we may be warranted in perceiving an efflorescence in philological reasoning at certain periods in Indian history—the early modern centuries witnessed philological undertakings of the magnitude of Sāyaṇa's Ṛgveda commentary[10] and the hermeneutic acrobatics of Nīlakaṇṭha Caturdhara[11]—there is nothing new, or *navya,* about philology as so defined for the scholars of the seventeenth century.

On one hand, Hindu sectarian theology in early modern centuries did inherit the legacy of classical Sanskritic thought through reference to a common focal point—namely, the interpretation and exegesis of the Brahmasūtras—leading sectarian lineages to nominally demarcate their identity on the basis of ontological doctrine, whether "dualist," "nondualist," or some variation thereof. Equally impressive techniques of exegesis were marshaled to defend one interpretation over another; and yet, despite protests to the contrary, no faction managed to achieve even a marginal victory by common consensus. It was perhaps because of this philosophical stalemate—and, no doubt, the social and economic stakes of theological marginalization—that, as time progressed, sectarian debate began to overflow the boundaries of ontology as theologians, in search of some common ground for dialogue, began to question even the most fundamental rules of Sanskrit textuality and disciplinarity.

On the other hand, thinking from within traditional Sanskritic categories may tempt us to equate philology, for a Sanskrit-educated audience, with the strict confines of a single *śāstric* discipline: the hermeneutics of Pūrva Mīmāṃsā. Although traditionally viewed by doxographers as a discrete school of thought (*darśana*) in its own right, Pūrva Mīmāṃsā exercised a pervasive influence on the idea of textuality across disciplinary boundaries in India, so that it now seems redundant even to make the observation. For instance, the work of Lawrence McCrea (2009) demonstrates the foundational role played by Mīmāṃsā interpretive techniques in the development of Sanskrit literary theory (Alaṅkāraśāstra) as an academic discipline. Thus, the genuine centrality of Pūrva Mīmāṃsā to Sanskrit hermeneutics often leads to an impasse when the category of philology is applied to Sanskrit intellectual history as an etic theoretical lens. Anterior to the publication of sectarian philology in the sixteenth and seventeenth centuries, prominent sectarian theologians, including the fourteenth-century Lion among Poets and Logicians (Kavitārkikasiṃha), relied heavily on the theoretical apparatus of Pūrva Mīmāṃsā in his approach to textuality, even when attempting to dismiss the theological presuppositions of classical Mīmāṃsakas themselves.

And yet Vedānta Deśika approached much of his oeuvre with penetrating philological insight, developing an eye for the textual integrity of his tradition's scripture rarely seen in preceding centuries (Cox 2016). As with the case of European philology and its Renaissance humanist legacy, sectarian public philology of the seventeenth century owes a significant debt to a sort of scriptural "renaissance" undertaken by Vedānta Deśika and his contemporaries from various sectarian communities. Unsurprisingly, perhaps, it was during this period—between the eleventh and fourteenth centuries—that Śaivas and Vaiṣṇavas simultaneously embarked on a large-scale rapprochement of the sectarian scriptures of their lineage with a wider concept of Vedic—or Hindu—orthodoxy. Sectarian scripture in south India witnessed significant "textual drift"—or forgery, rather, depending on one's inclination—during this formative period. Śaiva scriptures such as the Sūtasaṃhitā gradually conformed to the south Indian religious landscape—placing new emphasis on Cidambaram, the center of Cōḻa-period Śaiva temple culture—and adopted a notably Vedānticized inflection to hybridize, perhaps for the first time, Śaiva religiosity with the teachings of the Upaniṣads. It is likely no accident that theologians such as Vedānta Deśika were inspired to develop new tools to think historically about the nature of scriptural authenticity.

What we witness in the sixteenth and seventeenth centuries, however, is an upsurge not simply of philology but intersectarian philology—pugnacious critiques of theological rivals on text-critical grounds. It is these moments of encounter that I aim to examine, tailoring to the Indian textual sphere the methods of discourse analysis, in the Foucauldian sense, not individual works but the irruption of philological concerns into the intersectarian circulation of philological polemic. Included in this discourse are the works of major intellectuals, which deserve to be remembered as classics of Indian theology in their own right, as well as the broader sphere of sectarian discourse as such: polemical pamphlets, student essays, and handbooks for debate, most of which lie unpublished in the manuscript libraries of south India. In fact, this circulation of pamphlets, many designed to prepare theologians for public debate, underscores the extent to which philology was not, simply speaking, a matter for the manuscript archive but a subject of increasing social significance. I aim, then, not only to bring unused source materials to light but also to explore the extent to which philological approaches to sectarian debate moved beyond the rarified circles of the intellectual giants to shape the contours of the south Indian religious landscape. In such circumstances, a wider discursive analysis of early modern textuality in India can illuminate substantive shifts in the south Indian religious ecology in a way that fails to emerge from adhering strictly to the scriptural classics.

How, then, did public philology shift the religious ecology of south Indian sectarian communities? Most evidently, major thinkers of the sixteenth century achieved what may be an unprecedented public circulation of their works through sectarian networks, prompting an explosion of interest in philological questions across all strata of discourse, from the most elevated to the most banal commentarial essay, a trend that continued even into the colonial era. Where doctrinaire theologians failed to defeat each other on strictly philological ground, they frequently returned to key questions of scriptural authenticity and meaning to undermine their opponents' foundational sources of knowledge and veridicality; over the course of a handful of generations, philology had become a pillar of the unspoken rules of polemical discourse. That is, sectarian theology came to be a matter not for the temple or literary salon but for public debate, circulating readily across regional and sectarian boundaries. More importantly, however, philology went public in early modern south India by inquiring directly into the role of sectarian identity in public space. Having surveyed the extent and scope of public philology as a discourse of intersectarian polemic, we will turn to its direct engagement with the world outside of the text, to illuminate through a concrete example how sectarian theologians aimed to reshape the boundaries between religious communities.

I begin, then, by highlighting three problematics that occupied the minds of scholars such as Nīlakaṇṭha, on the Smārta-Śaiva side, and his Vaiṣṇava rivals from the Mādhva and Śrīvaiṣṇava lineages. First, exegetes of rival traditions turned their attention to their respective scriptural canons, each negotiating standards of text criticism that might distinguish their own canon from that of their opponents. In particular, a lively debate surfaced regarding the validity of the Śaiva Purāṇas as authoritative scripture, necessitating a collective reconsideration of precisely what textual features of the Purāṇas as they had been transmitted signaled their authenticity as prescriptive revelation. Second, even the tools of interpretation came under fire in the seventeenth century, as disciplinary approaches of reading texts, such as Nyāya (logic) or Mīmāṃsā, were claimed as the exclusive property of one sectarian tradition or another. As a result, we observe an increasing methodological divide between Smārta-Śaivas, whose hermeneutics come to be equated strictly with the field of Pūrva Mīmāṃsā, and other lineages such as the Mādhvas, who claimed the school of Navya Nyāya as a distinctive domain of expertise. As a result, participants in these debates were forced to reason afresh about textual validity without the support of the knowledge systems that had sustained Sanskritic thought for centuries. And third, among the disciplinary approaches to textuality called into question during this period, the fields of etymology and lexicography came to occupy something of a contentious place in the domain of scriptural interpretation, and we witness a rise in fascination with etymological acrobatics (including catalogues of hundreds of "valid" Pāṇinian etymologies of the names of deities) along with a well-deserved skepticism of the utility of such an analytic approach. One issue that proved a hotbed of contention was the proper spelling of the name Nārāyaṇa; the debate generated countless polemical tracts claiming to adjudicate the valid referents of the name on etymological ground.

UNSTABLE RECENSIONS: THE CONTESTED AUTHORITY OF THE ŚAIVA PURĀṆAS

In his commentary Kauṇḍa Bhaṭṭa's *Padārthadīpikā* (The illumination of categories), an early modern treatise on formal logic, Gīrvāṇendra Dīkṣita, son of Nīlakaṇṭha Dīkṣita, embarks on an apparently peculiar digression while addressing the *maṅgala* verses of the work.[12] He begins his commentary by explaining,

> By the term "black and white" is meant a thing that consists of both Hari and Hara, because, in the epics and Purāṇas, oftentimes Śiva is described as appearing [white] like a pure crystal, and Viṣṇu as appearing [black] like a dark cloud.
>
> But one might wonder, "How can this be the case? Hari and Hara cannot possibly be nondifferent, as their difference is established by numerous authoritative means of knowledge." In fact, the nondifference of Hari and Hara is understood from numerous Purāṇic statements such as the following:
>
>> Śiva alone is Hari manifest, Hari alone is Śiva himself.
>> The man who sees a difference between the two goes to Hell.[13]
>
> The difference [between them] is understood to be conditional, but the opposite [i.e., their nondifference being conditional] is inconceivable. We understand their difference to be conditional based on the previously exemplified statement "sattva, rajas, and tamas" itself; we do not likewise observe a statement of the conditionality of nondifference. Thus, the nondifference of Hari and Hara is absolutely real.[14]

In the context of a hairsplitting commentary on the niceties of logical syllogisms, it may seem odd that Gīrvāṇendra would foreground such a seemingly irrelevant theological dispute. And yet he seems intent on locating in Kauṇḍa Bhaṭṭa's *maṅgala* verse a particular theological vision—the nondifference of Śiva and Viṣṇu—that had become a matter of some contention in the south over the preceding generations, even more so than in Kauṇḍa Bhaṭṭa's social circles in Benares.[15] Why, we might wonder, was a descendant of south India's most staunchly Śaiva intellectual families so determined to demonstrate the equality of Śiva and Viṣṇu, even when the matter bore little relevance to the discussion at hand? As it turns out, his motivations were likely much more complex than an irenic vision of religious pluralism. Rather, for a Śaiva Advaitin, inheriting the intellectual legacy of Appayya Dīkṣita, the nonduality of the two sectarian deities was a contentious claim in Gīrvāṇendra's generation, and one that certainly would not have been endorsed by his Mādhva or Śrīvaiṣṇava rivals, who were keen to demonstrate their ontological difference—and, as a consequence, the status of Viṣṇu as supreme deity. Thus, the appeal to their unity by partisan Śaivas was a deliberate counterattack on Vaiṣṇava sectarian polemics.

The debate Gīrvāṇendra alludes to at the outset of his commentary is treated at much greater length by his own father, Nīlakaṇṭha, in his *Śivatattvarahasya*, or "The Secret of the Principles of Śiva." Primarily structured as a commentary on a popular Śaiva hymn, "The Thousand and Eight Names of Śiva," Nīlakaṇṭha's *Śivatattvarahasya* also contains one of the most sophisticated and philologically sensitive sectarian tracts that have come down to us today. In this extended preface, Nīlakaṇṭha addresses a subject that was causing his Smārta-Śaiva contemporaries a fair amount of consternation—namely, the accusation, most likely leveled by his Śrīvaiṣṇava contemporaries, that the Śaiva Purāṇas were invalid textual authorities because of their intrinsically *tāmasa* character. *Tamas*, indeed, was the lowest of the three "qualities" of matter that the Sāṅkhya school of Indian philosophy proposed as the building blocks of the universe, associated generally with sloth, torpor, and moral degeneracy. And yet this accusation is founded on a serious hermeneutical impasse, one that was recognized equally by both parties with a greater trepidation than most authors of earlier periods—namely, that the Purāṇas contradict themselves. Given the numerous internal inconsistencies and blatant contradictions between Purāṇas that were thought to be equally authoritative, how could they all be salvaged as valid scriptural authorities? In response to this dilemma, the Śrīvaiṣṇava community had arrived at an expedient explanatory device, one that can be traced back to the time of Rāmānuja, but which had, by the seventeenth century, taken on an altogether new systematicity and precision.

Nīlakaṇṭha puts the matter eloquently into the mouth of an unnamed opponent (*pūrvapakṣin*), a traditional strategy of Sanskrit philosophical prose that allows the author to demolish the case of a hypothetical adversary. In Nīlakaṇṭha's words, his opponent lays out the case against the Śaiva Purāṇas as follows:

> Here, some people say that there is no validity to the Names contained in the Skanda Purāṇa, because the Skānda, and so forth, are not valid sources of knowledge given that they are *tāmasa* Purāṇas. After all, Brahmā, the author of the Purāṇas, in some eons was predominated by *sattva*, in some by *rajas*, and in some by *tamas*; when he was predominated by *sattva*, he composed Vaiṣṇava Purāṇas, when he was predominated by *rajas* Brāhma Purāṇas, when predominated by *tamas* Śaiva Purāṇas. And thus, the Śaiva Purāṇas, composed by a Brahmā who was blinded by *tamas*, are completely nonauthoritative like deluded prattle. But the Vaiṣṇava Purāṇas, composed by a Brahmā predominated by *sattva*, are authoritative, like the statements of a learned person.[16]

This line of argumentation—which had understandably proven popular in a polarized sectarian environment—can be traced back to the works of Rāmānuja himself, albeit in embryonic form. In the *Vedārthasaṅgraha* (Compilation on the meaning of the Vedas), his problematic of inquiry is precisely the same: Why do the scriptural passages contradict each other, and what do we do about it? He writes, "If one were to ask, 'How can it be that Vedic statements, which are unauthored, are mutually contradictory?' then, as previously stated, there is actually no contradiction because a unitary purport [*tātparya*] can be determined." In this context, Rāmānuja quotes the same Purāṇic passage above (suggesting a direct influence on Nīlakaṇṭha's own imagined opponent), demarcating the same tripartite division among the Purāṇas based on their eon of composition and the *guṇa* predominating that particular eon. He moves on quickly, however, to proposing his better-known "adjectival" exegesis of the names of Śiva in the Upaniṣads: interpreting Śvetāśvatara Upaniṣad 3.11, *śāśvataṃ śivam acyutam*, he pointedly maintains that the name Śiva is nothing but a modifier of Viṣṇu—Acyuta—indicating his auspiciousness.[17]

What does not concern Rāmānuja to any significant degree, however, is the strict opposition between Śaiva and Vaiṣṇava Purāṇas. For Nīlakaṇṭha's imagined opponent, operating in a society in which sectarian tensions have reached new heights, it is the antagonism between the two bodies of scripture that is central. Clever as Rāmānuja's interpretation of the name *Śiva* may be, Nīlakaṇṭha's opponent shows no interest in it and, instead, expands upon the Tāmasic nature of the Śaiva Purāṇas at great length, arguing that it is the reliability of the speaker, Brahmā, that determines the relative authority of Śaiva and Vaiṣṇava Purāṇas. Evidently the passage cited by Rāmānuja struck him as an ideal battle ground for exposing the relative merits of Śaiva and Vaiṣṇava theology—not on philosophical grounds but based on the textual integrity of their respective scriptures.

Expanding on his initial complaint about the speaker's unreliability, Nīlakaṇṭha's opponent compiles a list of seven textual deficiencies that vitiate the scriptural authority of the Śaiva Purāṇas. He summarizes his case as follows:

> Thus, the Śaiva Purāṇas are nonauthoritative (1) because the speaker has the fault of being *tāmasa*, (2) because of contradiction with scripture, (3) because of internal contradiction [*svavyāghātāt*], (4) because the meaning of its own statement is not corroborated by another Purāṇa that is accepted as a valid authority[,] ... (5) because it is clear that the intention of describing the greatness of the *liṅga* [Liṅgamāhātmya] as stated in the Liṅga Purāṇa has come forth sequentially from a question concerned with a particular topic,[18] (6) because the Kūrma Purāṇa, and so forth, are well known to have lost their original recensions [*naṣṭakośatvāt*], and (7) because of the possibility of interpolation because of their excessive prolixity.[19]

Intriguingly, none of the reasons adduced by the opponent for his distrust of the Śaiva Purāṇas has any bearing on the content, or doctrine, expressed by them. Rather, with each of the reasons Nīlakaṇṭha attempts to supersede doctrinal differences by appealing to an ostensibly shared sense of philological reasoning as to what ought to constitute an authoritative text, and what features of such a text may show proof of corruption or instability. If our author were a contemporary critical editor, his criteria for textual authenticity would by and large be accepted by academic audiences as eminently plausible, when translated into the idiom of modern philological practice.

In particular, reason six will catch the eye of any contemporary textual scholar: is it truly possible that seventeenth-century intellectuals had developed a sophisticated model of the diachronic fluctuation of texts through circulation and accumulation of variants? By Nīlakaṇṭha's day, commentators had been using terms such as *pāṭha* for centuries to indicate their awareness of variant readings in classic works of poetry. Here, however, Nīlakaṇṭha's opponent employs a rather unusual and striking term, *naṣṭakośa*, which has little in the way of precedent in Sanskrit discourse before the intellectual giants of second-millennium south India.[20] Its resonance, however, is unmistakable: the Śaiva Purāṇas, our unnamed opponent argues, have lost their original recensions—that is, the original "manuscript copies" of their authentic (divinely authored) textualized form have been lost. Succinctly, when first enunciated by their speaker, the Śaiva Purāṇas were known to have contained a vast number of verses, as several putatively original citations attest. The versions accepted as canonical by the opponent's contemporaries possess far fewer verses, which suggests, quite logically, that the remaining verses have been lost over time. Thus the received text can be presumed to bear little resemblance to the original, divinely authored Purāṇa that one might have considered authoritative.

Nīlakaṇṭha's reply illuminates the issue in more detail, illustrating his clear awareness that texts, whether revealed or not, have a history and, as historically bounded entities, are subject to loss and transformation:

And, as for the argument [that the Śaiva Purāṇas are not authoritative] because it is well known that the Kūrma and so forth have lost their original recensions, this also is insubstantial. For, the Brāhmī Saṃhitā, which consists of six thousand verses, is still available [*pracarati*]—it is not at all lost. If you maintain that the portion over and beyond the Brāhmī Saṃhitā is lost, consisting of eleven thousand verses from within the text of seventeen thousand verses known to have belonged to the Matsya Purāṇa, then let it be, who says it is not? After all, we are not citing any verses from there. But there is no ground for excessive doubt concerning further loss within the Saṃhitā that has come down to us as scripture. If some further portion is said to be "lost," then any other Saṃhitā could also be conceived of as "lost," given that there would be no deciding factor for discriminating what has been lost and what has not.

If you argue that the portion we have received could have been written by anyone—then, no, because there is no basis for this. For, it is not the case that if some has been destroyed then all of it must be destroyed, nor if some has remained then all must remain; nor, clearly, do either you or I have even a grain of discomfort the size of a sesame seed with regard to the grammar of Pāṇini occasioned by the Aindra Grammar's having been lost. That being the case, even with regard to the Viṣṇu

Purāṇa, it would wind up being very difficult to refute the anxiety about its extant six thousand verses, conjoined with the seventeen thousand verses of it that have been lost from within the twenty-three thousand verses we come to know of from the words of the Matsya Purāṇa.[21]

Here we find Nīlakaṇṭha wrestling with what many would consider to be a cogent objection to the Matsya Purāṇa's textual integrity: the Purāṇa has evidently suffered from poor transmission, which caused nearly two-thirds of the text to be lost, and consequently one might wonder whether the remaining portion has also been inaccurately transmitted. The debate, then, concerns the effect of textual transmission on the viability of scripture as a source of authoritative knowledge. Nīlakaṇṭha argues, as many of us would, that we cannot afford to abandon fragmentary textual traditions even if we can no longer recover a comprehensive picture of their recension histories, much less the form of works as originally enunciated.

Another of the opponent's objections may strike us as odd at first glance—namely, his suspicion of the Liṅgamāhātmya—but in fact a very similar form of reasoning is used by textual scholars even today to track interpolations in classical texts. The Liṅga Purāṇa, Nīlakaṇṭha's opponent argues, fails to conform to the traditional generic constraints of Purāṇic texts because it includes a number of interludes in which the characters raise lines of discussion that are seemingly irrelevant to abstract questions of ultimate truth, such as the nature and function of the *śivaliṅga,* the aniconic image of the god Śiva employed in ritual worship.[22] In his opponent's analysis, these passages seem to concern matters so highly specific and foreign to our expectations as to suggest a particular time and place of interpolation. Nīlakaṇṭha, for his part, agrees that a general internal coherence must exist for us to accept a Purāṇa as free from interpolations, but he maintains that the initial question itself around which the text is structured is not by itself sufficient to determine its unitary intentionality (*tātparya*). Such questions, he argues, often illuminate the bias and limitations of the questioner rather than the ultimate truth promulgated by the Purāṇa. In fact, if seemingly tangential questions were sufficient to overturn the authority of scripture, even the most-prized narratives of Vaiṣṇava devotion would be called into question. The Bhāgavata Purāṇa itself, Nīlakaṇṭha notes, begins with a similar exhortation: "Sūta, you know—we beseech you. By whose will was the Lord, master of the Yādavas, born of Devakī and Vasudeva?"[23]

Although much can be said about Nīlakaṇṭha's argument, two aspects of the debate on both sides are of particular interest in the present context. First, we witness a sustained and philologically sensitive inquiry into a particular textual problematic—that is, which features of textual structure facilitate comprehension of the overall purport (*tātparya*) of a text, and what bearing does this purport have on our assessment of the text's recension history? Such dialogue flourished in the sixteenth and seventeenth centuries; we may recall here the Mādhva-Śaiva debate on *upakrama* versus *upasaṃhāra*—the relative priority of the beginning or end of a text for determining its intentionality—a subject that rose considerably in popularity in response to the work of Appayya Dīkṣita. Second, we observe a kind of empiricist leaning in both opponents' readiness to exemplify passages that problematize common assumptions about the Purāṇic genre and how it communicates authoritative knowledge. In both cases, our sectarian intellectuals employ philological reasoning to push the boundaries of normative textual practice—and yet the enunciatory context is not the traditional disciplines of text criticism but the sectarian polemical tracts themselves. It is the new intellectual space opened up through the irruption of sectarian polemics that provided an ideal venue for philology to reach new heights, in many cases moving beyond the language and problematics in which textual interpretation had been posed for centuries through the classical Sanskritic knowledge systems.

In the final analysis, we should be clear that philology in the sixteenth and seventeenth centuries flourished through the vehicle of sectarian theology, and its applications were by and large theological in their agenda. We would deceive ourselves in expecting to uncover a neutral, "secular" space in which philological reasoning developed free from external commitments. Indeed, the European case would caution us against expecting philology and theology to keep separate company. To name but a single instance, Isaac Casaubon, one of early modern Europe's first groundbreaking philologians—who recognized that the hermetic revelations so foundational to Renaissance thinking were in fact anachronistic apocrypha postdating the biblical texts by several centuries—was both a classicist and a Huguenot theologian by trade, carrying out his intellectual work in the service of an antipapist agenda.[24] In the Indian case, it was the theological off-shoots of philology that truly took root in public discourse, moving beyond the most sophisticated of scholarly discourses to affect the motivations and predispositions of Sanskritic culture across the south Indian religious landscape. After all, it was not Nīlakaṇṭha's definition of prolixity that his son Gīrvāṇendra alluded to in his commentary on the *Padārthadīpikā* but, rather, the relevance of the three Sāṃkhya *guṇas* to casting doubt on the speaker of the Śaiva Purāṇas and, hence, their authority as scripture.

As it is perhaps this critique that troubles Nīlakaṇṭha the most—that the Śaiva Purāṇas are inherently *tāmasa*—he advances a revised theological model of the speakers of the various Purāṇas from the standpoint of his Śaiva Advaita philosophical leanings. Rather than disputing the Purāṇic attestations of a tripartite division in the Purāṇas and the *guṇas* of their speakers, Nīlakaṇṭha circumvents the entire paradigm by postulating Śiva as the unitary creator of the Trimūrti—Viṣṇu, Brahmā, and Rudra—with Paramaśiva in the purest and most abstract sense being absolutely distinct from the embodied or qualified (*saguṇa*) form, Rudra, who was delegated to speak the *tāmasa* Purāṇas. By making this case, Nīlakaṇṭha aims not only to secure Śaiva immunity from a hierarchical paradigm that favors the supremacy of Viṣṇu—and one that has significant textual evidence to back it up, at that—but also to salvage the unitary authoritativeness of the Purāṇic corpus as a whole, irrespective of sectarian affiliation. He proposes his *siddhānta* as follows:

> And, as for the argument that the Vaiṣṇava Purāṇas are authoritative because they lack the seven previously mentioned faults of the Śaiva Purāṇas—with regard to this, the proposition [*pratijñā*] of the syllogism is valid, but the reason [*hetu*] is not worthy of being investigated. . . . Even if others were to argue that the Śaiva and Vaiṣṇava Purāṇas have been situated as mutually opposed and, thus, because of that mutual opposition the Vaiṣṇava Purāṇas could be said to be invalid, given that our aim is to inform about the truth, it would not be reasonable for us to do so. For, the fact that others have erred does not mean that one must err oneself. Thus is introduced the established conclusion [*siddhānta*] that sets forth the validity of all Purāṇas.
>
> And as for what was argued—[that the Śaiva Purāṇas are not authoritative] owing to internal contradiction—this is refuted for precisely the same reason. There is not even a whiff of internal contradiction, because the origin of Rudra from Nārāyaṇa concerns the origin of the Rudra endowed with qualities, whereas the Trimūrti originates from Paramaśiva.[25]

Thus, Nīlakaṇṭha effectively deflects the textual evidence marshaled by his Vaiṣṇava rival through a strategy of creative subversion, repositioning the Śiva of the Śaiva religion outside of the hierarchical paradigm Vaiṣṇavas had deduced through close readings of the Purāṇas. A strategy such as this bears not only theological but sociological implications as well, positioning the Brahminical Śaiva community, which had begun to style itself explicitly as "Smārta," to appeal to a transcendent Hindu orthodoxy that conceptually denied the sectarian social structure from which it had arisen. In fact, despite the incisive philological insights of both Nīlakaṇṭha and his opponent, theological models such as these left an indelible impact on the sectarian discourse of subsequent generations. Over the course of the following century, Smārta-Śaivas enthusiastically adopted this conceptual distinction between their chosen deity, Paramaśiva, and the *saguṇa* Rudra of the Trimūrti, and they relegated the latter to the same subordinate plane of existence as Viṣṇu himself. This rhetoric soon attained such popularity that it became purely a matter of convention to assert, at the outset of Śaiva sectarian tracts, the transcendent status of Paramaśiva, the true Śaiva deity. Take for example the following *maṅgala* verses from the *Īśavilāsa* of "Appayya Dīkṣita" and the *Madhvamukhacapeṭikā*,[26] two Śaiva polemical works conspicuously prefaced with this same formula:

> By whose command Brahmā is the creator of the universe and Hari
> the protector,

And the destroyer is known as Kālarudra, homage to him, who
  bears the Pināka bow.[27]

I bow to the nondual Śiva, *distinct from the Trimūrti,* the cause of
  creation and so forth, who provides all refuge,
Knowable from the Vedānta throughout the entire universe, for the
  pacification of a veritable flood of obstacles.[28]

"TRANSGRESSING THE BOUNDARIES" OF DISCIPLINARITY: THE SECTARIANIZATION OF CLASSICAL KNOWLEDGE SYSTEMS

By the sixteenth century in south India, as with the majority of the subcontinent, the idea of *newness* had thoroughly captivated intellectual discourse—whether novelty of form, substance, or indeed of scholarly methodology. It is no accident, in fact, that schools of thought whose very names proclaimed the virtue of newness had come into sudden vogue across sectarian lines. Such is the case, most notably, with Navya Nyāya, or "New Dialectics," an emergent discipline whose influence reached nearly every corner of Sanskrit intellectual discourse, sectarian theology being no exception. Take, for instance, the following aphorism, cited by the Mādhva theologian Nārāyaṇācārya in his *Advaitakālānala* (The armageddon of Advaita), a systematic diatribe countering the *Madhvatantramukhamardana* (Crushing the face of Madhva's doctrine) of the Smārta-Śaiva polymath Appayya Dīkṣita:

> Statements endowed with logical reasoning are admissible even
>   from a child.
> Anything else should be abandoned like grass, even if spoken by
>   Brahmā.[29]

According to Nārāyaṇācārya, what Appayya lacked, succinctly, was logical reasoning. As an outspoken proponent of Madhva's Dvaita (dualist) theology, Nārāyaṇācārya embarked on his polemical project, the *Advaitakālānala,* not merely to defend a dualist model of ontology but also to champion the revolutionary dialectical models of Navya Nyāya philosophy. Navya Nyāya, although perhaps better known for its origin and efflorescence in Bengal following the influential thirteenth-century *Tattvacintāmaṇi* (Crest jewel of principles) of Gaṅgeśa, had made a second home for itself among the prominent logicians of the Mādhva lineage, who were justly renowned by contemporaries for their unsurpassed mastery of the discipline. This trend perhaps reached its zenith under the pioneering dialectical endeavors of Vyāsa Tīrtha, whose metaphysical tracts, with such names as the *Nyāyāmṛta* (The nectar of logic) and the *Tarkatāṇḍava* (The dance of reasoning), began to evoke an invariable concomitance between Navya Nyāya and the

Mādhva tradition itself. In subsequent generations, Vyāsa Tīrtha was succeeded by prolific scholars such as Vijayīndra Tīrtha, who continued the Navya Nyāya legacy with his Nyāya-*mauktikamālā*, Nyāya-*saṅgraha*, Nyāyādhvadipikā,[30] among many others—which, even when not directly concerned with formal logic, relentlessly evoke the semiotic authority of the "New Dialectics."

Even outside of the Vaiṣṇava fold, critics of Madhva's doctrine gravitated toward the Mādhva predilection for formal logic, seizing every opportunity to impugn the rationality of the school's founder. Among the most memorable critiques of Madhva's dualism, Appayya Dīkṣita's *Madhvatantramukhamardana* caricatures Madhva as no less than an intellectual fraud, delusional enough to believe himself an incarnation of the wind god, Vāyu. Appayya further contends that among the scriptural passages Madhva cites, many were simply fabricated out of thin air (*svakapolakalpita,* or literally, "fashioned from his own cheek"),[31] and the remainder interpreted so tortuously as to defy even the limits of plausibility. He elaborates: "Such Ṛgvedic mantras are demonstrated to refer to the triad of incarnations of Vāyu that he himself has made up, and so forth—thus we witness the wholesale transgression of the boundaries of reasonable authority [*prāmāṇikamaryādollaṅghanam*]."[32] Appayya then continues to adduce a version of the very aphorism Mādhvas themselves cite with pride, censuring not merely the theological doctrine of his Mādhva opponents but equally their attachment to logical reasoning as the cornerstone of academic inquiry.

> Now, on the principle "Speech endowed with *reason* is to be accepted, not [mere] venerability," we would give credit to his doctrine if we could discern in it *anything reasonable*. But such is not the case. For, generally, in his doctrine, statements that are ascertained from his own heart alone are supported, rather than commonly held principles. And those principles that *are* exhibited are extremely carelessly observed, applied here and there at will. Even the boundaries of Pūrva Mīmāṃsā are led astray through interpretations of *disharmony* [*asāmañjasya*]. Generally speaking, words are used completely inappropriately. His versification cannot possibly be construed syntactically, and more often than not the meters do not exist.[33]

While railing against the methodological preoccupations of his opponents, Appayya reveals his own disciplinary leanings as well. Although considered by all a polymath—a master of all disciplines (*sarvatantrasvatantra*)—Appayya, to the best of our knowledge, never once composed a treatise on formal logic. Rather, he cultivated a particular expertise in the field of Mīmāṃsā, or Vedic exegesis, a discipline that had centuries before attained the status of a general hermeneutics, its principles adopted widely across the Sanskrit knowledge systems. Beyond developing a simple mastery of the field, Appayya also pioneered a sustained inquiry into the status of Mīmāṃsā as a discipline, negotiating the complexity of its relationship with Vedānta philosophy, or Uttara Mīmāṃsā.[34] Despite the discursive prestige accorded to Navya Nyāya terminology by the sixteenth century, his prose shows few traces of its unmistakable philosophical idiom.[35] And perhaps most tellingly, with his provocatively titled treatise on Mīmāṃsā, the *Vidhirasāyana* (The elixir of injunction), Appayya proclaimed to his contemporaries that the entire discipline of Mīmāṃsā was in need of resuscitation—and that he, specifically, would provide the remedy.[36]

In short, Appayya's primary concern, beyond Madhva's alleged carelessness with source criticism, is that the integrity of the boundaries—or the operative rules—of Mīmāṃsā hermeneutics not be compromised through haphazard textual interpretations. By describing Madhva's reading strategies as "disharmonious" (*asāmañjasyenaiva*), Appayya further demarcates himself as an avowed insider in Mīmāṃsā hermeneutics: the principle of *sāmanjyasya*, or "harmony," is a Mīmāṃsaka axiom that requires interpreters, wherever possible, to understand texts as harmonious intentional communications, free from internal contradiction. Such subtle gestures were by no means lost on his Mādhva contemporaries. Given that their Smārta-Śaiva opponent had so thoroughly identified himself with the inner workings of the Mīmāṃsā system, they began to look for strategies to dismantle not merely Appayya's own arguments but also the very universality of Mīmāṃsā's hermeneutical apparatus.

What precisely was the relationship, then, between Mādhva faith and formal logic, Śaiva scripture and Mīmāṃsā exegesis? Disciplinarity, it seems, was no longer coterminous with the object of inquiry for the Sanskrit knowledge systems in early modern south India. One did not become a Mīmāṃsaka, in this climate, merely to understand the meaning of the Vedas, nor a Naiyāyika to master syllogistic reasoning. Rather, by the sixteenth century, during the floruit of Appayya Dīkṣita, the first stages of a sectarianization of the means of knowledge took place, as discipline-specific approaches to textuality came to be claimed as the property of competing religious traditions. To be a Mādhva theologian in this period, one had little choice but to apply oneself to the study of Navya Nyāya; and over the course of time, Mīmāṃsā acquired an intimate association with the social circles of the Smārta-Śaivas, such that by the following centuries prominent Mādhvas expressed a wholehearted disdain for the interpretive maxims of Mīmāṃsā philosophy.

By the time of Vijayīndra Tīrtha, a genuine skepticism had begun to arise in Mādhva circles concerning the general applicability of Mīmāṃsā hermeneutics. Although Vijayīndra himself had authored works of the Mīmāṃsā school, he evidently felt no compunction, as did Appayya, regarding the "transgressing" of its "boundaries" in the service of Dvaita theology. In his *Turīyaśivakhaṇḍana* (Crushing the transcendent-fourth Śiva), for instance, Vijayīndra even celebrates the virtue of transgressing Mīmāṃsaka boundaries, which, he contends, was in fact a deliberate and strategic decision on the part of the Mādhva school:

It is unreasonable to say that the boundary of Pūrva Mīmāṃsā is led astray by such improper application. By saying that the statements of our Teacher [Madhva] were arrived at merely by his own fancy, one acts like a frog in a well. Only the principles shown by our Teacher possess the fortitude of intellect, and not those shown by others. The disharmonious application of the boundaries of Pūrva Mīmāṃsā is in fact precisely our doctrine.[37]

It is Nārāyaṇācārya, however, who finally threw down the gauntlet, in his *Advaitakālānala*, calling for the wholesale rejection of Mīmāṃsaka reading strategies outside of the narrow confines of Vedic ritual exegesis. Structured as a systematic counterattack on Appayya's *Madhvatantramukhamardana*, the *Advaitakālānala* rejects each one of Appayya's allegations in turn, including the notorious issue of Madhva's recovery—or fabrication—of little-known scriptures. As one may predict, Nārāyaṇācārya was prepared with an equally incisive counterattack for each of Appayya's allegations, attempting to renegotiate the limits of what constitutes acceptable scriptural authority and how we can reliably trust the authenticity of an attested source. In making his case, Nārāyaṇācārya exhibits much of the heightened philological sensitivity marshaled by his near contemporary, Nīlakaṇṭha Dīkṣita, in his *Śivatattvarahasya*, never hesitating to bring critical scrutiny to fundamental questions of source criticism.

Take, for instance, the question of metrical flaw, still employed today as a key text-critical principle for determining whether a verse or text has been modified or poorly transmitted over the centuries. Madhva's sources, Appayya tells us, are consistently riddled with metrical errors; thus, we are forced to doubt the faithfulness of their transmission and, as a result, their reliability as authoritative scripture. Nārāyaṇācārya takes a firm and principled stand on the matter based on the legacy of classical Sanskrit metrics, claiming that an innumerable array of variant verse forms are in fact metrically permitted, and, hence, a deviant metrical form cannot be reliably accepted as a criterion for the corruption of a verse. In fact, he reminds us quite correctly that the Mahābhārata is full of metrically deviant verses, all of which are accepted equally as authoritative by his contemporaries. He elaborates:

> For instance, the meter known as *jagatī* consists of twelve syllables, and there are 4,096 mutually distinct subtypes because of their derivations based on their sequential formation of heavy and light syllables. Names, such as *vaṃśastha*, *drutavilambita*, and so forth, have been designated for a few among them. Such is the case for a single meter; as there may be a greater number of syllables in a given meter, an individual meter may exceed a lakh [of subtypes]. And as for those [well-known] meters such as *śārdūlavikrīḍita* and *sragdharā*, these are applied specifically per verse or per foot. It is not that a single specific meter is demanded by all four lines of a verse.[38]

On the question of metrical flaw, Nārāyaṇācārya is by no means timid in attempting to disarm not only Appayya's arguments but even his principal tools of textual interpretation. What engages his attention throughout the majority of the *Advaitakālānala*, however, is not metrics but Mīmāṃsā. Preoccupying himself with the analytical power of Mīmāṃsā maxims, and the limits of their applicability, Nārāyaṇācārya calls into question the essential nature of disciplinarity in Sanskrit *śāstra* and the extratextual sectarian significance of disciplinary divisions. Appayya, for his part, being an accomplished Mīmāṃsaka with an ingenious sense of the hermeneutic potential of Mīmāṃsā strategies of interpretation, launches his attacks on Madhva by way of highly specific Mīmāṃsaka principles. Take, for instance, the first verse of the *Madhvatantramukhamardana*—quite likely intended both as an intellectual witticism and as a genuine attack on the scriptural foundations of dualist theology. He writes,

> To those who define the subject of the Brahmasūtras as "Śiva or
>   Viṣṇu,"
> It is agreed—we who worship *nirguṇa* brahman accept the *saguṇa* as
>   well.
> Little contradiction arises for us, who know the *na hi nindā* maxim.
> Nor should any other interpretation of the Sūtras be suppressed by
>   you.[39]

The *na hi nindā* maxim is an interpretive principle paraphrased directly from the *Mīmāṃsāsūtrabhāṣya* (2.4.20) of Śabara, who aims to resolve the potential contradictions in ritual procedure resulting from Vedic passages that appear to censure (*nindā*) a particular sequence of actions. Such blame, Śabara contends, does not prohibit what seems to be prohibited, but rather simply allows room for some other possibility. As he writes, "Blame, after all, is not employed to blame the blameworthy, but rather to praise something other than what is blamed (*na hi nindā nindyaṃ ninditum prayujyate, kiṃ tarhi ninditād itarat praśaṃsitum*). As such, what is understood is not a prohibition of what is blamed but rather an injunction of something else."[40]

Appayya, for his part, extracts the *na hi nindā* maxim from its Vedic ritual context and adapts it for the resolution of apparent logical contradictions in other scriptures, such as the sectarian Purāṇas and the Brahmasūtras. Any scriptural statement that appears to castigate either Śiva or Viṣṇu—or even to deny the non-dualistic nature of the world—may simply be interpreted as an optional, contingent description of the true state of affairs. Individual deities, for example, may be equated with the nondual brahman as *saguṇa* manifestations on the force of this same maxim. Apparently exasperated by this approach, Nārāyaṇācārya not only maintains that Appayya's particular uses of Mīmāṃsā hermeneutics are inapplicable as a critique of Madhva's doctrine of dualism, or as a means to determine the identity of or difference between Śiva and Viṣṇu, but he also goes much further and throws into question the more general validity of Pūrva Mīmāṃsā itself as an approach to textual interpretation outside of the narrow confines of Vedic ritual procedure. As he remarks aphoristically in one of his verses: "Mīmāṃsā, set forth to resolve the contradiction among statements occupying the peak of scripture, is in this case entirely fruitless."[41]

By reducing the consequences of the *na hi nindā* maxim to absurdity, what Nārāyaṇācārya aims to elucidate is the danger involved in haphazardly applying hermeneutical principles without careful attention to what those principles logically entail. When any critical statement can be explained away as optionality, scripture is rendered unable to negate heretical doctrines in simple, declarative statements. Even genuine philosophical refutation becomes logically impossible. By thus attempting to outlaw Mīmāṃsā reading practices in the arena of sectarian debate, Nārāyaṇācārya reveals the growing division between the very tools of textual interpretation employed by rival sectarian traditions. In fact, rather than agreeing on a single shared medium for debate, the two rival traditions began to demarcate certain textual approaches as essentially their own property, distancing themselves from attack and counterattack by attempting to invalidate their opponents' reading practices. In fact, Nārāyaṇācārya enthusiastically accepts Appayya's allegations that Madhva "transgresses the boundaries" of Mīmāṃsā, construing this transgressive maneuver as the culmination of the Mādhva school's mastery of syllogistic logic. No school of philosophy, even Mīmāṃsā, he argues, ought to be accepted as the arbiter of all intellectual activity. Were this the case, one who failed to accept the primacy of "primordial matter" (*prakṛti*) would "transgress" the precepts of the Sāṅkhya school of philosophy, and one who failed to accept the ontological inherence of properties in objects would "transgress" the principles of Vaiśeṣika.

> And as for the claim that even the boundaries of Pūrva Mīmāṃsā are being led astray by improper argumentation, then our response is that we are not the servants of the Pūrva Mīmāṃsakas. We'll proceed with whatever boundaries we like. But rather—
>
> > Statements endowed with logical reasoning are admissible even from a child.
> > Anything else should be abandoned like grass, even if spoken by Brahmā.
>
> Based on this principle, we accept what is reasonable, and we abandon what is unreasonable. This is an ornament, not a fault, for those who propound independent systems of thought. Otherwise, by failing to accept the ontological category of inherence, one would transgress the boundaries of Kaṇāda's [Vaiśeṣika] system, and by failing to accept the primacy of *prakṛti*, one would transgress the boundaries of Sāṃkhya; thus, we by no means consider this a fault. But rather, how could we not perceive you yourself—who have accepted the singularity of the self, the universal brahman, the falsehood of the world, and the fact that the Veda teaches falsehood— as having transgressed the boundaries of all systems apart from the Buddhists.[42]

In short, Nārāyaṇācārya turns Appayya's allegation on its head—transgressing the hermeneutics of Pūrva Mīmāṃsā is no fault at all but rather a dearly held principle of argumentation and interpretation. Despite—or perhaps even because of—the vehemence of his argumentation, Nārāyaṇācārya manages both to solidify the boundaries between their respective sectarian communities and, in the process, to draw widespread scrutiny across sectarian boundaries to the very reading practices that had been taken for granted for centuries as the foundations of textual interpretation. As a result, the source material of sectarian debate became the source of a widespread reconsideration of textual interpretation itself, as intellectuals from all camps contributed to an incisive reconsideration of just how the texts they had long taken for granted really do mean what we think they mean.

THE MANY MEANINGS OF *NĀRĀYAṆA*: ETYMOLOGY AND LEXICOGRAPHY IN INTERSECTARIAN DEBATE

As a tradition justly renowned for its rigorous analysis of the form and function of language, Sanskrit textual culture has always made room for etymology. Commentators in all subdisciplines habitually gravitated toward both historical etymology—namely, the morphological derivation of words provided by Pāṇinian grammar—and various techniques of semantic etymology, such as Yāska's Nirukta, a school of thought devoted to deriving the meaning of Vedic texts from the level of the word upward. Both Pāṇinian Vyākaraṇa and Nairuktika etymology continued to flourish throughout the second millennium in south India, particularly as exegetical tools for defending sectarian-specific interpretations of scripture. Among noteworthy sectarian iconoclasts, Madhva in particular initiated a number of new and controversial approaches to Vedic exegesis, demarcating new boundaries for the scope and applicability of etymological analysis. In order to establish Viṣṇu himself as the "great purport," or *mahātātparya*, of Vedic scripture, Madhva proposed new parameters for the very meaning of Vedic words themselves. Viṣṇu, he argued, being the sole entity in possession of all perfect attributes (*guṇaparipūrṇatva*), could literally be denoted by every single word in the Vedic corpus (*sarvaśabdavācyatva*), each of which held the capacity to signify one of his unique properties.[43]

In light of these contentious claims, it is no wonder that Madhva's dialectic strategies sparked centuries of debate across south India as to the limits and proper applications of etymological analysis. As sectarian tensions escalated in subsequent centuries, theologians of all lineages seized upon this new permissiveness to elevate etymological speculation to new heights. Succinctly, we witness two distinctive trends in the approach to word meaning over the early modern centuries, cultivated expressly for the purpose of proving the superiority of one sect over another. First, theologians cultivated a predilection for what we might call "extreme etymology." Reminiscent of the passion for *śleṣa*, or extreme feats of language, that spread like wildfire among the literary circles of south India in particular,[44] sectarian advocates strove to outdo their competitors in the complexity or even sheer number of etymologies they could defensibly derive from the name of their chosen deity.

One noteworthy example is a remarkable composition by the notable Mādhva theologian Vijayīndra Tīrtha, the *Nārāyaṇaśabdārthanirvacana* (Etymology of the meaning of the word Nārāyaṇa). Circulated as a pamphlet-sized handbook for the possible derivations for this popular name of Viṣṇu, the *Nārāyaṇaśabdārthanirvacana* assembles well over one hundred (126, to be precise) etymological explanations for the name *Nārāyaṇa,* all conforming precisely to the strictures of Pāṇinian grammatical analysis. Through such etymological feats, Vijayīndra effectively unites the supposed legitimacy of Pāṇinian grammatical derivation with a Nirukta-like freedom to derive any semantic meaning demanded by the commentator's theological agenda. Elsewhere, Vijayīndra Tīrtha proves capable of subordinating even the most obvious primary word meanings to his creative etymologies. For instance, in his *Turīyaśivakhaṇḍana*—a treatise aimed explicitly at refuting the existence of a "transcendent fourth" Paramaśiva—Vijayīndra defends his characteristically Mādhva claim that *all* names of deities in the Vedic corpus ought to be interpreted primarily as signifiers of the god Viṣṇu, a principle he extracts from the Ṛgvedic passage "yo devānāṃ nāmadhā eka eva," construed rather problematically by Madhva as "He who is the one single name of all the gods." As he writes, "And moreover, through examination of the scriptural citation 'yo devānāṃ nāmadhā eka eva,' one establishes the conclusion that Nārāyaṇa alone is the single chief purport of the names of all gods. Otherwise, one would be forced to block the primary signification of the restrictive limitation: *one single name.*"[45]

In fact, the names of deities themselves, such as Nārāyaṇa, had become prime objects of contestation for entire generations of sectarian polemicists.[46] Names of individual deities do occur frequently in Vedic and Purāṇic literature, but by the sixteenth century many of these names had long since acquired a conventional association with one of the two principal sectarian deities of Vaidika Hindus. In such a context, given Vedic statements declaring that both "Īśāna" and "Nārāyaṇa" are the supreme deity, the sole source of the universe, it is all but inevitable that commentators should resort to strategic etymology to demonstrate that one or the other does *not* signify Śiva or Viṣṇu, respectively, as custom would hold. As a result, etymological virtuosity soon became a prized commodity among prominent theologians who wished to establish the absolute supremacy of one sectarian deity over the other.

The name *Nārāyaṇa* in particular came to occupy a central strategic position in these debates, as Vaiṣṇava expositors struggled to secure the name exclusively for Viṣṇu, and Śaiva commentators contrived some alternative explanation for why the name referred either to a transcendent Paramaśiva exclusively or to all three deities of the Trimūrti—Brahmā, Viṣṇu, and Rudra-Śiva. Moreover, their explanations of how *Nārāyaṇa* means what they propose it means draw on the heights of grammatical, etymological, and philological reasoning from across disciplines. One has only to survey the *New Catalogus Catalogorum* or any of the major manuscript libraries to observe a proliferation of treatises concerned with *ṇa-tva,* or the grammatical rules prompting retroflection of the nasal *n* in Sanskrit words and compounds, their origins concentrated quite specifically in early modern south India.[47] In essence, this peculiar fascination was no disinterested collective inquiry into morphological grammar; rather, the aim was to establish why *Nārāyaṇa* exhibited its retroflection in the final syllable, and what the implications of this retroflex were for the meaning of this highly contested name.

On the other hand—perhaps in response to such feats of extreme etymology— more circumspect theologians began to direct a critical gaze toward both the very concept of word meaning and the tools traditionally used to ascertain that meaning. If etymology can truly establish that a word signifies any deity or quality desired, what explanatory value does it possess? And, if traditional meanings of words and names can easily be undermined by etymological sleight of hand, of what use is a dictionary that tells us that *Nārāyaṇa* means "Viṣṇu"? It is this critical reflectivity toward disciplinary approaches to word meaning that occupied the attention of many of Appayya's, Vijayīndra's, and Nārāyaṇācārya's near contemporaries. Particularly noteworthy in this regard is a dialogical exchange between a Smārta-Śaiva exegete, Govinda Nāyaka, and a Vaiṣṇava rival whose name remains unknown, in which the two debate the true meaning of the name *Nārāyaṇa* and the disciplinary approaches suitable for arriving at its true meaning.

Both the original Smārta treatise and the Vaiṣṇava response, which replies directly to the Smārta work in question, have been preserved in the same bundle at the Adyar Library and Research Centre in Chennai,[48] providing us with a unique opportunity to witness sectarian polemical exchange in action. What is most fascinating about this exchange, however, is that each opponent integrates a programmatic methodological statement into the substance of his claim, differing not only as to *what* the name *Nārāyaṇa* means but also *how* we can justifiably discern its signification. On the Smārta side, Govinda Nāyaka advocates etymology as the principal authority for determining word meaning, whereas his Vaiṣṇava interlocutor defends lexicography as the deciding factor in adjudicating signification. In the process, we meet with a substantive exchange regarding the relative merits of etymology and lexicography themselves as knowledge systems and tools for sectarian debate.

The first of these works, the *Nārāyaṇaśabdasādhāraṇya* of Govinda Nāyaka, advocates the Smārta position, arguing that the name *Nārāyaṇa* simultaneously signifies each deity of the Trimūrti—Brahmā, Viṣṇu, and Rudra-Śiva. He declares his intention plainly at the outset of the pamphlet: "It is well-known in literature such as the Purāṇas that, based on the conventional usage by the learned and etymology, the term *Nārāyaṇa* is expressive of the Trimūrti—that is, Brahmā, Viṣṇu, and Śiva." As evidence for this rather bold assertion, Govinda Nāyaka proceeds to exemplify creative etymologies that construe the name *Nārāyaṇa* as referring to each of the three deities, corroborating these etymologies with Purāṇic citations that narrate these same meanings in well-known mythological episodes. Like the clever etymologies of Vijayīndra Tīrtha, Govinda Nāyaka's glosses hinge on pedantic references to such unlikely Sanskrit lexemes as *ṇa*, a "word" that possesses the virtue of simultaneously accounting for the peculiar retroflexion in the compound *Nārāyaṇa*. Drawing on the various attested meanings of *ṇa*, for instance, he explains the name *Nārāyaṇa* as follows: "*Nāra* is the aggregate of individual souls, or *nara*-s. The one from whom liberation [is given] to that [aggregate] [is Nārāyaṇa]. *Ṇa*, in fact, indicates liberation, as attested in the *Ratnamālā*: '*Ṇa* refers to a lotus or knowledge.' The dative case ending is not elided."[49] And subsequently: "Or, *Nārāyaṇa* refers to the *ṇa*, or 'lover,' of the *nāra*, the aggregate of women in Vraja. The dative case ending is not elided, as in the compound 'lover to Ahalyā.'[50] The word ṇa, in the *Ratnamālā*, is said to refer to a lover, Bhairava, a thorn, or a sound."[51]

In the above examples, the name *Nārāyaṇa* is construed in the conventionally accepted sense, as an alternative name for Viṣṇu. The true force of Govinda Nāyaka's argument comes into view, however, when he applies the same etymological strategies to render the name *Nārāyaṇa* capable of signifying Brahmā, Viṣṇu, and Śiva equally. Just as the name was construed above to signify "the lover of the women of Vraja," a meaning that unmistakably refers to the Vaiṣṇava theology of Kṛṣṇa, the same name, he argues, can be derived to reveal hidden references to the canonical mythology of Śiva or Brahmā. These references, in turn, once revealed, demonstrate a genuine ontological capacity within the name *Nārāyaṇa* to bring to mind the gods Śiva and Brahmā to the same degree as Viṣṇu. Take, for instance, the following alternative etymologies, which evoke the motifs of Śiva as Gaṅgādhara, bearer of the river Ganges, and Brahmā as originating from the lotus-navel of Viṣṇu:

> Or, [Śiva is so called] because of his being the abode of the water of the Gaṅgā—or *nāra*. *Nāra*s are clearly defined as "waters" in the Kūrma Purāṇa. In various locations in the Purāṇas, the word *Nārāyaṇa* is revealed as referring to Śiva.[52]

> Now is clarified the fact that the word *Nārāyaṇa* can also refer to the Four-Faced [Brahmā]. . . . He of whom the lotus stalks, or *nāla*, arising from [Viṣṇu's] navel are *ayanas*—that is, they take the form of paths for coming and going. *Ayana* is used in the sense of "refuge" or "path." In the Śiva Purāṇa, [we encounter such a usage of the term *nāla*]: "O sage, having gone on each *nāla* for a hundred years, he mounted the lotus by means of the path of the *nāla*, O sage.[53]

This approach is no mere parlor trick; rather, the author intends to advance a genuine argument about the intrinsic signifying capacity of the name *Nārāyaṇa*, which, in turn, holds serious implications for the orthodox Vaidika pedigree of non-Vaiṣṇava Hindu sects. Etymology, traditionally, is a fundamental criterion for the signifying capacity (*śakti*) of a word. By attesting valid Pāṇinian etymologies of the sacred name *Nārāyaṇa* that unambiguously evoke Śiva and Brahmā, Govinda Nāyaka implies that the Vedas themselves, when using the name *Nārāyaṇa*, simultaneously inculcate the authority of each of the three deities of the Trimūrti through the signifying capacity (*śakti*) of that single name. On this basis, Śaivas would be able to advance a Vedic exegetical defense of the transcendence of a unitary Paramaśiva, who is beyond name and form, encompassing all three subordinate deities—including Viṣṇu, who is referred to directly by the name *Nārāyaṇa*. Govinda Nāyaka himself hints at just such an implication: "Or, all names may apply to all deities, because the three are reflections of one consciousness."[54] In essence, the project is to undercut the Mādhva concept of *sarvaśabdavācyatva*, "being signified by all names," from the Vedas, so that it refers not to Viṣṇu but to the nondual, absolute Paramaśiva. And furthermore, if all three deities can be proven ontologically equivalent on etymological grounds, there can be no possibility of presuming an inherent difference in the Purāṇas of Śaiva, Brāhma, and Vaiṣṇava origin on the grounds of their respective authorship alone.

In the second of the two tracts, the *Nārāyaṇaśabdanirukti*, an anonymous Vaiṣṇava polemicist attempts to refute these claims, maintaining that the name *Nārāyaṇa* refers exclusively to Viṣṇu in common parlance. Taking refuge in the old maxim "Customary usage supersedes etymology" (*rūḍhir yogam apaharati*), the author contends that etymological sophistry bears no relationship to the actual semantic function of a word, whether in scripture or worldly discourse. To the contrary, if one were free to provide alternative etymological explanations for any scriptural term, including names of deities, chaos would result, especially in the domain of ritual. Given that particular religious observances are prescribed in Purāṇic scriptures as appropriate for the worship of each individual deity, one would be free to substitute any of the ritual instructions or implements at will simply by replacing the name *Śiva* with *Viṣṇu*. As our Vaiṣṇava polemicist warns us:

> Then, the following could be said: a statement that prohibits worshipping Viṣṇu with unhusked barleycorns would signify the prohibition of worshipping Śiva with unhusked barleycorns. A statement prescribing *darśan* of Śiva at dusk would prescribe the *darśan* of Viṣṇu at dusk. A statement that prescribes the observance of a vow for Viṣṇu on the Ekādaśī (the eleventh day of the lunar fortnight) would then prescribe the observance of that vow for Śiva on the Ekādaśī, and so forth. Because the consequence would be entailed that all rituals described in the Purāṇas, and so forth, could be practiced however one desires, the differential arrangements of Vedic practices would be dissolved, and no sin would accrue to those who practiced in whatever manner they wished.[55]

Clearly, for both interlocutors, the etymology of the name *Nārāyaṇa* was by no means a matter restricted to academic pedantry; rather, both sides believed the issue had wide-ranging consequences for the regulation of public religious observances across sectarian lines. Philology, in short, facilitated the adjudication of religious practice. For our present purposes, however, what is most interesting is the conceptual consequences of this polemical interaction—that is, the pressure that exchanges such as this one placed on those who would reflect on core textual practices of textual interpretation within the Sanskrit knowledge systems. In the present scenario, Govinda Nāyaka and his Vaiṣṇava opponent did not rest their cases at the proposal and refutation of individual etymologies; rather, their exchange overflowed the boundaries of pure polemic, sparking deeper theoretical reflections about the utility of etymological modes of interpretation. Govinda Nāyaka, for his part, defends the practice of "extreme etymology" on theoretical grounds, dismissing not only the maxim "Customary usage supersedes etymology" but also the discipline of lexicography itself and its authority with regard to word meaning. On the limitations of the standard Sanskrit lexicon, Govinda Nāyaka writes,

> One might argue that because [the word *Nārāyaṇa*] appears in lexicons as referring to Viṣṇu in such passages as "Viṣṇu, Nārāyaṇa, Kṛṣṇa," and so forth, it cannot refer commonly to the triad of deities—this is not correct. What is commonly known from a lexicon, after all, serves merely for the education of children. Otherwise, words not included [in the lexicon] could not possibly refer to Viṣṇu. Precisely the same would be true as well for words referring to Brahmā and Śiva. . . .
>
> Therefore, because words such as *Nārāyaṇa* are revealed in the Purāṇas as referring to the triad of deities, it should be understood that such words are construed through a restriction of their signifying power as referring to Viṣṇu [alone]. For that very reason, Kaiyaṭa has explained that a word, which possesses multiple signifying capacities, is applied to a signified entity by means of the delimitation of the word's signifying power. Such is the case with the application of the word *twice-born*, which signifies a member of the three classes, to the Brahmin in particular owing to the currency of this usage among the ignorant—after all, it is revealed in the Nāradīya: "'twice-borns' are Brahmins, Kṣatriyas, and Vaiśyas." Likewise, when the words *Brahmin* or *Smārta* are employed, although they signify Smārtas, Vaiṣṇavas, Mādhvas, [and] Śaivas, only Smārtas are understood, rather than Vaiṣṇavas and the rest, owing to the currency of such usage among the ignorant. And the same occurs as well with the word *Nārāyaṇa*.[56]

At first glance, Govinda Nāyaka's argument may strike the reader as intuitively plausible. After all, does a word acquire its power to convey meaning simply because its definition appears in a dictionary? To the contrary, authors of lexicons have selected the principal definitions of words so as to meet the needs of a rather restricted audience—namely, those who have no prior acquaintance with a word, and who thus require a straightforward indication of its most frequently attested meaning. Moreover, if a specific idiomatic sense of a word has gained currency in popular discourse, lexicons will be more likely to point readers toward this specific meaning rather than toward the full range of the word's denotative capacity. This is the case with words such as the term *Smārta,* which, in classical literature signified all individuals learned in the *smṛtis,* but which in early modern south India came to refer exclusively to one particular sectarian community. Theoretically speaking, Govinda Nāyaka refers to this linguistic phenomenon as the "restriction" of a word's signifying capacity (*śakti*). And by restricting the signification of a word for a particular purpose, he argues, one cannot genuinely curtail the word's capacity to denote a wide range of meanings in various contexts.

Where Govinda Nāyaka's opponent differs, however, is on the very nature of lexicography as a discipline. Specifically, he draws our attention to the intensely philological practice of compiling a dictionary, an enterprise that requires a sustained engagement with living speech communities as well as with the extensive canon of texts written in the Sanskrit language. A lexicon is not, ideally speaking, simply a collection of signposts for the ignorant; rather, producers of dictionaries aim to compile the range of meanings attested for a word across all extant genres of textuality, orienting the discerning reader both to the statistically most significant meanings and those specialized senses of words that are restricted to particular contexts. Presented with such a lexicon—that is, one that has been compiled through an exhaustive philological analysis of all major textual genres—no responsible exegete should ascribe a meaning to a Purāṇic name that has never before been attested in the history of Sanskrit textuality. And if a passage attesting an improbable meaning for a term happens to be found, it would more than warrant suspicion of interpolation, particularly in a Purāṇic corpus biased toward the sectarian faction the citation favors. As our Vaiṣṇava polemicist argues,

> For, a lexicon does not of its own accord restrict the signifying power of a word, generally used by prior authors in various senses, to a single object. Nor does it state that a word generally employed by prior authors in a restricted set of senses can in fact be taken in a variety of senses. Rather, it states that a word possesses signifying capacities with regard to precisely those meanings for which it has attained currency, which are not contrary to general usage, and do not provoke the scorn of learned people—because, like grammar, lexicography is subordinate to actual usage. Otherwise, a lexicon would not be usable by all people. Thus, a lexicon of its own accord clearly defines the conventional meaning, which has become current owing to repeated usage by a multitude of people, so that it may be easily understood.[57]

In other words, to explain that words such as *Nārāyaṇa* have one commonly accepted meaning does not require a theoretical appeal to the "restriction" of signifying power. Rather, critical reasoning and extensive reading across genres is sufficient to alert the discerning mind that *Nārāyaṇa* simply does not mean "the one who bears the river Ganges" in any naturally occurring citation. While, conveniently for the Vaiṣṇava case, words such as Śiva (auspicious), Īśāna (Lord),

Maheśvara (Great Lord), and other names of the god Śiva regularly function as descriptive adjectives in the Mahābhārata, the Bhāgavata Purāṇa, and other religious texts, "words such as *Nārāyaṇa*," the Vaiṣṇava polemicist maintains, "despite their intrinsic generalizability, *do not* occur in general usage in such narrative passages as referring to something other than *Nārāyaṇa*, either independently or as qualifying adjectives. . . . The word *Nārāyaṇa* is not observed to be employed in the sense of *Śiva*, and so forth, anywhere *except in the statements you have exemplified.*"[58] Extreme etymology, quite simply, stretches the common sense of philology beyond all reasonable credulity. Our author rests his case, concluding by impugning the textual integrity of the passages from the Śaiva Purāṇas that Govinda Nāyaka cites in defense of his alternative etymologies of *Nārāyaṇa*:

> The employed usages that you have cited as conveying the fact that the word *Nārāyaṇa* refers to Śiva are *not* exemplified in texts such as the *Nīlakaṇṭha Bhāṣya*, *Śivārkamaṇidīpikā*, *Śivastutisūktimālikā*, *Śivatattvaviveka*, and *Śaivakarṇāmṛta*,[59] [which were written] by followers of the Śaiva doctrine who are extremely self-interested, for the purpose of establishing that the word *Nārāyaṇa* refers to Śiva. Nor do we exemplify them when attempting to refute them, a process that involves recording each individual line contained in those texts. Moreover, because in the Mahābhārata, and other works as well, interpolations are observed, it is difficult to avoid the doubt that interpolations may exist in extremely prolix works such as the Śiva Purāṇa and the Skanda Purāṇa, as these works are generally compiled by Śaivas alone. After all, fabricated texts on the greatness of sacred centers, which concern *modern temples* and other sites, are being composed and attributed precisely to the Skanda Purāṇa, the Śiva Purāṇa, and so forth. Thus the passages you cite are not Purāṇic at all.[60]

Indeed, our author's final allegation is genuinely credible: early modern south India had witnessed the emergence of Purāṇic factories, of sorts, fabricating a mythological past (sacred "narratives of place," or *talapurāṇams*, Skt. *sthalapurāṇas*) for devotional sites across the Tamil country—Madurai being no exception, as will be discussed in the next chapter. As the Vaiṣṇava counterattack on the *Nārāyaṇaśabdanirukti* reaches its logical conclusion, readers are led to the same state of guarded skepticism that Nīlakaṇṭha Dīkṣita encounters in his *Śivatattvarahasya*. When implausible proof texts surface in debate, sectarian philologians apply a renewed critical gaze to the textual integrity of sectarian scripture itself, warning against the ever-present reality of textual drift and, consequently, the dangers interpolation can pose for responsible scriptural exegesis. Throughout this exchange, Govinda Nāyaka and our anonymous Vaiṣṇava polemicist advance arguments far removed from the doctrinal claims of sectarian theology. In search of common ground for contestation, both opponents have turned instead to the disciplinary tools of textual hermeneutics, generating an informed reconsideration of the limits of two key approaches to semantic analysis. Each of the two, etymology and lexicography, although supported by centuries of classical learning, appear to the eyes of early modern polemicists as themselves contingent analytic devices, subject to application only within the restricted confines of cautious philological reasoning.

PHILOLOGY IN THE PUBLIC SPHERE: THE PRACTICAL APPLICATIONS OF TEXTUAL CRITICISM

Despite their passing preoccupation with lexicons and retroflexes, sixteenth- and seventeenth-century scholars had become increasingly fascinated with the social significance of public sectarian comportment. Markers of membership in a particular sectarian community became the object of new contestation and critical inquiry, and creativity in the hermeneutic feats employed to justify the usage of these insignia rose dramatically. Take, for instance, the practice of applying the *tripuṇḍra*—three stripes of ash—to the forehead to publicly signal one's identity as an orthodox Śaiva. Early modern Smārta-Śaivas, such as Appayya Dīkṣita and Nīlakaṇṭha Dīkṣita, had adopted a line of scriptural defense for the practice of applying the *tripuṇḍra* that hinges on a striking interpretation of a verse from the Śvetāśvatara Upaniṣad, one that has generated as much controversy among seventeenth-century *śāstrin*s as among contemporary scholars:

> By the power of austerity and the grace of god, the learned
> Śvetāśvatara
> Knew brahman and proclaimed to the *atyāśramin*s that pure
> Supreme, worshipped by the company of sages.[61]

The key term in this verse is *atyāśramin*. Many contemporary translators adopt an additive approach to construing this perplexing term, rendering "*ati-āśrama*," as "beyond the *āśrama*s," that is, having transcended the four stages of life.[62] And indeed, speculation from within the Sanskrit knowledge systems seems to justify this interpretation. Advaitin theologians, beginning with Śaṅkarācārya, adopted terms such as *atyāśramin* to speak of a class of renunciants, often *jīvanmukta*s (those liberated while alive), who had passed beyond the strictures of the traditional social order.[63] More recently, however, leading scholars of early Śaivism have discovered that the term *atyāśrama*, in its original usage, in fact is closely associated with a group of Atimārgic Pāśupatas.[64] That is, Śaiva scriptures, as early as the Niśvāsamūlasūtra (ca. fifth century C.E.), speak of two principal subsets of Śaiva lineages: the Atimārga—in subsequent centuries including such groups as the Pāñcārthika Pāśupatas, Kāpālikas, and Kālāmukhas—and the Mantramārga, commonly associated with Āgamic Śaivism (such as the Śaiva Siddhānta). Among the former, initiates are said to adopt a practice known either as the *atyāśrama* vow (*atyāśramavrata*) or the Great Pāśupata vow (*mahāpāśupatavrata*), an observance that later Śaiva exegetes understand quite rightly to involve smearing the entire body in ash (*bhasmoddhūlana*).

Among Western Indologists, the recovery of this Śaiva sense of *atyāśrama*—and the religious sensibilities it was intended to evoke—figures among the more noteworthy discoveries of the past decades. Nevertheless, equal credit must be granted to the Smārta-Śaiva philologians of the early modern period, who themselves had recovered the same historical sense of the term *atyāśramin*, which had fallen into ambiguity for earlier Advaita Vedānta philosophers. Having amassed Upaniṣadic, Purāṇic, and Āgamic citations that contained the troubling term, Smārta polemicists ascertained correctly that the *atyāśramavrata* and *pāśupatavrata* were synonymous and involved the practice of smearing the body with ash. By the seventeenth century, however, Nīlakaṇṭha and his colleagues had added a polemical twist to their interpretation of this problematic term, claiming that *atyāśrama* literally referred not to the smearing of ash but, more specifically, to the prescription to apply the *tripuṇḍra* to the forehead, the Śaiva sectarian *tilaka*. By doing so, they had essentially uncovered a Vaidika proof text for a distinctively Śaiva sectarian practice—a practice, in fact, that publicly demarcated one's identity as an orthodox Śaiva.

Nīlakaṇṭha Dīkṣita explores the matter in some detail in his *Saubhāgyacandrātapa*, his unpublished manual of Śrīvidyā ritual, outlining the scriptural injunctions for the application of the *tripuṇḍra*:

> In the Śvetāśvatara Upaniṣad, it is revealed:

> "By the power of austerity and the grace of god, the learned
>   Śvetāśvatara,
> knower of brahman, proclaimed to the *atyāśramins* that pure Supreme, enjoyed by the company of sages."[65]

> On this matter, at the end of the procedure for applying the *tripuṇḍra* is revealed the following statement in the Brahmottarakhaṇḍa:

> "Supreme gnosis, capable of severing transmigration, belongs to
>   those alone
> By whom was practiced long ago this *atyāśrama dharma*.

> The fact that the bearing of the *tripuṇḍra* is established here to be expressed by the term *atyāśrama* is corroborated by the following praise of instruction in the knowledge of brahman in the Kālāgnirudropaniṣad, which establishes [the bearing of the *tripuṇḍra*] as a prerequisite knowledge of brahman:

> "He should make three straight lines: this *śāmbhava* vow is described by the knowers of the Veda in all the Vedas. One who desires liberation should practice it for the cessation of rebirth. Whichever learned celibate student, householder, forest dweller, or ascetic makes such a *tripuṇḍra* with ash is purified of all unforgivable sins."[66]

Vaiṣṇavas, as one might imagine, were by no means satisfied with this line of reasoning and took great pains to provide alternative explanations. Take, for instance, the celebrated Mādhva scholar Vijayīndra Tīrtha, who, in his *Turīyaśivakhaṇḍana*, expresses some trepidation regarding the prevalent Śaiva interpretation of the term *atyāśrama*: "Some people, however, accepting the meaning of the term *atyāśrama* as stated in the *smṛti*s on the force of contextualization and so forth, say that it refers to the eligibility for a certain kind of knowledge. Suffice it to say that we will explain when deliberating on the statement from the Atharvaśiras why smearing with ash, bearing the *tripuṇḍra*, and so forth *do not* constitute a prerequisite for the knowledge of brahman."[67]

Vijayīndra Tīrtha, it appears, was well aware of the ground Śaivas sought to gain through their philological endeavors, and had taken steps to counter their claims. By his use of the phrase *prakaraṇādivaśāt* (on the force of contextualization and so forth), Vijayīndra again appears to prefigure Nārāyaṇācārya in expressing a distrust of Mīmāṃsaka strategies of interpretation, which, as Nārāyaṇācārya had claimed, facilitate counterintuitive—and often simply unreasonable—construals of scripture. By way of reply, he proposes a much more conservative interpretation, founded not on historical precedent but on the strictures of Pāṇinian grammar. Compounded from the prefix *ati* and a well-known word for the Brahminical stages of life, a term such as *atyāśrama*, according to Vijayīndra, cannot plausibly be interpreted in a sense so distant from its historical etymological derivation. Drawing on Pāṇini's Sūtra 1.04.095 (*atir atikramaṇe*), he maintains that, "in the Kaivalya Upaniṣad, the word *atyāśrama* as well, appearing at the beginning and end of the text, ought reasonably to be construed as referring to the stage of life of the ascetic. It is not reasonable to hope to prove on the strength of even this term that the Kaivalya Upaniṣad is about Śiva."[68]

And yet Vijayīndra's words of caution did little to restrain the philological inquiry of his Śaiva opponents; in fact, Śaivas of the next generation would take their inquiry a step further, launching a comprehensive inquiry into the historical attestations of the term *atyāśrama* in *śruti* and Purāṇic narrative. Echoing Nīlakaṇṭha's own position, a remarkably similar argument surfaces perhaps a century later in a lengthy polemical tome titled the *Īśavilāsa*, composed by one "Appayya Dīkṣita"[69]—most likely not identical with the sixteenth-century polymath of the same name. The author of the *Īśavilāsa* presents an exhaustive study of the relevant scriptures,[70] establishing from his encyclopedic array of citations that the terms *atyāśramavrata*, *pāśupatavrata*, and *śirovrata* are synonymous, and that they refer to the practice of applying the *tripuṇḍra* as well as to smearing the body with ash. Building on this philological apparatus, however, he takes his conclusion a step further. This Appayya Dīkṣita arrives at the conclusion that those who wish to know brahman are not only enjoined explicitly by scripture to apply the *tripuṇḍra* but also expressly forbidden from applying any other sectarian insignia, including the *ūrdhvapuṇḍra*, the Vaiṣṇava sectarian *tilaka*. As our author writes, "Thus, because the vow of the *tripuṇḍra* and of the smearing with ash literally prohibits bearing another *puṇḍra*, the numerous other statements prohibiting the *ūrdhvapuṇḍra* based on this, found in the Vaśiṣṭha and Liṅga Purāṇas, the Parāśara Upapurāṇa, the Mānava[dharmaśāstra], the Sūtasaṃhitā, and the Sāmba Purāṇa are not written here so as to avoid prolixity."[71]

Among the verses "Appayya Dīkṣita" cites in defense of his argument is an intriguing narrative episode he unearthed from the Kūrma Purāṇa, in which the sage Śvetāśvatara himself—notorious from the original attestation of *atyāśramin* in the Śvetāśvatara Upaniṣad, described here as the "Mahāpāśupata"[72]—arrives wearing only a loincloth, his body smeared with ash, and instructs King Suśīla in the practice of the *atyāśrama* vow, which the texts equate with the "entire essence of the Vedas."[73] From this Kūrma Purāṇa passage, our author concludes the "Pāśupata" and *atyāśrama* vow refer commonly to a single practice that involves the bearing of ash, mandated by a veritable constellation of reliable scriptures and incumbent on members of all castes who wish to attain knowledge of brahman.[74] While partisan in the extreme, Appayya's argument speaks to a genuine philological perseverance—a willingness to return straight to the sources to uncover the roots of sectarian practice in his own day and age. This, in fact, is precisely what he discovered. The Kūrma passage in question provides us with a remnant of a Vedicized Pāśupata lineage that derived its own authority from the sage Śvetāśvatara, an ideal figurehead, as the Vaidika scripture named for him provides a genuine defense of Pāśupata Śaivism.[75] As a member of a much later movement of Vaidika Śaivas, "Appayya" came to this same conclusion, marshaling his text-critical analysis in support of the polemical ambitions of his contemporary sectarian community.

Bearing the *tripuṇḍra*, in other words, was fashioned as a foundational precept of public orthopraxy through the textual inquiries of public philologians. But how would this precept apply to those who had adopted esoteric religious commitments? In other words, among orthoprax Smārta-Śaivas, what mark ought a practitioner of Śrīvidyā to display? Nīlakaṇṭha addresses the issue at some length in his *Saubhāgyacandrātapa*:

> Now one might object: "Bearing the *tripuṇḍra* applies to worshippers of Śiva, but devotees of the goddess ought not to apply ashes. . . . If such is argued, then because the *tripuṇḍra* of ash is prescribed as a component of the worship of Śiva along with the goddess [Sāmba] in the Kaivalyopaniṣad, . . . and since I myself will establish in the fourth chapter that *Śrīvidyā practitioners are in fact worshippers of Śiva* along with the goddess, it is absolutely necessary for them as well to apply the *tripuṇḍra*.
>
> Or, if one were to ask as well whether the restriction to smear one's body with sandalwood paste ought to be accepted by devotees of the goddess, I say no. For as is well known, one ought to bear whatever signifiers are appropriate to the deity one

worships, since the essence of the Tantras enjoins these things: the bearing of garlands of forest flowers and such by Vaiṣṇavas, and the bearing of *rudrākṣas* by Śaivas. This principle is known in worldly affairs also, as among the retinue of the king and so forth. Thus, in this instance, devotees of the goddess, known as the "Ornamented Queen," auspicious by her full ornamentation of yellow sandal paste, ought also to generally adopt such ornamental attire; this is the essence of the Śākta Tantras. . . . And this attire should not be understood as forbidden to Smārtas.

But, as it is stated in the Kūrma Purāṇa, . . . attire that unsettles worldly people is forbidden. Whatever attire upsets worldly people in a particular place or at a particular time ought to be abandoned, accepting [attire] insofar as it serves the welfare of the world. Thus, in a region populated by simpletons, one should evoke all of this only mentally—one need not show anything externally. It is with this very intention that the *Lalitopākhyāna* stated, "Or, mentally visualized ornamentation."[76]

Nīlakaṇṭha's concern for public appearances in this passage is striking, and all the more so as he appears to be dialoguing directly with an actual group of Śākta contemporaries who were somewhat more exclusivist in their interpretation of Śākta scripture and, certainly, more overt in their public proclamation of identity. As Nīlakaṇṭha himself, on the other hand, is both a devoted practitioner of Śrīvidyā and a staunchly orthodox Śaiva Brahmin, his aim is to synthesize the two categories to whatever extent possible both in theory and practice. Not only does he believe that Śrīvidyā practitioners ought to comport themselves purely as orthodox Smārta-Śaivas in public, bearing only the *tripuṇḍra* and adopting no other external display of their identity, but he also goes so far as to make the categorical claim that Śrīvidyā practitioners *simply are* Smārta-Śaivas by definition.

The *tripuṇḍra,* as it turns out, was by no means the only sectarian marker that had become an issue of broad public contestation. A similar controversy was generated by the practice of bearing of the signs of Viṣṇu branded on one's body, or *taptamudrādharaṇa,* a practice adopted by the Mādhva Vaiṣṇavas that garnered extensive critique both from other Vaiṣṇava traditions and from Smārta-Śaivas. These branded insignia generated a widespread public controversy, as theologians from each camp returned to their scriptures to interrogate the legitimacy of the practice of branding among orthodox, Vedic Hindus. In fact, even Appayya Dīkṣita himself is reputed to have authored a work titled the *Taptamudrākhaṇḍana,* "The Demolition of Branded Insignia." One particularly poignant diatribe on the issue was composed by a certain Vijayarāmārya, titled the *Pākhaṇḍacapeṭikā* (The slap in the face of heretics). It does not take much perusal to glean something of the vehemence of his stance:

And thus, through recourse to groundless statements that contradict scripture, fabricated by the Mādhvas and others and having the mere semblance of Vedic orthodoxy, fools practice the bearing of branded insignia, their minds deluded by the impressions produced by great sins amassed in previous births. Thus they attain a low caste status; at the end of the cosmic dissolution they will enjoy all the fruits of hell.

And that is precisely why there are a thousand statements existing in various locations that prohibit those with Vedic eligibility to bear branded insignia and prescribe an expiation for bearing them, indicating that hell, and so forth, will result when one fails to perform this expiation. Among these, we exemplify only a sampling.[77]

In short, abstract as they may be on paper, or palm leaf, these philological projects hold major implications for our understanding of the public religious culture of Hindu sectarianism. Whether branded on the arm or smeared on the forehead with ash, sectarian insignia were no small matter for the many southern theologians who were committed to advertising the Vaidika orthodoxy of their chosen sect in public circles. These *tilaka*s, borne directly on the foreheads of sectarian affiliates, delineate a polarized public space in which dialogical partners move not as equals but as embodied signifiers of their religious identity. Bodily displays of identity—and their associated performances—I suggest, served as a primary point of transference between the realms of theology, as a strictly textual enterprise, and religious culture as enacted by practitioners. As a result, the vast upsurge in interest we witness in *philological* topics, such as the textual foundations of the *tilaka* and branding, confront us with the potential ability of theological debate to shift the terrain of religious community formations. Far from constructing a value-neutral space of public exchange, the philological inquiries of Smārta-Śaivas and their rivals visibly demarcated the boundaries between competing sectarian communities. Individuals could instantly distinguish coreligionists from outsiders on the basis of such insignia, which served as indexical signs of one's community of affiliation. As a result, echoes of the exchanges between Śaiva and Vaiṣṇava scholars have left an indelible impression on the religious landscape of south India, fostering a visual demarcation of religious difference.

What, then, is *new*—or, one might even say, *modern*—about the sectarian marks borne by Śaivas and Vaiṣṇavas in the seventeenth century? In fact, such insignia were used to mark the bodies of practitioners of both Brahminical Hinduism and non-Brahminical religions from the earliest stages of Indian history. The *tripuṇḍra*, for instance, as our Smārta-Śaivas came to recognize, descends directly from the practices of early Pāśupata ascetics, Śaiva renunciants whose ash-covered limbs were instantly emblematic of their social identity. And yet a closer look reveals a crucial shift in the function of bearing ash between the height of Pāśupata asceticism in the early first millennium and the seventeenth century. As renunciants, Pāśupata ascetics engaged in a soteriological practice aimed at liberating the individual soul from the chains of human existence, and the bearing of ash itself was among the tools designed to sever those chains. Pāśupatas chose to bathe in ash and, likewise, to feign insanity, engaging in lewd displays in public places, not to inform outsiders of their identity, but to cultivate a particular state of being divorced from social reality, which, they believed, would lead directly to liberation. In fact, more advanced Pāśupata practitioners were instructed to conceal the signs used to mark the body in order to maintain their internal state without the support of external signifiers. What Pāśupata were engaging in, then, was a process of mimesis—of first imitating, then internalizing the characteristic features of the god Śiva in order to transform the initiate into Śiva himself.

In the Western context, a similar process has been discussed by the theorist Giorgio Agamben, who locates a direct parallel between the outward appearance of early Christian monastics and their spiritual state of being, both represented by the word *habitus*. Agamben writes, "To inhabit together thus meant for the monks to share, not simply a place or a style of dress, but first of all a *habitus*. The monk is in this sense a man who lives in the mode of 'inhabiting,' according to a rule and a form of life. It is certain, nevertheless, that cenoby represents the attempt to make habit and form of life coincide in an absolute and total *habitus,* in which it would not be possible to distinguish between dress and way of life."[78]

Much like the Pāśupatas, early Christian monks, according to Agamben, adopted external signifiers, such as the habit, to integrate their way of life with their external appearance. The result, for both, was a personal transformation predicated upon their embodiment, quite literally, of a system of values. In subsequent traditions, however, such as the Franciscan community, theologians began to distinguish between the rules of monastic life, strictures that were meant to be obeyed, and the way of life or inner disposition cultivated as a component of monastic practice. It is this conceptual distinction, Agamben argues, between one's chosen way of life and the rules one follows in public that laid the foundation for the emergence, in the Western tradition, of the idea of public space. This shared public space, in Enlightenment Europe, came to be governed by a common set of rules, adhered to by all participants regardless of their inner convictions. In the Hindu context, early Pāśupata theologians would have found such a concept completely antithetical to the aims of their soteriological practice. And yet this idea of public space is not so distant from the religious public that seventeenth-century Śaiva theologians aimed to cultivate through their public theology.

In essence, there was something distinctly *new* about the role that sectarian markers, such as the *tilaka,* played in defining the boundaries of public space. Unlike in the European case, however, we can speak most accurately not of a public sphere but of *publics* in the plural, as theologians of each community took initiative in reshaping the rules that governed public engagement of devotees and their interactions with those outside the tradition. With this distinction in mind, we begin to find a resolution to the contrast with which we began the present chapter: namely, the bifurcation of Nīlakaṇṭha's religious commitments, privately a devotee of the goddess, publicly a proponent of Smārta-Śaiva orthodoxy. To be a practitioner of Śrīvidyā had little impact on the public comportment of an orthodox Śaiva Hindu, in the mind of Smārta-Śaiva theologians such as Nīlakaṇṭha Dīkṣita. One could bear the *tripuṇḍra,* the Śaiva *tilaka,* in public while maintaining one's personal devotion to the goddess as foundational to one's sense of religious identity.

But if the public theology of the seventeenth century was in fact something *new*, was it also in any meaningful sense *modern?* The religious publics shaped by Nīlakaṇṭha and his colleagues are just that—religiously inflected public spaces defined almost exclusively by practices most scholars would consider decidedly religious in nature. In the canons of classical theory, however, modernity is habitually associated with a teleological trajectory of secularization, such that the terms *public* and *secular* have become prescriptively equated with each other in Western discourse. Even in more recent years, theorists have attempted to define the singularity of modernity, epitomized by the European Enlightenment, as founded upon the limitation of religion in public space. Take, for instance, the work of Charles Taylor (2007), who contends that "almost everyone" would characterize our moment in time as a fundamentally secular age, regardless of one's geographical and cultural point of reference. The secularity of a society, Taylor argues, may imply a virtual evacuation of religion from public space; or in some cases, it may imply the establishment of a socially sanctioned option to eschew belief in a higher power or participation in religious ritual, an option exercised by a significant percent of the population. And yet in the context of early modern India, as well as India today, the character and function of public space diverges sharply from either of these criteria.

In the post-Enlightenment Western world, an individual is said to engage with the larger social world as an *unmarked citizen,* a position of agency unaltered by the individual's identity, whether social, cultural, or religious. While this concept of the universal individual has rightly come under fire by Western theorists in recent decades, it is safe to say that, in India, one typically engages with society not as an unmarked but as a *marked citizen,* qualified by features of caste, gender, regional, and religious identity. In south India, by wearing a Śaiva *tilaka,* a person visibly marks himself as a participant in a certain religious public, as one who is likely to frequent certain temples, observe certain festivals, and accept the authority of certain sacred texts. It tells us little, however, about other aspects of his religious identity, aspects that may prove more integral to understanding his conception of the world or the experience of the divine he professes. It tells us little about the personal ritual practices he has adopted to structure his daily life, or about the saints or deities with whom he cultivates a particular relationship. In the case of Nīlakaṇṭha Dīkṣita, his public appearance would tell us nothing about his devotional relationship with his preceptor, Gīrvāṇendra Sarasvatī, or about the Śrīvidyā Tantric ritual he practiced to bring about a union with the divine in the form of the goddess Lalitā Tripurasundarī.

Thus, while themselves cultivating a particular devotional experience, theologians such as Nīlakaṇṭha worked in public circles to constitute the boundaries of a community of marked individuals: Śaivas in public, but very possibly something else in the privacy of their homes. What, then, do scholars of religion have to gain by understanding this layering of public and private religion, a key feature of

Hindu religious identity since the early modern centuries? These religious publics, shaped by sectarian Hindu communities, point to an important qualification for our efforts to define Hinduism as a unitary religion. By examining the emergence of the distinct religious publics of early modern south India, I aim to demonstrate that in a fundamental sense, Hinduism has not been homologized. With its multiple religious publics coexisting in the same geographic space, and with its division between public and private modes of religiosity, Hinduism is a religion structured around diversity and bifurcated identities. In modern Indian society, these multiple religious publics make room for difference not by erasing religion in the public sphere but by publicizing it, so to speak, to facilitate the coexistence of diverse realities. The Smārta-Śaiva tradition, in short, epitomizes a popular adage, circulated for centuries, that encapsulates the multilayered experience of Hindu religious identity: "A Vaiṣṇava in public, a Śaiva in the home, a Śākta in the heart.

4

The Language Games of Śiva

Mapping Text and Space in Public Religious Culture

By what process does a text—a product of the written word—depart from the materiality of a palm-leaf manuscript to enter, irrevocably, the domain of public culture? What does it mean for a religious text, a compendium of sacred mythology, to go public, to seemingly cut beyond local publics defined by caste, religion, and even language? These are questions, on one hand, about the sheer dynamics of circulation, the material factors facilitating the spread of knowledge. But on the other hand, these selfsame questions interrogate the very nature of the public itself in early modern India—of space and its relation to the public religious culture that enlivens it with a shared sense of significance.

For the majority of Madurai's modern-day residents, no work of literature better captures the spirit of the city than does the *Tiruviḷaiyāṭal Purāṇam* (*TVP*), or the "Sacred Games of Śiva." The *TVP* threads together sixty-four mythological vignettes illustrating Śiva's divine intervention—in other words, his cosmic play (Skt. *līlā*, Tamil *viḷaiyāṭal*)—in the city of Madurai. In the process, the "Sacred Games" effectively maps Madurai's *religious* landscape onto the *spatial* terrain of the city itself, so that its defining topography comes to be seen as shaped by Śiva's sacred play. It was here, indeed, by the banks of the river that defines the old city, that Śiva set down (*vai*) his hand (*kai*) on the ground to quench the thirst of an unruly wedding guest, bringing forth the gushing torrents of Madurai's Vaikai River. Likewise, on the outskirts of town, to this very day stands the distinctively elephant-shaped Yānaimalai mountain, an elephantine war machine launched by the Jains of Madurai as they assailed their Śaiva adversaries, frozen in place by Sundareśvara, the "Beautiful Lord" Śiva come to earth in the form of Madurai's king. It is Śiva himself who dwells, alongside his green-skinned consort Mīnākṣī,

137

at the spatial and ritual heart of the city, Madurai's Mīnākṣī-Sundareśvara Temple, located at the center of both text and landscape. Above all, the temple is home to one of the most extravagant ritual performances in contemporary south India: the wedding of Mīnākṣī and Sundareśvara, the most celebrated of the sixty-four sacred games, brought to life in an annual festival that attracts throngs of pilgrims during the month of Cittirai (April/May).[1]

And yet, before the sixteenth century, these narratives were scarcely known outside of the elite circles of Tamil literati. One cannot help but wonder, then, how it happened that Madurai as a city came to be *entextualized* by a single work of Tamil literature. Indeed, the seventeenth-century *Tiruviḷaiyāṭal Purāṇam* of Parañcōti Muṉivar has come to be accepted by popular religious culture and temple authorities alike as the sole canonical instantiation of the sixty-four sacred games.[2] First premiered before a public audience in the Mīnākṣī-Sundareśvara Temple itself, Parañcōti's *TVP* is a text inseparable from its context. Parañcōti composed his masterpiece, more than likely, during the reign of Tirumalai Nāyaka, post-Vijayangara regent of Madurai, whose enthusiasm for temple renovation had radically transformed the visual contours of the city center. Writing at a pivotal moment in the city's history, Parañcōti had every reason to sing the praises of Madurai as sacred center and center of power, and his extended prologues on the incomparability of Madurai and Mīnākṣī's temple leave little doubt as to his affections for his hometown. His exposition of the sacred marriage, rhetorical centerpiece of the epic and liturgical centerpiece of the temple's annual calendar, waxes eloquent for nearly two hundred verses about the jeweled wedding pavilions and garlands of basil and *campaka* flowers, down to the minute details of the ceremony's ritual implements, as if to evoke a panorama that was, literally, lived reality to his readers. The *TVP*, succinctly, is a textual icon that points directly to the lived space of the city of Madurai.

A similar cycle of sixty-four "Sacred Games of Śiva" was first compiled around the thirteenth century by Perumparrapuliyūr Nampi.[3] Although certain individual episodes we find in Nampi's work had surfaced on various earlier occasions in Tamil literary history,[4] no evidence survives to indicate that a complete canon of Śiva's sixty-four divine sports had ever been previously compiled. Writing in Cidambaram, the medieval seat of Śaivism in Tamil Nadu, Nampi fashioned his *TVP* in a register of verse that intersected seamlessly with the tail end of the more classicized and ornamentalizing Cōla period literary culture.[5] He claimed initiation under a Śaiva pontiff, a certain Paramajñānaśivan operating out of the Māḷikai Maṭam,[6] a Śaiva monastery in the vicinity of Cidambaram. As a result, it may come as no surprise that Nampi's verse fuses a high Tamil literary idiom with the ethos of earlier Śaiva devotional (bhakti) hymns, in which both Madurai and Cidambaram were integrated into a network of Śaiva sacred sites spread across the Tamil landscape. Perhaps no aspect of the text better illustrates the divergence of Nampi's interest from that of Parañcōti than his treatment of the Sacred Marriage. In Nampi's work, the ceremony itself is relegated to a mere eight verses. Śiva concludes the wedding ceremony by graciously taking political command of the Pandian kingdom, his in-laws' estate, for he deems a mere woman, such as Mīnākṣī, obviously unfit to rule. The entire event, in fact, is entirely devoid of emotional affect. It is only in the following story, in which the sage Patañjali petitions Śiva to perform his cosmic dance in the city of Madurai—replicating the sacred center of Cidambaram's Golden Hall in his second, colonized home, the Silver Hall of the Madurai Mīnākṣī temple—that Madurai becomes a truly sacred city. Himself a foreigner to the cultural heartland of southern Tamil Nadu, Nampi reimagines Madurai as an embodiment of a translocal Tamil Śaivism, with little intent to engage with either the landscape or local populace of Madurai itself. As such, Nampi's work lends itself to interpretation as a novel and creative work of literature, synthesizing the scattered material of cultural memory into a textual artifact capable of entering, for the first time, the sphere of elite, translocal vernacular literature.

And yet, as we shall see, the "Sacred Games of Śiva" boasts a lengthy history of creation and re-creation, making it perhaps the most fluid literary motif in south Indian history, remarkable for its facility in traversing boundaries of language, class, sect, and locality. Originally—as it was for Nampi—*TVP* had been simply a text, with no pretensions to achieving scriptural authority or to being woven into the fabric of everyday life. Whereas the legends had previously been known only to premodern Tamil literati through the work of Nampi itself, the "Sacred Games of Śiva" irrupted suddenly into a more general popularity across the Tamil region in the sixteenth and seventeenth centuries, a period in which the genre of the Tamil *talapurāṇam* (sacred narrative of place; Skt.: *sthalapurāṇa*) surged in popularity in conjunction with the rising social, cultural, and economic prominence of the south Indian temple complex. Written for an entirely distinct literary and cultural milieu, a work like Parañcōti's thus speaks at once to an audience of literati and to popular enthusiasts already captivated by the cultural dynamism of the Madurai Nāyaka regime and the newfound social capital of the Mīnākṣī-Sundareśvara Temple. Over time, Parañcōti's rendering of the work became such a fixture of the religious culture of Madurai that it entirely eclipsed any public memory of Nampi's *TVP*, which remained an obscure fragment of literary history until (and perhaps even after) it resurfaced in the early twentieth century through the editorial craft of U. Ve. Caminataiyar.

Indeed, within the span of a single century, the *Tiruviḷaiyāṭal Purāṇam* made the transition from a highly delimited legend of place, restricted to the classics of Tamil literary culture, to a canonical fixture of Śaiva religiosity across south India, visually reenacted in sacred sites across the Tamil country. Over the course of a mere handful of decades, a narrative that had previously attracted little imitation prompted numerous transcreations in Tamil, Telugu, and Sanskrit, with Marathi and Kannada versions soon to follow. The legends even began to surface in temple murals, statuary, and public calendrical festivals in Madurai and beyond, a far cry from the hallowed halls of elite literary societies. The "Sacred Games of Śiva," one might argue, have permanently entered the public domain of the people of Madurai and, in fact, have become a pillar of the city's public religious culture.

In contemporary discourse on the public and publicity, the multiplicity of publics—or public spheres—has met with unproblematic acceptance in the aftermath of a spate of critiques responding to the English translation (1989) of Habermas's seminal work *The Structural Transformation of the Public Sphere.* The public in the singular—itself a largely imagined construct—is made multiple, recent theorists suggest, by the emergence of *counterpublics,* a term employed by Nancy Fraser (1991) and Michael Warner (2002), among others, to highlight the sites of subaltern resistance to a dominant cultural paradigm, where public discourse fragments to give voice to subordinated identities of gender, ethnicity, or sexuality. Likewise, in the south Indian context, to describe the "Sacred Games" in Madurai as a fixture of public culture in the singular immediately raises the question of who, precisely, constitutes such a public. More often than not, the working assumption of most interpreters would be to presume that such a public is simply coterminous with Brahminical normativity. In such a formulation, Brahminism is unproblematically treated as the South Asian equivalent of the bourgeois public sphere. Like its European analogue, which presumes that only an educated, enfranchised populace constitutes such a public, an Indian "bourgeois public sphere" would exclude the majority of Madurai's population.

But does such a framework fit with the evidence at hand, or was the situation on the ground more complex? In early modern south India, *publics* were likewise indubitably multiple, but the factors that delimit one from another remain obscure. Did Vēḷāḷas—considered Śūdras by Hindu legal code, despite their considerable wealth and social prestige—belong to the same public as Smārta Brahmins? Given south India's history of linguistic—and literary—pluralism, did native speakers of Tamil belong to the same public as speakers of Telugu? Did the Śaivas of Madurai, frequenters of the Madurai Mīnākṣī temple, belong to the same religious public as the Vaiṣṇavas who attended the rival Aḻakar Temple just outside the city?

When speaking of religious publics in early modern south India, we have seen, over the preceding chapters, that Hinduism—as an umbrella category for describing multiple religious traditions—was never fashioned as a social imaginary distinct from the sectarian communities it comprised. No concept of *the* religious public had yet been constructed among south Indian Hindus, much less one that equitably incorporated Muslims, Christians, or Jains in the Tamil country. Arguably, indeed, the singular notion of *the public* as such, founded as it was upon a disembodied, normativizing conception of communicative reason, proves conceptually intractable in the South Asian domain and, perhaps, ultimately incommensurable with the nature of publicity in early modern India. The religious publics of early modern south India, then—coterminous, to a large extent, with the sectarian networks of Śaiva and Vaiṣṇava religious communities—were not counterpublics in the strict sense, were provided with no overarching public in the singular in defiance of which they might aim to construct a particularized, subaltern identity.

How, then, did the "Sacred Games of Śiva" manage to transcend the boundaries of south India's multiple public spheres, differentiated along lines of caste, language, and religion? By excavating its multilingual textual history, I aim to narrate the journey of the *TVP* from text to public culture, a trajectory that left few boundaries uncrossed—particularly the boundary of language. While originally a classic of refined Tamil literature, the *TVP* gained widespread traction only when detached from its original moorings in temporally and culturally distinct literary culture to circulate across Madurai's multiple publics through a discursive process of literary—and even visual—re-creation. Emerging first as an aesthetic fashion among cultured elites writing in Tamil, Telugu, *and* Sanskrit, the narratives began to surface within a matter of decades in temple murals, statuary, and calendrical festivals, thus entering the public domain irreversibly. Their becoming public, and transcending the text, thus, has quite a bit to do with the appeal it generated first among reading publics in multiple languages, followed by its visual and performative enshrinement in public space. In this light, the publication of the text itself can only be "read"—figuratively speaking—through its evocations in temple art, architecture, and public festivals, a fashion that *followed*, rather than preceded, its irruption into the spheres of south India's literary publics.

While the precolonial textual archive often occludes dynamics of extratextual circulation, the "Sacred Games" may prove an exception to the rule, entering public discourse with remarkable visibility by the mid-seventeenth century. Take, for instance, the benedictory verse to a seventeenth-century grammatical work attributed to the renowned polymath Appayya Dīkṣita, the *Prākṛtamaṇidīpikā*,[7] a handbook designed to promote literacy in the Prakrit language among Sanskrit playwrights:

> May that battle of the Pandian princess with Parameśvara
> At the time of their marriage protect [you],
> In which victory belonged to both equally—
> Marvelous in that Śiva and Śivā both obtained each other.[8]

Although somewhat unexpected in a didactic work on Prakrit grammar, the verse at hand refers unmistakably to the most widely known of Śiva's sports in Madurai: his wedding to Mīnākṣī, who had taken birth in Madurai as the Pandian princess Taṭātakai. When the child, much to her father's chagrin, was born with an extra breast, the sage Agastya assured the family that if the girl were raised as the crown prince and trained in warfare, the extraneous breast would disappear as soon as she first encountered her future husband. In time, the young Taṭātakai grew to maturity and set out to conquer the directions, finally ascending toward Mount Kailāsa to defeat Śiva himself on the battlefield. Upon beholding her opponent, Taṭātakai's third breast disappeared and she bashfully laid down her weapons in deference to her future husband, after which the pair proceeded to Madurai to make arrangements for their wedding. Given the ellipticality of his verse, Appayya must have expected his readership—scholars and poets working within the Sanskrit knowledge systems—to readily supply the remainder of the narrative, despite its vernacular literary origins. Evidently, by the seventeenth century, the "Sacred Games" had achieved a certain currency among cultured audiences outside the Tamil literary fold.

As a point of comparison, another intriguing reference to the "Sacred Games" preserved in Madurai's Jesuit chronicles demonstrates beyond a doubt that less than a century later, the *TVP* narratives had spread far beyond the confines of courtly literary communities. Writing in 1700, a certain P. Pierre Martin describes the storytelling activities of a local Madurai woman as follows:

> Her sixty-year-old mother distinguishes herself by her skill in winning souls for Jesus Christ; I want to quote an example for you. Before her conversion, she was firmly devoted to her sect and knew by heart all the fables of her idols. Her delight was to recount them and she did so with grace; her neighbors had no sweeter recreation than to come and sit around her to listen to them. As soon as she had received baptism, she invited her friends, who hastily rushed up to her and begged her to recite some *Game* of Śiva. "Oh! Those are just old stories," responded our good storyteller, "but I'm going to give you one that is really something else! It's completely new; I've only known it myself for several days. If you listen to me with attention, I will let you know the place where we go after death, where our friends and ancestors have gone, where we will go in turn."[9]

Considering that, although the Jesuit author of the above letter held little interest in the content of the woman's "idolatrous" narratives, he was able to readily classify them as "Games of Śiva" suggests that the *TVP* legends had made the transition from literary text to popular mythology by the end of the seventeenth century, such that the cycle had become virtually synonymous with oral Śaiva narrative for her captive audience. A respected elder by the year 1700, this woman came of age in a Madurai that had only recently witnessed the widespread temple renovation program of Tirumalai Nāyaka (1623–1659), who famously restructured the annual Cittirai Festival and instituted a number of calendrical observances to publicly showcase episodes of the *TVP*.[10] Narratives that may have been just beginning to rise to popularity in her youth had become for her, by 1700, the "old stories."

By the end of the seventeenth century, then, text had transitioned to public religious culture: the *TVP* was no longer a classic of Tamil literature but popular mythology that had percolated into public conversation at social gatherings. But before the *TVP* had truly become a public phenomenon, it had begun to spread like wildfire among literary elites writing in multiple languages, giving rise to a veritable explosion of variant narratives. Fortunately, the literary and documentary archive of the early modern Tamil country provides ample resources for re-embedding Parañcōti's *TVP* within its original enunciatory context. What we meet with, in fact, is not a singular text—the *TVP* of Parañcōti—but a discursive sphere. The "Sacred Games" had so thoroughly captivated the literary imagination of the epoch that, by the middle of the seventeenth century, the *narrative cycle* inspired quite a number of transcreations not only in Tamil but in Telugu and Sanskrit as well, a surprising number of which preceded the premiere of Parañcōti's masterpiece. By examining this profusion of textual variants, we can learn to read the *TVP* less as an isolated work of creative genius that inexplicably caught hold of public imagination and more as a discursive act, conditioned and made possible by a network of multilingual circulation. It was this process, in fact, that eventually resulted in the public reception of Parañcōti's *Tiruviḷaiyāṭal Purāṇam* as the singular *talapurāṇam* of Madurai, relegating its competitors to the footnotes of history.

Language boundaries, in everyday wisdom, are conceived of as permeable only through the concerted effort of translation, an intention to make the local intelligible beyond the intimate boundaries of a speech community. How—and why—did the *TVP* begin to circulate so seamlessly across Tamil, Telugu, and Sanskrit speech communities, with Kannada and Marathi soon to follow? As Ludwig Wittgenstein famously made clear, there is no such thing as a private language—all languages are by definition public by virtue of their invocation of a set of shared, intersubjective insights about reality. The games of language we play, conditioned by socially shared conventions and rules, cannot help but give rise to the very acts of communication they make possible, and the sacred games of Śiva are no exception. By examining the dynamics of language, circulation, and textuality during this formative period (ca. 1550–1650) when the *TVP* irrevocably broke from the constraints of the palm-leaf manuscript, we can see how a text gone public can transition from emerging object of literary interest to public religious canon, simultaneously fixed and open for critical response. It is this process of multilingual circulation, codification, and publication, succinctly, that interests us—and that is what I describe as the "Language Games of Śiva."

MANY *TIRUVIḶAIYĀṬAL PURĀṆAMS*: THE INVENTION OF THE *STHALAPURĀṆA* OF MADURAI

The literary sphere of the seventeenth-century Tamil region, while situated unambiguously in India's Vernacular Millennium,[11] fostered a number of flourishing literary traditions, not least among them a prolific network of cosmopolitan Sanskrit literati. Indeed, in the wake of the fragmentation of the Vijayanagara Empire, the Nāyaka kingdoms of Madurai and Tanjavur, heirs in the Tamil country to its cultural prestige, continued Vijayangara's liberal patronage of poets writing in both Sanskrit and the vernacular. Operating in such close quarters and competing for patronage and performance opportunities, the poets of the Nāyaka-period literary sphere,[12] whether writing in Tamil, Telugu, or Sanskrit, necessarily developed an acute awareness of each other's presence. Such an awareness is often overtly manifested in their literary creations, which show ample evidence of intertextual influence and response.

Perhaps unsurprisingly, some of these poets held less than favorable opinions of their competitors. Take, for instance, this verse by Nīlakaṇṭha Dīkṣita from his Sanskrit *mahākāvya,* or classical epic, the *Śivalīlārṇava,*[13] or "The Ocean of the Games of Śiva":

> Through the decadence of the Kali Yuga, having strayed from the
> Path of suggestion [*vyaṅgyapatham*] dear to the learned, disregard-
>   ing scripture,
> [Bad poets] have acquired a taste for poetic feats [*citra*] of word and
>   meaning—
> Much like the passion of hicks for vernacular texts.[14]

Such disapproval of vernacular literature may seem unremarkable coming from Nīlakaṇṭha Dīkṣita, descendant of one of India's most learned Brahmin intellectual families, ranked among the most celebrated Sanskrit poets of the second millennium—were it not for the fact that this statement *itself* appears in what is in fact an adaptation of a vernacular text, narrating in the form of a Sanskrit epic the *Tiruviḷaiyāṭal Purāṇam,* the sixty-four "Sacred Games of Śiva" in Madurai. When reembedded in its immediate discursive context, then, Nīlakaṇṭha's *Śivalīlārṇava* opens up a number of questions about the role of language choice in a diverse, multilingual society such as south India after the rise of vernacularism. Bronner and Shulman (2006), for instance, raise just such a question in their article, "'A Cloud Turned Goose': Sanskrit in the Vernacular Millennium." Masterfully excavating the multilingual resonances in a number of seventeenth-century works of Sanskrit literature from the Tamil country, Bronner and Shulman demonstrate beyond a doubt that the Sanskrit literary tradition in the South had become thoroughly conversant with, and in some ways dependent upon, the thematic and stylistic conventions of the vernacular. Whether the *Śivalīlārṇava* was truly intended to harmonize with a preexisting vernacular literary canon, however, deserves a more nuanced consideration.[15] Indeed, Bronner and Shulman interpret the *Śivalīlārṇava* as something of a replica of the Tamil original, largely conforming to its intentionality and cultural agenda. By describing the text as a "rendition of an earlier Tamil equivalent," the authors presume, perhaps inadvertently, that the text's only intention was to "give voice" to a vernacular world that was preexistent in its entirety—and, by implication, essentially timeless.[16]

As we shall see, in the process of recasting the *Tiruviḷaiyāṭal Purāṇam* narrative, the *Śivalīlārṇava* did incorporate quite a number of cultural allusions familiar primarily to an educated Tamil readership. It is not every day, after all, that we meet with elegant depictions in literary Sanskrit of the founding of the Tamil Caṅkam or of the exploits of the Tamil Śaiva bhakti saints Ñānacampantar and Māṇikkavācakar, which Nīlakaṇṭha faithfully included in his Sanskrit rendition of these sixty-four popular Tamil legends. To view Nīlakaṇṭha, however, as faithfully transcribing a Tamil idiom in Sanskrit would misread the bold and often subversive intent of the text. Indeed, the first canto of the *Śivalīlārṇava* consists almost entirely of a highly specific literary-theoretical critique of Nīlakaṇṭha's fellow *Sanskrit* poets. We find here, for instance, a sarcastic diatribe against much of second-millennium (post-Mammaṭa) trends in poetic practice, such as the near-exclusive reliance on feats of language fashionable in the Nāyaka courts in which the formal properties of poetry are privileged over its content. Nīlakaṇṭha expresses disdain, for instance, for *citra kāvya*—pictorial poetry (think Apollinaire in twentieth-century France)—and *yamaka*, a type of paronomasia that repeats the same sequence of syllables in entirely different words. Indeed, the very suggestion that poetry should be founded upon feats of language rather than the beauty of suggested meaning was anathema to Nīlakaṇṭha:

> In the Kṛta Yuga, suggestion [*vyañjanā*] became incarnate;
> In the Treta Yuga, it became subordinated [*guṇībabhūva*];
> In the third age, there were feats of meaning [*arthacitra*];
> And in the fourth age, a profusion of twinning rhymes [*yamaka*].

> Indeed, having ascended to the overlordship of poetry,
> The resolute do not delight in mere feats of language [*śabdacitra*].
> Having reached the abode of celestial women in heaven,
> How could any one-eyed woman be worth approaching?

> Did the creator fill the mouths of the feebleminded with garlic,
> And sprinkle bitter neem juice?
> If not, from whence comes the putrid odor and acridity
> When speech is issuing forth from them?[17]

In these verses, Nīlakaṇṭha's polemic can be read intelligibly only within the context of a thoroughly Sanskritic conversation on aesthetics, specifically invoking the authority of the eighth-century literary theorist Ānandavardhana, who made the case in his masterwork, the *Dhvanyāloka* (The illumination of implicature), that poetry was made beautiful only by the complex interplay of literal and suggested meaning.[18] As with the entirety of the first canto of the *Śivalīlārṇava*, this discourse was evidently intended for an audience not only proficient in Sanskrit but also thoroughly versed in the canon of Sanskrit literary theory. How can we make sense of this canto as figuring into a text that ostensibly celebrates the heritage of a distinctively Tamil vernacular culture? Given that such a polemic would have been all but unintelligible to anyone outside the orbit of the cosmopolitan Sanskrit literary tradition, it may not be accurate to claim that the *Śivalīlārṇava* simply "participated along with" the vernacular in Nīlakaṇṭha's day and age. To make such a suggestion, as Bronner and Shulman have done, presumes that vernacular literature in general operated out of a unified intentionality—that of "inventing and elaborating . . . cultural identities."[19] And given that Nīlakaṇṭha was a notorious satirist, first-rate literary mind, and public figure in the literary salon and court of Madurai, his own intentionality in composing the *Śivalīlārṇava* is far from cut-and-dried.

To more fully appreciate what may have motivated Nīlakaṇṭha to compose a unique and interstitial work requires, above all, a nuanced understanding of its enunciatory context—in this case, both the institutional structure of the multilingual literary sphere in which it took part, and the textual history of the Tamil "original," the *Tiruviḷaiyāṭal Purāṇam*. The Nāyaka period of south India in particular, a period of rapid social and political transformation, provides us with an ideal arena to explore such questions. A multilingual literary sphere such as this, which fostered multiple vernacular traditions (namely, Tamil and Telugu) with competing sources of institutional sponsorship and patronage, allows us to bracket the Sanskrit-vernacular binary in favor of a model that situates multilingual literary production within its diverse social and institutional settings. It also illuminates the social embeddedness of Sanskrit literary and intellectual discourse, as exemplified by the particular case of Nīlakaṇṭha Dīkṣita. Nīlakaṇṭha's *Śivalīlārṇava* is no accident of literary genius outside of time and space, but an active response to the multidimensional social and literary milieu in which his *mahākāvya* was deliberately articulated.

Just how many *Tiruviḷaiyāṭal Purāṇam*s are there? What little scholarship has been devoted to the subject is unequivocal:[20] there are *two TVPs*, the lesser-known *TVP* of Perumparrapuliyūr Nampi, dated most convincingly to the late thirteenth century, and the celebrated *TVP* of Parañcōti Muṉivar, belonging most likely to the late sixteenth or early seventeenth century.[21] The latter, comprising nearly twice the number of verses found in Nampi's version, incorporated a number of innovations that distinguish it from its "original" counterpart, substantially reordering of the sequence of games and replacing three of Nampi's sixty-four episodes with entirely distinct narratives. In addition to these two primary Tamil variants, a single Sanskrit Purāṇic rendering has been attested, the Hālāsya Māhātmya, which, given the radical proliferation of manuscripts transmitted in numerous south Indian scripts, seems to have been transmitted widely across the southern half of the subcontinent since at least the eighteenth century.[22] In short, given our current knowledge of the *TVP*'s textual history, previous scholarship on the work(s) has focused nearly exclusively on two issues: a narratological comparison of the two Tamil *purāṇams*, and the adjudication of the relative priority of Parañcōti's *TVP* and the Hālāsya Māhātmya. The latter, by virtue of its Sanskrit Purāṇic pedigree, is by and large presumed to have preceded the *TVP*, with very little evidence adduced to support this conclusion.

Our textual archive, however, renders the actual number of *Tiruviḷaiyāṭal Purāṇams* somewhat more ambiguous. Nampi, for his part, nowhere refers to his own work under the title *Tiruviḷaiyāṭal Purāṇam*, claiming simply to have "spoken the sixty-four Sacred Games of Cokkaṉ" (*cokkaṉ viḷaiyāṭa laṟu pattu nāṉkuñ coṉṉēṉ*) contained in the "great *purāṇam* of Madurai" (*māmaturaip purāṇam*).[23] This may come as no surprise given its relatively early date compared to most representatives of the mature *talapurāṇam* genre, which truly established itself as a fixture of Tamil literary practice around the fifteenth and sixteenth centuries. More tellingly, however, our earliest-known literary references to Nampi's *purāṇam* seem similarly uninterested in designating the work as the *Tiruviḷaiyāṭal Purāṇam*. One such work, the *Payakaramālai* (Skt. *Bhayaharamālā*), refers to its project of rendering Nampi's work in a brief garland of sixty-four verses in the following terms:

> Rejoicing, I complete reciting all sixty-four of the primordial sports
> of Our Lord,
> Praising Perumpaṟṟapuliyūr Nampi, chief among the Kauṇḍinya
> Gotra,
> Ruling over Celli garlanded with beautiful lotus flowers.
>
> Is it not the case, in the Kappinci land in the region bearing the
> fertility of rain clouds,
> I speak the sixty-four sports of the one garlanded in mountain
> ebony flowers
> Of Nampi of the famous Tillai, ruling over the auspicious southern
> town of Celli,
> Adjoining the place known as Caturvedimangalam of Paraśurāma.[24]

In short, our literary archive provides us with little evidence to discern whether Nampi's composition acquired its title from within the tradition or as a result of a superimposition of modern scholarship linking it directly with Parañcōti's better-known rendering of the narrative. To break with the arbitrary pairing of the two *TVP*s, then, permits us to narrow our scope of inquiry from the ahistorical domain of myth criticism, shifting our focus away from purely narratological concerns such as the sequence of episodes in favor of a more socially embedded approach to texts and literary institutions. In fact, our textual archive tells a different story: we meet with no complete retellings of the "Sacred Games" between the lifetime of Nampi and the mid-sixteenth century, after which point we witness a sudden explosion of variant narratives crossing linguistic and social boundaries. The most significant of these pre-Parañcōti variants, in fact, is not in Tamil at all but in Telugu: the *Cokkanātha Caritramu* (The story of Cokkanātha) of Tiruvēṅgaḷakavi (circa 1540).[25] This unique work was patronized by the pair of subchieftains Pedda Rāma and Cinna Rāma, who operated out of southern Tamil Nadu in the vicinity of Ramnad, significantly removed from Madurai's cultural orbit. Nevertheless, the Telugu *Cokkanātha Caritramu* is arguably the earliest example of a complete translation—or perhaps more accurately "transcreation"—of the full sixty-four sacred games postdating the thirteenth-century Nampi.[26] Indeed, much like Nampi, as a member of the vernacular literary elite residing at a distance from Madurai itself, Tiruvēṅgaḷakavi held little interest—either regional or rhetorical—in sacralizing the landscape of Madurai.

A number of fairly early works, dating to the first half of the sixteenth century, show an increased fascination with the *TVP* narrative. The *Tiruvuccāttānar Nāṉmaṇimālai* of Nociyūr Palaṉiyappaṉ Cervaikkārar (Tamil, circa 1527), for instance, while largely concerned with other matters, includes a chapter that condenses Nampi's ordering of the sacred games into an easily digestible set of verses. Likewise, the *Kālahasti Māhātmyamu* of Dhurjaṭi (Telugu, circa 1509–1529), authored by a poet traditionally revered as one of eight literary celebrities (*aṣṭadiggajulu*) of the Vijayanagara court of Kṛṣṇadevarāya, incorporates—possibly for the first time—a cycle of the Tamil *Tiruviḷaiyāṭal* legends into a Telugu text.[27] Within the domain of Madurai itself, the *Maduraic Cokkanātar Ulā* of Purāṇa Tirumalainātar (Tamil, early sixteenth century), belongs to the Ulā genre of Tamil literature, a literary form centered on the motif of the formal public procession of a ruler or deity in a particular locality—in the present instance, Cokkanātar or Sundareśvara of Madurai. While recounting the procession of Sundareśvara through the streets of Madurai, the *Cokkanātar Ulā* sprinkles allusions to several of the games of Śiva.

By the mid- to late sixteenth century, we begin to encounter a number of complete renditions of the sixty-four games in multiple languages—including the *Cokkanātha Caritramu*—which thus predate Parañcōti's own masterpiece but often survive in fragmentary condition with numerous corruptions. Many have been all but forgotten by the scholars of Tamil or Telugu literary history. Take for instance, the *Cuntara Pāṇṭiyam* (The story of Sundara Pandian) of Aṉatāri (late sixteenth century), a virtually unstudied retelling of the "Sacred Games" in his incarnation as the Pandian ruler Sundareśvara, a work that despite its intriguing digressionary discussions of subtle body yoga and Śākta devotionalism, has only barely survived to this day. How many other authors like Aṉatāri set out to retell the "Sacred Games" only to have the manuscripts of their compositions dismissed by their colleagues or lost to subsequent generations?[28] We also encounter abortive attempts at alternative *talapurāṇams* of Madurai that subsume the "Sacred Games" under an entirely different narrative frame. The *Katampavaṉapurāṇam* (The purāṇa of the Kadamba Forest) of Vīmanāta Paṇṭitar, for instance claims to narrate the sacred history of the city from an entirely different stream of textual transmission, one that ostensibly was adapted from a Sanskrit work variously referred to as the *Kadambavanapurāṇa* or, synonymously, the *Nīpāraṇyapurāṇa*. Previous scholarship has assumed a somewhat earlier date for this work, as it incorporates within a structurally distinct mythological framework a single chapter that catalogues the sacred games according to Nampi's earlier sequence. This argument, however, neglects the fact that its author, Vīmanāta Paṇṭitar, refers directly to Parañcōti in the opening verses of the composition, adopting an almost apologetic tone for his audacity in putting forth another contender for Madurai's official *talapurāṇam*:

> Even after the existence of the *Tiruviḷaiyāṭal Purāṇam* flourishing
>   suitably with the sixty-four
> Told by the great Parañcōti Muṉivar of excellent fame through the
>   grace of Śiva,
> I commence to narrate in a manner in eleven chapters with fame
>   known across the earth surrounded by water,
> Having recited the story of the Sacred Games of the One Who Is
>   Like a Remedy, through the customs that grace the assembly.[29]

But precisely what sort of textual culture accompanied the *TVP*'s rise from obscurity to a place among the literary elite of multiple language communities? Why were these texts written, and was their enunciatory effect the same in Tamil, Sanskrit, and Telugu? In fact, it was not only the languages but also the institutions of literary circulation that had diverged radically in south India by the sixteenth century, leading to the emergence of distinct literary spheres that often intersected but operated out of disparate commitments in the domains of literature, politics, and devotion.

THE SITES OF MULTILINGUAL LITERARY
PRODUCTION IN NĀYAKA-PERIOD SOUTH INDIA

By the very definition of the genre, the Tamil *talapurāṇam*, a narrative of place, deals with the unique soteriological properties and divine exploits associated with a precise locality in the Tamil country. As these legends, more often than not, owe relatively little to the pan-Indic corpus of Sanskrit *purāṇas*, one might expect that authors of Tamil *talapurāṇams*, composed primarily of narratives that are strictly Tamil in geographical and cultural origin, would look no further than the extensive literary and devotional archive accumulated by well over a millennium of Tamil textual history. Nevertheless, from the very inception of the Tamil *talapurāṇam* genre, poets evidently felt compelled to provide these temporally and geographically delimited narratives with a stamp of approval from the transregional Sanskritic tradition by framing their compositions as translations, or perhaps transcreations, from original Sanskrit exempla. Such was the case with Nampi's *TVP*, one of the earliest-known examples of the *talapurāṇam* genre, which, despite the obviously Tamil origins of many of its episodes, Nampi informs us, was not originally transmitted in Tamil at all. Nampi claims, rather, to have drawn on an otherwise unattested Sanskrit "text" known as the Sārasamuccaya, contained in the Uttaramahāpurāṇa.[30] Based on the title—even setting aside its absence in manuscript history—there is good reason to doubt that an excerpt titled the "Compilation of Essences" (Sārasamuccaya) in the "Other Great Purāṇa" (Uttaramahāpurāṇa) ever existed at all.

The relationship between Sanskrit and vernacular in the early modern Tamil South, succinctly, may not be quite as cut-and-dried as it appears. Regardless of how strongly Nīlakaṇṭha Dīkṣita may have personally disapproved, the Nāyaka-period Tamil country belonged unmistakably to what Pollock (1998b) has termed the "Vernacular Millennium"; and in fact, vernacular literature flourished there in abundance. Not only did the region continue to foster its vibrant and prolific heritage of Tamil literary production, but also Nāyaka rulers, hailing from Andhra and formerly employed under the Vijayanagara Empire, imported along with their political rule a predilection for Telugu literature, which began to take root in the far South through their continued patronage. Of course, the social and political functions of vernacularization had been fully present in the Tamil region since the height of Cōḻa rule, when Tamil literature began to assume the role of the primary medium for royal encomium, adopting numerous stylistic and tropic features from the preexisting Sanskrit cosmopolitan tradition. Moreover, high Cōḻa literature was indubitably a courtly phenomenon, produced and publicized within the central networks of the empire's ruling elite and often directly underwriting the interests of royal power.

The vernacular of the Nāyaka period, however, took shape within a sphere of multiple competing cultural currents, creating a dynamic in which the emulation and implementation of received literary models did not flow unilaterally from the cosmopolitan to the vernacular, from the transregional to the language of place. In fact, literary classics were often adapted from one vernacular to another,[31] and just as often from the vernacular back into Sanskrit.[32] While the cosmopolitan vernacular, so to speak, often accompanies a certain documented social trajectory, much less is known about the sort of extratextual environment that would support such a multidirectional sphere of literary influence.

Given this apparent fluidity of interchange between competing literary currents—that is, given the ease with which the *content* of the literary craft traversed the boundaries of language—should we presume an equally fluid *social structure* facilitating the production and transmission of literary texts across distinct language-based communities? Certainly, the answer to this question varies considerably by geographical region, even during the time frame we have been referring to as India's "early modern" period (ca. 1500–1800). Literary production in the Nāyaka-period Tamil country need not have operated within institutional frameworks equivalent to those of the seventeenth-century Rājput courts of Rajasthan or anywhere else in the Indian subcontinent. The situation in south India, however, is further complicated by the coexistence of multiple vernacular traditions within a shared geographical and cultural space. In such a context, Pollock's model of the vernacular age might suggest that the competing vernacular literatures of south India ought to have equally inherited certain constitutive features of the Sanskrit cosmopolitan paradigm. For instance, we might expect, in the present case, that Tamil and Telugu works of literature were patronized at the same Nāyaka courts, performed in the same venues, and influenced equally by the rhetoric and values of the Sanskrit literary tradition.

With its broad appeal across linguistic lines, the *TVP* and its numerous multilingual variants provide us with an ideal arena where we may explore the extent to which these assumptions hold true for the south Indian case. Fortunately, the texts in question speak for themselves, providing information about their contexts of patronage and performance both explicitly and implicitly through the rhetorical tropes they invoke. Take, for instance, the following verse from the introduction to the *Cuntara Pāṇṭiyam*:

> Aṉatāri of the town of Vayarpati, in the court of
> The king Tiruviruntavaṉ in Kallur, offered in pure Tamil
> The Sanskrit text about the Nāyaka of Madurai Cuntara Pāṇṭiyaṉ,
> On the six-legged seat [*aṟukāṟpīṭam*] with jewels emitting rays of
>   light.[33]

What precisely is this "six-legged seat" that Aṉatāri so specifically foregrounds at the outset of his work? The remainder of the *Cuntara Pāṇṭiyam* provides us with no further clues, but fortunately Aṉatāri is not the only one of our authors to mention just such a six-legged seat with the same emphatic placement in the introductory verses of a work. In fact, the first verse of Parañcōti's *TVP* is structured around a fourfold pun on the term *aṟukāṟpīṭam*, suggesting that the term is more than an idiosyncratic turn of phrase:

> Like the nectar, the treasure presented [*araṅkēṟṟum*] by Māl who
>   had churned the ocean, exalted on his serpent seat [*aṟukāṟpīṭam*],
> Having sung in rare Tamil the greatness of Madurai where the
>   female beetles [*aṟukāṟpēṭu*] play music,

> Parañcōti Muṉi premiered [*araṅkēṟṟiṉāṉ*] [this work] from the six-
> legged seat [*aṟukārpīṭam*] surrounded by the gods in the
> Sanctuary of Cokkanātha, whose crown is dignified by the glory of a
> six-strand topknot [*aṟukārpīṭu*].[34]

Not only does Parañcōti inform us here of the location of his "six-legged seat"—that is, in the interior of the Madurai temple's shrine (*caṉṉati/sannidhi*) dedicated to Śiva as Sundareśvara or Cokkanātha—but he also connects this particular ritual platform directly with the institution of the literary premiere, or *araṅkēṟṟam*. The *araṅkēṟṟam*, as a literary-performative institution, survived well into the nineteenth century,[35] as a central pillar of preprint culture Tamil literary practice.[36] Seventeenth-century evidence suggests unambiguously that the *araṅkēṟṟam* was an established institution of Tamil literary performance in the period; one notable instance is an extant correspondence written by the poet Antakakkavi to his patron inviting him to the *araṅkēṟṟam* of his forthcoming work.[37] What we learn here, however, is that in the Nāyaka-period literary sphere in which Parañcōti premiered his highly influential *TVP*, the *araṅkēṟṟam* of a *talapurāṇam*, and possibly of other works bearing on the sacred sites of the Tamil Śaiva religious landscape, seems to have been directly facilitated by temple institutions. Thus, as Parañcōti informs us quite clearly, his *TVP* was debuted in the Madurai temple within the central shrine of Sundareśvara itself. Further evidence is supplied by the repeated mention of the *aṟukārpīṭam*, evidently a type of ceremonial platform on which a poet sat when premiering his work.[38] Although little memory remains today about just what type of material artifact the *aṟukārpīṭam* was and how it was employed in literary performance, sufficient evidence exists to confirm that such a platform did (or perhaps still does) exist in the Mīṉākṣī-Sundareśvara Temple,[39] if not also in similar Śaiva temples elsewhere in Tamil Nadu. Succinctly, Parañcōti informs us here that his *TVP* was presented publicly within a ceremonial-performative context that linked the text's literary virtues with the temple itself as a venue of performance, a politico-religious institution that structured the social prestige of literary patronage.

But just who were these sponsors of the literary works, such as Parañcōti's, that were publicly premiered at major temple sites? In some cases, temple officials or priests seem to have played an instrumental role in encouraging an author to embark on composing a sacerdotal literary work in the Tamil language, ostensibly translated from a Sanskrit original. Vīmanāta Paṇṭitar, author of the *Katampavaṉapurāṇam*, for instance, describes his impetus to begin his work in just such a fashion, claiming that the temple priests (*talattōr*) requested that he translate into Tamil the Sanskrit Purāṇa on the greatness of the Kadambavana, the Kadamba forest that preceded the urbanized landscape of Madurai:

> When the temple priests [*talattōr*]—endowed with a fame that that
> has risen to flourish across the prosperous earth

> That is suitable to those who worship of the Lord who lives in
>   southern Madurai of singular fertility—said to tell in the southern
>   language,
> With love that perceives clearly, the northern book on the Greatness
>   of the cool Katampa forest fertile with beauty,
> I commenced to narrate through His grace, with verdantly flourish-
>   ing garlands of verse in the Viruttam meter.[40]

That said, as the regional megatemples of south India—such as the Madurai temple—had by this period become significant centers of political and economic exchange, we should not underestimate the impetus for subordinate chieftains to participate as exhaustively as possible in this transactional network. Numerous other authors, such as Aṉatāri, author of the *Cuntara Pāṇṭiyam,* cite as individual patrons of their works, not the Nāyaka kings of Madurai or Tanjavur, but generally their subvassals who had established smaller regional courts at various locations throughout the Tamil region. This decentralized form of patronage is a distinctive feature of what has been described, though not without some trepidation, as the feudal political structure of the Nāyaka regimes. From the Vijayanagara period onward, the term *nāyaka* was applied to describe a regional feudatory ruler subservient to the centralized authority of the empire. Even after Madurai and Tanjavur had attained functional independence from the declining Vijayangara state, the term was retained as a key feature of political discourse, first perhaps as a rhetorical gesture of humility but later as a functional description of the similar political hierarchy that had emerged under the Nāyaka regimes themselves. Nāyaka vassals, too, often referred to themselves by the title *nāyaka,* and breakaway states frequently emerged in competition with the generally prevailing authority of Madurai and Tanjavur. This increasingly decentralized political structure appears to have provided subchieftains and subordinate officers with a heightened incentive to engage directly in the patronage of Tamil literature, especially works of more overtly theological import that offered avenues for advancement in the competitive prestige economy centered on major temple institutions.[41]

Such was the case with Aṉatāri, author of the *Cuntara Pāṇṭiyam,* who in the above verse describes his patron as a certain subordinate officer, Tiruviruntavaṉ of Kallur. He then further elaborates the complex chain of hierarchy that linked his direct patron, Tiruviruntavaṉ, with the centralized Nāyaka authority of Madurai under Kacci Vīrappa Nāyaka, apparently through the mediation of a certain tertiary figure, Cevvanti, who held some official role at the Madurai court and evidently held favor among the Nāyaka as well:

> The truthful southern one, Tiruviruntāṉ Cavuntaraṉ—friend of
> Cevvanti of the *sabhā,* who is endowed with the favor of such a man,
>   surrounded by sovereigns,

> Known as the king Kacci Vīrappa—said to tell with a southern
>   treatise
> The story flourishing in the language of the gods; thus I undertook
>   to tell it.[42]

Such was the case as well for the author of the *Cokkanātar Ulā,* Purāṇa Tirumalaināṭar, who names as his patron Vīramāraṉ, functionary or ruler in a certain locality known as Mulaicai, whose anniversary of rule he celebrates with the composition of the work in question, narrativizing the occasion as the impetus for Cokkanātha's public procession:

> On the day commemorating the affectionate rule of the earth,
> Surrounded by the ocean, by Vīramāraṉ, of southern Mulaicai of the
>   Vedic books,
> The primordial sovereign god, the Lord residing of Madurai
>   Tiruvālavāy,
> Graciously came in procession.[43]

In short, whereas patronage may in some cases have derived from temple officials directly, in most cases it was more likely granted by various subvassals of the Nāyaka rulers or upstart rivals at minor courts who aimed to enhance their standing in the economy of ritual exchange centered on honors distributed by the Mīnākṣī-Sundareśvara Temple. A third factor, however, that significantly influenced the structures of literary circulation among Tamil Śaiva poets of the sixteenth and seventeenth centuries was participation in the devotional networks of prominent Tamil Śaiva monastic centers, such as Tarumapuram or Tiruvavatuturai. These monastic centers had increased dramatically in economic social prominence over the preceding centuries[44] and, by the sixteenth and seventeenth centuries, seem to have provided a crucial venue for circulating of literary works and fostering poetic talent among those who wished to participate in Tamil literary circles.[45] Cultivating a distinctively Tamil Śaiva identity in contrast to the Sanskritic lineages of the Śaiva Siddhānta,[46] these monasteries attracted mainly lay participants of Vēḷāḷa social origin.[47] While Vēḷāḷa castes were technically considered Śūdra in origin, their representatives had often attained an elevated social standing in this period as major landholders and managers of agricultural property.[48]

It is no accident, in fact, that the vast majority of Śaiva poets writing in Tamil during this period who provide us with any biographical information explicitly professed a Vēḷāḷa caste origin[49] as well as affiliation with spiritual preceptors of the Tamil Śaiva lineages. Among the authors of *TVP* variant narratives, a prime example is Vīmanāta Paṇṭitar, author of the *Katampavaṉapurāṇam,* who directly links his poetic endeavors with his caste origin:

> I aim to expound the ancient book, the Purāṇam of the forest of
>   young Katampa trees with golden blossoms, by the nectarean
>   grace of the Lord,
> While sweetly singing poets recite, in fertile Tamil, in the manner
>   stated by Agastya, sage of the Potiyam mountain.
> I, Vīmanātaṉ of Ilambur, who gives renown to the Lord with the
>   great lotus eyes, the fame of the southern king,
> Examining thoroughly the Purāṇam that inquires into the true path,
>   I compose the great devotion of the Vēḷāḷas of the clan of the river
>   Gaṅgā.[50]

It was not merely caste alone, however, that provided a social foundation for the continued patronage of Tamil literature; rather, it required the mediation of monastic institutions that structured their ideological self-representation on the Vēḷāḷa heritage of its founders and lay participants. It is perhaps no surprise, then, that Vēḷāḷa authors of Tamil Śaiva literature in this period often participated openly and actively in the development of these increasingly prominent devotional centers. The prototypic example of such a poet is Kumārakurupara, a seventeenth-century contemporary of Tirumalai Nāyaka who authored numerous works dedicated primarily to the goddess Mīnākṣī of Madurai.[51] After a long-standing connection with the *maṭam*s at Tarumapuram and Tiruvavatuturai, Kumārakurupara is believed to have been sent northward by his lineage preceptors to establish a branch *maṭam* of the Tamil Śaiva tradition in Varanasi. From among authors of the *TVP* corpus, one highly specific reference speaks to the sectarian allegiance of the family of Purāṇa Tirumalaināṭar, author of the *Cokkanāṭar Ulā*. His son, in his grammatical work the *Citamparappāṭiyal,* informs us of his family's close affiliation with the Tamil Śaiva lineage,[52] referring unmistakably to the lineage's founder, Meykaṇṭar, and even suggesting that he composed the work in question at the behest of a later preceptorial figure, Tatuvañāṉaprakācar (Skt. Tattvajñānaprakāśa):

> Meykaṇṭāṉ of Veṇṇai, whose gardens flourish with flowers,
> Having come as Tatuvañāṉaprakācar, who adorns Kanchi with fame,
> By the grace of him who said to tell it, so that the meters may flourish,
> Having praised his feet, I apportion the *Citamparappāṭiyal.*[53]

A great deal of research remains to be done on the influence of Tamil Śaiva monasteries on both the literary sphere of early modern Tamil Nadu and its expression in public religious culture, despite their social influence and avid patronage of religious expression in diverse media. For instance, a significant portion of temple mural paintings produced during the sixteenth and seventeenth centuries was sponsored directly by highly ranked administrators or members of these same Tamil Śaiva monasteries.[54] In short, present evidence strongly suggests that the

Tamil literary sphere of the sixteenth and seventeenth centuries had become intimately intertwined with the Tamil Śaiva monastic lineages as an institutional foundation for literary patronage and circulation. The dynamics of Tamil textuality in the early modern Tamil country, then, were markedly distinct from what we observe in the case of both Telugu and Sanskrit literature of the period: Tamil literariness, in early modern Madurai, was centered upon its production, performance, and circulation within the Śaiva monastery.

The patronage of Telugu literature, on the other hand, even within the same time frame and geographical region, diverges significantly from the Tamil case. One striking example, for instance, is the *Cokkanātha Caritramu* of Tiruvēṅgaḷakavi, a text that relates the same cycle of narratives but with a rhetoric that marks its social location as distinct from that of its Tamil counterparts. This unique work was patronized by a pair of subchieftains, Pedda Rāma and Cinna Rāma,[55] who operated out of southern Tamil Nadu in the vicinity of Ramnad. It is arguably the earliest example of a complete translation—or perhaps more accurately "transcreation"—of the complete sixty-four sacred games of Śiva into a language other than Tamil, and it dates to the mid-sixteenth century and likely predates the most influential renderings of the narrative, the *TVP* of Parañcōti and the *Hālāsya Māhātmya*. As a result, this previously unstudied work stands well-positioned to expand our perspective on the institutional foundations and linguistic media of literary circulation during this period.

In terms of patronage, the *Cokkanātha Caritramu,* much like a number of the Tamil texts of the period, was sponsored by relatively minor chieftains from a subregional court to the south of Madurai. Its performative rhetoric, however, is quite different from that of its Tamil counterparts, explicitly evoking the imagery and prestige of a courtly literary *sabhā*—a world where kings are attended with yak-tail fans and offered an uninterrupted flow of betel leaf. One might even describe the setting as "secular" in this case, as the work betrays no connection with any temple-based or monastic institution but, rather, emphasizes the aestheticized political power of its patrons. As we can glean from the following passage, Pedda Rāma and Cinna Rāma felt that their worldly prestige stood to benefit considerably from attracting skilled Telugu poets hailing from long-celebrated literary families:

> "Praiseworthy among the Bhaṭa lineage, like green camphor,
> The son of Tipparāja, Tiruvēṅgaluṇḍu, clever at propagating through
>   narrative"—
> When he was so informed, that king of men Cinna Rāma,
> Then, with great joy, called me and welcomed me with respect,
> Praising me and offering me betel—
> "O faultless person, the younger brother of your grandfather,
>   Timmarāja,
> Exalted across the entire earth, received the name
> 'King of Green Camphor' from Prauḍharāya [of Vijayanagara]—

Timmarāja begat Tipparāja, who extolled kings brilliantly.
You, an Indra among poets, who are praised by the noble,
Are the son of that literary connoisseur [*rasika*].
You have a mind dexterous in the play of illustrious poetry.

Therefore, compose a poem for me, and make it known across the
    earth—
In the Dvipada style, with clarity, as a great exemplar,
So that it shines in the minds of great poets,
Such that they praise it in their minds with sweet sentences—
About the sixty-four sports of the one of stainless, auspicious acts,
The Lord of Madurai, in the Andhra language,
Dedicated to the name of Pedda Rāma,
An Indra for the grandness of his good deeds."[56]

In this respect, the *Cokkanātha Caritramu,* unlike the Tamil texts we have examined, is undoubtedly an heir to the political, social, and literary values of the Sanskrit cosmopolis. Unsurprisingly, the linguistic register as well is highly Sanskritized, and we meet with a celebration of cosmopolitan literary history in the guise of the traditional *kavi praśaṃsā* (praise of previous poets), not only of the great celebrities of the Telugu literary world but of the Sanskrit tradition as well:

Having extolled all the poets existing on the earth
With true sentences of praise shining with true devotion—
Those by the names of Vyāsa, Vālmīki, Mahākavi Kāḷidāsa,
Bhavabhūti, Daṇḍi, Māghu, Bhīma of Vēmulavāḍa,[57] Nannaya,
Tikkana, Erṟana, Śrīnātha—making effort with great devotion
To compose such a work by which work I obtain the desired aim.[58]

Succinctly, it is the Telugu literary sphere that has inherited many of the more overtly political functions of aestheticized discourse in Nāyaka-period south India. The same pattern holds true for the central Nāyaka courts of Madurai and Tanjavur,[59] which extensively patronized works of Telugu literature but rarely works in Tamil, a strategy that was perhaps intended in part as a political statement of hegemony by a dynasty still perceived by the local populace as foreign in origin, Telugu speakers by heritage rather than Tamil. The Nāyaka rulers of Tanjavur in particular were not only avid connoisseurs of Telugu verse but also themselves active participants in the literary sphere. A prime example is Raghunātha Nāyaka,[60] who as a child was showered in gold (*kanakābhiṣeka*) for his extemporaneous *yakṣagāna* drama, and who continued throughout his career to craft ornate renditions of the Sanskrit classics, including a Telugu adaptation of the *Naiṣadhīyacarita.* In fact, for the Tanjavur Nāyakas, literary talent was primarily a royal virtue embodied in the king's own persona. This royal embodiment of poetic virtuosity was iconically represented by the Śāradā Dhvajamu, the "literary banner" gracing the court to announce, for instance, that no poet could surpass the poetic prowess of Vīrarāghava Nāyaka,[61] Tanjavur's king, a prolific author of exclusively Telugu compositions. Language, in short, was a central determining factor of literary excellence at the Nāyaka courts. For the duration of the Nāyaka regimes, cosmopolitan courtly literature remained the exclusive property of Telugu and Sanskrit rather than Tamil, the true vernacular of the region, which had successfully carved out for itself an independent institutional domain.

Given the preceding evidence—that is, in light of the multicentric structure of literary production in the Nāyaka period—how can we explain the increasing popularity of the *TVP* across the boundaries of language and place? Previous scholarship has speculated that the *TVP* owed its popularity directly to Tirumalai Nāyaka, thought to have been a likely patron for Parañcōti's celebrated re-creation of the legends, but the sixteenth-century evidence renders this conclusion highly improbable. And yet, given the diverse attributions of patronage for these works, no single regime or ruler can be held responsible for their circulation, including—as counterintuitive as it may seem—the Nāyaka rulers of Madurai, in light of the central iconicity the legends eventually attained as signifiers of Madurai's cultural heritage and religious authority. Alternatively, as many of the narratives record exploits of the quasi-historical rulers of the Pandian dynasty, one might have suspected an incentive for the southern Pandians of Tenkasi to encourage the production and circulation of a narrative that eulogizes the ancient Pandian dynasty. No evidence, however, is available to support such a hypothesis. As a result, we are left to posit a much more complex discursive dynamic by which literary influence and interchange traveled fluidly beyond the boundaries of social institutions and regional polities, a process deserving of further research and inquiry.

Although an intriguing phenomenon in its own right, the multiplicity of institutional sites that supported literary production in the Nāyaka period also bears significant implications for our understanding of how literary themes are developed, circulated, and disseminated into the domain of public culture. The *TVP* is simply one example of a narrative that grew to maturity and attained its now cherished place in cultural memory by navigating this multicentric, multilingual literary milieu. As a literary theme that received substantial attention throughout the sixteenth century across the boundaries of language, institution, and locality, the *TVP* appears to defy a number of our normative assumptions about how works of literature attain a position of social or cultural prominence, whether through the genius of an individual poet or through the direct patronage of a single political ruler or other social agent wishing to legitimize his claim to authority. In fact, the *TVP*'s widespread dissemination throughout the sixteenth century—and this presuming a flawed and incomplete historical archive—defies the very possibility of reading its reemergence in the Nāyaka period as a top-down act of political legitimation. To the contrary, Tirumalai Nāyaka interventions coincide closely with the period of textual codification witnessed in the following decades, as the *TVP* began to circulate outside the boundaries of elite literary circles, entering the domain of popular literary culture.

TWIN TEXTS: THE CANONIZATION OF THE *TIRUVIḺAIYĀṬAL PURĀṆAM*

Most importantly for our purposes, none of the works noted above appear to be indebted to either of the two exemplars of the *TVP* genre given historical primacy by existing scholarly literature, namely the *TVP* of Parañcōti and the Sanskrit Hālāsya Māhātmya, allegedly the direct sources for all representations of the "Sacred Games" in the centuries after Nampi. In fact, two of the most interesting of these works, the *Cuntara Pāṇṭiyam* and the *Cokkanātha Caritramu,* are sufficiently similar on structural grounds to that of Parañcōti's *TVP* to suggest the genuine emergence of a shared template for narrative improvisation. But the works diverge in crucial respects, bringing seriously into question the presupposition that all of the texts could have been adapted unilaterally from a single point of origin. Reactions in the scholarly literature have varied considerably, ranging from that of Harman (1987a), who has emphasized the purely rhetorical role of Sanskrit "originals" in Tamil Purāṇic composition, to those of Jeyechandrun (1985) and Wilden (2014), who virtually assume that Parañcōti translated the Hālāsya Māhātmya directly into Tamil. And yet, to date, I have not once encountered a single citation of the Hālāsya Māhātmya originating earlier than the late seventeenth century.[62] Internal textual evidence, on the other hand, speaks volumes about this issue, but only when Parañcōti's *TVP* and the Hālāsya Māhātmya are brought into dialogue with a much broader spectrum of contemporary literary production. As I argue below, the suspiciously similar contents of Parañcōti's *TVP* and the Hālāsya Māhātmya pair them as "twin texts," so to speak, strongly suggesting at the very least that the Hālāsya Māhātmya could not have been known to any vernacular poets before Parañcōti.

Beyond the *Cokkanātha Caritramu*'s inclusion of three of Nampi's original games, perhaps the work's most suggestively interstitial feature is its "elision" of the prolific Purāṇic frame narratives that feature prominently in both Parañcōti's *TVP* and the HM. While the *Cokkanātha Caritramu,* much like Nampi's earlier *TVP,* undertakes a streamlined narration of each of the sixty-four games, showing no predilection for mythological elaboration, the latter canonical narrative is scattered with mythological backstories and nonnarrative materials—from ancient curses to applied religious observances (*vratas*) and spontaneous *stotras*—as one would expect from the texture of a typical Sanskrit Purāṇa. Some of these digressions, such as the apparently irrelevant Somavāravrata chapter in the HM and the *stotra* sung by Patañjali upon witnessing Śiva's dance after the sacred marriage in Madurai, feature only in the HM and no other known variants. Most mythological addenda, however, although preserved identically in both Parañcōti's *TVP* and the HM, appear in no other early rendering of the "Sacred Games," including the *Cokkanātha Caritramu*, which otherwise conforms closely in narrative structure to the later *TVP* and the HM.[63] Combined with his inclusion of Nampi's three original episodes, however, Tiruvēṅgaḷakavi's apparent unawareness of *any* of the later Purāṇic frame narratives strongly suggests that he did not have either the HM or Parañcōti's *TVP* available as a model when composing the *Cokkanātha Caritramu*. Moreover, given his deep respect for Sanskritic culture (such as a lengthy digression on the virtues of sixteenth-century Varanasi), heavily Sanskritized vocabulary, and the Purāṇic narrative style employed in his introductory frame, it is highly unlikely that Tiruvēṅkaḷakavi would have neglected entirely these new additions had he indeed "translated" the HM into Telugu.

One prime example of such a mythological excursion, and a fairly controversial one at that, sets the stage for the origin story of the Tamil Caṅkam and is featured prominently in both Parañcōti's *TVP* and the HM, a series of narratives that eulogize the prehistoric efflorescence of Tamil literary culture in the city of Madurai. Although this particular narrative is unattested before the *TVP* and the HM, its distinctive features in the HM have been cited as evidence for both the priority and relative antiquity of that work by scholars of Tamil literary history such as David Shulman (2001). Our story begins with Brahmā and his three wives, who have set out on a pilgrimage to Varanasi to bathe in the Ganges together. Upon their arrival at the sacred river, Sarasvatī's attention is suddenly diverted by the melodies of a celestial musician of sorts, and she abandons the task at hand in pursuit of the unseen singer. When she returns to rejoin her husband and cowives Gāyatrī and Sāvitrī, Sarasvatī discovers that Brahmā and the others have already completed their ablutions, and Brahmā is distinctly displeased at her unexplained absence at the crucial moment of ritual purification. Angered at her apparent irresponsibility, Brahmā curses her to undergo forty-eight mortal births in recompense for her lapse. When Sarasvatī, distraught, begs Brahmā to relent, he modifies the curse so that she will be born simultaneously as the poets of the Tamil Caṅkam represented by the forty-eight letters of the alphabet, accompanied by Śiva as the forty-ninth poet, the embodied form of the letter *a*. In Parañcōti's words:

> When she said, "You who have crossed beyond the travails of the
>   flesh, shall I,
> Who am your companion in this rare life, truly be cast into a mortal
>   womb?"
> Seeing the lady of the white lotus, in which the bees submerged in
>   its honey, who

Sounded the Vedas, the four-faced leader spoke, in order to soothe
   her distress:

"Let it be that the forty-eight letters, renowned among the
Fifty-one, known as those beginning with *ā* and ending with *ha,*
Having become forty-eight poets, will be incarnated from your
   body,
With its budding breasts, in the world surrounded by the excavated
   sea.

Permeating all of the letters appearing as such, enlivening [*uyttiṭum*]
   them so that they appear
With various motions [*iyakkam*],[64] having acquired a natural form
   suitable to the
Body [*mey*] of each of them, the Lord who flows as the primacy
   belonging to the letter *a*
Is, indeed, our Lord of the Ālavāy of the Three Tamils, in just such a
   manner.

Each of them having become a single scholar, adopting a sacred
   form,
Having ascended to the great jeweled seat of the Caṅkam, and
He, having become the forty-ninth, manifesting erudition to each in
   their hearts,
They will guard poetic learning with delight," said the Lotus-Born
   Lord.[65]

And as similarly recounted in the HM:

Then, the Speaker of Speech, afraid, bowed and touched
The pair of lotus feet of her husband with her hands, and petitioned
   him:

"All of this rebuking was done by me out of ignorance.
Forgive me, Ocean of Compassion! Look upon me with your side-
   long glance."

[Brahmā replied:]
"I, petitioned, along with my vehicle again and again by Brāhmī
have given a counter curse to that Bhāratī out of compassion.

The letters from *a* to *sa*, consisting of speech, which have come forth
   from your body,
of clever intellect, will be born together on the earth with different
   forms.

The all-pervasive Lord Sadāśiva, bearing the form of the letter *ha*,
Shall become a single lord of poets in the midst of those clever-
    minded ones.
And the forty-nine the true poets of the Sangham.[66]

Aside from the often noted confusion about the total number of letters, which may result in part from the ambiguities of cross-linguistic transmission,[67] the most salient feature of this mythological prehistory is that the Caṅkam poets have been symbolically encoded as the incarnate letters of the *Sanskrit* alphabet, which together are said to comprise the body of Sarasvatī herself, the power of language. Shulman (2001), for instance, argues that this esoteric imagery provides unambiguous evidence that the HM originated from an older, pan-Sanskritic Śākta theological system,[68] which was later imperfectly transmitted into the Tamil cultural sphere in Parañcōti's *TVP*, resulting in a denuding of the HM's specifically Sanskritic Śākta vocabulary. It is true, in fact, that this episode, as well as numerous other passages in the HM, are heavily overlaid with Śākta terminology, from the reference to the *saṅghaphalaka*—the Caṅkam plank, the seat of the poets in the assembly hall—as a *vidyāpīṭha* or *mātṛkāpīṭha*[69] to references to a set of *navaśakti*s, or nine fierce goddesses, who are somewhat less coherently integrated into the overall plot of the Purāṇa.[70] Unfortunately, none of these terms are truly tradition-specific enough to evince a definitive origin in any pan-Sanskritic tradition of esoteric Śāktism, much less, as Shulman contends, within an unspecified Śākta lineage from the northwest of the Indian subcontinent.

We do, on the other hand, find numerous exact parallels to the Śākta terminology of the HM from within the Tamil Śaiva canon itself, suggesting that we need not look as far afield for their origin as Shulman has contended. In particular, the Tirumantiram, which notoriously preserves numerous remnants of a proto-Śrīvidyā esotericism that seems to originate in the Kashmiri Śākta-Śaiva traditions exported to the South, repeatedly invokes the set of fifty-one letters of the alphabet as central elements of its various *yantra*s and other esoteric imagery. On several occasions, we also find reference to Śiva as embodying the foremost of these syllables, the letter *a*:

From the beginning she is the life of the fifty-one
Letters that constitute the alphabets.
The bejeweled one is with Śiva
In the *cakra* of the letters.[71]

Chambers are twenty-five; each contains two letters;
Letters enclosed are fifty; the commencing letter is *A*;
Kṣa is the final letter; to the fifty is added *Oṃ*.
In all, fifty-one letters are inscribed in the chambers.[72]

Although the Tirumantiram was most likely composed centuries before Parañcōti's *TVP*,[73] as the tenth book of the Tamil Śaiva canon, its imagery understandably maintained widespread popularity among Parañcōti's contemporaries, even surfacing in publicly available works of Tamil Purāṇic literature. The trope of the fifty-one letters, for instance, makes an appearance in the *Cuntara Pāṇṭiyam* as well, entirely disconnected from any mention of the Caṅkam or its myth of origin:

> We bow, to escape the ocean of existence, to the raft that is the pair
>   of feet marked with the *cakra*
> Of that very Cokkaṉ of the beautiful twelve-petaled lotus
>   [*dvādaśānta*], of which the radiance is ripened
> In the void that has come together as Śiva and Śakti, *nāda*
>   [resonance] and *bindu* [drop],
> Where the various lotuses—whose petals are fifty-one letters—
>   unfold in a single syllable.

Given these striking parallels, the esoteric imagery that may seem to betray an extralocal origin for the Sanskrit HM in fact evokes the flavor of a distinctively Tamil Śākta-Śaivism, leaving little remaining doubt that the HM emerged not from any pan-Indic Sanskrit tradition but directly from the Tamil Śaiva textual culture of the early to mid-second millennium. Although preserving a number of originally Sanskrit features—from the inclusion of the letter *kṣa* in the alphabet to translocal yogic terminology such as *nāda, bindu,* and *dvādaśānta*—the imagery of the Tirumantiram had been adopted and reworked for centuries within the confines of the Tamil Śaiva tradition. Far from blending uneasily with Tamil Śaiva theology as Shulman would have it, the fifty-one letters play a central role in a subtle cosmology that had been accepted centuries earlier into the core repertoire of Tamil Śākta-Śaiva tradition, remaining in circulation through the seventeenth century and beyond.

This being the case, the frame narrative of the Tamil Caṅkam cycle simply cannot indicate an earlier, extra-Tamil origin for the HM. To the contrary, the fact that both the HM and Parañcōti's *TVP* preserve such a memorable and idiosyncratic Purāṇic accretion in nearly identical form—one that is attested by no other known variant dating to the sixteenth century—establishes beyond doubt that the circumstances of their composition were directly linked, but within a much more delimited time frame than previously suspected. The twin texts appear to postdate the *Cokkanātha Caritramu* of the mid-sixteenth century, which closely resembles the later narrative structure but includes none of the Purāṇic accretions and preserves Nampi's earlier episodes, which were forgotten by later audiences. All evidence considered, the HM was most likely re-Sanskritized directly from Parañcōti's fabulously successful *TVP* shortly after its composition in response to demands for a Sanskrit original, although it remains possible that the Sanskrit Purāṇic version was "found"—that is, commissioned—and employed as a model for Parañcōti's work. In any case, it is beyond a doubt that the Sanskrit HM never circulated in south Indian literary venues before Parañcōti's *TVP* had substantially influenced the public culture of Madurai and the temple of Mīnākṣī and Sundareśvara.

Some decades later, however, Nīlakaṇṭha Dīkṣita, luminary of the Sanskrit literary society of Madurai, had personally gained access to the HM, a fact that can be gleaned through a careful reading of his own rendition of the "Sacred Games" as a Sanskrit *mahākāvya*, his *Śivalīlārṇava*. In the course of the Caṅkam cycle of episodes, after the goddess Sarasvatī had taken incarnation as the forty-eight Caṅkam poets in Madurai, the current Pandian ruler, Campaka Pāṇḍya (so named for his well-known preference for the fragrance of *campaka* flowers), had encountered a troubling dilemma. During the course of an intimate evening with his newly wed queen, Campaka Pāṇḍya discovered that her hair was endowed with a rather distinctive fragrance and began to contemplate its origin. The king was so troubled by his uncertainty that he promptly announced a prize of a purse of gold coins for any poet who could produce a compelling and eloquent verse explaining whether or not a woman's hair can produce such a fragrance without the presence of flowers or artificial perfumes. The prize-winning verse, which Śiva himself composed and entrusted to a young Brahmin bachelor named Tarumi, was widely understood from the earliest attestations of the Caṅkam narratives to be a genuine Caṅkam-period verse preserved in one of the anthologies, the *Kuṟuntokai:*

> O bee with your hidden wings, you have lived a life in search of honey.
> So tell me truly from what you have seen.
> Among all the flowers you know, is there one that smells more sweet
> Than the hair of this woman with her peacock gait and close-set teeth
> And ancient eternal love?[74]

In the course of adapting this episode, the necessity naturally arose for both Nīlakaṇṭha and the author of the HM to translate this verse into Sanskrit, preserving in the process a distinct linguistic texture from the surrounding narration. Beyond any possible coincidence, however, both the HM and the *Śivalīlārṇava* employ precisely the same verse,[75] in *āryā* meter, as a translation for the Tamil of the second stanza of the *Kuṟuntokai:*

> O bee, you know the fragrances of flowers. Tell me truly today:
> What fragrance can compare with the fragrance in the locks of a
>   noble woman's hair?[76]

Nīlakaṇṭha's *Śivalīlārṇava* (ca. 1625–1650), then, provides a definitive *terminus ante quem* for the twin canonical renderings of the "Sacred Games," the HM and Parañcōti's *TVP*, which as a conjoined pair may have been composed a mere decade or two before. From a strictly literary historical standpoint, this exercise in dating may appear somewhat inconsequential. From the standpoint of political history, however, the idea that the publicly acclaimed versions of the "Sacred Games" should have originated during this particular period demands a consideration of the narrative's role in Nāyaka statecraft and in the city of Madurai, a cultural capital rapidly transforming under the influence of the Madurai Nāyaka regime. Following the reign of Viśvanātha Nāyaka (1529–1564), who by the end of his career had achieved de facto independence from the declining Vijayanagara Empire, the religio-political landscape of Madurai took on a newfound importance for the agenda of the Madurai Nāyakas, who may well have found it advantageous to highlight the rich cultural legacy of the ancient Pandian capital at the heart of their kingdom. Given the political, economic, and cultural significance of the south Indian temple complex during this period, the cultural renaissance instituted by the successors of Viśvanātha Nāyaka naturally began with an expansion of the most influential regional temples—particularly the Mīnākṣī-Sundareśvara Temple, the geographical and cultural center of Madurai.

"THE PASSION OF HICKS FOR VERNACULAR TEXTS": THE *ŚIVALĪLĀRṆAVA* OF NĪLAKAṆṬHA DĪKṢITA

The "Sacred Games of Śiva" had become a pillar of local culture and religion and, in the literary sphere, a theme primarily inviting response rather than active recreation. Perhaps the most influential of these responses, articulated during the height of the public codification of the *TVP*, came from the pen of none other than Nīlakaṇṭha Dīkṣita himself, one of the most celebrated figures in the literary and courtly circles of Madurai during the reign of Tirumalai Nāyaka. A closer look at his response—a Sanskrit *mahākāvya*, the *Śivalīlārṇava*—will illuminate the dynamics of response to an emergent fixture of popular culture and to the place of Sanskrit language and literature within the multilingual, multicentric literary sphere of seventeenth-century Madurai. Succinctly, Nīlakaṇṭha appears to have served as a sort of premodern public intellectual, remembered primarily for his interventions in the local and regional circulation of Sanskrit discourse. Indeed, his bold style and idiom display a degree of intellectual freedom than is typically associated with court poets of the cosmopolitan Sanskrit world order. Although unquestionably surviving through royal patronage, Nīlakaṇṭha never once deigned to mention the name of his patron in a single one of his works, a far cry from the politicization of Sanskrit aesthetic discourse regnant in Indic courtly culture for well over a millennium. And yet, we never meet with mention of a *Tirumalābhyudaya* (Victory of Tirumalai Nāyaka) to match the *Raghunāthavilāsa* (The play of Raghunātha Nāyaka) of Nīlakaṇṭha's rival to the north, Rājacūḍāmaṇi Dīkṣita, patronized by the Nāyaka court of Tanjavur. Rather, Nīlakaṇṭha's literary style is fiercely nonconformist and unrelentingly satirical, humorously highlighting the social degeneracy of his contemporaries as well as the decadence he perceived in Nāyaka period Sanskrit literature. Given this precedent, it should perhaps come as no surprise at all that Nīlakaṇṭha was bold enough to adapt into Sanskrit the most popular vernacular work of his day, the *Tiruviḷaiyāṭal Purāṇam*, while simultaneously denouncing the very idea of vernacular literariness: "[Bad poets] have acquired a taste for poetic feats [*citra*] of word and meaning—*much like the passion of hicks for vernacular texts.*"[77]

Much like Nīlakaṇṭha's other works of *kāvya*, the *Śivalīlārṇava* is replete with hints of its author's intention and deliberately incisive wit. Indeed, the precedent of Nīlakaṇṭha's idiosyncratic style, as well as the historical evidence of his public visibility in mid-seventeenth-century Madurai, would caution us against neglecting these hints of Nīlakaṇṭha's contrarian ambitions by reading the *Śivalīlārṇava* as a passive fulfillment of royal commission or subservience to popular fashion. Similarly, we would be ill advised to read the *Śivalīlārṇava*, rather presumptuously, as a mere "translation" of a timeless—and essentially ahistorical—work of vernacular literature, thus reducing Nīlakaṇṭha's agenda to faithful replication of the original Tamil. This is not to say, however, that Nīlakaṇṭha approached the narrative of Śiva's sacred games with anything less than the highest respect. To the contrary, as a fiercely loyal devotee of Mīnākṣī, he exhibits a deep and sincere reverence for her earthly manifestation and sport with Śiva throughout the *kāvya*. This reverence, however, is directed in Nīlakaṇṭha's voice to a canonical narrative that has been deliberately divorced from its original linguistic context. Distancing himself from "the passion of hicks for vernacular texts," Nīlakaṇṭha has represented a traditionally Tamil legend that, for him, derives none of its virtue from an intrinsic connection to Tamil language or culture.

In the case of the *Śivalīlārṇava*, the re-Sanskritization of a vernacular work of literature reversed the typical historical dynamic of vernacularization: rather than the expected localization of the transregional, we witness a deliberate deregionalization of local culture. It is unquestionably true that the Sanskrit of seventeenth-century south India regularly addressed itself to local concerns, but not necessarily in acquiescence or outright adulation. In fact, that Sanskrit literature remained a vital medium of discourse implies, by definition, that Sanskrit remained a vehicle for contestation as well as imitation. The *Śivalīlārṇava*, then, exemplifies an intriguing inversion of the vernacular by the still-vibrant values and presuppositions of a Sanskritic worldview. In the case at hand, two particularly noteworthy features stand out in Nīlakaṇṭha's treatment of traditionally Tamil motifs, both of which deserve further exploration: first, Nīlakaṇṭha defiantly inserts the distinctive idiom of Sanskrit intellectual discourse into explicitly non-Sanskritic contexts; and second, he intentionally reads the canonical repertoire of Tamil Śaivism through the lens of the Sanskrit Śaiva tradition, as if to claim these legends for a Smārta-Śaiva orthodoxy that challenged the language and caste boundaries distinctive to the Tamil Śaiva community.

Certainly, it is no easy task to denude such a regionally inflected cycle of legends of its regional character, or even to "transregionalize" it—that is, to render it accessible to a cultured audience beyond the confines of its locality of origin. And like many Tamil works of the period, the *TVP* is emphatically Tamil in its ideology and literary texture. Among the sixty-four games of Śiva, several bear the overt impressions of a thousand years of Tamil literary and devotional history, reworking narratives from the Periya Purāṇam and other mainstays of the Śaiva canon that had long become ingrained in public memory. References to the Tamil Caṅkam, or to the Tamil Śaiva bhakti saints, for instance, would scarcely seem intelligible when translated out of a regional cultural framework. And yet, Nīlakaṇṭha proves himself exceptionally talented at rendering the core narratives of Tamil Śaiva culture in the idiom of elite Sanskritic, and even *śāstric,* discourse.

Perhaps the best example of Nīlakaṇṭha's creative inversion of his material is his rendition of the Tamil Caṅkam cycle: indeed, where better to comment on the role of vernacular literature than while narrating the origin of India's most celebrated vernacular literary academy? Before the *TVP* renaissance in Madurai, the preceding centuries had witnessed numerous literary and commentarial attempts to recover the quasi-historical origins of Tamil literature as it first emerged in Madurai's prehistorical golden age, each of which took for granted the unique virtues of an intrinsically Tamil literary aesthetic. In Nīlakaṇṭha's voice, however, the poets of the Tamil Caṅkam speak like Sanskrit *śāstrins,* intimately conversant with the history of Sanskrit thought from literary theory to Vedic hermeneutics. In just this spirit, the Caṅkam cycle of the *Śivalīlārṇava* begins with an encounter between the forty-eight Caṅkam poets, incarnated from Sarasvatī as the letters of the Sanskrit alphabet, and a host of "bad poets" (*kukavis*) who attempt to harass the Caṅkam poets with specious arguments derived from a deeply flawed understanding of Sanskrit literary aesthetics (Alaṅkāraśāstra):

> Several nonpoets, the worst of scholars, and other bad poets, who
>   had made an agreement,
> Struck up a specious quarrel with those poets who had no match in
>   the [triple] worlds:
>
> "'Word and meaning, free from faults, ornamented, and of supreme
>   virtue'—[*śabdārthau doṣanirmuktau sālaṅkārau guṇottarau*]
> To those poets who define poetry as such, we fold our hands in
>   salute.
>
> What could be more flawed than the highest misdeeds of a lover,
>   described in verse?
> Indeed, that is why the prattling of poetry [*kāvyānām ālāpaḥ*] is cast
>   off by the learned.

Then again, others conceive of flaws and virtues [*guṇadoṣāḥ*] based
    on their own whim.
One may as well investigate crows' teeth and take up rustic village
    sayings.

The nonsensicality of poems that have no syntactical construal is
    hard to break through,
Like sentences about sprinkling with fire; how do people delude
    themselves with them?

If suggestion [*vyañjanā*] were accepted as a modality of language,
    conveying various meanings
While freed from all constraints, should not a prostitute be consid-
    ered a wife?

Let fire be 'implied' [*dhvanyate*] by smoke; let a pot be 'implied' by
    the eye.
If meaning 'implies' a meaning, what consistency is there to the
    means of knowledge?"[78]

After these and other spurious arguments pieced together from disconnected
fragments of literary theory and logic—each of which would have been immediately recognizable to a Sanskrit-educated audience—Nīlakaṇṭha draws the dialogue to a close with his signature sarcastic wit:

"If the meaning of poetic statements conveys pleasure, even when
    distasteful,
Then listen with delight to your own censure composed by poets:

'Ah! The ripening of suggested emotion [*bhāvavyakti*]! Ah! Con-
    cealed flavor [*rasa*]!'
With moist tears streaming from their falsely squinted eyes,
Their hair bristling repeatedly as if undigested food were churning
    in their guts—
How has the earth been pervaded by poets, those thick-witted
    beasts!"

Their pride wounded by those juveniles who in such a manner
Continued prattling on repeatedly, long disciplined in deviant doc-
    trine,
Unwilling to listen to a single word of rebuttal,
Those best of poets betook themselves to the Moon-Crested Lord
    for refuge.[79]

Thus, in Nīlakaṇṭha's rendition, it is a barrage of third-rate literary theorists
that prompts the Caṅkam poets to petition Śiva for the celebrated Caṅkam plank

(*caṅkappalakai,* Skt. *saṅghaphalakam*),[80] a magical device that automatically assesses the true aptitude of a poet. A small wooden platform measuring one square *muḻam* in length,[81] the Caṅkam plank expands when approached by a genuinely learned poet, thus seating all forty-eight members of the Tamil literary academy and excluding all others. The same narrative outcome occurs in the *Śivalīlārṇava* as in Parañcōti's *TVP*; and yet, it may come as a surprise to witness the Caṅkam poets debating in a language and idiom foreign to their actual literary practice (both historically and in cultural memory). Were Nīlakaṇṭha interested in either accurately depicting or extolling the legacy of the Tamil academy, many centuries of Tamil grammar and literary theory might have provided him with a foundation for contextualizing the narrative within the cultural ethos typically evoked by hagiographers and historians from within the Tamil tradition. As a point of contrast, Parañcōti's *TVP* not only actively celebrates the distinctively Tamil character of the Tamil Caṅkam but also takes great pains to adorn the Caṅkam cycle of games with direct references to Tamil literary theory. In Parañcōti's version, in fact, this set of episodes foregrounds the role of Agastya, the prototypically southern sage, whom legend regards not only as the primordial Tamil grammarian but also as the instructor of the Caṅkam poets themselves. When Agastya was first dispatched by Śiva to the Tamil country, he confirmed his own role in the origin myth of Tamil literary culture:

> Preparing to take leave, he requested one thing:
> "They say the land I am going to, the Tamil land [*tamiḻ nāṭu*], is full
>   of verse [*toṭai*].
> As all the people dwelling in this land have researched sweet Tamil
>   [*iṉṟamiḻ*] and possess its knowledge,
> I ought to be able to give a reply to those who ask.
>
> So that the flaws of my thinking may leave me, Father,
> Please graciously grant me a work on the poetics (*iyaṉūl*) of refined
>   Tamil [*centamiḻ*],
> So that it may be clear to such a one, you have bestowed the first
>   treatise [*mutaṉūl*]."
> After he had understood, he said "I see your feet—I am your
>   servant, O Eternal One!"[82]

In addition to the clear ethos of linguistic pride prevalent in Tamil literary self-reflection, this passage incorporates a number of references to Tamil grammatical theory, from *iyal tamiḻ*—literally "natural Tamil," referring broadly to Tamil composition extending beyond the bounds of prosody strictly speaking, one of the "three Tamils" (*muttamiḻ*)—to *centamiḻ,* a common laudatory expression for the literary register of the language. The remainder of the passage only increases in technicality, celebrating Agastya's knowledge of the "two prefaces," "seven tenets," "four meanings," "ten faults," "nine beauties," and "eight *yuktis*."[83] Parañcōti further manages to narrativize the origin of the southern sage's legendary treatise on grammar, the *Akattiyam,* referred to above as the "primordial treatise" (*mutaṉūl*), a work believed by many commentators to have preceded the *Tolkāppiyam.* For Parañcōti, it was specifically this body of knowledge that constituted the learning of the Caṅkam poets: an intrinsically Tamil corpus of literary and grammatical theory innately suited to both the language of their compositions and their cultural identity as icons of Madurai's Tamil heritage.

Not to be outdone by his near contemporary, Nīlakaṇṭha attributes a high degree of specialized knowledge to the Caṅkam poets—not of Tamil grammar but of Sanskrit *śāstra,* specifically of Mīmāṃsā hermeneutics. As we have seen previously, further into the Caṅkam legends, the king of Madurai, Campaka Pāṇḍya, had promised a rich reward to the poet who could present him with a verse convincingly explaining the fragrance of his queen's hair. It was the young Brahmin named Tarumi, offering as his contribution a verse that Śiva had composed and revealed to him, who was awarded the prize. Green with envy, the illustrious Caṅkam poet Nakkīrar immediately demanded that Tarumi's prize be rescinded on account of a literary flaw in the verse, arguing that poetic convention did not allow one to attribute fragrance to a woman's tresses unadorned by flowers or fragrant oils. Upon hearing this insult, Śiva himself appeared before Nakkīrar and demanded an explanation for his insolence. Nakkīrar stood his ground and insisted upon the flaw, even when Śiva manifested his true form, complete with five heads and a third eye that threatened to burn the defiant poet to ashes. While the debate ends here for most versions of the narrative, Nīlakaṇṭha inserted a few more choice insults, through which Nakkīrar foolhardily claims superiority over Śiva himself based on his encyclopedic knowledge of Sanskrit hermeneutics:

> Although a devotee, seeing that great wonder Kīra rebuked him
>   once again.
> Stronger yet than the innate delusion of fools is the delusion contained in the semblance of intellect:
>
> "Given that your own works, which have attained the great audacity
>   of being called 'scripture,'
> Are intelligible only when those such as myself describe another
>   intentionality [*tātparyāntaravarṇanena*]
> And applying suppletion, inversion, contextualization, extraction,
>   and conjunction, [*adhyāhāraviparyayaprakaraṇotkarṣānuṣaṅgā-*
>   *dibhiḥ*]
> Keep this in mind and don't look to find fault with my poems, O
>   Paśupati!"[84]

Hearing Nakkīrar's audacity, it is no wonder that Śiva responded by scorching his assailant with his third eye and sending him flying into the Golden Lotus Tank of the Madurai temple. The interpretive techniques Nīlakaṇṭha enumerates here, drawn from the Pūrva Mīmāṃsā school of Vedic exegesis—*adhyāhāra, viparyaya, prakaraṇa, utkarṣa,* and *anuṣaṅga*[85]—are highly specific terms of art, by no means common knowledge to those who are not thoroughly acquainted with Sanskrit philosophical discourse. One can only imagine that this misrepresentation of Nakkīrar's identity would have struck Nīlakaṇṭha's audience as intimately familiar, evoking the resonances of their own discursive community, while simultaneously comically absurd when applied to a legendary figure of the Tamil academy. I contend that Nīlakaṇṭha's ambition in this passage is not one of simple cultural translation, replacing Tamil idiom with terms more familiar to an audience of Sanskrit scholars. The terms in question, first of all, are not equivalent; hence, "translation" as a category is an unlikely candidate for the situation at hand. What we witness here is more of a full-scale recoding of the narrative context, as Nīlakaṇṭha deliberately divorces the characters from a cultural context that is not merely original to the legends but also fundamental to their rhetorical intent, the reinforcement of the intrinsic Tamil-ness of the history and sociality of the city of Madurai.

What is at stake, then, in Nīlakaṇṭha's attempt to remove the Tamil from the Tamil Caṅkam? His motivation certainly appears to be more complex than sheer antagonism or cultural bigotry, as he quite readily asserts in passing that the Caṅkam poets are learned in the *dramiḍasūtrarahasya,* the "secret of the Southern Sūtra" (possibly referring to the *Tolkāppiyam*). Further, despite his incisive wit, Nīlakaṇṭha never abandons his core stance of reverence toward the sacred site of Madurai, the abode of his chosen deity Mīnākṣī, and its legendary history as manifested in the divine sports of Śiva. In fact, Nīlakaṇṭha's interpretation of some of the *TVP*'s outwardly devotional episodes illuminates more clearly his attitude toward distinctively Tamil cultural and religious motifs. A number of the episodes in the "Sacred Games" directly concern the central devotional figures of the Tamil Śaiva Siddhānta tradition, including the Tamil bhakti saints Ñāṉacampantar (Jñānasambandha) and Māṇikkavācakar, whose Tamil-language compositions form an integral part of the Tamil Śaiva canon. Once again, Nīlakaṇṭha's portrayal of these saints in no way lacks the reverence one would expect him to display toward the foremost devotees of the local Śaiva tradition, whom the legends at hand portray as carrying out the miracles of Śiva and Mīnākṣī at the heart of the Madurai temple. He refers most commonly, for instance, to Ñāṉacampantar with honorifics such as "Emperor among Spiritual Teachers" (*deśikasarvabhauma*). Nevertheless, Nīlakaṇṭha's respect for their status as icons of Śaiva devotionalism does not stop him from shifting the emphasis away from the Tamil language of the devotees' compositions and the distinctive regionality of their cultural legacy. That is, for Nīlakaṇṭha, the Emperor among Spiritual Teachers was simultaneously the Teacher of the Precepts of the Vedānta (*trayyantasiddhāntaguru*),[86] who comported himself like an orthodox Smārta-Śaiva (*atyāśramastha*).[87]

Take, for instance, the ubiquitous legend of the confrontation between the Śaivas and Jains in ancient Madurai, a narrative most commonly associated with Cekkiḻār's Periya Purāṇam but retold in the *TVP*s of Nampi and Parañcōti as well. In this episode, misfortune had befallen the Śaivas of Madurai as the city was overrun by Jains; even the king himself had converted to Jainism. And yet, when the king was overtaken by a seemingly incurable fever, only the Śaiva saint Ñānacampantar was able to bring him relief by anointing him with sacred Śaiva ash. Upon witnessing the extent of Jain domination in Śiva's sacred city, Ñānacampantar resolved to shed light on the errancy of their doctrine by challenging them to an ordeal, failing which the Jains were to willingly commit suicide by impaling themselves on stakes. According to both Parañcōti and the HM, Jñānasambandar and a representative of his Jain rivals each released a palm-leaf manuscript into a fire; on Ñānacampantar's leaf was written one of his own devotional poems, which are now preserved in the Tēvāram, the first seven books of the Tirumuṟai, while the Jain representative cast into the flames a palm leaf with an array of magical mantras. Unsurprisingly, the Jain palm leaf was incinerated, while Ñānacampantar's poem survived unscathed.

Nīlakaṇṭha's version of this particular ordeal proceeds similarly, but with one crucial modification:

> Abandoning all their exempla, fortified by hermeneutics and logic,
> Overstepping the bounds of all reason, those fools came together,
>   desiring to conquer him [Ñānacampantar] by ordeal.
>
> "The Śākya seer has seen that nonviolence alone can dispel all the
>   afflictions of *saṃsāra*.[88] Maheśa must not be worshipped; ash is
>   not auspicious."
> Thus, the Arhats wrote their own thesis.
>
> "The Vedas are the authority, along with the Kāmika and so forth.
>   Śaṅkara alone is the One Lord of the universe. Those desiring
>   liberation on earth must bear ash alone."
> Thus, the teacher wrote his own thesis.[89]

By shifting the ordeal to a test of doctrinal confession alone, an important detail has been elided from the narrative. Now that Ñānacampantar (or Sambandhanātha, as Nīlakaṇṭha refers to him) no longer wins the ordeal on the strength of his own composition, nothing in Nīlakaṇṭha's version signals that Ñānacampantar was revered primarily as a devotional poet, much less that his compositions were written in Tamil rather than Sanskrit. To the contrary, we find the bhakti saint endorsing the inerrant validity of the Sanskrit scriptures, ranging from the Vedas themselves to the Kāmika Āgama and other scriptures of the Sanskrit Śaiva Siddhānta tradition, which Nīlakaṇṭha himself considered indispensable for the Advaita-inflected Śaivism growing in popularity among the Smārta Brahmins of his circle. Given that the Sanskrit and Tamil Śaiva Siddhānta lineages had maintained institutionally and doctrinally distinct profiles for centuries before Nīlakaṇṭha's own floruit, conflating the scriptural corpus of the two is no mere oversight. Rather, Nīlakaṇṭha has transformed Ñānacampantar's character into that of a Sanskrit-educated scholastic ritualist rather than a Tamil devotional poet, a profile we would expect to see attributed to an Aghoraśiva rather than a poet of the Tēvāram.

In fact, the deliberateness of Nīlakaṇṭha's recasting of Ñānacampantar's legacy becomes unmistakable as this narrative continues, when the Pandian begs the Śaiva preceptor for initiation upon seeing the humiliating defeat of his Jain advisors. Although no previous version of the episode recounts any details of this initiation, Nīlakaṇṭha inserts a technically accurate account of a Saiddhāntika initiation as typically described in the Sanskrit Āgamas:

> The Pāṇḍya, who had surrendered in refuge to Sambandhanātha
>   upon seeing this ordeal,
> Asked for the initiation that cuts through all sin, capable of bestow-
>   ing the knowledge of Śiva.
>
> Purifying his six paths [ṣaḍadhvanaḥ] and his five kalās, that em-
>   peror of preceptors
> Entered his body effortlessly, although it had been defiled with a
>   heterodox initiation.
> Having entered his body, purifying him by uniting with his channels
>   [nāḍīsandhāna],
> That guru, an ocean of compassion, extracted his caste [jātiṃ
>   samuddhṛtya] and installed in him the knowledge of Śiva.
>
> Having bestowed his own body, wealth, and heart at his lotus feet,
>   the Pāṇḍya
> Ruled the earth on the Śaiva path, worshipping the Lord with the
>   Half-Moon Crest.
>
> When that Lord of the people ascended to the state of Śiva, all his
>   offspring were
> Devoted to Śiva, intent on Śiva's mantra, and proficient in the nec-
>   tarous essence of the knowledge of Śaiva Āgama.[90]

Through Nīlakaṇṭha's erudite attempts at inversion, Ñānacampantar is transformed from a bhakti saint into a ritually accomplished Śivācārya of the Sanskrit Śaiva Siddhānta, effortlessly performing the esoteric procedures for entering the body of his pupil through the subtle channels (*nāḍīsandhāna*) and removing his birth caste,[91] replacing the core of his identity with the knowledge of Śiva. His emphasis on the removal of caste, *jātyuddharaṇa*, as integral to Śaiva initiation is particularly intriguing, as the concept had fallen out of favor with the more conservative branches of the Sanskrit scholastic tradition, who preferred to align the Siddhānta with orthodox Brahminical social values. Nīlakaṇṭha, for his part, does not hesitate to endorse the practice, which entails the belief that all Śaiva initiates of a certain stature[92] have been ontologically elevated above caste distinctions.[93] Evidently, although Nīlakaṇṭha's literary aesthetic endorses the near-exclusive valuation of the Sanskrit language and intellectual tradition, his conservatism in language choice does not equate with a conservatism in caste consciousness. The polemics of twentieth-century Tamil politicians notwithstanding, Sanskrit in Tamil Nadu did not always herald a social agenda of outright Brahminical supremacy. That is, the structure of multilingual literary practice does not correlate simplistically with social structure.

In fact, it is precisely the issue of caste, and its removal, that most directly unites Nīlakaṇṭha with his institutional rivals of the Tamil Śaiva lineages. Owing to the social constituency of the Tamil Śaiva community in Nīlakaṇṭha's day, ascetic preceptors traditionally hailed from a Vēḷāḷa background, technically a Śūdra caste, which rendered them ineligible for preceptorial initiation according to the traditional strictures of Brahminical legal literature.[94] Unsurprisingly, the Vēḷāḷa lineages were keen to defend their legitimacy on textual as well as de facto political and economic grounds. One unique textual artifact of the mid- to late seventeenth century makes this case explicitly: the *Varṇāśramacandrikā* of Tiruvampaḷatēcikar (a near contemporary of Nīlakaṇṭha Dīkṣita),[95] the only known Tamil Śaiva treatise to be written in Sanskrit. In this intriguingly belligerent work, Tiruvampaḷatēcikar openly advocates the ordination of Śūdras to the lineage seat, scouring the textual history of Śaivism in Sanskrit to identify a vast array of precedents for this practice. The evidence he assembles aligns perfectly with Nīlakaṇṭha's own views of Śaiva initiation, suggesting that Nīlakaṇṭha was far more aligned with his times than language politics alone might lead one to suspect:

> The *homa* for extracting caste [*jātyuddharaṇa*], whether individually
>   or by the hundreds,
> Indeed incinerates Śūdra caste identity with fire, O six-faced one.[96]

Ironically, it is not only traditional Āgamic sources that figure prominently in the Sanskrit citations of Tiruvampaḷatēcikar. The *Varṇāśramacandrikā* is also the earliest known work to cite the Hālāsya Māhātmya, a text that, as we have seen, had recently entered the Sanskrit textual corpus through the mediation of the "Tamil vernacular." And yet, writing in the late seventeenth century, a Vēḷāḷa preceptor could cite the HM as an authoritative reference grounding the doctrines of the

Tamil Śaiva community in the purported legal standards of a transregional Śaiva orthodoxy. Owing in no small part to the cross-linguistic circulation of works such as the HM and Nīlakaṇṭha's *Śivalīlārṇava,* the Sanskrit-vernacular dichotomy in the Tamil country had truly come to function as a circular network of intertextual influence, resulting in a multicentric discursive sphere that reconstituted the shape of social and religious communities, such as the Tamil and Sanskrit Śaiva Siddhānta.

FROM TEXT TO PUBLIC RELIGIOUS CULTURE: THE *TIRUVIḶAIYĀṬAL PURĀṆAM* IN SEVENTEENTH-CENTURY MADURAI

In the introduction to his edition of the *Cokkanātar Ulā,* U. Ve. Caminataiyar, father of the modern renaissance in Tamil literary studies, recounts a popular anecdote concerning how the text's author, Purāṇa Tirumalainātar, came to receive his rather peculiar nom de plume.[97] Far better known for his other surviving composition, the *Citampara Purāṇam,* Tirumalainātar is said to have been petitioned by the elders and devotees of the Cidambaram Śaiva community to translate the surviving Sanskrit scriptural canon recounting the sacred history of Cidambaram into Tamil. Not having access to a suitable Sanskrit original, our would-be translator set off for the mountain country (*malaināṭu*), where he discovered a single, incomplete manuscript of the Sanskrit *Cidambara Purāṇa* and proceeded to translate the extant portion into the form of an equivalent Tamil *talapurāṇam.* Although Tirumalainātar remained grievously disappointed at being unable to locate the entire Sanskrit original, the temple priests were so gratified by his efforts and the quality of his final product that they appended the prefix "Purāṇa" to his title in commemoration of the *Citampara Purāṇam.*

While we sadly lack any documentary evidence to confirm that sixteenth- and seventeenth-century Tamil poets actively sought out Sanskrit manuscripts on which to anchor the authority of their Tamil compositions, more recent accounts confirm that such was common practice in the nineteenth century. For instance, a similar anecdote recorded by U. Ve. Caminataiyar outlines the process by which his own teacher, Minatcicuntara Pillai, renowned scholar of Tamil literature, set out to produce a Tamil *talapurāṇam* of Kumbakonam at the request of local monastic authorities:

At that time Civakurunātapiḷḷai, who was the *tahṣīldār* [collector] in Kumpakoṇam, and other Śaiva dignitaries thought, "Let us ask this master poet to compose the purāṇa of Kumpakoṇam in Tamil verse." At their request, he [Tiricirapuram Mīṇāṭcīcuntaram Piḷḷai] came to Kumpakoṇam from Tiruvāvaṭuturai in 1865 and took up residence with his retinue in the building of the Tiruvāvaṭuturai mutt in Peṭṭai Street. He first had the Kumpakoṇam purāṇa translated from Sanskrit into

Tamil prose; in this he was aided by Maṇṭapam Nārāyaṇa Cāstirikaḷ Mutaliyār, a scholar of the Caṅkarācāriyar Mutt. Afterward he began to compose the purāṇa in verse form. He would compose the verses orally, and from time to time one of his pupils, Tirumaṅkalakkuṭi Ceṣaiyaṅkār, would write them down. Short parts of the purāṇa used to be prepared each day in the morning and given their first formal recitation in the afternoon in the *maṇḍapa* in the front of the shrine of Ādikumbheśvara [Śiva at Kumpakoṇam]. Many came to take pleasure in the recitation. . . .

When the *araṅkerram* [debut] of the Kumpakoṇam purāṇa was completed, the dignitaries of that city gave him a shawl, a silk upper garment, [other] garments and gifts, and two thousand rupees collected from the public. They had the manuscript of the purāṇa mounted upon an elephant and taken around the town instate. Then several of the dignitaries purchased and donated a covered palanquin, made Piḷḷai sit in it, and carried it themselves for some distance. Thus they demonstrated the love they felt for the Tamil language and the custom of olden times.[98]

What is the significance, then, of Minatcicuntara Pillai's story to our understanding of public religious culture in seventeenth-century Madurai? What we witness in this vignette is nothing less than the creation of public canon, narrated from the perspective of onlookers who witnessed the debut of his Tamil Purāṇam and accepted its legends as an authoritative précis of Kumbakonam's sacred legacy. For Pillai as well as for the seventeenth-century Parañcōti, the birth of a *talapurāṇam* was a social affair, imbricated with the monastic and temple institutions where the text was composed, debuted before a public audience, and commemorated by local elites with the bestowing of ritual honors. It is a process that takes place in time and space, fusing new meaning onto the sites it commemorates, which become legible for future generations of devotees. Space itself, in temple and monastic complexes, becomes entextualized with the emergent public canon—what previous generations of scholars have described as "sacred space." And yet, this sacred space is anything but the hermetically sealed "sacred," set apart from the phenomenal experience of the mundane realm. It remains, rather, a *public* space—a site for the reproduction of public religious culture, available for response, reenactment, and contestation.

Indeed, religious spaces across the Tamil country were in the midst of a radical reentextualization in the sixteenth and seventeenth centuries: the materiality of religious sites itself was transformed through massive temple-building campaigns, and the newly refurbished temple complexes were indexed with fresh mythological narratives. Succinctly, we witness a remarkable upsurge both in the production and renovation of Hindu temples and in the composition of *talapurāṇams* in Tamil to invest them with canonical meaning. In excavating the history of the *talapurāṇam* genre, David Shulman (1976) notes that the vast majority of these texts lack the pedigree of the Tamil classics but were composed, primarily, during the sixteenth and seventeenth centuries, the very moment when the Nāyaka regents of the Tamil country were renewing their alliance with sacerdotal power by endowing new temple building projects at the heart of their domains. The Madurai Mīnākṣī-Sundareśvara Temple is no exception: after the succession of Viśvanātha Nāyaka to the throne of Madurai in the mid-sixteenth century, the early generations of Nāyaka rulers set to remapping the sacred landscape at the center of Madurai, transforming the architectural visage of the temple with the addition of new temple towers (*gopurams*) and pavilions (*maṇḍapams*), but imprinting it with signifiers of an entirely new mythology: namely, the sixty-four "Sacred Games of Śiva" in Madurai.

Broadly speaking, the expansion of the Mīnākṣī-Sundareśvara Temple under the Madurai Nāyakas took place in three principal phases.[99] Between 1570 and 1600, the temple attained its present shape with the construction of the external wall and four *gopurams* of the outermost third *prākāra* along with the four *gopurams* of the second *prākāra*. Subsequently, the early decades of the seventeenth century witnessed further accretions, such as the Thousand-Pillared Pavilion (Āyirakkāl Maṇṭapam). The remaining structural innovations that grace the temple today were commissioned during the reign of Tirumalai Nāyaka (1623–1659), whose efforts earned him a reputation as the chief architect behind the entire program of temple expansion. Tirumalai Nāyaka's innovations include the Putu Maṇṭapam, or "New Maṇḍapa," an external festival pavilion adjacent to the eastern side of the temple complex, and the towering Rāya Gōpuram, which although never completed was intended to upstage all similar temple *gopurams* across the southern half of the subcontinent.

The early Nāyakas did not restrict themselves, however, to expanding the physical edifice of the temple complex. Beginning around the early seventeenth century—that is, during the latter two phases of temple renovation—the Madurai Nāyakas began to enrich the symbolic face of the Mīnākṣī-Sundareśvara Temple as well with sculptural and pictorial representations drawn from unprecedented literary sources, particularly the *Tiruviḷaiyāṭal Purāṇam*.[100] In fact, no such image can be reliably dated to prior phases of temple construction.[101] In short, the early to mid-seventeenth century witnessed an explosion of interest in graphic as well as performative portrayals of the "Sacred Games" throughout the Madurai temple complex. Sculptural depictions of four of the games were displayed in the early seventeenth-century Āyirakkāl Maṇṭapam, and six in Tirumalai Nāyaka's Putu Maṇṭapam shortly thereafter. The seventeenth century also witnessed the first complete sequence of mural paintings—a genre of representation popular in Nāyaka-period temple art—of all sixty-four sacred games, displayed quite prominently alongside the Golden Lotus Tank (*poṟṟāmaraik-kuḷam*) in front of the shrine of Mīnākṣī, the ritual heart of the temple. Moreover, an intriguing detail of the "Sacred Games" statuary reveals that the temple improvements took place simultaneously with, rather than subsequent to, the codification of the *Tiruviḷaiyāṭal*

Purāṇam itself. In both the Āyirakkāl Maṇṭapam and the Putu Maṇṭapam, a statue appears depicting a game in which Śiva as a tiger feeds a deer, a legend that appears in early versions of the "Sacred Games" but which has been elided in Parañcōti's *TVP* and the Hālāsya Māhātmya. The publicization of the "Sacred Games," in short, was part and parcel of its canonization; it is very likely that Parañcōti composed his masterpiece while the statues were being erected, or afterward, and his work certainly had not been fully accepted as canon by the time of the construction of the Putu Maṇṭapam around 1630.

Furthermore, and perhaps most importantly, as the *TVP* began to enter the visual landscape of the Madurai temple, Tirumalai Nāyaka instituted a series of calendrical festivals showcasing several of the "Sacred Games" in public performance. In terms of the codification of public religious culture, however, Tirumalai Nāyaka's most influential innovation was the Putu Maṇṭapam itself, designed to host many of the temple's festivals outside of the temple walls, externalizing a previously internal, delimited space that may not have been physically accessible to residents of Madurai in numerous caste communities. Indeed, these new calendrical festivals captured the attention of the temple's ritual officiants when describing the contributions of Tirumalai Nāyaka to the Madurai temple complex. The *Stāṇikarvaralāṟu,* one of our most detailed sources of the temple's history, chronicles the changing ritual duties within various factions of the temple priesthood over the centuries and, in the process, draws particular attention to the new centrality accorded to the performances of the sacred games under the leadership of Tirumalai Nāyaka:

> Lord Tirumalai Nāyaka, having great devotion to Mīnākṣī and Sundareśvara, on a day in which the goddess became pleased, established an endowment under the arbitration of Ayya Dīkṣita, instructing that the sacred games be conducted in the manner established by the Purāṇas at the hands of the temple priests as follows: for Sadāśiva Bhaṭṭa, the Game of Chopping the Body, the Selling of Bangles, Carrying Earth for Sweetmeat; and for Kulaśekhara Bhaṭṭa, the Bestowing of the Purse [of gold coins], the Game of Turning Horses into Foxes,[102] the Raising up of the Elephant; and several other games divided evenly. Having granted an endowment ordering that several games be accomplished at the hands of the subordinates, he had them conducted such that happiness would arise at witnessing the spectacle.[103]

Spectacle, in fact, is just what the "Sacred Games" had become by the mid-seventeenth century, as visual and performative media rendered the narratives of Śiva's miraculous exploits immediately accessible to a diverse and even nonliterate public. Among the numerous games reenacted in public ceremonies, however, it was the Sacred Marriage of Śiva and Mīnākṣī that would leave the most visible imprint on Madurai's public religious culture. Tirumalai Nāyaka's most radical adjustment to the festival calendar was, undoubtedly, to unite the wedding of Madurai's divine couple with the overwhelmingly popular Cittirai Festival—in which the city's resident Vaiṣṇava deity, Aḷakar, made his annual procession to the river Vaikai, pausing in his journey to bestow temple honors on the dominant caste groups of the Madurai region. According to prior legend, Aḷakar had journeyed from his temple home several miles outside of town to the middle of the Vaikai River for the express purpose of liberating the sage Muṇḍaka from a curse that entrapped him in the body of a frog, an act of grace that Madurai's Vaiṣṇava residents had previously commemorated each year in the month of Cittirai (April/May). When the annual Cittirai Festival was conjoined with the Sacred Marriage, Viṣṇu as Aḷakar, whom the "Sacred Games" represented as the brother of Mīnākṣī, was understood to be entrusted with the task of performing the marriage rites for Śiva and his bride. As local legend has it, Aḷakar reaches the center of the river Vaikai only to realize that the marriage has already taken place without him, and in retaliation he grudgingly returns to his temple without setting eyes upon the divine couple, pausing along the way to spend the night with his paramour, a Muslim courtesan.

By re-creating the Cittirai Festival, then, Tirumalai Nāyaka managed to draw unprecedented attention to the legend that best encapsulates the royal heritage of Madurai, whose kings are the descendants of Śiva and Mīnākṣī themselves. Simultaneously, he positioned Madurai's most popular religious festival as a virtually unprecedented site for social and religious integration, creating a festival space that accommodated the interests of diverse caste communities, from Smārta Brahmins to the Kaḷḷar devotees of Lord Aḷakar, and blended the theologies of Śaiva and Vaiṣṇava devotionalism. Other favorites among the sixty-four games must have also quickly entered the repertoire of Madurai's residents, as by and large the same games depicted in temple statuary—publicly available year round as sites of memory—were dramatized yearly with festival processions and even mimetic reenactments of Śiva's divine interventions.[104] Indeed, each of the minor festivals enacting Śiva's sacred games, managed by representatives of rival priestly families of the Madurai temple, provided substantive incentive among elite families to compete for the attention of a wider public.

Facilitated by Tirumalai Nāyaka's royal interventions, then, an increasingly popular literary motif rapidly achieved widespread circulation far beyond the literary domain. That the *TVP* legends did, in fact, circulate is evident from the rapidity with which sequences of the sacred games began to appear in temple mural paintings across the Tamil region, demonstrating the broad appeal the narratives had achieved even outside of their domain of immediate reference, Madurai, the city in which the miracles were originally enacted.[105] Similar mural sequences, for instance, mirroring the sixty-four panels emblazoned on the Madurai temple outside the Golden Lotus Tank, had appeared in the Naṭarāja Temple of Cidambaram by the late seventeenth century and in the Bṛhadīśvara Temple in Tanjavur by the eighteenth century. Likewise, the "Sacred Games" soon became a common

FIGURE 4. A temple priest prepares a festival image to commemorate the sacred game in which Śiva grants liberation to a crane.

fixture of the material culture of religion in Madurai and beyond, replicated on temple carts across the region, festival textiles for chariots (*tērcilai*), and miniature paintings. Succinctly, the "Sacred Games of Śiva" were legible, for the majority of Madurai's seventeenth-century residents, not from the text of the *Tiruviḷaiyāṭal Purāṇam* but from the material culture of the Mīnākṣī-Sundareśvara Temple and from participation in the collective reenactments of the legends in temple festivals. In the words of Kim Knott (2005, 43) on the production of religious space, the enactment of the "Sacred Games" does not "take place," but "makes place," encoding the temple's visual facade with religious significance proper to multiple distinct communities.

What, then, does religious space—what the classical history of religions has referred to as "sacred space"—have to do with public religious culture, with the religious values or frames of reference cultivated by individuals from diverse social and sectarian backgrounds across the city of Madurai? Looking at the temple as public space—a space in which publics move, a space in which publics are created—is a crucial step in transcending both Western and modernist presuppositions that would unproblematically equate religion with the private sphere, the internal domain of affect or belief. Discounting the truly interior spaces of ritual worship, such as the *garbhagṛhas*, or inner "wombs" of the temple accessible only to trained priests, the temple pavilions (*maṇḍapas*) in which festivals are performed serve as physical sites for public gatherings and enactments of shared religious sensibilities. A temple in south India, it must be remembered, is constantly bustling with crowds in motion. Indeed, much of the physical space of the Madurai temple, as with the majority of sacred sites across south Asia, incorporates what the Western imagination has understood as nonreligious public space, from shopping complexes to casual gatherings for social conversation. As a result, the images inscribed on such a space, whether murals or statuary, create an ideal readership of visual media by cultivating a collective public frame of reference. Such images, in other words, are nothing less than social agents, exerting an active influence on the human agents who move through spaces inflected by their signifying capacity.[106]

To understand how new religious concepts and values come to be publicly accessible, or come to constitute a cornerstone of a particular public culture, then, depends fundamentally on theorizing the public as inhabiting a particular space, constituted in no small part by the visual signifiers that inhabit that space. Space, in its very materiality, as recent theorists have recognized, is by its very nature a socially imbricated category. Indeed, the materialist turn in religious studies and the humanities at large has become sensitive to space not simply as the Kantian precondition for human cognition but as a site for the signification and contestation of cultural values. From the vantage point of early seventeenth-century Madurai, space—both within the temple and throughout the city at large—was in the process of being overlaid with new conceptual resonance. With the visual inscription of the "Sacred Games of Śiva" in temple art and architecture, devotees of Mīnākṣī who traversed the temple halls and circumambulated the Golden Lotus Tank were now confronted with contested claims as to the significance of their spatial practice—that is, their lived engagement with socially significant spaces. But at this particular juncture in history, the "Sacred Games" did not yet fully belong to what Henri Lefebvre (1992, 33) would call "representations of space"—that is, the normative and fully articulated conventions for how temple space ought to be interpreted. To the contrary, the public space of the Madurai temple complex can best be characterized as "representational space"—a lived space of public contestation, capable of being contested by counterhegemonic interest groups who aim to overlay shared space with localized layers of meaning.

By the late seventeenth century, the *Tiruviḷaiyāṭal Purāṇam* had become a household name, and yet the legends were able to permeate the religious ecology of Madurai without disrupting its delicate balance—that is, by appealing to the diverse religious publics of Madurai, whether Śaiva or Vaiṣṇava, whether Smārta, Vēḷāḷa, or Kaḷḷar. The temple itself, then, did not homogenize the publics of Madurai, separated as they were by the boundaries of caste, language, and sect, but facilitated the overlaying and intersection of parallel public spheres. Its explosion into literary fashion, as we have seen, took place across multiple literary publics, facilitated by media of performance and patronage centered on the temple site itself. Likewise, its departure from the textual form and entry into public culture was a process mediated by a transference of shared meaning from the written word to visual and performative text. What took place during this period in Madurai was not merely the birth of a narrative, or even the birth of a religious canon, but the *entextualization* of public space. The "Sacred Games of Śiva" were not simply encoded in the memory of a collective populace but were canonized in physical public space, accessible in that they can be read, reinterpreted, and reenacted over time. The temple became not a space outside of time but a nexus for the temporal and spatial encoding of meaning, a space in which people moved through and performed meaning—a spatial nexus for the overlaying of multiple parallel publics.

Conclusion

A Prehistory of Hindu Pluralism

A CONTINUING LEGACY: THE MAKING OF A HINDU SECTARIAN COMMUNITY

Who invented Smārta-Śaivism? Was the tradition created *ex nihilo* through the abstract discourses of an intellectual elite, or did it emerge organically through the unfolding of social dynamics over the course of the early modern centuries? As with the purported "invention" of Hinduism, to identify the moment and circumstances of birth of a particular sectarian tradition raises a number of vexing theoretical questions about historical causation—the process by which a genuinely new cultural edifice comes into being. My aim in this work has been to sketch the unmistakable impressions of public theology on the embodied, socially embedded boundaries of Smārta religious life, its role in shaping emerging modes of religious identity—a process that cannot be reduced either to hegemonic domination or to elitist fancy. Indeed, the impact of Smārta-Śaivism on contemporary religious culture in Tamil Nadu extends far beyond the boundaries of *maṭha* or *sampradāya,* "monastery" or "lineage." Much in the way that the "Sacred Games of Śiva," the distinctive legend of place of Madurai, has historicizable discursive origins in the public theology of the seventeenth century, the same can be said for the wider public Smārta culture of the Tamil region. The subsequent inauguration of a public regional culture, from the Śrīvidyā inflection of Carnatic music (Shulman 2014) to the public esotericism of contemporary Chennai (Kachroo 2015), bears the distinct impressions of the actors and events of early modernity.

The Smārta-Śaiva community—with its perduring alliance between Śaṅkarācārya renunciant lineages, the monastic institutions they maintain, associated temple complexes such as the Kāmākṣī Temple of Kanchipuram, and a laity comprised largely of south Indian Smārta Brahmins—an integral feature of Tamil Smārta culture today, began to emerge under specific and eminently observable social circumstances in the sixteenth and seventeenth centuries. As I have documented throughout this book, the intellectuals who found themselves in the midst of this rapidly emerging network were by no means passive observers; rather, they actively contributed to the constitution of the network itself and the continual rethinking of its dimensions and boundaries. Precisely by doing so, in fact, Nīlakaṇṭha and his colleagues forged systems of religious meaning that opened new avenues for public religious participation in the Smārta community and, concomitantly, new models for lived religious identity. Although seemingly confined to palm leaves and paper through the medium of written text, the intellectual work of these scholars played a foundational role in the conceptual constitution of the emergent Smārta system, articulating new boundaries for the orthodoxy and orthopraxy of participant devotees, stabilizing the social structure of the system by delimiting it from competing sectarian systems, such as the more transgressive Śākta esoteric lineages or the vibrant Vaiṣṇava traditions of the region.[1] Niklas Luhmann (1995), indeed, insightfully observes that systems, composed of socially embedded institutions, cohere not on the basis of institutions alone but, rather, through the shades of meaning they acquire through the communicative endeavors of social agents. Such meaning supplies the very rationale for preserving religious institutions—and the religious publics they cultivate—in the face of constant competition from neighboring communities and perpetual fluctuations in the fabric of society. It is no surprise, then, that court-sponsored intellectuals of the seventeenth century should have exerted their most formative influence on extratextual life through their work as public theologians.

Indeed, the public memory of their influence in shaping the boundaries of a new religious community is palpable throughout the writings of their descendants, from the eighteenth century down to the present day. Take, for instance, the following excerpt from the decidedly southern Purāṇa, the Śivarahasya: As the text-critical acumen of our early modern theologians has taught us, some Purāṇic extracts offer representations of seemingly modern phenomena and so warrant suspicion of interpolation. Some passages, however, occasion no room for doubt. The following vignette allays our fears that the practice of scriptural forgery may have somehow diminished under early colonial rule:

> All twice-borns will be devoted to barbarous conduct, poor,
> And of meager intellect. In such a world, a sage will be born.
> O Śivā, Śaṅkara, born from a portion of me, the greatest of the
>   devotees of Śiva,
> Will take incarnation in the Kali Yuga, along with four students.
> He will bring about the destruction of the groves of heretics on
>   earth.

To him I have given the wisdom of the Upaniṣads, O Maheśvarī.
In the same Kali Yuga, O Great Goddess, the twice-born named
    Haradatta[2]
Will be born on the surface of the earth to chastise the non-Śaivas.
There will also be a certain [Appayya] Dīkṣita, a god on earth, a por-
    tion of me, O Ambikā,
Ceaselessly engaged in radiant practices, born in a Śaiva Sāmaveda
    lineage.
And other Bhaktas, O Mistress of the Gods, in the Cēra, Cōla, and
    Pāṇḍya countries,
Supremely devoted to me, will be born in all castes:
Sundara, Jñānasambandha, and likewise, Māṇikyavācaka.[3]

Śaṅkara, Haradatta, and Appayya Dīkṣita: in this eighteenth- or nineteenth-century Purāṇic accretion, the Smārta-Śaiva legacy has rewritten the canon of saints of the Tamil country, elevating the progenitors of the Smārta tradition above the common "devotees" of Śiva, the Tamil Śaiva bhakti saints. This particular passage, in fact, was adduced as the prototypic source text for the divinity of Appayya Dīkṣita by his nineteenth-century biographer, Śivānanda Yogīndra, born Śeṣa Dīkṣita. The tradition he inspired, however, reaches far beyond the printed pages of his classic chronicle to inform the religious identity of the present-day Dīkṣita family, who pride themselves on their descent from a genuine *aṃśāvatāra*, or partial incarnation,[4] of Śiva.

Intriguingly, hagiography, if not history, has never ceased to remember the formative theological influence of Appayya and Nīlakaṇṭha on the nascent Smārta-Śaiva community. From within the tradition, such hagiography blurs the line between theology and Indological scholarship. Spokesmen for the Appayya Deekshithendrar Granthavali Prakasana Samithi, for instance, advertise the intellectual legacy of their forefather in polyglot newsletters with theologically inflected taglines such as "Srimad Appayya Deekshithendrar is regarded as the aparavathara of Srimad Sankara Bhaghavathapadal and also revered in this country, as an incarnation of Iswara."[5] The divine status of these scholars is commemorated most frequently, however, by means of narrative. Short anecdotes depicting the exploits of Appayya and Nīlakaṇṭha have circulated over the course of multiple generations, preserved with the stamp of authority of their influential biographers. Swami Sivananda,[6] founder of the Divine Life Society, to name one highly visible example, includes both Appayya and Nīlakaṇṭha in his *Lives of Saints*, in the company of Jesus and the Buddha, Śaṅkara and Vidyāraṇya. His narratives, moreover, capture something of the deeply sectarianized climate in which the scholars actually moved, hinting at the highly charged community boundaries that solidified over the course of their lifetimes. Such is the case with this memorable account—forced English versification and all—of Appayya's ostensive pilgrimage to Tirupati, stronghold of south India Vaiṣṇavism par excellence:

> Once to Tirupathi the sage
> Went on a lonely pilgrimage,
> And there the Mahant to him told:
> "Enter not the fane; it can't hold
> Within its precinct a Saivite;
> To enter here you have no right."
> Wrath was the saint and quietly he
> By occult power did o'ernight change
> The fane's image of Lord Vishnu
> To Siva. The Mahant turned blue
> When in the morn he, aghast, saw
> Vishnu's image changed to Siva.
> To the great sage he now did run
> And of him humbly beg pardon,
> And asked the image be restored
> To the shape he loved and adored.
> Such was the great saint Appayya,
> An incarnation of Siva,
> Whom men still love and have reverence
> For his wisdom and intelligence. (Sivananda 1947, 313)

Such stories abound in the public memory of Nīlakaṇṭha and Appayya's descendants: Appayya leaves his body in Cidambaram in the presence of Naṭarāja, Nīlakaṇṭha is granted the gift of sight by Mīnākṣī, Ratnakheṭa Dīkṣita garners the favor of Kāmākṣī in Kanchipuram. More often than not, these episodes have been dismissed out of hand by contemporary Indologists as an impediment to reconstructing a lost intellectual history. In this case, however, beneath hagiographical adulation lies a kernel of historical fact: these narratives serve as communal sites of memory for the socioreligious transformations of the sixteenth and seventeenth centuries, the systemic restructuring of the religious landscape that had been publicly facilitated to no small degree by Appayya, Nīlakaṇṭha, and their intellectual contemporaries. A few generations before the fact, these narratives superimpose the same Smārta-Śaiva culture that was born from their public theological interventions. These stories are replete with rivalry between Śiva and Viṣṇu, the veneration of Śaṅkarācārya ascetics, the adulation of Kāmākṣī and Mīnākṣī, and initiation into the mystery of Śrīvidyā. Like most hagiographies, the exploits of Appayya and Nīlakaṇṭha tell us less about their actual biographies than about the lives they shaped in future generations, when such motifs were no longer novel inventions but fixtures of the fabric of Smārta religiosity.

As a point of fact, neither the cultural icons of south Indian Smārtism nor the everyday religious practice of the community could be conceived of today, in their present shape, were it not for the theological innovations of Appayya's and Nīlakaṇṭha's social circles. For instance, the tradition of Carnatic music would not have been the same without the Śrīvidyā-inflected *kirtans* of Tyāgarāja and Muttusvāmī Dīkṣitar,[7] whose compositions practically constitute the canon. Nor is it an accident that among the ranks of influential scholars in twentieth-century Tamil Nadu, many were devotees of the Kanchi and Sringeri Śaṅkarācārya lineages, initiates in Śrīvidyā ritual practice, or descendants of the Dīkṣitas themselves. Indeed, the very same P. P. S. Sastri who is responsible for orchestrating the preservation of Nīlakaṇṭha's *Saubhāgyacandrātapa* was also the chief contributor to the editing of the southern recension of the Mahābhārata. The authority of the Śrīvidyā Society of Mylapore, at one time the defining institution of Chennai's quintessential Brahmin neighborhood, rests squarely on the shoulders of Appayya and Nīlakaṇṭha; and the neighboring academic bookstore, Jayalakṣmī Indological Bookhouse, maintains itself largely through the sale of Śrīvidyā scriptures and *paddhatis*, consumed voraciously by local intelligentsia. The Sanskrit curriculum in Tamil Nadu pairs the transregional classics of Kālidāsa with the highly regional centuries of the mute poet Mūkakavi,[8] a devotee of Kāmākṣī, largely unknown to Sanskrit literature beyond the Tamil region but celebrated with reverence as an icon of Sanskrit Smārta culture.

That this particular confluence of cultural currents is prototypically Smārta in character—that is, that these features are universally definitive of Smārta-Śaiva religious culture—is captured eloquently by Sankara Rama Sastri, remembered as one of the most prolific critical editors of works of *kāvya* and Alaṅkāraśāstra of the period. Speaking for the twentieth-century Śrīvidyā practitioners of Chennai, Sastri writes, in his Sanskrit introduction to a handbook of Śrīvidyā ritual, the *Śrīvidyāsaparyāpaddhati*:

> This [tradition] was first taught by Paraśiva, the primordial Lord, to the auspicious goddess. Partisanship to this tantra, which independently aggregates the entirety of the aims of man, was manifested by the Blessed Feet of Śrī Śaṅkarācārya, composing the *Saundaryalaharī*, which encapsulated the entirety of Mantraśāstra, and the commentary on the Lalitātriśatī. The ancient great poets, crest jewels of the Vedic tradition, such as Kālidāsa and Mūkakavi, and those of more proximate times, such as Nīlakaṇṭha Dīkṣita, had firmly secured their affections to the pair of lotus feet of the goddess, as is celebrated repeatedly by numerous anecdotes. It has also been ascertained that Vidyāraṇya and others, although the highest of preceptors of the knowledge of Advaita, engaged in the practice of Śrīvidyā. It is well-known by word of mouth that the great treatise on Mantraśāstra, titled *The Forest of Wisdom*, was composed by the sage Vidyāraṇya, and likewise, the treatise on Mantraśāstra known as the *Parimala* was written by the illustrious Appayya Dīkṣita. These two works,

however, are no longer extant. Through an unbroken succession in sequence from the Blessed Feet of Ādi Śaṅkarācārya, the worship of the Śrīcakra, performed in various locations in the monasteries of the Śaṅkarācārya lineages, establishes beyond a doubt the Vaidika status of the tradition of the fifteen-syllable Śrīvidyā mantra.

For, the great goddess Rājarājeśvarī, the supreme deity of Śrīvidyā, known by the name of Kāmākṣī as she adorns the domain of Kanchipuram, has been worshipped by many thousands of the leading traditions of *śruti* and *smṛti;* likewise with Mīnākṣī, illuminating the city of Madurai, who is renowned as the Advisor (Mantriṇī) in the Śrīvidyā tradition, and the goddess referred to as Akhilāṇḍeśvarī, lighting up the sacred site of Jambukeśvara, who indeed is known in Mantraśāstra as the Chastiser (Daṇḍinī), bearing titles such as Daṇḍanāthā, and likewise, Śrī Kanyākumārī, illumining the sacred site of Kanyakumari, who indeed in Śrīvidyā is renowned by the name of the three-syllabled goddess Bālā. Every single twice-born who is intent on the practices of the *śruti*s and *smṛti*s worships daily the mother of the Vedas, Sāvitrī. This is precisely why it is commonly said that *all twice-borns on earth are externally Śaivas, and internally Śāktas.* Therefore, the Śrīvidyā tradition itself is included within the Smārta tradition.[9]

The peculiar aphorism cited here bears repeating, as its theological import cannot be underestimated: as S. R. Sastri informs us: "All twice-borns on earth are externally Śaivas and internally Śāktas." The above passage outlines the conceptual, historical, and geographical territory of a homogenized, unified Smārta sectarian tradition. While modern Smārta religiosity is orthodox Śaiva in its public image and was founded on Śrīvidyā esotericism at its core, it is anchored on the authority of the figures who were narrativized in the seventeenth century as the progenitors of Smārta-Śaivism, such as Śaṅkarācārya and Kālidāsa, and those who set in motion those very narratives, such as Appayya and Nīlakaṇṭha Dīkṣita. And for the Smārtas of present-day Tamil Nadu, Smārta-Śaivism is as intimately bound up with Tamil geography as with the intellectual heritage of Śaṅkara: Śrīvidyā, in its highest abstractions, abides for south Indian Smārtas in the embodied form of the newly domesticated Śākta sacred sites of the Tamil country, where scripture maps perfectly onto spatial territory.

In practice as well as in theory, the legacy of Nīlakaṇṭha's generation synecdochically invokes the characteristic Smārta-Śaiva religiosity preserved by Nīlakaṇṭha's contemporary descendants. Nearly twenty years ago, the residents of Palamadai, the ancestral *agrahāra* of Nīlakaṇṭha's lineage in southern Tamil Nadu near Tirunelveli, honored the memory of their illustrious forefather by allocating a plot of land in the village as a branch *maṭha* of the Śaṅkarācārya lineage of Sringeri. The inauguration ceremony was graced by the presence of Sringeri's Jagadguru Bhāratī Tīrtha Svāmigaḷ, whom present-day descendants of Nīlakaṇṭha have commonly accepted as family guru. In the adjoining shrine to the village's Maṅgalanāyakī Temple, presently venerated as Nīlakaṇṭha's *samādhi* shrine, rests a set of three photographs: a reproduction of a mural painting of Appayya bequeathing scriptural manuscripts to Nīlakaṇṭha, flanked by portraits of the two most recent Jagadgurus of the Sringeri lineage, Bhāratī Tīrtha and Abhinava Vidyātīrtha. Three and a half centuries later, now that Brahmin scholars are no longer sponsored by local rulers to compose works of Sanskrit poetry and philosophy, some things have changed very little for the descendants of early modern south India's leading intellectuals. A hereditary devotional relationship with Śaṅkarācārya preceptors remains to this day a cornerstone of the religious observances of both Appayya's family, who profess allegiance to the Śaṅkarācāryas of the Kāñcī Kāmakoṭi Pīṭha, and of Nīlakaṇṭha's, devotees of the Sringeri Śaṅkarācārya lineage who continue to accept Mīnākṣī as their *kuladevatā,* many of whom recite the *Lalitāsahasranāmastotra* on a daily basis.[10]

Through this book, I have endeavored to capture the process of public theology in the making—the point of intersection between discourse and social system. I have chosen to highlight three instances of theological trajectories—genuinely revolutionary in the scope of their agenda—that exerted a fundamental influence on the future shape of Smārta-Śaiva sectarianism. I chronicle the birth of the formative features of Smārta-Śaiva religiosity from within the sectarian community itself. On one hand an epoch-making development in the history of Indian religion and intellectual life, the birth of the Smārta sectarian tradition also provides an optimal illustration of the widespread acceleration of Hindu sectarianism throughout the centuries of the early modern era, in south India and beyond. When placed in the context of a wider sectarian community in the process of coming into existence, these works begin to speak with a cohesive voice, telling the story of the earliest articulations of the religious values that came to structure the experience of an enduring religious tradition. It is not merely the historical facticity of the Smārta tradition—and the circumstances of its origin—that I have aimed to elucidate in this book; it is also, more crucially, the process of its emergence. Public theology, I contend, provides us with a powerful model for accounting for both the diverse, multivalent texture of Hindu religious experience and the historically contingent phenomena—the genuine theological efforts—that allowed these traditions to assume the shape we observe today.

THE BANYAN TREE: EARLY MODERN SECTARIANISM
AND MODERN PLURALISM

On September 11, 1893, Swami Vivekananda, disciple of Ramakrishna Paramahamsa and history's best-known advocate of Hindu Universalism, defined Hinduism for the World Parliament of Religions in Chicago as a religion qualified primarily by "tolerance and universal acceptance." Ironically, though obviously owing to no intention of his own, his speech prefigured by more than one hundred years a date that resonates for modern audiences with the specter not of tolerance but terrorism. This coincidence was not lost on Prime Minister Narendra Modi, who addressed a crowd in New York City on precisely the same date in 2014 in New York City. Modi proclaimed, "There are 2 images of 11th September: one of the trail of destruction in 2001 and the other the message of Swami Vivekananda in 1893. Had we followed Swami Ji's message, history would never have witnessed such dastardly acts as we saw on 11th September 2001 in [the] USA."[11] Much can be made of the politics behind Modi's invocation of this striking coincidence. For our own purposes, however, the message that Vivekananda delivered that day not only actively promotes a "neo-Hinduism" replete with European influence, as is well known, but also reflects back to the Western world a polemical critique of difference as dissent. In Vivekananda's own words: "Sectarianism, bigotry, and its horrible descendant, fanaticism, have long possessed this beautiful earth. They have filled the earth with violence, drenched it often and often with human blood, destroyed civilization, and sent whole nations to despair."[12]

Sectarianism, bigotry, fanaticism, violence: these synonyms, in the late-nineteenth-century Anglophone imaginaire, reveal just how much discursive space was shared between the Orientalist scholarship of Sir M. Monier-Williams just a decade earlier, in 1883, and the religious worldview of the high-caste Hindus at the height of the Bengali Renaissance. Sectarianism, as defined by Monier-Williams, the exclusive worship of Śiva or Viṣṇu, was an insidious and divisive form of re-ligion that threatened the integrity of a primordial Brahmanical whole. Such an impetus to erase difference comes across most clearly in Vivekananda's speech through the key scriptural verses he cites in support of a Hindu Universalism that, in his view, transcended time and space: "As the different streams having their sources in different places all mingle their water in the sea, so, O Lord, the different paths which men take through different tendencies, various though they appear, crooked or straight, all lead to thee." By no means a coincidence, Vivekananda did not attribute a source to this scriptural citation, which in his mind speaks to a Hinduism free from sectarian division. The passage in question, however, hap-pens to be drawn from verse seven of the *Śivamahimnaḥ Stotram,* "Hymn to the Glory of Śiva," recited for centuries by sectarian Śaivas, the quintessential text that strategically subordinates all other religious traditions to Śaiva orthodoxy. In full, the verse reads:

> The Vedas, Sāṅkhya, Yoga, the Pāśupata doctrine, and the Vaiṣṇava:
> Where authorities are divided, one says, "This is highest," another,
>   "That is beneficial,"
> Due to such variegation of the tastes of men, who enjoy straight or
>   crooked paths.
> *You alone* [Śiva] are the destination, as the ocean is the destination
>   of the waters.[13]

Implicit in the rhetoric of this verse, as we observed in chapter 1, is an inclusivism that appears to welcome with one hand while excluding with the other. Vaiṣṇavas, followers of Sāṅkhya and Yoga, Pāśupatas—not to be conflated with the author's own branch of Śaivism—and Vedic Brahmins, we learn, are all solidly established on the path to truth, a truth that happens to be known as "Śiva." A remarkably similar strategy is omnipresent in the discourse of early modern Śaivism in south India, when Śaivas routinely moved to incorporate Vaiṣṇavism under their own umbrella through the rubric of the Trimūrti, the triple form of divinity. Brahmā, Viṣṇu, and Rudra, in other words, the triad of deities governing creation, sustenance, and dissolution, are simply the manifestations of an overarching divine principle known as Paramaśiva. Vivekananda, essentially, in seeking out source material to promote a homogenized Hinduism, had the ambiguous fortune to invoke a verse that in its original discursive context conveys precisely the opposite message—namely, the supremacy of the Śaiva religion. As Wilhelm Halbfass has written, encapsulating a well-worn argument advanced by Paul Hacker: "'Inclusivism' is the practice of claiming for, and thus including in, one's own religion or world-view what belongs in reality to another, foreign or competing system. It is the subordinating identification of the other, the foreign, with parts or preliminary stages of one's own sphere."[14] Such inclusivism, succinctly, may not ultimately provide the ideal metaphor for the peaceable coexistence of multiple religious traditions.

And yet Hindu pluralism, in contrast to the endemic communalism of postindependence India, itself has genuine roots in the subcontinent's precolonial heritage. In his 2007 monograph *A Vision for Hinduism: Beyond Hindu Nationalism*, Jeffrey Long articulates a vision for a Hindu religious pluralism founded on just this model of inclusivism. Long prefaces his remarks cautiously with the caveat that Western pluralists have levied harsh criticism against the idea of inclusivism on the grounds that its rhetoric generally reads as paternalistic, condescending to "include" the diversity of religious Others encountered by the religious mainstream. And yet, what Long successfully clarifies is the genuine theological work done by Vivekananda and his contemporaries in constructing a viable pluralistic worldview that holds meaning for practitioners past and present. Inclusivistic pluralism, for many, is a sincerely held theological commitment and can viably be promoted as a genuinely emic Hindu pluralism. Emic as this inclusivism may be, however, in the sense of originating within the Indian subcontinent, Vivekananda's particular brand of pluralism is also historically contingent, inconceivable apart from the encounter between the British and Indian intelligentsia that precipitated the Bengali Renaissance. While it is by no means accurate to claim that Vivekananda's theology was "invented" by the British, its historical origins lent themselves to participation in a particular political trajectory. The concept of tolerance, as C. S. Adcock (2014) has demonstrated, a well-known mainstay of Gandhian secularism, served a particular and timely political function, disaggregating questions of caste from the consolidation of an ethos of Hindu majoritarianism. It is no wonder, perhaps, that many observers associate this form of tolerant inclusivism with right-wing Hindu extremism: to be tolerant, succinctly, implies a claim to the authority to tolerate someone else. As a result, inclusivist pluralism, justly or unjustly, is often tarred with the same brush that condemns the sanctioning of communalist violence.

In contrast, etic models of secularist pluralism run afoul of a more pervasive problem—namely, the legacy of European imperialism, a parochialism that lives on in the adjudication of religious difference around the globe. In spite of the burgeoning literature on the multiplicity of global secularisms,[15] excavating the influence of non-Western models of religion as a human right or religion and governmentality,[16] Eurocentrism is alive and well in contemporary discourse on Indian pluralism. Across disciplines of scholarship, pluralism, succinctly, generally falls under the purview of a healthy civil society—a mode of sociality prescriptively modeled after the canons of liberal political theory, the heritage of the European Enlightenment. Where religion is viewed as anathema to public space, its very eruption into visibility is said to signal the dangers of incipient outbursts of violence. Such a scenario is perhaps best exemplified by the stringent standards of the French *laïcité,* in which even the public presence of a Muslim headscarf threatens the singularity of normative civil society—a uniformity literally inconceivable in the Indian subcontinent. Pluralism, in this light, is measured by the rubric of parliamentary democracy, quantified by participation in the political process and the frequency of civil unrest, or the lack thereof. One encounters this ethics of pluralism, for instance, in a compilation of essays edited by Wendy Doniger and Martha Nussbaum (2015) under the title *Pluralism and Democracy in India*—a pair which the authors cast as prescriptively intertwined in their vision for a pluralist Hinduism in the new millennium. In the introduction to the volume, the authors outline a program by which the Indian State can "foster a healthy democratic public culture" by "encouraging civil society institutions that provide a counterweight to the rabid but highly effective groups organized by the Hindu Right."[17]

This book offers no prescriptions for the practice of Hinduism, or for how India can best address the changing needs of a multireligious population. Nevertheless, the past, though it may be a foreign country, is no mere object of curiosity to be studied for personal edification. Although I have approached the origins of Hindu sectarianism in this book on strictly historical grounds, its excavation bears significant potential to speak to the formative antecedents of a distinctively Hindu pluralism through what Foucault describes as a genealogy of the present. The religious inclusivism the Hindu Right has inherited from Vivekananda and his contemporaries, while Hindu in the sense of belonging to the lifeworlds of numerous Hindus today, bears little resemblance to the practice of Hinduism before colonial intervention. In fact, this inclusivism actively obfuscates our understanding of the precolonial diversity of Hinduism and its distinctive engagement with public space. Likewise, viewing history through the lens of a prescriptive Western-centric pluralism predisposes us to read the archive of the Indian past for its deviance from the standards of Euro-American secularism and from the canons of the Enlightenment to which it serves as invariable telos. Thus, in the words of Wendy Doniger, the Mughal emperor Akbar was a pluralist who aimed to "transcend all sectarian differences and unite his disparate subjects,"[18] one of the invariable wings of the good-Muslim, bad-Muslim binary of Akbar and Aurangzeb perpetuated by colonial historiography. And yet when read outside this entrenched metanarrative, Akbar's patronage facilitated the institutional realization of a markedly different sort of pluralism: by endowing separate temples for the Vallabha and Gauḍīya Sampradāyas of Vaiṣṇava Hindus,[19] Akbar and his successors sponsored, though perhaps unwittingly, the efforts made by these communities to establish distinct public and institutional domains. From the gaze of early modern India, sectarianism and pluralism were not opposites: they were fundamentally intertwined.

If this book offers no religious prescriptions, still less does it propose a political agenda—in contrast, perhaps, to Doniger and Nussbaum's vision for revitalizing Indian civil society. The task of advocating religious pluralism in a nation wrought with communalist violence and fundamentalism is far beyond the scope of the present work. Nevertheless, if we have learned anything from the past decades of banned books, crumbling mosques, and hurt feelings, we cannot help but reckon with the fact that the past is always political. Undoubtedly, the way in which we as scholars choose to represent the history of Hinduism has real-world consequences. As a result, it may not be unreasonable to reach for some measure of optimism in recovering a particular Hindu past—not *the* Hindu past, as no single voice can capture such an entity—that speaks to a genuinely emic religious pluralism, one that is at once neither founded upon universalism or exclusivism, nor modeled as a modular transplant of European civil society. Indeed, Hindu pluralism, in historical context, is genealogically independent of European magnanimity; it is not an Other forged in the crucible of colonial subjugation. It is a conceptual, and institutional, approach to internal diversity that cannot be reduced to a singular axis of hegemony.

We are at the point, then, when we can revisit the following questions: What is modern, and distinctively South Asian, about the pluralistic landscape that emerged in India, not in the aftermath, but before colonialism, at the dawn of modernity? How more generally can we understand this new relationship between religion and publicity, in which public space is polarized by the movement of individuals embodying their sectarian identities? To be sure, religious pluralism in south India, as in many contemporary societies, implied at the minimum a plurality of religious institutions, Hindu and otherwise: sectarian communities in south

India were underwritten by a pluralistic economic and legal landscape, as distinct sectarian institutions competed as regionwide landlords and power brokers. This sheer plurality of religions, for many theorists, was sufficient to mark India as a highly pluralistic society: Ernst Troeltsch, bringing our exploration full circle, argues that Hinduism and Buddhism were the earliest advocates of religious pluralism, granting the individual the right to choose his own personal faith. And yet, in India, religion itself is rarely a matter of belief, a propositional assent to the existence of deities or the authority of a particular temple or saint.

Pluralism, in early modern south India, like religion itself, is an embodied, spatial practice; when religious identity is not the internal affair of a private, unmarked citizen, religious pluralism itself is performed in public space. The story of Hindu pluralism is no utopia; by no means is it free of inequities and injustices. And yet, attending to Hinduism's emic legacy of religious pluralism allows us to heed the advice, proffered by Martha Nussbaum among others,[20] to refrain from labeling any one vision as India's "real" or "authentic" image. When speaking of Hinduism—a religious unity that first emerged as inherently plural, a fusion of the myriad Śaiva, Vaiṣṇava, Śākta, and other religious identities—it is simply impossible to speak of an authentic Hinduism in the singular. Pluralizing Hinduism, then, is not a strategic project, designed to render audible its numerous subaltern voices—although this is undoubtedly a legitimate concern—but rather a recognition that its composite history makes it impossible to select any doctrine, practice, or identity as a Hindu "ideal type." Indeed, it is the spatial enactment of religious pluralism that formed the foundation of early modern south India's multiple religious publics, making possible a multicentric negotiation of power, identity, and truth. In essence, the sectarian religious publics of early modern south India provide us with an opportunity to rethink the very criteria for a non-Western pluralism, founded not on the prescriptive model of a Western civil society but on a historically descriptive account of the role of religion in public space.

The Sixty-Four Games of Śiva

The following is a brief summary of each episode of the Sacred Games according to Parañcōti's sequence. For a fuller rendition of the narratives, see Holt (2007) and Dessigane et al. (1960).

1. Indra's Sin Is Removed (*intiraṉ paḻi tīrtta paṭalam*)
   The god Indra, having incurred the sin of Brahminicide by killing the demons Viśvarūpa and Vṛtra, is relieved of his sin after having discovered a *śivaliṅga* in a *katampa* forest and having bathed in its sacred pool.

2. Removing Airāvata's Curse (*veḷḷaiyāṉaic cāpatīrtta paṭalam*)
   Indra's white elephant Airāvata is cursed by the sage Durvāsas for trampling on a flower garland gifted to Durvāsas by Śiva. Airāvata is forced to descend to earth and is cleansed of his sin by worshipping at the same *śivaliṅga* in the *katampa* forest.

3. Establishing the Sacred City (*tirunakaran kaṇṭa paṭalam*)
   A merchant named Dhanañjaya chances upon the *śivaliṅga* in the *katampa* forest while traveling for business. After he reports his discovery of the shrine to the king Kulaśekhara Pāṇḍya, Śiva comes to the Pandian ruler in a dream and commands him to clear the *katampa* forest and build the city of Madurai.

4. The Incarnation of Taṭātakai (*taṭātakaippirāṭṭiyār tiruvavatārap paṭalam*)
   The Pandian king Malayadhvaja performs a sacrifice to obtain a son, but instead a daughter is born with three breasts. He is instructed by divine guidance to raise her as a son, knowing that her third breast will disappear when she meets her future husband.

5. The Sacred Marriage (*tirumaṇap paṭalam*)
   Princess Taṭātakai, having inherited the Pandian kingdom, embarks on the traditional conquest of the directions. She defeats all enemies effortlessly, until she leads an assault on Śiva at Mount Kailāsa. When she beholds Śiva, her third breast disappears, and a divine wedding later ensues in Madurai.

6. Dancing in the Silver Hall (*veḷḷiyampalat tirukūttāṭiya paṭalam*)
   Following the divine marriage, the sages Patañjali and Vyāghrapāda respectfully refuse to eat until they receive *darśan* of Śiva's sacred dance, traditionally held at the Golden Hall in Cidambaram. Śiva obliges by replicating his dance in the Silver Hall of the Madurai temple.

7. Feeding Guṇḍodara (*kuṇṭōtaraṉukku aṉṉamiṭṭa paṭalam*)
   One of Śiva's Gaṇa attendants, named Guṇḍodara, devours the remainder of the vast wedding feast.

8. Calling the Rice Pits and the Vaikai River (*aṉṉakkuḻiyum vaikaiyum aḻaitta paṭalam*)
   Having devoured vast amounts of rice, Guṇḍodara begs for water, and Śiva responds by placing (*vai*) his hand (*kai*) on the ground to create the Vaikai River.

9. Calling the Seven Seas (*ēḻukaṭal aḻaitta paṭalam*)
   Queen Kāñcanamālā, Taṭātakai's mother, wishes to make a pilgrimage to bathe in the ocean. Śiva summons the seven seas into a tank in the vicinity of Madurai to fulfill her desire.

10. Calling Malayadhvaja (*malayattuvacaṉaiy aḻaitta paṭalam*)
    The late king Malayadhvaja returns from heaven to bathe in the seven seas with his wife, Kāñcanamālā.

11. The Incarnation of Ugravarman Pāṇḍya (*ukkirapāṇṭiyaṉ tiruvavatārap paṭalam*)
    Taṭātakai gives birth to a son, Ugravarman Pāṇḍya, incarnation of Murukaṉ.

12. Giving a Mace, Spear, and Armband to Ugravarman Pāṇḍya (*ukkirapāṇṭiyaṉukku vēl vaḷai ceṇṭu koṭutta paṭalam*)
    Ugravarman Pāṇḍya marries the daughter of the Cōḻa king and receives divinely empowered weapons from his father.

13. Throwing the Spear at the Ocean (*kaṭalcuvara vēlviṭṭa paṭalam*)
    Having received orders from his father, Śiva, in a dream, Ugravarman Pāṇḍya throws his spear at the ocean to prevent it from encroaching upon the city.

14. Throwing the Armband at Indra's Crown (*intiraṉ muṭimēl vaḷaiy eṟinta paṭalam*)
    Following a long drought, Ugravarman Pāṇḍya and the Cōḻa and Cēra kings approach Indra to petition him for rain. Ugravarman, son of Śiva, refuses to humble himself before Indra; when Indra, angered, attacks him, he throws his armband at Indra's thunderbolt, stopping it in midair.

15. Hitting Mount Meru with the Mace (*mēruvaic ceṇṭāl aṭitta paṭalam*)
    During another drought, Ugravarman prays to Śiva, who instructs him to travel to Mount Meru and hit the mountain with his mace. Having done so,

Ugravarman discovers a hidden fortune that alleviates the suffering of his kingdom.

16. Granting the Truth of the Vedas (*vētattukkup poruḷ aruḷic ceyta paṭalam*)
When the Brahmins of Madurai are chanting the Vedas without comprehending them, Śiva appears before them in the form of Dakṣiṇāmūrti to instruct them, teaching that the Vedas and the *śivaliṅga* are one.

17. Selling Rubies (*māṇikkam viṟṟa paṭalam*)
When the royal ministers discover that rubies are missing from the Pandian prince's crown before his coronation, Śiva takes the form of a jewel merchant to replace the rubies.

18. Drying Up Varuṇa's Ocean (*varuṇaṉ viṭṭa kaṭalai vaṟṟac ceyta paṭalam*)
Varuṇa, the god of the ocean, makes a pilgrimage to Madurai to cure his stomachache. When the ocean threatens to inundate Madurai as a result, Śiva calls the clouds to dry up the water.

19. The City with Four Barriers (*nāṉmāṭakkūṭalāṉa paṭalam*)
When Varuṇa again threatens Madurai with a torrential storm, Śiva commands the king Abhiṣekha Pāṇḍya to construct four barriers to protect the city.

20. Becoming an All-Powerful Ascetic (*cittar*) (*ellām valla cittarāṉa paṭalam*)
Śiva takes the form of an ascetic, performing numerous miracles throughout Madurai.

21. Feeding the Stone Elephant Sugarcane (*kallāṉaikkuk karumparuttiya paṭalam*)
Śiva, disguised as an ascetic, impresses king Abhiṣekha Pāṇḍya by causing a stone elephant in the Madurai temple to come to life and eat a stalk of sugarcane.

22. Killing the Elephant (*yāṉaiy eyta paṭalam*)
When the Cōḻa king dispatches Jain magicians to assault Madurai with enchanted siege weapons, Śiva becomes an archer and shoots the rampaging elephant, turning it into stone and creating the mountain Yāṉaimalai.

23. The Old Man Becomes a Boy (*virutta kumārapālarāṉa paṭalam*)
Śiva takes the form of an ascetic to bring comfort to his devotee, Gaurī, who is experiencing domestic strife in her marriage to a Vaiṣṇava. When Gaurī offers food to the old ascetic, Śiva transforms himself into a young Śaiva Brahmin boy.

24. Changing the Leg and Dancing (*kāṉmāṟiy āṭiṉa paṭalam*)
When the king Rājaśekhara Pāṇḍya expresses sorrow at seeing the dancing Śiva in the Madurai temple strain his leg by always dancing on the same foot, Śiva miraculously transforms the temple image so that it dances on the other foot.

25. Fearing Slander (*paḻiyañciṉa paṭalam*)
When a Brahmin accuses a hunter of murdering the Brahmin's wife, King Kulottuṅga Pāṇḍya prays to Śiva for guidance in administering justice. Śiva reveals to the king how the attendants of Yama, god of death, had arranged the Brahmin's wife's demise, proving the hunter's innocence.

26. Absolving the Great Sin (*māpātakan tīrtta paṭalam*)
Śiva grants clemency to a Brahmin boy guilty of incest and patricide, demonstrating his compassion toward even the worst of sinners.

27. Cutting the Limbs (*aṅkam veṭṭiṉa paṭalam*)
Śiva confronts in battle a young sword-fighting instructor who disrespects his teacher and approaches his teacher's wife with lust. Śiva then cuts the young man's body into pieces.

28. Killing the Elephant (*nāgam eyta paṭalam*)
The Jain magicians of Madurai summon a giant serpent demon to kill the Pandian king by poisoning him with his venom. Śiva cures the king by releasing drops of nectar from the crescent moon in his hair, purifying the city of Madurai.

29. Killing the Magical Cow (*māyappacuvai vataitta paṭalam*)
When the Jains dispatch a crazed cow demon to wreak havoc in the city of Madurai, Śiva's bull, Nandi, defeats it.

30. Revealing the Truth (*meykkāṭṭiṭṭa paṭalam*)
When an enemy army attacks the Pandian kingdom, King Kulabhūṣaṇa Pāṇḍya appoints his general, Cuntaracamantar, to raise an army in a single day. Cuntaracamantar petitions Śiva for assistance, and Śiva himself arrives mounted on horseback and surrounded by a massive army.

31. Granting the Inexhaustible Bag of Gold (*ulavākkiḻiy aruḷiya paṭalam*)
By disrespecting the Brahmins of his kingdom, Kulabhūṣaṇa leads Madurai into poverty and despair. When the king prays to Śiva for a remedy, Śiva appears before him in a dream and grants him a bottomless bag of gold.

32. Selling Bangles (*vaḷaiyal viṟṟa paṭalam*)
The sages' wives whom Śiva had seduced in the Dakṣa forest are reborn, owing to their impropriety, as women of the Vanikar caste in Madurai. Because their bangles had previously fallen off as a result of the women's longing for Śiva, the god appears in Madurai in the form of a bangle seller to replace them.

33. Teaching the Eight Great Siddhis (*aṭṭamācittiy upatecitta paṭalam*)
Śiva teaches the eight great *siddhi*s (magical powers), commonly mentioned in Tantric texts, to the Kārttikeya Yakṣīs, instructing them to meditate on the goddess to master these powers.

34. Placing the Mark of the Bull (*viṭaiyilacciṉaiy iṭṭa paṭalam*)
In a dream, Śiva promises to grant his *darśan* to the Cōḻa king Kāṭuveṭṭiya during his pilgrimage to Madurai. Onlookers later discover a bull symbol emblazoned on the north gate of the Madurai temple, where Śiva had personally escorted the Cōḻa king into the shrine for *darśan*.

35. Placing the Watershed (*taṇṇīrpantal vaitta paṭalam*)
When the Cōḻa Kāṭuveṭṭiya conspires with the Pandian king's brother to overthrow the kingdom of Madurai, Śiva magically multiplies the Pandian troops on the battlefield, leading to a landslide victory. He constructs a watershed amid

the Pandian forces, appearing among the troops himself as a servant offering
water.

36. Doing Alchemy (*iracavātañ ceyta paṭalam*)
The housewife Poṉṉaṉaiyāḷ is deeply devoted to Śiva, offering all of her earnings
to feed his ascetic devotees, yet she longs for a statue of Śiva to worship. Śiva appears before her as an ascetic and miraculously transforms her copper pots into
gold, which she then has made into a *mūrti* of Śiva to be installed in the temple.

37. The Cōḻa King Falls into a Pit (*cōḻaṉai maṭuvil vīṭṭiya paṭalam*)
Because the Pandian king has spent his treasury on worshipping Śiva, his
standing army has diminished, inviting a Cōḻa invasion. During the battle, Śiva
causes the Cōḻa king to fall into a pit, onto the Pandian king's spear.

38. Granting the Unemptying Paddy Container (*ulavākkōṭṭaiy aruḷiya paṭalam*)
Having invested all of his harvest in offerings of charity, despite great famine,
the farmer Nallaṉ, falling into poverty, decides to commit suicide. When he
comes before Śiva in the temple to offer his life, Śiva grants him a bottomless
container of paddy.

39. Filing a Case for the Uncle (*māmaṉākavantu vaḻakkuraitta paṭalam*)
When a wealthy merchant renounces the world, leaving his fortune to his
nephew, relatives appropriate the money from the boy. Śiva appears in court in
the form of the merchant to demand that the relatives return the wealth to the
boy and his mother.

40. Showing Śiva's Heaven to Varaguṇa Pāṇḍya (*varakuṇaṉukkuc civalōkaṅ kāṭṭiya
paṭalam*)
Śiva grants Varaguṇa Pāṇḍya a vision of the heavenly realms, having rescued
him from the accidental sin of Brahminicide and facilitated his defeat of the
Cōḻa army.

41. Selling Firewood (*viṟaku viṟṟa paṭalam*)
To settle a dispute between a musician devotee, Bāṇabhadra, and his rival, Śiva
takes the form of a firewood seller. Śiva claims to have been rejected as un-
worthy of discipleship under Bāṇabhadra, while performing divine music that
astounds the onlookers.

42. Giving the Sacred Letter (*tirumukaṅ koṭutta paṭalam*)
After Śiva has stolen much of the Pandian king's wealth to distribute to his poor
devotees, he sends Bāṇabhadra on a mission to the Cēra king, who gifts him the
entirety of his treasury to return to Madurai.

43. Giving the Plank (*palakaiy iṭṭa paṭalam*)
Because of Bāṇabhadra's ceaseless devotion in singing to Śiva in the temple every
night, Śiva procures for him a golden, jewel-encrusted seat on which to sing.

44. Winning the Music Contest (*icaivātu veṉṟa paṭalam*)
When Bāṇabhadra's wife quarrels with the king's mistress, the mistress sets up
a music competition between Bāṇabhadra's wife and a Laṅkan singer. Śiva arranges victory for Bāṇabhadra's wife.

45. Giving the Breast to Piglets (*paṉrikkuṭṭikku mulai koṭutta paṭalam*)
Śiva transforms himself into a mother sow to give milk to a family of orphaned piglets, changing their bodies into those of men.

46. Changing the Piglets into Ministers (*paṉrikkuṭṭikalai mantirikaḷākkiya paṭalam*)
Śiva explains his actions by appointing the twelve pig-faced men as royal ministers.

47. Teaching the Blackbird (*karikkuruvikkupatēcañ ceyta paṭalam*)
When a blackbird makes a pilgrimage to bathe in Madurai's temple tank, Śiva initiates him with his divine mantra. Previously, the blackbird had been a man, reborn as a blackbird owing to his misdeeds.

48. Giving Liberation to the Crane (*nāraikku mutti koṭutta paṭalam*)
A crane bathing in the temple tank declines, out of piety, to eat the sacred fish, and Śiva grants him liberation as a boon.

49. Becoming the City Encircled by a Snake (*tiruvālavāyāṉa paṭalam*)
When the Pandian king requests a marker for the city's boundaries, Śiva releases the snake encircling his wrist to surround the city, marking its outskirts.

50. Shooting the Arrow Named for the Beautiful Lord (*cuntarappēr ampeyta paṭalam*)
Defending Madurai against the invading Cōḻa army, Śiva takes the form of an archer to lead the Pandian army, shooting divine arrows that slaughter the Cōḻa soldiers en masse.

51. Giving the Caṅkam Plank (*caṅkappalakai koṭutta paṭalam*)
The poets of the Tamil Caṅkam are incarnated from Sarasvatī in Madurai owing to a curse. Śiva grants them a magical plank that expands, but only far enough to allow those with poetic talent to sit upon it.

52. Giving the Prize to Tarumi (*tarumikkup poṟkiḻiy aḷitta paṭalam*)
When a young Brahmin bachelor, Tarumi, cannot afford a dowry, Śiva arranges for him to win the king's poetry contest by granting him the winning verse. The Caṅkam poet Nakkīrar attempts to find fault with Śiva's verse, and Śiva throws him into the temple tank in retaliation.

53. Lifting Nakkīrar to the Shore (*kīraṉaik karaiy ēṟṟiya paṭalam*)
Śiva rescues Nakkīrar from the tank and forgives his audacity, at which point Nakkīrar's pride is humbled.

54. Teaching Grammar to Nakkīrar (*kīraṉukku ilakkaṇam upatēcitta paṭalam*)
Because of Nakkīrar's deficient knowledge of grammar and poetics, Śiva dispatches the sage Agastya to alleviate his ignorance.

55. Resolving the Caṅkam Poets' Quarrel (*caṅkattār kalakaṉ tīrtta paṭalam*)
When the Caṅkam poets cannot agree on the relative value of their compositions, Śiva appoints the merchant Dhanapati, an incarnation of Murukaṉ, as judge.

56. The Poet Iṭaikkāṭar's Resentment (*iṭaikkāṭan piṇakkut tīrtta paṭalam*)
    The Pandian king disrespects a Tamil composition of the poet Iṭaikkāṭar, and
    Śiva, taking offense, departs from Madurai along with his *liṅga,* returning only
    when the king begs forgiveness.

57. Throwing the Fishing Net (*valai vīciṉa paṭalam*)
    The goddess is not listening when Śiva instructs her in the meaning of the
    Vedas, so Śiva curses her to be born in a fishermen's community, and curses
    his bull, Nandi, to become a shark. Śiva takes incarnation to capture that shark
    with a net when it terrorizes the fishing community.

58. Teaching Māṇikkavācakar (*vātavūraṭikaḷukku upatēcitta paṭalam*)
    The young Māṇikkavācakar, a gifted servant of the Pandian king, is dispatched
    by the king with money to buy horses. During his journey, Śiva appears to the
    young man and initiates him, at which point he is overcome with devotion.

59. Foxes Become Horses (*nari pariyākkiya paṭalam*)
    Māṇikkavācakar has spent the funds given to him on service to Śiva, and the
    king is angered when the requested horses do not materialize. In response to
    Māṇikkavācakar's prayers, Śiva transforms all the foxes in the forest into horses
    for the king.

60. Horses Become Foxes (*pari nariyākkiya paṭalam*)
    Although the king is pleased with his new horses, at midnight the horses trans-
    form back into foxes. In order to save his devotee from punishment, Śiva floods
    the Vaikai River to distract the soldiers.

61. Carrying Earth (*maṇ cumanta paṭalam*)
    When the citizens of Madurai are drafted to dam the Vaikai River, an eighty-
    year-old sweetmeats vendor is unable to work. Śiva volunteers to take her place
    but falls asleep at the docks. The dockworker strikes Śiva's body with a blow that
    resounds throughout the city.

62. Curing the Pandian King's Fever (*pāṇṭiyaṉ curan tīrtta paṭalam*)
    The Pandian king converts to Jainism and, as a result, falls ill with a virulent
    fever. The Śaiva saint Ñāṉacampantar cures him with sacred ash, converting
    him back to Śaivism.

63. Mounting the Jains on Stakes (*camaṇaraik kaḻuv ēṟṟiya*)
    The Jains, in anger, challenge Campantar to an ordeal to prove the veracity of their
    doctrine. Upon failing in the task, they proceeded to impale themselves on stakes.

64. Calling the Vaṉṉi Tree, Well, and Linga (*vaṉṉiyum kiṇaṟum iliṅkamum aḻaitta
    paṭalam)*
    Campantar resurrects a young boy killed by a snakebite, and marries him to the
    girl who had summoned the saint to save the boy's life. The only witnesses to
    the marriage, a *vaṉṉi* tree, well, and *liṅga,* magically appear to save the girl from
    ostracization at the hands of her cowife.

NOTES

INTRODUCTION

1. Names have been changed.

2. Such works include W. C. Smith (1962), Dalmia (1995), Stietencron (1989), Hawley (1991), B. K. Smith (1989), and numerous others.

3. This position has been most notably advocated by Andrew Nicholson in his book *Unifying Hinduism: Philosophy and Identity in Indian Intellectual History* (2010). See also Pennington (2005), van der Veer (1994), and Lorenzen (1995, 1999), to name a few.

4. The Sanskrit *śloka* reads: "prāmāṇyabuddhir vedeṣu sādhanānām anekatā | upāsyānām aniyama etat dharmasya lakṣaṇam ||" Quoted in Inamdar (1983).

5. I speak primarily of the Āgamic Śaivism of the Mantramārga. See chapter 1 for a more detailed discussion of the transformation of Śaivism from a hegemonic, pan-Indian religion to a sect of an overarching Hindu orthodoxy.

6. Ernst Troeltsch (1931) here draws on Max Weber's distinction between *Kirche* and *Sekte* outlined in his *Die Wirtschaftethik der Weltreligionen* (1915–1919). See also Srilata Raman (2007, 180n2) for an alternative definition proposed by Louis Dumont.

7. See Hawley (2015) for a deconstruction of the very idea of the "bhakti movement."

8. Novetzke (2016).

9. Monier-Williams, *Brāhmanism and Hinduism* (1891, 60).

10. Masuzawa, *The Invention of World Religions* (2005).

11. See Subrahmaniam, *South Indian Temple Inscriptions*, 3:393, for the Tamil text of this inscription from the Varadarāja temple in Kanchipuram, recorded as ARE no. 584 of 1919.

12. Bronner (2007).

13. vidvadguror vihitaviśvajidadhvarasya śrīsarvatomukhamahāvratayājisūnoḥ | śrīraṅgarājamakhinaḥ śritacandramauḷir asty appai dīkṣita iti prathitas tanūjaḥ || yena śrīcinnabommakṣitipabalabhidaḥ kīrtir avyāhatāsīt yaś ca śrīkaṇṭhabhāṣyaṃ

paramaśivamatasthāpanāyoddadhāra | tena śrīraṅgarājādhvarivaratanayenāppayajvādhi-
penākāri prauḍhonnatāgraṃ rajatagirinibhaṃ kālakaṇṭheśadhāma || This inscription is re-
corded in "Report on South Indian Epigraphy" as number 395 of 1991. The text is published
in Y. M. Sastri (1929, 148–149), and Ramesan (1972, 25–26). Y. Mahalinga Sastri recom-
mends emending the original "yena," the first word of the second *pāda* of v. 2, to "yaś ca."
Sastri also believes this verse to be the original composition of Appayya Dīkṣita himself, as
portions of it appear elsewhere in the author's oeuvre.

14. svasti śrī śakābdaṃ 1504 kku mēl collā niṉṟu citrabhānu varuṣam svāmi
kālakaṇṭheśvararuṭa kōvililē śrīkaṇṭhabhāṣyam aiññūṟu vidvāṃsarukku paṭipikka
atukku śivārkamaṇidīpikaivyākhyānamum paṇṇi vēlūr cinnabomma nāyakkar kayyilē
kanakābhiṣekamum paṇṇi viccukkoṇṭu atukkuppiṉ vēlūrilē śivārkamaṇidīpikaiyum aiññūṟu
vidvāṃsarukku paṭippikka cinnabomma nāyakkar kayyilē svarṇaṅkaḷum agrahāraṅgaḷum
paṭaippiccu prativirājyaṃ [i.e., pṛthivīrājyam] paṇṇiviccu nyāyarakṣāmaṇi kalpataruparimala mutalāṉa nūṟu prabandha paṇṇiṉa appaidīkṣitaruṭa kṛti inta śivālayam śubham astu. See
the preceding footnote for the published inscription. The Sanskrit verses and Maṇipravāḷa
prose are followed by the signatures of a number of scholars who served as witnesses.

15. We also find the variant "Śrīkaṇṭhamatapratiṣṭhāpanācārya." This *biruda* also appears in the colophon of the first *pariccheda* of Nīlakaṇṭha's *Saubhāgyacandrātapa*.

16. For example: ata evāsmaddīkṣitaiḥ śivārcanacandrikāyām uktam—rājānaḥ
strībālā roginaḥ pravāsinaś ca śītodakena snānāśaktāv uṣṇodakena snānaṃ kuryuḥ.
The *Śivārcanacandrikā* is one of Nīlakaṇṭha's primary sourcebooks for daily Śaiva ritual
practice.

17. "Bathed in gold on account of his *Śivārkamaṇidīpikā*, he was praised by Samarapuṅgava
Yajvan as follows: At the time of his unction in gold, on the pretext of heaping up gold
all around him, King Cinnabomma made a golden water basin for the wish-fulfilling
tree of stainless wisdom, Appayya Dīkṣita." (tad api jñāyate yad eṣa śivārkamaṇidīpikāva-
sānalabdhakanakasnānaḥ praśaṃsitaḥ samarapuṅgavayajvanā yathā—hemābhiṣekasamaye
parito niṣaṇṇasauvarṇasaṃhatimiṣāc cinabommabhūpaḥ | appayyadīkṣitamaṇer
anavadyavidyākalpadrumasya kurute kanakālavālam || [*Nalacaritranāṭaka*, pgs. 4–5]). The
work Nīlakaṇṭha cites here, Samarapuṅgava's *Yātrāprabandha*, is structured as a biographical
travelogue and commemorates the pilgrimage of the author's elder brother to Varanasi. In
a similar vein, Ramesan cites another anonymous poet as having described Appayya as follows, stressing once again the centrality of Śaiva theology to his scholarly work: nānādeśana-
rendramaṇḍalamahāyatnātidūrībhavat-kādācitkapadāravindavinater appayyayajvaprabhoḥ
| śaivotkarṣapariṣkṛtair aharahaḥ sūktaiḥ sudhālālitaiḥ phullatkarṇaputasya bommanṛpateḥ
puṇyāni gaṇyāni kim ||

18. śaivaśāstravidāṃ śreṣṭhaḥ śrīmān appayyadīkṣitaḥ | citrakūṭe jitārātiraśobhata
mahāyaśāḥ || advaitadīpikābhikhyaṃ granthaṃ appayadīkṣitaḥ | cakāra bhagavad[d]veṣī
śaivadharmarataḥ sadā || (*Prapannāmṛtam*, 126.13). advaitadīpikābhikhyaṃ granthaṃ
appayyadīkṣitaḥ | cakāra bhagavad[d]veṣī śaivadharmarataḥ sadā || (126.14).

19. vidhāya tātayācāryas tatpañcamatabhañjanam | śrīrāmānujasiddhāntam avyāhatam
apālayat || mahācāryo mahātejāḥ sa kṛtvā caṇḍamārutam | avyāhataṃ yatīndrasya taṃ
siddhāntam apālayat || (*Prapannāmṛtam*, 126.17).

20. For more details on these texts, see Minkowski (2010), "I'll Wash Out Your Mouth
with My Boot," a study of the sectarian controversies in seventeenth- and eighteenth-

century Benares concerning the authenticity of the Bhāgavata Purāṇa. Chronological and stylistic evidence makes it clear that this trend in north Indian sectarian debate was borrowed directly from the South, particularly by way of Bhānuji Dīkṣita/Rāmāśrama, son of Bhaṭṭoji Dīkṣita, pupil of Appayya Dīkṣita.

21. See also Pauwels (2009).

22. See LaRocque (2004) for this argument. LaRocque, however, somewhat overextends the historical reach of his evidence in painting a portrait of early modern Vaiṣṇavism and Jainism as ideological supports of a protocapitalist economy, which he literally equates with Weber's Protestant ethic.

23. Horstmann (2006, 2009).

24. Luhmann (1995, 21).

25. Translation by Vasudeva (2005).

26. For a qualification of the argument that Appayya Dīkṣita reinvented south Indian Śaivism through a recovery of Śrīkaṇṭha's Brahmasūtrabhāṣya, see Fisher (2017), which draws attention to the debts Appayya owes to Vīraśaiva theologians in the Andhra and Tamil regions.

27. See, for instance, Victoria Kahn (2014) for a "return to secularism" as the intrinsic feature of a singular modernity inherited from western Europe; and see Gregory (2012) on the argument for the causal relationship between the Protestant Reformation and secularism.

28. On distinctively Indian manifestations of secularism in the twentieth century and beyond, see for instance Asad (1993) and Bilgrami (2014).

29. Among counterexamples that can be proposed, Kabir and other *nirguṇa bhakti* saints, I would argue, do not fit this description. Disavowing ritualism or affiliation with particular communities is not the same as rejecting religion as a category.

30. It is important to distinguish sectarian conflict from the armed militarism of religious renunciants who served as mercenaries in north India (Pinch 2006). See Clémentin-Ojha (1999) for a colonial-period example of more properly sectarian conflict.

31. Venkatkrishnan (2015).

32. Lutgendorf (2012).

33. O'Hanlon (2011).

34. On the prescription that religious dialogue be fostered in intercommunal "civic centers," see Doniger and Nussbaum (2015).

35. Hudson (1977, 1989), Davis (2004).

36. A more recent history of the Tamil Brahmin community's trials and transformations in the twentieth century can be found in Fuller and Narasimhan (2014), *Tamil Brahmins: The Making of a Middle Class*. Those unfamiliar with the religious landscape of Tamil Nadu should note that the term can be misleading: by no means are all Tamil Brahmins Śaiva, nor were Smārta Brahmins in a position of relative social dominance in the seventeenth century let alone today, an intellectual rather than political or economic elite.

37. Fuller and Narasimhan (2014) discuss the social structure of Tamil Brahminism in the early twentieth century, what they describe as the "making of a middle class." On the religious culture of the contemporary Smārta-Śaiva Brahmin community, see Douglas Brooks (1992b), as well as Leela Prasad (2007), a lively ethnographic account, if not specifically grounded in the Tamil south.

38. See in particular Clark (2006) on the history of the Sringeri Śaṅkarācārya *maṭha*.

1. HINDU SECTARIANISM

sa svāmī mama daivataṃ taditaro nāmnāpi nāmnāyate. This line occupies the final *pāda* of each verse of the *Śivotkarṣamañjarī*.

1. yaṃ śaivāḥ samupāsate śiva iti brahmeti vedāntino bauddhā buddha iti pramāṇapaṭavaḥ karteti naiyāyikāḥ | arhaṃś ceti ha jainaśāsanamatiḥ karmeti mīmāṃsakāḥ so 'yaṃ vo vidadhātu vāñchitaphalaṃ srīkeśavas sa[rva]dā || Rice, *Epigraphical Carnatica*, 5:99.

2. The *Śivamahimnaḥ Stotram* is included in the vast majority of ecumenical, Śaiva, and Smārta modern collections of Sanskrit devotional hymns and has been the subject of dozens of commentaries, though only Madhusūdana Sarasvatī's has been published. See *Śivamahimnaḥ Stotram,* edited by W. Norman Brown (1965), for edition and translation. Most likely produced by a community of Śaivas who adhered neither to the Śaiva Siddhānta nor to the older traditions of the Pāñcārthika Pāśupatas, the text was certainly extant and in circulation by 985 C.E., when we find it inscribed on the walls of the Amareśvara temple in Omakareshwara in central Madhya Pradhesh.

3. *Śivamahimnaḥ Stotram,* v. 7: trayī sāṃkhyaṃ yogaḥ paśupatimataṃ vaiṣṇavam iti prabhinne prasthāne param idam adaḥ pathyam iti ca / rucīnāṃ vaicitryād ṛjukuṭilanānāpathajuṣāṃ nṛṇām eko gamyas tvam asi payasām arṇava iva.

4. In fact, to the best of our knowledge, most Pāśupatas, such as Kauṇḍinya, author of our earliest surviving scholastic work of the tradition, did not accept the authority of the Vedas at all, despite the fact that Pāśupatism is typically considered to be a "Hindu" tradition.

5. B. K. Smith (1989, 13–14). Emphasis in original.

6. For more detail on Śaiva postmortuary rituals, see Sanderson (1995) and Mirnig (2009). Acharya (2010) offers an edition and translation of a Pāśupata postmortuary ritual manual. The procedures for the brushing of the teeth, *dantadhāvana,* in most Śaiva handbooks, or *paddhatis,* recapitulate the core discussion of the matter in Manu, often with more elaborate systematization. See, for example, Brunner-Lachaux (1963, 1985) for richly annotated discussions of the routine Śaiva purification practices to be performed in preparation for worship and their intertextual relationship with the Dharmaśāstras.

7. Consisting of eight major works composed over the course of the first millennium of the Common Era, the Śivadharma corpus offers us unparalleled insight into the practices and theology of lay Śaivas as well as into the social practices and institutional culture of transregional Śaiva communities in the first millennium. The subject of several forthcoming studies, as well as an ongoing collaborative research project headed by Peter Bisschop and Florinda de Simini aimed at producing critical editions of the texts, most of the scholarship on this subject remains unpublished. Important exceptions include two early surveys by R. C. Hazra (1985) of the Calcutta manuscripts of the Śivadharma and Śivadharmottara— which offer some conjectures on the dates of the work—as well as an additional survey of the Śivadharmottara by Paolo Magnone (2005), which provides some useful insight but offers an implausible chronology and context for the work's origin. Jason Schwartz (2012) offers a concise but significant reading of the contempt that the texts display toward Vaidika religions, as well as a treatment of their devotional theology. Finally, Alexis Sanderson's (2009) theorization of the Śaiva Age is deeply informed by this corpus, and citations from these texts are presented without much comment in his most recent essays. Peter Bisschop has

noted that the Śivadharma is likely a work of the early fifth century and the Śivadharmottara probably was largely composed in the seventh or early eighth century (personal communication, New Delhi, 2012). A transcript of the Śivadharma, misidentified as Śivadharmottara, has been published on the web by the Muktabodha Indological Archive. Another key text of the corpus, erroneously identified as the Śivopaniṣad, was included by Adyar in *Unpublished Upaniṣads* (1933). Finally, Yogi Nara Hari Nath, the Nāth Maṭhādhipati of Mṛgasthalī in Nepal, published a handwritten transcription, accompanied by his own learned commentary in mixed Sanskrit and Nepali, of five works of the corpus (1979).

8. tasmāc chataguṇaṃ puṇyaṃ śive mṛtpātradānataḥ / hemapātrantu yad datvā puṇyaṃ syādvedapārage // agnihotrāśc a vedāś ca yajñāś ca bahudakṣiṇāḥ / śivaliṅgārcanasyaite koṭyaṃśenāpi no samāḥ (Śivadharma 5.88, 7.2). Likewise, the following verse presents us with a theme and variation on the above message, seemingly extolling Vaidika religious practice while in fact strictly distinguishing the community of Śaiva devotees, Śivabhaktas, from non-Śaiva Brahminical practitioners: "Śiva is the Veda; the Veda is Śiva. The one who studies the Veda is Sadāśiva. Therefore, the devotees of Śiva ought to give charitably to one learned in the Vedas, according to capacity." vedaḥ śivaḥ śivo vedaḥ vedādhyāyī sadāśivaḥ / tasmād vedavide deyaṃ śivabhaktair yathābalam (Śivadharma 4.12).

9. The Niśvāsa corpus (of which the first volume has been recently published by the Institut français de Pondichéry) includes the earliest foundational texts of the Śaiva Siddhānta and seems to provide the textual foundation for Tantric religion in general, as the corpus has come to serve as the primary resource for the redaction of quintessential Bhairava Āgamas, such as the Svacchanda Tantra, as well as key works of the Trika, such as the Mālinīvijayottara. The first work in the corpus, Niśvāsatattvasaṃhitā (c. fifth century C.E.) was likely composed in western Gujarat and displays some evidence of a textual relationship with the Śivadharma. Dominic Goodall, working in collaboration with a team of Indologists trained by Alexis Sanderson, has produced critical editions of at least four of these texts, which have been made available to me by Somadeva Vasudeva. During my stay in Pondicherry, I had the privilege of reading with Dominic Goodall selections from the Niśvāsaguhya—a heterogeneous work with a number of distinct strata, with the Niśvāsaguhya comprising the latest strata—including some interpolations from as late as the eighth century. The first volume of the Niśvāsatattvasaṃhitā, edited by Dominic Goodall and a number of his colleagues, has recently been released (2015). The Niśvāsa has also been discussed in Sanderson (2006), Goodall and Isaacson (2007), Vasudeva (2012), and the dissertation of Hatley (2007).

10. For instance: vedasiddhāntaśāstrāṇāṃ bauddhārahaṃtavādināṃ | advayaṃ kathitaṃ teṣāṃ na te jānanti mohitā || Note that the Aiśa register of the Kūlasāra often fails to conform to the strictures of Pāṇinian grammar.

11. purāṇaṃ bhāratam vedaḥ śāstrāṇi sumahānti ca | āyuṣaḥ kṣayaṇāḥ sarve dharmo 'lpo granthavistaraḥ ||

12. Śivadharma 1.36: na me priyaś caturvedī madbhaktaḥ śvapaco 'pi vā | tasmai deyaṃ tato grāhyaṃ sa saṃpūjyo yathā hy aham || Compare this with the ubiquitous rhetoric of the Bhāgavata Purāṇa, extolling the Dog-cooker who has become a devotee of Viṣṇu. This very same verse reappears regularly in later Śaiva literature and was adopted by Vaiṣṇava bhakti theologians as well (cf. Gopāla Bhaṭṭa, *Haribhaktivilāsa,* 10.127). See Schwartz (2012).

13. anenaiva vidhānena dīkṣitā ye varānane || brāhmaṇāḥ kṣatriyā vaiśyāḥ śūdrāś cānye 'thavā priye | sarve te samadharmāṇaḥ śivadharme niyojitāḥ || sarve jaṭādharāḥ proktā bhasmoddhūlitavigrahāḥ | ekapaṅktibhujaḥ sarve samayinas tu varānane || putrakāṇāṃ bhaved ekā sādhakānāṃ tathā bhavet | cumbakānāṃ bhaved ekā na prāgjātivibhedataḥ || ekaiva sā smṛtā jātir bhairavīyā śivāvyayā | tantram etat samāśritya prāgjātiṃ na hy udīrayet || putrakāṇāṃ sādhakānāṃ tathā samayinām api | prāgjātyudīraṇād devi prāyaścittībhaven naraḥ || dinatrayaṃ tu rudrasya pañcāhaṃ keśavasya ca | pitāmahasya pakṣaikaṃ narake pacyate tu saḥ || avivekī bhavet tasmād yad icched uttamāṃ gatim | Svacchandatantra, 4.539–545. Cf. Niśvāsakārikā 12.161ff.

14. While these practices are treated in great detail in most Tantric literature, Flood (2006) offers a particularly clear overview of their function in Tantric ritual.

15. Much as will later be the case in regard to the interpretation of the Vedānta Sūtras, various early Tantric communities, while sharing a common reference point in the form of these practices, differed drastically in their interpretation of the philosophical and ontological implications of what it means for us to say that the practitioner "transforms himself into the god" in order to perform ritual actions, and what the implications of this are for our understanding of human nature. The early Pāśupatas seem to have been ontological pluralists, believing that an originally distinctive human practitioner replaces the substances that constitute his body with the substance that makes up Śiva, thereby becoming logically identical with him. Śaiva Siddhānta theologians, in contrast, being strict dualists, believed that, at best, a liberated practitioner becomes transformed into "a Śiva," remaining logically and ontologically distinct from Śiva himself, if for no other reason than the fact that his liberation took place within historical time, and thus he, unlike the Lord, has a point of origin.

16. Trilocanaśiva was the disciple of both Aghoraśiva of Cidambaram and Jñānaśambhu of Varanasi, perhaps the two most important Śaiva Siddhānta theologians of his day. He is most famous for his commentary on the *Somaśambhupaddhati*, which has been cited extensively by Brunner-Lachaux (1963) in her annotated translation of the work. Goodall (2000) offers a historical contextualization of these figures in his review of Brunner-Lachaux's work.

17. ekapaṅktiḥ sadā varjyā bhojane bhinnajātibhiḥ || bhuñjāno 'jñānato vipraḥ kṣatraviṭśūdrajātibhiḥ | jñātvā viramya madhye tadācānto bahurūpakam || japed daśa ca viṃśac ca triṃśac caiva yathākramam | bhojanānte yadi jñānam ekadvitriśataṃ kramāt || ajñātajātibhiḥ paṅktau bhuktvā tattriśataṃ japet | apāṅkteyais tathājñeyair aparair anulomajaiḥ || . . . śūdrādyucchiṣṭasaṃspṛṣṭaṃ spṛṣṭaṃ vāpyantyajātibhiḥ || bhuktvā svabhāvaduṣṭānnaṃ kriyāsparśanadūṣitam | bhuktvā snāto nirāhāraḥ pañcagavyaṃ pibed api || Trilocanaśiva, *Prāyaścittasamuccaya*, v. 220–223, 231–232 (Goodall and Sathyanarayanan 2014).

18. In later Śaiva procedures for *prāyaścitta* such as Trilocanaśiva's *Prāyaścittasamuccaya*, all manner of sins come to be addressed purely through the repetition of the Aghora *mantra*, rather than through an array of mantras tailored for distinct applications as in early Śaiva literature. Dominic Goodall, personal communication.

19. For instance, the Sarvajñānottara, a Saiddhāntika scripture, shows quite a number of such nondualist accretions dating to the middle of the second millennium. After this point, the Sarvajñānottara came to be used as a key proof text for Saiddhāntika theologians who advocated the pervasive trend toward nondualism within both the Tamil and the Śaiva lineages during this period.

20. The Bhojadeva who authored the *Tattvaprakāśa* has often been erroneously conflated with King Bhoja of Dhārā, author of the *Sarasvatīkaṇṭhābharaṇa* and other works.

21. jayatīti. sarvasmād upari vartate ity arthaḥ. kutaḥ. asya vigrahasyottaravigrahavadut pattināśādyabhāvāt. tac ca vedamayatvād vedasya ca nityatvād iti.

22. This Aghoraśiva is the same as the author of the *Mahotsavavidhi*, which has been edited and translated by Richard Davis (2010). For further information on Aghoraśiva, see Davis (1986–1992).

23. cidghana eko vyāpī nityaḥ satatoditaḥ prabhuḥ śāntaḥ | jayati jagadekabījaṃ sarvānugrāhakaḥ śambhuḥ ||

24. tatra   tāvad   ācāryaḥ   prāripsitasya   prakaraṇasyāvighnaparisamāptyarth am   siddhāntaśāstrapravṛttinimittaṃ   sakalatattvātītaṃ   niṣkalaṃ   paramaśivam ādyayā "ryayā stauti—cidghana iti. cicchabdenātra jñānakriye vakṣyete. tad uktaṃ śrīmanmṛgendre—caitanyaṃ dṛkkriyārūpam iti. cid eva ghanaṃ deho yasya sa cidghanaḥ. na tu karmakālādīśvaravādinām iva jaḍaḥ, acetanasya cetanādhiṣṭhānaṃ vinā pravṛttyayogāt. na cāsya baindavaśarīrādyupagamo yuktaḥ, anīśvaratvaprasaṅgāt. tasya ca kartrantarāpekṣāyāṃ svakartṛkatve 'nyakartṛkatve vā 'navasthāprasaṅgāc ca . . . vyāpī sarvagataḥ na tu kṣapaṇakādīnām iva śarīraparimitaḥ, saṅkocavikāsadharmī vā, tādṛśasyā- cetanatvānityatvādidoṣaprasaṅgāt. nityaḥ ādyantarahitaḥ. na tu bauddhādīnām iva kṣaṇikaḥ, utpattikāla eva naśyatas tasya jagatkartṛkatvāsaṃbhavāt. nanu muktātmāno 'py evaṃbhūtā evāta āha—satatoditaḥ. nityamuktaḥ. na tu muktātmāna iveśvarāntaraprasādamuktaḥ, anavasthāprasaṅgāt. . . . sarvānugrāhakaḥ. anugrahaś cātropalakṣaṇaṃ sṛṣṭyāder api. ataś ca sṛṣṭisthitisaṃhāratirobhāvānugrahākhyaiḥ pañcabhiḥ kṛtyaiḥ sarveṣām ātmanāṃ bhogamokṣaprada ity arthaḥ.

25. tathā   hi—jñānaṃ   tāvad   aparokṣabhūtam   apavargakāraṇam.   āparokṣyaṃ ca   nididhyāsanenāvidyāsaṃskāratiraskāre   saty   udbhavati.   nididhyāsanaṃ   ca śravaṇamananābhyāṃ śivātmajñāne saṃjāte sambhavati. te cāntaḥkaraṇaśuddhitaḥ saṃjāyete.   sā   kāmyapratiṣiddhakarmaparihāreṇa   nityanaimittikakarmānuṣṭhā- nād bhavati. . . . kāmanāśrutayaś caihikaphalāḥ citrayā yajeta paśukāmaḥ ityādaya aihikaphalaniviṣṭacittān viprān vaidikamārge pravartayituṃ pravṛttāḥ, svargaphalāś ca tadutsukān iti. ye ca śatrunāśotsukās tān vaidikamārge pravartayituṃ śyenā[ci?] rādyabhicārakarmavidhayaś ceti. tataś ca vihitasnānapāpakṣayakarmānuṣṭhānānvādhānāgni- hotrādinā kramāt manaḥśuddhisambhave sati kāmanānivṛttau nityanaimittikakarmānuṣṭhā- nād ātmavividiṣārūpāntaḥkaraṇa-śuddhyudbhave śravaṇamananābhyāṃ śivātmajñāne saṃjāte nididhyāsanābhyāsād avidyātatsaṃskārāpanayanāntaraṃ śivātmāparokṣye sati mokṣa iti. taduktaṃ mokṣadharmādau—sarvatra vihito dharmaḥ svargaḥ satyaphalodayaḥ. bahudvārasya dharmasya nehāsti viphalā kriyā iti. atra ye maheśvaraniyukte śraute smārte vā karmaṇi pravartante, te mucyante; ye tu na pravartante, te saṃsaranti.

26. For Rāmakaṇṭha II as theologian see Goodall (1998). For Rāmakaṇṭha II as philoso- pher see Watson (2006).

27. *Paramokṣanirāsakārikā*, 3.4.1. Translation by Alex Watson et al. (2013). Rāmakaṇṭha appears to be particularly fond of the verse he quotes after this *kārikā*, as it reappears else- where in his oeuvre, in the *Nareśvaraparīkṣāprakāśa*.

28. Note that Śrīkaṇṭha originally describes his position as a Śaiva Viśiṣṭādvaita, on the model of Rāmānuja's *sampradāya*, which was rapidly gaining momentum among the

intellectual circles of Śrīkaṇṭha's day. In contrast, Appayya vacillates between a commitment to the partisan Śaiva stance of Śrīkaṇṭha's Śaiva Advaita "school" and the emerging orthodox position that Advaita Vedānta itself had begun to occupy in Smārta-Śaiva society.

29. See McCrea (2016) for the argument that Appayya singlehandedly reinvented Śrīkaṇṭha's Śaiva Advaita. For evidence to the contrary, see Fisher (2017) for the case that nondual Śaiva Vedānta (Śivādvaita) in Tamil Nadu owes its origins to the wholesale import of the Śaktiviśiṣṭādvaita, or Śivādvaita philosophy of the Sanskritic (Ārādhya) Vīraśaivas, whose core lineage was based at Śrīśailam in present-day Andhra Pradesh.

30. The scriptural locus for this meditation is Chāndogya Upaniṣad 8.1.1–8.1.5.

31. daharavidyāniṣṭho 'yam ācāryaḥ. ata eva tasyāṃ rūpasamarthakam ṛtaṃ satyaṃ paraṃ brahmeti mantram iha bhāṣye punaḥ punar ādarātiśayād vyākhyāsyati. kāmādyadhikaraṇe ca svayaṃ daravidyāpriyatvāt sarvāsu paravidyāsu daharavidyotkṛṣṭeti vakṣyati. ataḥ svaśākhāmnātadaharavidyāyāṃ viśeṣyanirdeśakena padena svopāsyaṃ namaskāryam nirdiśati paramātmana iti. śrūyate hi taitirīyopaniṣadi—tasyāḥ śikhāyā madhye paramātmā vyavasthitaḥ. iti. kecana sa paramātmā śivād anya iti kathayantaḥ parān bhramayanti tadanuvartanena sādhavo mā bhramiṣur ity abhipretya viśinaṣṭi śivāyeti. daharavidyopāsyaḥ paramātmā śiva evety ācāryaḥ śārīrādhikaraṇe nipuṇataram upapādayiṣyati. Appayya comments here on the verse oṃ namo 'haṃpadārthāya lokānāṃ siddhihetave | saccidānandarūpāya śivāya paramātmane ||

32. Vidyāsu śrutir utkṛṣṭā rudraikādaśinī śrutau | tatra pañcākṣarī tasyāṃ śiva ity akṣaradvayam || The Śrīrudram, a hymn found in all recensions of the Yajur Veda, which had been central to the ritual practice of Śaivism long before the sixteenth century, is in fact the first textualized occurrence of the *pañcākṣarī mantra: oṃ namaḥ śivāya.* See also Gonda (1980).

33. For the case of Vijayanagar, see Valerie Stoker's (2011) work on competition between Vaiṣṇava sectarian communities for royal patronage at major temple sites such as Tirupati.

34. Rao and McCrea have organized a multiyear research group under the name "Age of Vedānta," which inquires into historical explanations for Vedānta's rise to unprecedented prominence in the late-medieval period. Preliminary essays produced by this project have been published in the *Journal of Hindu Studies* 8(1), 2015. Outside of the domain of systematic philosophy, the work of Jason Schwartz (forthcoming), likewise, convincingly locates a new of universalization of Hindu dharma emerging in thirteenth-century Maharashtra, in which diverse religious communities were reimagined as founded on a common theory of personhood and adhering to shared juridical, ritual, and theological canons.

35. Although we have not had the opportunity to examine the historical trajectory of Vaiṣṇavism in the present context, we need not assume that Vaiṣṇavism's path to "becoming Hindu" followed the same trajectory as that of Śaivism. Inquiry into early Vaiṣṇavism is sadly impeded by an incomplete textual archive. In many cases, the discursive history of early Vaiṣṇavism seems to bear a divergent relation to Vedic traditions, such that from an exceptionally early period, we find numerous examples of Vaiṣṇavism's attempt to present the worship of Viṣṇu as enjoined by a lost *śākhā* of the Vedas. See for instance Robert Leach (2013) on the influence of the Ekayāna or Pañcarātra Vaiṣṇavas of the Mahābhārata—especially evidenced in the Nārāyaṇīya—on the later Pañcarātra, or "Tantric" Vaiṣṇava tradition.

36. Rāmānuja, *Vedārthasaṅgraha:* kecid brahmakalpāḥ saṃkīrṇāḥ kecit sattvaprāyāḥ kecid rajaḥ-prāyā kecit tamaḥprāyā iti kalpavibhāgam uktvā sattva rajastamomayānāṃ

tattvānāṃ māhātmyavarṇanaṃ ca tatkalpaproktapurāṇeṣu sattvādiguṇamayena brahmaṇā kriyata iti coktam. yathoktaṃ mātsye—yasmin kalpe tu yat proktaṃ purāṇaṃ brahmaṇā purā | tasya tasya tu māhātmyaṃ tatsvarūpeṇa varṇyate || iti. viśeṣataś coktam—agneḥ śivasya māhātmyaṃ tāmaseṣu prakīrtyate | rājaseṣu ca māhātmyam adhikaṃ brahmaṇo viduḥ || sāttvikeṣu ca kalpeṣu māhātmyam adhikaṃ hareḥ | I have not been able to locate this quote in the Matsya Purāṇa. In fact, as we will see in chapter 3, many sectarian theologians actively contested the textual integrity of the Matsya and other sectarian Purāṇas owing to their frequent interpolations.

37. See Nicholson (2015, 180, 1.44). See also Nicholson 2005a on Vijñānabhikṣu's Vaiṣṇava affiliation.

38. Vijñānabhikṣu, commentary on the Īśvara Gītā (Nicholson 2005b, 312): purāṇādau māyāvādaparyantānāṃ bahūnāṃ pāṣaṇḍaśāstrānāṃ śivakṛtatvasmaraṇāt. viṣṇos tu buddhirūpeṇa pāṣaṇḍaśāstrakartṛtvaṃ na svābhāvikaṃ kiṃtu śivapreraṇād eva cakāra mohaśāstrāṇi keśavo 'pi.

39. See chapter 4 for a further discussion of Nīlakaṇṭha's ostensive job title and duties at the court of Tirumalai Nāyaka.

40. Known works of Nīlakaṇṭha Dīkṣita include three *mahākāvyas* (*Śivalīlārṇava, Gaṅgāvataraṇa, Mukundavilāsa*), a number of *laghukāvyas* and *stotras* (*Kalivaḍambana, Sabhārañjana, Anyāpadeśaśataka, Ānandasāgarastava, Vairāgyaśataka, Śāntivilāsa, Gurutattvamālikā*), a drama titled the *Nalacaritranāṭaka,* and one *campū* (*Nīlakaṇṭhavijayacampū*).

41. The *Mahābhāṣyapradīpaprakāśa* is not published, and I have not been able to access a usable manuscript of the work. Two manuscript copies are recorded as being held in the Government Oriental Manuscripts Library in Chennai: a Telugu-script palm leaf manuscript and a Devanāgarī paper transcript. The transcript is currently "missing," and the palm leaf manuscript is so badly damaged as to be virtually unusable. Another manuscript is said to be located at the Sarasvati Bhavan Library in Varanasi, which I have not been able to consult.

42. See chapter 2 for further discussion of the *Saubhāgyacandrātapa* and Gīrvāṇendra Sarasvatī, and chapter 3 for the *Śivatattvarahasya.*

43. This series of ten Nāyaka portrait sculptures, culminating with that of Tirumalai Nāyaka as the most recent of the sequence, have been documented in detail in Branfoot (2001, 2007, 2011). Previous generations of scholarship made use of these portrait sculptures strictly as an aid to documenting the chronology of Nāyaka political history.

44. See for instance Pollock (2001, 2005) and O'Hanlon (2010, 2011).

45. yaṃ bhāṣyaṃ mahad adhyajīgapad ṛṣiḥ śrīcokkanāthādhvarī yo rāmasya ca nīlakaṇṭhamakhinā bāṇastavaṃ kāritaḥ | vyācaṣṭe kila rāmabhadramakhinas tasyāptaśiṣyaḥ kṛtī bhaumīndraṃ sa hi veṅkaṭeśvarakaviḥ yasyāṃ nibaddhaṃ yaśaḥ || Tanjavur Maharaja Serfoji's Sarasvati Mahal Library, Ms. No. 3827, Veṅkaṭeśvara Kavi, *Patañjalicaritravyākhyā,* v. 4.

46. sa svāmī mama daivataṃ taditaro nāmnāpi nāmnāyate |

47. As is made evident by the title of Rāmabhadra's hymn, the *Rāmabāṇastava,* and indeed by his very name, Rāmabhadra Dīkṣita held a particular fondness for Rāma, his *iṣṭadevatā*—an affiliation not uncommon among south Indian Śaivas, as, incidentally, was true of Tyāgarāja as well. His choice of personal deity in no way precluded him from participating in Smārta-Śaiva religious circles, which, as we will see in the next chapter, consisted

centrally of cultivating a devotional relationship with the Śaṅkarācārya preceptors of the northern Tamil country.

48. These are Tanjavur Maharaja Serfoji's Sarasvati Mahal Library, Ms. No. 6924 (chapter 9 of the *Dinakarabhaṭṭīya*) and No. 6862 (chapter 1 of the *Śāstramālāvyākhyāna*), respectively.

49. Aside from the Tamil chronicles, the *Talavaralāṟu* and *Stānikarvaralāṟu,* and the versified records of temple renovations (*Tiruppaṇivivaram* and *Tiruppaṇimālai*), our earliest "surviving" historical records of Madurai affairs, a collection of Marathi documents originally maintained in the Mackenzie Collection, have been indefinitely misplaced by the Government Oriental Manuscripts Library in Chennai. At the time of my visit in January of 2012, the staff was unable to locate these documents, all contained in a single bound volume.

50. "Stānikarvaralāṟu," pg. 268: ulakuṭaya perumāḷ maṭātipattiyattukku maṭṭum maṇitarkaḷ illaiy eṉṟu colla atai nammuṭaiya kuruvākiya kēcavatīṭcata ayyaravarkaḷukkup paṇṇuvikkiṟom eṉṟu karttākkaḷ muttuvīrappaṉāyakkar ayyaṉavarkaḷ tiruvākkuppirantatu.

51. Rāghavendra Tīrtha (ca. 1595–1671) served as pontiff of the Śrī Vijayendra Maṭha in Kumbakonam from 1624 to 1671, according to the attestation of his nephew Nārāyaṇācārya in his hagiographical account, the *Rāghavendra Vijaya*. For further details on his life and works, see B. N. K. Sharma (2000, 479–490).

52. Vādīndra Tīrtha, *Guruguṇastava*, v. 34: [tantra]śrīnīlakaṇṭhābhidhamakhimaṇinā bhaṭṭatantrānubandhe granthe [y]āvat tvadīye kariṇi guṇavidāropite 'bhyarhaṇāya | kīrtis te rāghavendra vratisumatimaṇe nūnam anyūnavegād diṅnāgān ārurukṣuḥ svayam api sahasādhāvad aṣṭau digantāt || Some dispute exists regarding the proper reading of the first two syllables, which are often reported as "mantrī," suggesting that Nīlakaṇṭha held the official title of *mantrin* under Tirumalai Nāyaka. Filliozat (1967) accepts this reading. Furthermore, the commentator on the *Guruguṇastava* of Vādīndra Tīrtha preserves the reading "tantraśrī." Note also that titles such as Dīkṣita and Makhin, which appear in the present verse, were used interchangeably by Smārta Brahmins in the Tamil region during this period.

53. Taylor, ed. and trans., *Oriental Historical Manuscripts*, 1835, 149–150. intappirakāram nēmukam paṇṇiṉa uṭaṉē aṭacey varuṣam vayyāci mācam—pūrvapaṭcammukkūrattampaṇṇiṉārkaḷ. Atu mutal vēlaiyaḷa aticākkirataiyāyp piṟaputittam vantu kaṇppārppatiṉālē aticākkirataiyāy naṭantutu. Mūṉṉutāka teppakkuḷam veṭṭukuṟapōtu naṭuvilē uttāraṇamāy orukeṉapati utaiyamāṉār avaraik kōvilil yeḷuntaruḷappaṇṇi viccārkaḷ vacanta maṇṭapam tūṉ nāṭṭukuṟapōtu yēkapātamūṟtti vāṇicciyirukkuṟa tuṇai naṭappaṭāteṉaru cīmaiyil uḷḷa vayiṣiṉavāḷukku caiyavāḷukkum vākkuvātamāy ākumācamvaraikkum vivacāram yēviṉa cuvāmi muṉṉilaikki naṭantutu appāla caivacittānti appātīṭcatā vayiṣṇar ayyātīṭcatāyyaṉavarkaḷ aṉekam kiṟantaṅkaḷp pāttu.

54. The issue of honorifics has also led to some confusion in the genealogy of the Dīkṣitas and other South Indian Brahmin intellectual families. Most genealogical studies refer to a number of individuals within a family simply as "Appa," "Appayya," or "Āccān" (Skt. Ācārya), leading to some confusion regarding the numerous "Appayya Dīkṣitas" and "Āccān Dīkṣitas" in Nīlakaṇṭha's immediate family. Josi (1977), for instance, proposes, based on family history, that Appayya Dīkṣita's given name was Vināyaka Subrahmaṇiya. The Ayya Dīkṣita referred to in this passage, being a Vaiṣṇava, is evidently distinct from the one

referred to in the *Stāṉikarvaralāṟu* regarding the *Tiruviḷaiyāṭal* festivals. Beyond this, we have little basis for conjecturing the identity of these two individuals. Some, such as Mahalinga Sastri, have hypothesized that Appa Dīkṣita here ought to be identical to the famous Appayya Dīkṣita, but this proposal results in insoluble chronological difficulties.

55. Consider, for instance, the Brahmin ministers Madanna and Akkanna of the seventeenth-century Golkonda sultanate in the Deccan, who nearly succeeded in overthrowing the state and personally seizing power. See Kruijtzer (2002) for further discussion. Concerning the spread of Persianate administrative practices prevalent in Golkonda at the time, Kruijtzer notes that the typical bilingual Persian *farmāns* issued by the brothers were unattested in the far South until eighteenth-century Maratha rule in Tanjavur. During the seventeenth century, neither Mughal nobility nor Maratha Brahmins were visibly present in the Nāyaka kingdoms, nor do we find mention of a class of individuals analogous to the Kāyasthas of North India.

56. Three copper-plate grants survive today testifying to a sustained relationship between the Madurai Nāyaka dynasty and a certain lineage of Brahmins of the Kauṇḍinya Gotra who maintained control of a monastery dedicated to the transgressive Śākta goddess Ekavīrā that was associated with the Jambukeśvara temple in Tiruvanaikka near Srirangam. Preceptors of this lineage appear to have referred to themselves as the Śrīkaṇṭha Ākāśavāsīs. For instance, copper plate 25 of 1937–1938, dated to Śaka 1584, records the following memory of the lineage's long-standing association with the Madurai Nāyakas: rāyarājamahāma[n]trīśiṣyo nāgappanāyakaḥ | tasyājani sutas so 'yaṃ viśvanāthākhyanāyakaḥ || svasevāniratasyāsya śiṣyasya vinīta tasya mudānvitaḥ | śrīkaṇṭhākāśaso tatpāṇḍyarājyaṃ dadau kila || labdhvā pañcākṣaraṃ tasmāt śrīkaṇṭhākāśavāsinaḥ | pañcagrāmān dadau tasya viśvanāthākhyanāyakaḥ || (Transcribed in July 2011 from the estampage currently held at the Archaeological Survey of India in Mysore.) The remainder of the grant, dating from Tirumalai Nāyaka's reign, goes on to detail in Telugu the villages granted to the Śrīkaṇṭha Ākāśavāsi Mahādeva Dīkṣitulu, which enabled the lineage to maintain a presence at a number of prominent Śaiva sites in the Tamil country, such as Jambukeśvara, Mātṛbhūteśvara, Rāmeśvara, and Cokkanāthapuram. In this section, Tirumalai Nāyaka is made to acknowledge his continuing family preceptorial relationship with the lineage: "mā vaṃśaṃ gurusvāmi āyina śrīkaṇṭhākāśavāsi vāri santati kaundinyagotraṃ katyāyina sūtraṃ yajuśākhā sāgni caturmahāvratavājapeyayājī mahādevadikṣitula vāraina mā gurusvāmi vāriki mā vaṃśakarta nāgamanāyadu vāri santati tirumalanāyaḍu vāru."

No such monastery exists today; the institution in question may have been replaced by the Śaṅkara *maṭha* now affiliated with the temple. Numerous stone inscriptions in the Jambukeśvara temple attest (all recorded 1937–1938) to the sizable influence of the Ākāśavāsīs over the Jambukeśvara temple, particularly two preceptors known as Mahādeva Dīkṣita and Sadāśiva Dīkṣita. Some even provide intriguing hints of their doctrinal position, such as repeated reference to the "three names of Śiva": Śiva, Śambhu, and Mahādeva. For instance: śivanāmatrayaṃ śivaśambhu mahādeva . . . kīrttanād [sic] eva gacchati | śivanāmatrayaṃ yas tu sakṛt paṭhati mānavaḥ | mahāpātakānāṃ pāttaiḥ mucyate nātra saṃśayaḥ || . . . aṣṭākṣarasvarūpatvāt nnāmatrayam udāhṛtam || śaivaṃ nnāmatrayaṃ loke jayati sma sanātanaṃ | sadāśivamakhindreṇa guruṇā saṃprakāśitaṃ|| (ARE 61 of 1937–1938).

57. In one of his publicly performed dramas, Nīlakaṇṭha's younger brother Atirātra Yajvan refers to his elder brother as master of the local literary society: "naṭī: kiṃnu

khu ehiṃtuhmāṇa eārisa kouhaṃlākāraṇam (kiṃ nu khalv idānīṃ yuṣmākam etādṛśakautūhalakāraṇam). sūtradhāraḥ: abhigatasabhānāyakalābhaḥ. naṭī: ko ṇu khu eso īdiso (ko nu khalv eṣa īdṛśaḥ.) sūtradhāraḥ: ayaṃ kila bharadvājakulapārāvārapārijātasakalakalāsāmrājyasiṃhāsanādhipatis tatrabhavataḥ śrīmato nārāyaṇādhvariṇas tapaḥparipākaḥ kartā kāvyānāṃ vyākartā tantrāṇām āhartā kratūnāṃ vyāhatā nṛpasabheṣu digantaraviśrāntakīrtir apāramahimā mānavākṛtiḥ sākṣād eva dākṣāyaṇīvallabhaḥ śrīkaṇṭhamatasarvasvavedī śrīnīlakaṇṭhādhvarī."

58. Our clearest source of information on this issue concerns the feudatory relationship between the Madurai Nāyakas and the emergent Setupati kingdom of Ramnad. Howes (1999) documents that this relationship was established on ritual as well as political grounds through the Śākta worship of Rājarājeśvarī, a statue of whom is said to have been given to the Setupati family by Tirumalai Nāyaka. Soon after, the Navarātri festival was initiated at Ramnad (as recorded in a copper-plate grant dating to 1659). A mural painting from the palace at Ramnad, preserved in the collection of the École française d'Extrême-Orient in Pondicherry, depicts Rājarājeśvarī bestowing the royal scepter upon the Setupati king, a ritual element integral to the royal celebration of Navarātri across South India.

59. See also Bronner (2015) for the memory of Appayya's identity as an incarnation of Śiva, which seems to have begun to circulate soon after his death.

60. Quoted from a recording made at Nīlakaṇṭha's *ārādhanā* in Palamadai, January 2011.

61. sa svāmī mama daivataṃ taditaro nāmnāpi nāmnāyate |

2. "JUST LIKE KĀLIDĀSA"

1. pāripārśvaka: adya srihālāsyacaitrotsavayātrāyām āryamiśrāḥ samāpatanti.

2. kavir ayaṃ kālidāsa iva svayam ambikādāsatayā tadājñām antareṇa niśvāsam api na karoti, kiṃ punar etādṛśaṃ prabandham.

3. Other sectarian networks prominent among court intellectuals in early modern South India include the Vaiṣṇava Mādhva and Śrīvaiṣṇava lineages. Much work remains to be done on the changing structure of these networks and their interactions. See for instance Stoker 2011; Rao 2014.

4. The earliest known manuscript of what might be termed proto-Śrīvidyā, the *Nityākaula,* a Tantric work devoted to the worship of a set of Nityā goddesses, is currently under study by Anya Golovkova, PhD candidate at Cornell University. Further work remains to be done on allied texts devoted to the Nityās, such as the *Ciñciṇīmatasārasamuccaya,* and other antecedent traditions such as those centered on Tripurabhairavī (Sanderson 2003– 2004, 367n50). See also Dyczkowski (2009, 3:179ff, 2:216–244).

5. The traditional dating of the *Tirumantiram,* extending back as far as the fifth to seventh century C.E., is, while accepted by Brooks and some others, historically inconceivable and incoherent outside of a Tamil nationalist agenda. See Goodall (2004, xxix). A date of the twelfth or thirteenth century is far more plausible. On the transmission of Śaiva and Śākta traditions from Kashmir to the Tamil country in the early second millennium, especially with regard to the Kālī Krama, an allied Śākta school, see Cox (2006).

6. Many of Bhāskararāya's contemporary lineage descendants trace his heritage and his Śrīvidyā ritual practice to the Andhra country, importing concepts that were not prevalent in Tamil Nadu in the seventeenth century.

7. Clark (2006) provides a thorough overview of our knowledge to date on the Śaṅkarācārya orders, especially the alliance between the Sringeri *maṭha* and the early Vijayanagara empire. See also Kulke (1993, 1985) for a cogent revisionist proposition on the changing self-representation of the Śaṅkarācārya lineage of Sringeri in the late Vijayangar period.

8. Śaṅkara, or Śaṅkarācārya, is the circa-eighth-century author of the *Brahmasūtrabhāṣya,* the foundational treatise of the Advaita (nondualist) school of Vedānta philosophy. Around the middle of the second millennium, monastic centers such as Sringeri in western Karnataka, closely allied with the founding rulers of the Vijayanagara empire, began to claim direct lineage descent from Śaṅkara himself, each successive preceptor taking the title Śaṅkarācārya.

9. Sanderson, "The Influence of Shaivism on Pala Buddhism." Further, the personal attendant of the recent Jagadguru of Sringeri, Candraśekhara Bhāratī, reports that, in one instance, a certain Satyānandanātha, who studied Vedānta with Jagadguru Saccidānanda Śivābhinava Bhāratī, personally initiated Candraśekhara Bhāratī into Śrīvidyā on the day before his ascension to the pontificate (Rao 1990).

10. bhagavatpādaiḥ aneḍamūkebhyaḥ laghucarcāstotradvayaṃ hastamastakasaṃyogamahimnā avāci. tanmahimnā bhagavatī pādāravindanirṇejanajalaṃ tanmukhe dattavatī. Elsewhere in the text, Lakṣmīdhara consistently refers to the *Laghu* and *Carcā Stotras*, part of the *Pañcastavī,* as the work of Kālidāsa.

11. ardhe tanor adrisutāmayo 'smīty ahaṃyunā kiṃ phalam ādiyūnā | gīrvāṇayogīndram upāsmahe taṃ sarvātmanā śailasutātmako yaḥ || *Śivalīlārṇava* (*ŚLA*) 1.5.

12. A manuscript of a work ascribed to Amareśvara Sarasvatī, remarkably enough a commentary on the *Prapañcasāra,* is currently held at the Punjab University Library, Lahore.

13. śaṅkaraś cāmarendraś ca viśveśvara iti trayaḥ | punantu māmakīṃ buddhim ācāryāḥ kṛpayā mudā || amarendrayatiś śiṣyo gīrvāṇendrasya yoginaḥ | tasya viśveśvaraḥ śiṣyo gīrvāṇendro 'ham asya tu || Bühnemann (2001) understands the original Gīrvāṇendra in the latter verse to be another name for Śaṅkara referred to in the former, but this seems implausible, as the convention at work in the first verse is the tradition of invoking first the founder of the lineage (in this case understood to be Śaṅkara) followed by the two preceding gurus in the lineage.

14. The Advaita authors and texts enumerated below are described in some detail by Minkowski (2011), who clearly articulates for the first time many of the lines of influence among early modern scholars of Advaita.

15. The Vedānta compositions of Nṛsiṃhāśramin include the *Bhedadhikkāra, Tattvaviveka, Advaitadīpikā,* and commentaries on the *Vedāntasāra* and *Saṃkṣepaśārīraka.*

16. See Minkowski (2011, 224) for a discussion of this evidence. Also worthy of note is that the Nṛsiṃhāśramin is credited as guru by Mahīdhara, the author of the *Mantramahodadhi,* the most respected work of Mantraśāstra in the north Indian sphere, comparable in influence to the *Prapañcasārasaṅgraha* in the South.

17. kalyāṇaguṇasampūrṇaṃ nirvāṇavibhavālayam | gīrvāṇendrasarasvatyāś caraṇaṃ śaraṇaṃ bhaje || (v. 4). The colophon to the first *pariccheda* also refers to Nṛsiṃhāśramin as the pupil of one Jagannāthāśramin, who, judging by the similarity of their titles, may have been the one who initiated him into *sannyāsa* (renunciation). The commentator

Nārāyaṇāśramin (himself Nṛsiṃhāśramin's immediate disciple) describes Gīrvāṇendra Sarasvatī as the author's "mantra guru." The distinction between *āśrama guru* and *mantra guru* may also aid in explaining what otherwise may seem like a troubling chronological inconsistency: how can Gīrvāṇendra Sarasvatī have been venerated as guru by Nīlakaṇṭha Dīkṣita as well as by Nṛsiṃhāśramin, who was a contemporary of his granduncle? Both Nīlakaṇṭha and Nṛsiṃhāśramin claim to have received a particular initiation from Gīrvāṇendra Sarasvatī by means of the bestowal of a mantra or *śaktipāta,* which may have taken place at any time during their lives. Furthermore, an intriguing verse from Nīlakaṇṭha's *Gurutattvamālikā* (verse 8, see below) appears to suggest that Gīrvāṇendra Sarasvatī was no longer alive during most of Nīlakaṇṭha's adult life, as Nīlakaṇṭha mourns not having the opportunity to serve him personally in his embodied form.

18. advaitapīṭhasthitadeśikaṃ taṃ hṛdyātmavidyāviśadāntaraṅgam | nityaṃ bhajāmo viśadasvarūpaṃ gīrvāṇayogīndragurum hṛdantaḥ || In the *Hariharādvaitabhūṣaṇa:* gīrvāṇendrayatīndrāṇāṃ caraṇāmburuhadvayam | svargāpavargadaṃ puṃsāṃ naumi vighnopaśāntaye ||

19. Documentary evidence does not yet permit us to establish the precise line of descent from Gīrvāṇendra Sarasvatī to the lineages of Kāñcī Kāmakoṭi Pīṭha or Upaniṣad Brahmendra. The Kanchi *maṭha*'s own lineage chronicles are historically dubious, as the lineage claims a precise list of preceptors going back so far as the early centuries B.C.E. On the grounds of the historical evidence available, critics argue that the Kāñcī Kāmakoṭi Pīṭha has existed in its present form only from the mid-eighteenth century onward. For this controversy see, for instance, Sarma (1987) and Venkatraman (1973). The relatively late origins of the present-day Kāñcī Kāmakoṭi Pīṭha do not, however, preclude us from inquiring into its formative antecedents.

Also worthy of note is an inscription recorded as ARE 443 of 1919, which attests that a village in the vicinity of Kanchipuram now known as Śuruṭṭil was once referred to as "Śaṅkarācāryapuram." The date of this inscription is unknown.

20. On the surviving manuscript evidence for this hymn, see Filliozat (1967).

21. On the six *adhvan*s enumerated by Nīlakaṇṭha, a common set of ontological categories in the Śaiva Siddhānta, see Filliozat (1967). The remainder of the hymn contains a number of technical references to Śaiva Siddhānta theology, such as a traditional visualization for the five faces of Sadāśiva.

22. *Gurutattvamālikā* (GTM) 5, 8, 9, 20. tattvasthānakalāpadākṣaramanūn śaivān ṣaḍ apy adhvanaḥ saṃśodhyaiva cirantanaiś ca gurubhiḥ kecid kvacit tāritāḥ | ekenaiva tu sārasaṃgrahakṛtivyaktena mantrādhvanā gīrvāṇendragurur viśṛṅkhalam avaty āprauḍhamūḍhaṃ jagat || svīkartuṃ caraṇodakaṃ caraṇayor mārṣṭuṃ rajaḥ pāvanaṃ mūrdhnā dhārayituṃ cirāya caraṇau hemābjasāmājikau | svāmin me januṣāṃ śatair api tṛṣā nāpaiti janmaiva tu dvaitīyīkam alabhyam eva bhavatā bhakteṣv acitte kṛtam || kṛcchrāṇi pradiśan sakṛc chravaṇataḥ kṛcchrāṇi hanti svataḥ karmāṇi grasate samūlam api naḥ karmāṇi siddhiṃ nayan | gīrvāṇendra iti śrutaḥ śrutiṣu yaḥ sarvāsu nirvāṇado mantro 'yaṃ caturakṣaro mama bhavatv āśvāsam āśvāsanam || antānantaśarīrabandhaparivāhopāttatattacchubhaprārabdhārthasamājabhāgyaphalito yaḥ śaktipātas taraḥ | nirṇīto yadi so 'pi deśikadayāpāṅgaprasaṅgavahas tattvaṃ tarhi guroḥ paraṃ kim api nety ākhyāta vītabhramāḥ ||

23. śrīmacchaṅkarapādasūktihṛdayāviṣkāraniṣṇātayā . . . kṛtyā | GTM 17.

24. See for instance Wallis, "The Descent of Power," 2008.

25. Rājacūḍāmaṇi Dīkṣita also composed a work titled the *Śaṅkarācāryatārāvali,* which does not appear to survive today but is attested by the author in his *Kāvyadarpaṇa.*

26. *Śaṅkarābhyudaya* (*ŚA*) 1.1, 1.5–10. asti svastikṛdastokaśastiś cūḍāmaṇir makhī | kartror viśvajitaḥ putraḥ kāmākṣīśrīnivāsayoḥ || kāvyaprakāśikāyāś ca yaḥ karoti sma darpaṇam | karṇāmṛtāgramānāni kāvyāni ca tathā śatam || śarvaryāś carame yāme śayānas sa kadācana | gīrvāṇendraguruṃ buddhyā gīrvāṇendram alokata || anugrahād āptavidyam amareśvarayoginaḥ | viśveśvarayatīśānavineyaṃ vinayojjvalam || paryāyaśaṅkarācāryaṃ pāre vācām avasthitam | prapañcasārapramukhaprabandhakṛtivedhasam || pratyagbrahmaikyanidhyānaprahasanmukhapaṅkajam | tattanmantrānusandhānatatparaṃ tamasaḥ param || kṛpayā coditas tena kṛpaṇānujighṛkṣuṇā | sa eṣa kurute kāvyaṃ śaṅkarābhyudayābhidham ||

27. The inscription in the Kālakaṇṭheśvara temple in Appayya's *agrahāram,* Adayapalam, includes mention of an endowment for general instruction in Śrīkaṇṭha's Śaiva Advaita. See chapter 3 for further details; see also Bronner (2007) on the educative function of many of Appayya's *stotras* (hymns).

28. Rāmabhadra was a reputed grammarian and author of the *Uṇādimaṇidīpikā,* having studied under Nīlakaṇṭha himself.

29. Despite Rāmabhadra's high praise, the original *Ācāryastavarāja* unfortunately does not appear to be extant today.

30. The mythical *cāṭaka* bird is said to drink only raindrops.

31. *ĀSR* 3, 4, 7, 41, 125. labdhaiḥ sādhukaviprabandhajaladhiṣv antaś ciraṃ majjatā śabdākhyair maṇibhiḥ patañjalivacaḥśāṇopalottejitaiḥ | yatnena grathitam mayā sumatayaḥ sarve 'pi kautūhalād ācāryastavarājabhūṣaṇam idaṃ paśyantu hṛṣyantu ca || yaḥ śāstreṣv akhileṣu śikṣitamatir yaḥ kāvyapāntho bhṛśaṃ yaḥ śakto 'timṛdu svayaṃ kavayituṃ yaś cānasūyākaṭuḥ | bhaktir yasya ca deśike sa jagati stotuṃ kṣamas tvāṃ vidann ācāryastavarāja mugdhahṛdayaḥ kvāhaṃ kva te varṇanam || brahmānandata eva janma bhavato rūpaṃ suvarṇojjvalaṃ trailokyaṃ ca kṛtaṃ vaśe paricayaḥ śāstreṣu sarveṣv api | ślāghante sudṛśaś ca saukhyajananīṃ śayyāṃ muhus tāvakīm ācāryastavarāja kas tava kaviḥ stotuṃ pragalbho guṇān || yatpūjāvasareṣu sūripariṣatkīrṇaiḥ sarojādibhiḥ pāṭalyaṃ dviguṇaṃ bibharti mṛdubhiḥ smeraiḥ prasūnotkaraiḥ | kṛṣṇānandamuneḥ padam tadadhikodbhāsi tvadāsañjane 'py ācāryastavarāja komalatamaṃ tvāṃ nūnam ākhyāti naḥ || jīvātur jagato 'pi cātakaśiśoḥ prītyai paraṃ vāridaḥ sarvāhlādakaro 'pi kairavamude jāgarti kāmaṃ śaśī | ācāryastavarāja viśvaviduṣām ānandanīyo bhavān prāyaḥ samprati rāmabhadrahṛdayollāsāya sannahyati ||

32. See below (the section titled "Śrīvidyā and Society in Nīlakaṇṭha Dīkṣita's *Saubhāgyacandrātapa*") for a brief overview of the history of the Śaiva Siddhānta, a prominent school of Tantric (Mantramārga) Śaivism.

33. One of a set of five hymns titled the *Pañcastavī,* the *Ambāstava* is in other regions commonly attributed to Śaṅkarācārya as well as to Kālidāsa.

34. See Bader (2000) for a thorough treatment of the extant Śaṅkaradigvijaya (Śaṅkara's conquest of the directions) narratives and their genealogical relationships.

35. *A Woorke concerning the trewnesse of the Christian Religion* (1587, 27). Cited in Yates (1964, 178).

36. Of course, there is no evidence that Kālidāsa himself was a Śākta. The false etymology of his name (Kālī-dāsa, "servant of the goddess Kālī"), as we will see, was accepted as valid by

Ardhanārīśvara Dīkṣita. Another Śākta work attributed to Kālidāsa is the *Cidgaganacandrikā,* a commentary on the *Krama Stotra* of Siddhanātha. Although cited as the work of Kālidāsa by Bhāskararāya, the *Cidgaganacandrikā* includes a self-attribution of authorship to one Srīvatsa, whom Rastogi (1979) dates to the twelfth century on the grounds of the dates of composition of the *Krama Stotra* and the earliest known citation of the *Cidgaganacandrikā* by Maheśvarānanda. In addition, South India in particular has attributed a number of Śākta hymns to the name of Kālidāsa, most popular among which is the *Śyāmalādaṇḍaka.*

37. Filliozat (1967), Josi (1977), Viswanathan (1982), and Unni (1995).

38. Iyer, "The Saubhāgyacandrātapa of Nīlakaṇṭha Dīkṣita," 1947; Sastri, "Two Rare Treatises on Saktism," 1942. Unfortunately, Iyer's cursory summary of the *Saubhāgyacandrātapa's* first chapter misrepresents the scope and ambitions of the work, portraying its thesis as that of an elementary work of Vedānta.

39. On various occasions Nīlakaṇṭha alludes to matters to be discussed at greater length in the succeeding chapters, referring to the *caturthapariccheda* and the *uttarapariccheda,* suggesting that at least five chapters were intended. The possible content of the chapters will be discussed in my critical edition of the text.

40. The colophon reads: iti śrīmadbharadvājakulajaladhikaustubha-śrīkaṇṭhamatapratiṣṭhāpanācārya-caturadhikaśataprabandhanivahika-śrīmanmahāvratayāji-śrīmadappayyadīkṣitasodarya-śrīmadāccādīkṣitapautreṇa śrīnārāyaṇadīkṣitātmajena bhūmidevīgarbhasambhavena śrīnīlakaṇṭhadīkṣitena viracite śrīsaubhāgyacandrātape prathamaḥ paricchedaḥ.

41. Although the text we possess today of the *Śivārcanacandrikā* was quoted verbatim by Nīlakaṇṭha in his *Saubhāgyacandrātapa,* the entire text seems to have been "borrowed" directly from the Kriyāsāra, a theological and ritual tract of the Śaktiviśiṣṭādvaita Vīraśaiva tradition (see Fisher, 2017). Note that the *Śivārcanacandrikā* in question is distinct from another work by the same title written by Śrīnivāsa Bhaṭṭa, a South Indian by heritage who had relocated to Benares and the Bundelkhand, his descendants later becoming influential *rājagurus* in Jaipur.

42. P. P. S. Sastri tells us that he had secured a Devanagari transcript of an original palm-leaf manuscript owned by a certain "Mr. Godbole" of Bombay. The current locations of both the original and transcript are sadly unknown. idaṃ ca saprapañcaṃ nirūpitam asmatpitāmahacaraṇaiḥ śivānandalaharyām iti neha kiñcid upapādanīyam. . . . sakalata-ntropasaṃhārakṣamasarvatantrasvatantra-śrīmūladevatāparivigraha-śrīnīlakaṇṭhadīkṣitair asmajjyeṣṭhacaraṇaiḥ śiṣyānugrahāya kṛtaṃ bahumīmāṃsānyāyaduravagāhaṃ saubhāgya-candrātapam anusṛtya vyavasthā pradarśyate.

43. asmatpitāmahacaraṇair apy eṣa eva pakṣo likhitaḥ śivārcanacandrikāyām, asmajjyeṣṭhacaraṇāś ca saubhāgyapaddhatyām ayam eva pakṣam aṅgīkṛtavantaḥ.

44. A traditional account of the Dīkṣita family is preserved in two nineteenth-century chronicles, the *Appayyadīkṣitendravijaya* and *Āccāndīkṣitavaṃśāvali.*

45. tvayy arpitaṃ prathamam appayayajvanaiva svātmārpaṇaṃ vidadhatā svakulaṃ sa-mastam | kā tvaṃ maheśi kuladāsam upekṣituṃ mām ko vānupāsitum ahaṃ kuladevatāṃ tvām || (*ĀSS* 43). The phrasing of Nīlakaṇṭha's verse alludes to a particular hymn composed by Appayya, the *Ātmārpaṇastuti.* While very little evidence exists to confirm Nīlakaṇṭha's assertion that Appayya himself professed a particular devotion to the goddess, descendants of the Dīkṣita family preserve this tradition through the narrative that Appayya

bequeathed to Nīlakaṇṭha his personal copy of the Devīmāhātmya. Appayya's *stotra,* the *Durgācandrakalāstuti,* does evince knowledge of Śākta practice, but nothing indicative of Śrīvidyā in particular.

46. Personal communication from several descendants of Nīlakaṇṭha Dīkṣita at his *ārādhanā* (the anniversary of the purported date of his death) in Palamadai, the family's *agrahāra,* or Brahmin village, which I attended in January 2011. According to the family, Nīlakaṇṭha and his descendants were granted the *agrahāra* by Tirumalai Nāyaka in compensation for his service as chief minister of Madurai. See chapter 4 for further discussion.

47. V. 75, 78: pāśuṃ sṛṇiṃ ca karayos tava bhāvayantaḥ saṃstambhayanti vaśayanti ca sarvalokān | cāpaṃ śaraṃ ca sakṛd amba tava smaranto bhūpālatāṃ dadhati bhogapathāvatīrṇāḥ || vidyātmano janani tāvakadantapaṅkter vaimalyam īdṛg iti varṇayituṃ kṣamaḥ kaḥ | tatsambhavā yad amalā vacasāṃ savitrī tanmūlakaṃ kaviyaśo 'pi tatas tarāṃ yat || Cf. *Lalitāsahasranāma,* v. 53–54: rāgasvarūpapāśāḍhyā krodhākārāṅkuśojjvalā || manorūpekṣukodaṇḍā pañcatanmātrasāyakā |; v. 61: śuddhavidyāṅkurākāradvijapaṅktidvayojjvalā |

48. See Khanna (1986) for the textual history of the early Kashmir school of Śrīvidyā and its engagement with Kashmiri Śaivite traditions.

49. The life and works of Bhāskararāya are discussed in detail by Brooks (1992a, 1990). Other Śrīvidyā adepts in south India founded their ritual system on the Paraśurāmakalpasūtra; on this lineage, see for instance Annette Wilke (2012).

50. As per current estimates for the dates of the earliest strata of the *Niśvāsatattvasaṃhitā,* the earliest surviving Saiddhāntika text (Goodall et al. 2015). For a concise summary of the rituals and doctrines of the Śaiva Siddhānta, see for instance Davis (1991) or Ishimatsu (1994).

51. Śaiva Siddhānta theologians are noted for their polemical refutation of Advaita Vedānta positions, in addition to those of other rival schools. See for instance the *Paramokṣanirāsakārikāvṛtti* of Bhaṭṭa Rāmakaṇṭha, commenting on the work of Sadyojyotis, in Watson et al. (2013).

52. Another example is the Saiddhāntika *Sarvajñānottara,* whose sixteenth-century recensions include a significant amount of nondualist material inspired by Advaita Vedānta (Goodall, personal communication). On the history of the Śivādvaita school, as well as the widespread colonization of south Indian Śaivism by nondual Vedānta, see Fisher (2017).

53. Saiddhāntika scriptures cited in the *Saubhāgyacandrātapa* include the Ajita, Aṃśumat, Kāmika, Karaṇa, Makuṭa, Mataṅgapārameśvara, Pauṣkara, Vīratantra, Suprabheda, Sūkṣma, Svāyambhuvam, Skandhakālottara, Acintyaviśvasādākhya, and the Śivadharma. In his *Śivatattvarahasya* he often cites the Vātulaśuddhāgama as well.

54. In his commentary on the name "Maheśvara," Nīlakaṇṭha writes: mahākāmeśvarādayo mūrtayaḥ kāścid atirahasyāḥ santi, tāś copadeśaikasamadhigamyā iti granthe na likhyante (pg. 42). Cf. Rājacūḍāmaṇi Dīkṣita, *Śaṅkarābhyudaya:* kalayāmi japāśoṇaṃ kāmeśvaramaheśvaram | (8.89).

55. His primary source, predictably, is the Śvetāśvatara Upaniṣad, a text accepted by nearly all later thinkers as a part of the original Upaniṣadic corpus but in fact composed by an early school of Pāśupatas, hence easily amenable to Śaiva interpretations.

56. evaṃ caivaṃbhūtacicchaktiviśiṣṭaśivajñānaṃ mokṣasādhanam iti sāmānyamukhapravṛttānām api śrutīnāṃ tātparyam avadhṛtam.

57. etena śivasyānupādānatvaṃ śakter jagadupādānatvaṃ cidātmakatvaṃ śivābhedaś cety etāvad api siddham.

58. tantreṣv eva vaidikatāntrikasamuccayasya kaṇṭharaveṇa pratipāditatvāt.

59. yady api bhaktiśabdo bhāvasādhanatayā upāsanāparyāyabhajanavācī. upāsanā dhyānaṃ nididhyāsanam iti paryāyaḥ. tatparasya caikena janmanā mokṣaḥ. udāhṛtavacanena śrutam. tathāpy upāsanāṅgabhūtārcanasya tathā tv aśravaṇe aṅginas tathātvaṃ kaimutikanyāyasiddham.

60. Nīlakaṇṭha elsewhere cites the Mahābhārata verse he alludes to here: purāṇaṃ dharmaśāstraṃ ca vedāḥ pāśupataṃ tathā | ājñāsiddhāni catvāri na hantavyāni hetubhiḥ || This appears to be a variant of verse 14.96.15 of the critical edition: bhārataṃ mānavo dharmo vedāḥ sāṅgaś cikitsitam | ājñāsiddhāni catvāri na hantavyāni hetubhiḥ || Note that Nīlakaṇṭha appears to treat the Mahābhārata as an authority on par with the other Purāṇic and Upaniṣadic passages cited, at least as concerns nonesoteric Vaidika matters.

61. āgamānām aprāmāṇyaśravaṇāt kathaṃ tato grāhyetikartavyateti cen na. na hy āgamasāmānyamapramāṇam iti tadvacanārthaḥ. . . . ityādinā pāśupatādyāgamānāṃ mahābhārata eva prāmāṇyavyavasthāpanād vaidikapūjāpekṣopahārasamarpakatvena teṣām api vedatulyatvāt. paraṃtu tatra ye vedaviruddhavāmācāropadeśaka . . . dapramāṇam.

62. The only monograph on the subject of the Brahmavidyās is the work of Narayanaswami Aiyar (1963). Itself simply a catalogue of the thirty-two currently accepted Brahmavidyās, the book begins to illuminate the history of the Brahmavidyā concept via the short introduction provided by V. Raghavan. While Śaṅkarācārya himself only briefly alluded to the concept of Brahmavidyās (śāṇḍilyādyā brahmavidyāḥ), several of these vidyās received heightened attention in south India beginning with the period of Rāmānuja in both Vaiṣṇava and Śaiva Vedāntic traditions.

63. In his Śivārkamaṇidīpikā (commentary on Śrīkaṇṭha's Brahmasūtrabhāṣya), Appayya takes care to assert that Śrīkaṇṭha is particularly fond of the Daharavidyā. Among contemporary practitioners in south India, one often encounters the assertion that Śrīvidyā can be equated directly with the Daharākāśavidyā, which might suggest a link between Appayya's emphasis on the Daharākāśavidyā and Śākta influences on the greater Śivādvaita tradition.

64. Śāntivilāsa, v. 8.

65. See Fisher (2017) for the genealogy of the Śivādvaita tradition before Appayya, from which he inherits his interest in subjects such as Cicchakti and the Daharavidyā. Suryanarayana Sastri has noted Appayya's own interest in these themes in his introduction to his edition of the Śivādvaitanirṇaya.

66. The significance of upāsana for Śaṅkarācārya has been described in detail in Dubois (2014).

67. In Nīlakaṇṭha's usage the term seems to refer to the Saiddhāntika Āgamas in general and not the particular class of Āgamas to which it typically refers.

68. Nīlakaṇṭha's views of the matter in the Saubhāgyacandrātapa can be profitably compared with a similar discussion by his north Indian contemporary, Kamalākara Bhaṭṭa, in his Śūdrakamalākara. See the forthcoming work of Jason Schwartz on the changing relationships between Dharmaśāstra and Tantric discourses.

69. See chapter 3 for further detail.

70. While little work has been done on the early history of Kaula Śrīvidyā in south India, Annette Wilke's (2012) work examines the standing of Kaula practice in the tradition of the Paraśurāmakalpasutra among Brahminical circles.

71. The *Ambāstava* is at least old enough to have been quoted by Maheśvarānanda in the *Mahārthamañjarī*, TSS ed., pg. 107.

72. Although we are able to locate historically a number of Ardhanārīśvara Dīkṣita's immediate family members, much less is known about his life and work. Brother of Keśava Dīkṣita and Rājacūḍāmaṇi Dīkṣita, he is believed to have educated his younger brother Rājacūḍāmaṇi in the *śāstras*. Other (now lost) works attributed to his name include the *Pārijātaharaṇa*, *Vivaraṇasāra*, *Satyāprīṇana*, and *Sāhityasarvasva*.

73. samudbhūtasthūlastanabharam uraś cāru hasitaṃ kaṭākṣe kandarpaḥ kusumitakadambadyutivapuḥ | harasya tvadbhrāntiṃ manasi *janayām āsa madano* bhavatyā ye bhaktāḥ pariṇatir amīṣām iyam ume ||

74. samudbhūtasthūlastanabharam uraś cāruhasitaṃ kaṭākṣe kandarpāḥ katicanakadambadyutivapuḥ | harasya tvadbhrāntiṃ manasi *janayantaḥ samayino* bhavatyā ye bhaktāḥ pariṇatir amīṣām iyam ume ||

75. Lakṣmīdhara appears to have spent his early years at the court of Gajapati Pratāparudra in Orissa, shifting later to the Vijayanagara court of Kṛṣṇadevarāya after the latter's defeat of the former, presumably circulating his Saundaryalaharī commentary among southern intellectual circles at this time. See Gode (1944).

76. Take, for instance, the Śaiva Siddhānta distinction between *samaya dīkṣā*, the first level of initiation, through which initiates are bound to adopt a certain *samaya*, or code of conduct, beyond that of external social convention, and *nirvāṇa dīkṣā*, a higher level of initiation that grants access to a more sophisticated soteriological technology.

77. The *pañcamakāra*s, a list of five traditionally impure substances that each begin with the letter *m*—*madya* (wine), *māṃsa* (meat), *matsya* (fish), *mudrā* (typically translated as "parched grain"), and *maithuna* (sexual intercourse)—is a common trope in many Tantric traditions.

78. The only other author identified as closely conforming to Lakṣmīdhara's views is one Rāmānanda, who composed commentaries on the Tripurā Upaniṣad and Tripurātāpinī Upaniṣad. See Brooks (1992a, 221n64). Rāmānanda likely postdates our generation of Smārta-Śaiva intellectuals, as none show any awareness of either of these Upaniṣads.

79. A number of additional structural phrases, such as "atra idam anusandheyaṃ" and "X-tamaśloka-vyākhyānāvasare vakṣyate," also appear quite regularly in both commentaries.

80. paśupatipāñcarātragaṇanāthakumāraśivāgamair mahitaḥ | viśvajidādikratukṛt sa ratnakheṭādhvaripuṅgavo jayati || śrī śrīnivāsamakhinas tasya putra mahāyaśāḥ | kāmākṣītanayaḥ śrīmān ardhanārīśvaraḥ sudhīḥ || tasmād adhītya śāstrāṇi pitus sarvāṇi sadguroḥ |ambasatavasya vyākhyānaṃ kurute gurusammatam || . . . śrīśaṅkarācāryakṛtau prabandhau saubhāgyavidyāsubhagodayākhyau | punaḥ punaḥ sādhu vicintya buddhyā tadadhvanā 'haṃ karavai nibandham ||

81. No text has yet been located bearing the name *Saubhāgyavidyā*. A number of Śrīvidyā works have been given the title "Subhagodaya" over the centuries, including a *Subhagodayastuti* attributed to Gauḍapāda, believed to have been the "grand-guru" of Śaṅkarācārya, and a much older work attributed to the Kashmiri Śrīvidyā theologian Śivānanda, cited by Amṛtānandanātha in his Dīpikā on the *Nityāṣoḍaśikārṇava* and Maheśvara in his *Mahārthamañjarīparimala*.

82. *ŚĀ* 1.57–62, 64. guror govindapādasya guṇarāśer anujñayā | viṣṇor nāmnāṃ sahasrasya vyatānīd bhāṣyam āditaḥ || mantrāgamamahāmbodhiṃ mathitvā buddhimanthataḥ |

prapañcasārapramukhaprabandhāmṛtam ādade || saubhāgyavidyām api tāṃ subhagodaya-
paddhatim | nirmame mantraśāstrārthanikṣepamaṇipeṭike || saguṇabrahmabodhaikasaktān
mandādhikāriṇaḥ | anugṛhṇann   athātānīd   asau   hariharastutīḥ || atantanīt
prakaraṇāny advaitātmaparāṇi saḥ | saundaryalaharīmukhyāḥ stutīr api paraḥ śatāḥ ||
karatalakalitādvayātmatattvaṃ kṣapitadurantacirantanapramoham | upacitam uditoditair
guṇaughair upaniṣadām ayam ujjahāra bhāṣyam || sa dvādaśe vayasi tatra samādhiniṣṭhair
brahmarṣibhiḥ   śrutiśiro bahudhā vicārya | śrīvyāsadeśikaśikhāmaṇisūtrarāśo bhavyaṃ
gabhīramadhuraṃ phaṇati sma bhāṣyam |

83. Lakṣmīdhara, commentary on the *Saundaryalaharī* (*LDh*), v. 1: iha khalu
śaṅkarabhagavatpūjyapādāḥ samayamatatattvavedinaḥ samayākhyāṃ candrakalāṃ śloka-
śatena prastuvanti.

84. The attribution of a *Saubhāgyacintāmaṇi* to Śaṅkarācārya is not attested elsewhere,
to my knowledge. Another Śrīvidyā work titled the *Saubhāgyacintāmaṇi*, apparently distinct from the one quoted by Ardhanārīśvara Dīkṣita, is attributed to the sage Durvāsas and
plays a central role in the liturgy of the Kāmākṣī temple in Kanchipuram.

85. None of these texts appear to be extant today, although the names Vasiṣṭhasaṃhitā
and Sanatkumārasaṃhitā have been claimed by other works, including a treatise on astron-
omy; a text titled the Sanatkumārasaṃhitā belongs to the corpus of Pañcarātra Āgama. That
Rājacūḍāmaṇi Dīkṣita, as well, accepts the set of five Saṃhitās as authoritative is suggested
in his *Śaṅkarābhyudaya*: sanakasanandanadhyeyā ghanakabarī bhātu śailarājasutā (v. 7.78).

86. *LDh*, v. 39, pgs. 77–78. śūdrāṇāṃ catuḥṣaṣṭhitantreṣv adhikāraḥ | evam
adhikārabhedam ajānānāḥ amīmāṃsakāḥ vyāmuhyanti|

87. *LDh*, v. 39, pg. 78. śubhāgamapañcake vaidikāgameṇaiva anuṣṭhānakalāpo nirūpitaḥ
| ayaṃ śubhāgamapañcakanirūpito mārgaḥ vasiṣṭhasanakaśukasanandanasanatkumāraiḥ
pañcabhiḥ munibhiḥ pradarśitaḥ | ayam eva samayācāra iti vyavahriyate | tathaivāsmābhir
api   śubhāgamapañcakānusāreṇa   samayamatam   avalambyaiva   bhagavatpādamatam
anusṛtya vyākhyā racitā |

88. A metanarrative central to the history of Śākta discourse in general is the steady
sublimation, at least in public settings, of overtly Kāpālika-inflected practices often occurring at the same time that a community is engaged in co-opting conceptual and ritual technology integral to these systems, such as formulations of Kuṇḍalinī yoga and the
newly conceived role of the ascetic Avadhūta, an unmarked naked ascetic who derives
his identity from engaging in such practice. Though debuting in Picumatabrahmayāmala,
both of these formulations become mainstays of early modern Brahminical ascetic traditions. Thus for example, references in the Tantras originally intended to allude to the
Brahmayāmala's *navākṣarī* mantra "Hail to the ferocious female skull bearer!" (hūṃ caṇḍe
kāpālini svāhā) are reinscribed as alluding solely to the Purāṇic mantra, associated with the
Devī Māhātmya (oṃ aiṃ hrīṃ klīṃ cāmuṇḍayai vicche), providing a public face for other
forms of Śāktism. Close inspection of the scriptural sources of the Kādi invoked by our
authors, however, call into question how much of this shift is dissembling, for Kāpālika-
inflected mantras, as well as deities, continue to be transmitted even in these orthodox
sources. See for example Rājacūḍāmaṇi's invocation of the wine-quaffing Mahākāla and
Mahākālī in the next section.

89. Work remains to be done on the social position of the Devīmāhātmya among
North Indian intellectuals of this same period, a number of whom, such as Nagojī Bhaṭṭa,

composed commentaries or practical manuals for its recitation (*prayogavidhi*). In Nepalese Śrīvidyā traditions, and most likely in north India as well, the Devīmāhātmya remained a cornerstone of liturgy even after it had been overshadowed by the Lalitāsahasranāma and associated scriptures in the South.

90. *LDh*, p. 16. viyatpūjyatvaṃ dvividhaṃ, daharākāśajaṃ bāhyākāśajaṃ ceti. bāhyākāśajaṃ nāma bāhyākāśāvakāśe pīṭhādau bhūrjapatraśuddhapaṭahemarajatādipaṭṭa le likhitvā samārādhanam. etad eva kaulapūjety āhur vṛddhāḥ. (*LDh*, v. 41, p. 116). śrīcakrasthitanavayonimadhygatayoniṃ bhūrjahemapaṭṭa-vastrapīṭhādau likhitvā pūrvakaulāḥ pūjayanti.

91. *LDh*, v. 41, pg. 122. yad uktaṃ subhagodaye—sūryamaṇḍalamadhyasthāṃ devīṃ tripurasundarīm | pāśāṅkuśa-dhanurbāṇahastāṃ dhyāyet susādhakaḥ || trailokyaṃ mohayed āśu varanārīgaṇair yutam || . . . atra samayināṃ bāhyapūjāniṣedhāt sūryamaṇḍalāntargatatvena pūjanaṃ niṣiddham ity āhuḥ tan na.

92. This hymn seems not to be extant. The concept of a hymn to the goddess's earrings may reflect the practice in Tamil Śaiva temple culture of installing Śrīcakras in the place of the earrings on the temple *mūrti,* best exemplified by the case of Akhilāṇḍeśvarī of the Jambukeśvara temple near Srirangam.

93. For instance, Lakṣmīdhara cites the following verse from the *Karṇāvataṃsastuti* in support of his claim that Samayins are to worship in the upper *cakra*s of the body: *ājñātmakadvidalapadmagate* tadānīṃ vidyunnibhe raviśaśiprayatotkaṭābhe | gaṇḍasthalapratiphalatkaradīpajālakarṇāvataṃsakalike kamalāyatākṣi ||

94. *Ambāstavavyākhyā* (ASV): samayināṃ bāhyapūjāyāḥ niṣiddhatvād antar eva pūjā kartavyā . . . subhagodaye kaulaśikṣāpaṭale—bāhyapūjāratāḥ kecit pāṣaṇḍā vedaninditāḥ | kaulāḥ kāpālikā mūlam āgamair avidhānataḥ || niṣiddhācaraṇāt pātaḥ teṣām iti hi me matam | tasmāt pīṭhārcanādīni vaidikānāṃ na vidyate || antaḥpūjāratāḥ santo vasiṣṭhasanakādayaḥ | vāñchitāṃ siddhim āpannās tasmād adhikam āntaram || atha cet karṣaṇādīni pratiṣṭhādīni cāgamaiḥ | ātharvaṇair athoktāni bādhitārthāni tāni kim || satyaṃ tāni tathoktāni svādhikārānuguṇyataḥ | mumukṣūṇāṃ na tatrāsti kiṃ pūjāyām adhikriyā || tasmāt samayinām antaścakreṣv evārcanādikam |

95. Even more tellingly, we meet with a number of striking rhetorical similarities between Ardhanārīśvara's improved *Subhagodaya* and the prose of Lakṣmīdhara's commentary. Take, for instance, the imagined opponent in the above passage, who questions the place of non-Smārta ritual procedures within the corpus of orthodox scripture, particularly rituals of ground preparation (*karṣaṇa*) and the installation of deities (*pratiṣṭhā*): "Now, if one objects that rituals for ground preparation, installation of deities, and so forth, as described by the Āgamas and Atharvaṇas, would be prohibited . . ." This very subject matter is raised by Lakṣmīdhara himself while delimiting the scriptures suitable for Samayin Śrīvidyā adepts, mentioning *karṣaṇa* and *pratiṣṭhā* specifically by name. Thus, not only does the seventeenth-century *Subhagodaya* explicitly and vehemently promote Lakṣmīdhara's notions of Samaya orthodoxy, but it also recycles language from disparate locations in his commentary. Evidently, the redactor of the *Subhagodaya* was quite familiar with Lakṣmīdhara's work and eager to respond to the more contentious points he raised.

Procedures for *karṣaṇa* rituals are a particular feature of South Indian Śaiva Siddhānta Āgama, a fact that Lakṣmīdhara as well seems to have noted, given that he attributes these procedures in particular to the Vātula, Vātulottara, and Kāmika Āgamas: *LDh*, v. 21, p. 76. vātulaṃ, vātulottaraṃ, kāmikaṃ ca tantratrayaṃ karṣaṇādipratiṣṭhāntavidhipratipādakam. tasmin tantratraye karṣaṇādipratiṣṭhāntā vidhayaḥ ekadeśe pratipāditāḥ | sa caikadeśo vaidikamārga eva. avasiṣṭhas tu avaidikaḥ.

96. *ASV:* śāktāḥ prathamo dvividhā. kaulāḥ samayinaś ceti. tatra kaulā dvividhāḥ. pūrvakaulā uttarakaulāś ceti. tatrāpi pūrvakaulās trividhā. mūlādhāraniṣṭhāḥ svādhiṣṭhā-naniṣṭhā ubhayaniṣṭhāś ceti. uttarakaulās tu caturvidhāḥ mātaṅgīvārāhībagalamu-khībhairavītantrasthāḥ. tad uktaṃ subhagodaye kālībhaṅgapaṭale—mūlādhāre svādhiṣṭhāne ca bhajanti kecaneśinīm | anyatarasmiṃs cānye tenaite pūrvakaulās trividhāḥ || mātaṅgīvārā-hīkālāmukhībhairavītantrāntarasthitāḥ | āntarapūjārahitā uttarakaulāś caturvidhāḥ jñeyāḥ || eteṣāṃ saptavidhānāṃ kaulānāṃ vigītācārāṇāṃ smaraṇam api pratyavāyahetuḥ kiṃ punas teṣām ācārapradarśanam. ataḥ prakṛtānupayuktatvāc ca nātra vistaraḥ kriyate.

97. Lakṣmīdhara glosses *Saundaryalaharī* v. 34 as an encoded representation of the doctrine of the Pūrva Kaulas, and v. 35 as that of the Uttara Kaulas.

98. samayinas tu caturvidhāḥ. bahiḥsvarṇādiracitacakravigrahādiṣu vaidikena vidhānenārcanaratāḥ, antarbahiścārcanaratāḥ, antar evārcanaratāḥ, arcanarahitāś ceti. atra ye asaṃjātayogābhyāsāḥ sādhakās te cakravigrahādau devīṃ vaidikair vidhānair ārādhayanti, ye tv īṣajjātayogasiddhayas te 'ntarbahiś ca pūjayanti, ye tu siddhayogās te 'ntar eva devīṃ arcayanti, ye tu prāptacittaśuddhayas teṣāṃ pūjāprakāraś ca pūrvam eva pratipāditaḥ.

99. This Śrīcakra is said to have been in possession of the family in Nīlakaṇṭha's *agrahāra* in Palamadai near Tirunelveli until about two decades ago, at which point it was donated to the personal *pūjā* of Jagadguru Bhāratī Tīrtha of Sringeri. When I visited Sringeri in August of 2011, I was able to observe the Gaṇeśa and *śivaliṅga* also pictured in this photo on the Jagadguru's public *pūjā*, but I was not permitted to see the Śrīcakra. This is unfortunate, as a great deal could be learned from the iconographic features of the Śrīcakra were a more precise image available.

100. *ASV:* iha khalu kālidāso mahākaviḥ sarvamaṅgalāprasādalabdhasarvavidyādhi patyas tām eva sarvamaṅgalām ekatrimśatā ślokair abhiṣṭauti. ASV: atha "ekatvam anekās tāḥ śaktayo yānty upādhitaḥ" ity uktarītyā layādinā śaktīnām abhedaṃ pratipādayan svasya kālidāsatvāt svābhimatāṃ kālīmūrtim abhiṣṭauti.

101. *ŚLA* 1.3: stanyena kaścit kavayāmbabhūva tāmbūlasāreṇa paro jananyāḥ | ahaṃ tato 'py unnatim āptukāmaḥ seve tato 'py unnatam akṣikoṇam || Nīlakaṇṭha here puns on the words *unnati* and *unnata,* suggesting that he will obtain even greater literary aptitude by worshipping the corners of the goddess's eyes, which are spatially elevated above her breasts and mouth. Ñānacampantar is famously said to have been breast-fed by Pārvatī as a young child when he wandered away from his parents while on pilgrimage, and Mūkakavi, as his name suggests, is believed to have been deaf and dumb before partaking of the *tāmbūla* spittle of the goddess. Little is known about the historical persona of Mūkakavi or about the origin the *Mūkapañcaśati* attributed to him, a set of five centuries on the goddess widely read in Tamil Nadu even today but rarely circulating in other regions.

102. Jonathan Bader's (2000) comprehensive overview of the Śaṅkaradigvijaya genre includes the *Śaṅkarābhyudaya* among the several works surveyed, but he remarkably makes no mention of its most distinctive features—namely its elevated poetic register and its deliberate, unmistakable references to Śrīvidyā iconography. Among his numerous contributions, Bader does, however, observe significant overlap between the *Śaṅkarābhyudaya*

and the Mādhavīya *Śaṅkaravijaya,* the most popular text of the genre, often attributed by its proponents to the fourteenth-century Vidyāraṇya, founder of the Sringeri Śaṅkarācārya lineage. Bader successfully demonstrates that the Mādhavīya *Śaṅkaravijaya* liberally appropriates verses from *all* previously extant chronicles (the total borrowed material comprising nearly two-thirds of the entire text), thus establishing its relatively late date of composition beyond any uncertainty. His analysis of the *Śaṅkarābhyudaya*'s contents, however, goes only so far as to record that in Rājacūḍāmaṇi's vision, Śaṅkara ends his pilgrimage and ascends to the Sarvajñapīṭha in Kanchipuram rather than in Kashmir.

103. Brahmāṇḍa Purāṇa 3.5.3–7. Note the explicit references not only to Kāmākṣī but to the Ekāmranātha Śaiva temple in Kanchipuram as well: agastyo nāma devarṣir vedavedāṅgapāragaḥ | . . . tasya cintayamānasya carato vasudhām imām | prāptam āsīn mahāpuṇyam kāñcīnagaram uttamam || tatra vāraṇaśailendram ekāmranilayaṃ śivam | kāmākṣīṃ karidoṣadhnīm apūjayad athātmavān ||

104. Aiyer and Venkataraman, *The Truth about the Kumbhakonam Mutt,* 51: "We are not concerned with the question of whether the Dikshita was a great man or whether he did or did not write a *Sankarabhyudaya.* The only relevant question is whether the *Sankarabhyudaya* put forward by the mutt is a genuine work and whether, even if it is, it can be relied upon as a historical work. It was published in the Sanskrit Journal *Sahridaya* years ago. It is not clear wherefrom the manuscript was obtained but it is known that the 7th and 8th sargas were supplied by the Kumbhakonam mutt. The Kavya is evidently incomplete. The correspondence between the slokas in this work and the *Madhaviya Sankara Vijaya* is not only striking but painfully astonishing. . . . It is quite patent that this Kavya was published years after the Madhaviya just to discredit the authenticity of the latter."

105. Such transcripts are available at the Government Oriental Manuscripts Library at the University of Madras, Adyar Library in Chennai, and at the Oriental Research Institute in Mysore.

106. I have been able to locate the Sringeri manuscript from the unpublished on-site handlist, which is not included in the *New Catalogus Catalogorum* citations, but I have not yet been permitted to consult the manuscript.

107. Rāmakṛṣṇa Sūri provides the details of his lineage of Bhāratī preceptors in the introductory verses to his commentary: śambhur bhūrikṛpānidhir jagad idaṃ dvaitādidurvādavat pāṣaṇḍoktibhir ākulaṃ sadamalakṣemaṃ vidhātuṃ kālau | yadrūpeṇa mahīm avātarad amūn advaitavidyāgurūn śrīmacchaṅkaranāmadheyabhagavatpādān hṛdā bhāvaye || namāmi sukhacidrūpabhāratīdivyapādukā | yadāśritā anāyāsāt taranti sma bhavārṇavam || śrīmaccidghanabhāratyākhyān praṇamāmi sevakā santaḥ | yatkāruṇyasudhāṃ budhau hṛṣad api labdhvā . . . vanti mahad amṛtam || praṇamāmy ānandaghanabhāratyākhyān mahāmunīn |

108. ŚA 7.78, 80.

109. In addition, the *Śaṅkarābhyudaya* never mentions a monastery at Kanchipuram, which would not have served the interests of Kanchi partisans interested in tampering with the text.

110. Anantānandagiri, *Śaṅkaravijaya,* chap. 35, pg. 256. Citations are drawn from the Calcutta (1868) edition, as the Madras (1971) edition suffers from considerable interpolation that took place over the intervening century. śrīcakrasya sivaśaktyaikyarūpatvāt vidyātmaikyam atyabhedād avasāyasiddhiḥ. tasmān muktikāṅkṣibhih sarvaiḥ śrīcakrapūjā kartavyeti dik.

tasmāt sarveṣāṃ mokṣaphalaprāptaye darśanād eva śrīcakraṃ bhavadbhir ācāryair nirmitam iti.

111. Anantānandagiri, *Śankaravijaya*, chap. 35, pgs. 256–257. trikoṇam aṣṭakoṇaṃ ca daśakoṇadvayaṃ tathā | caturdaśāraṃ caitāni śakticakrāṇi pañca ca || binduś cāṣṭadalaṃ padmaṃ tathā ṣoḍaśapatrakam | caturasraṃ caturdvāraṃ śivacakrāṇi tu kramāt || trikoṇabaindavaṃ śliṣṭam aṣṭāre 'ṣṭadalāmbujam | daśārayoḥ ṣoḍaśāraṃ bhūgṛhaṃ bhuvanāsrake || śaivānām api śāktānāṃ cakrāṇāṃ ca parasparam | avinābhāvasambandhaṃ yo jānāti sa cakravit || trikoṇarūpiṇī śaktir bindurūpaḥ sadāśivaḥ | avinābhāvasambandhaṃ tasmād bindutrikoṇayoḥ || evaṃ vibhāgam ajñātvā śrīcakraṃ yaḥ samarcayet | na tatphalam avāpnoti lalitāmbā na tuṣyati || Cf. Cidvilāsa, *Śankaravijayavilāsa*, 25.37–43: trikoṇam aṣṭakoṇam ca daśāradvitīyaṃ tathā | caturdaśāraṃ caitāni śakticakrāṇi pañca hi || binduś cāṣṭadalaṃ padmaṃ padmaṃ ṣoḍaśapatrakam | caturasraṃ caturdvāraṃ śivacakrāṇy anukramāt || trikoṇe baindavaṃ śliṣṭam aṣṭāre 'ṣṭadalāmbujam | dvādaśāraṃ ṣoḍaśāraṃ bhūgṛhaṃ bhuvanāsrakam || śaivānām api śāktānāṃ cakrāṇāṃ ca parasparam | avinābhāvasambandhaṃ yo jānāti sa cakravit || trikoṇarūpiṇī śaktir bindurūpaparaḥ śivaḥ | avinābhāvasambandhas tasmād bindutrikoṇayoḥ || evaṃ vibhāgam ajñātvā śrīcakraṃ yaḥ prapūjayet | na tatphalam avāpnoti lalitāmbā na tuṣyati ||

The significant number of variants in these two passages suggests they have been borrowed from a distinct textual source (i.e., Lalitopākhyāna) rather than transferred from one Śankaravijaya chronicle to the other.

112. taduktaṃ brahmāṇḍapurāṇe—trikoṇe baindavaṃ śliṣṭam aṣṭāre 'ṣṭadalāmbujam ity ārabhya, śaivānāṃ caiva śāktānāṃ cakrāṇāṃ ca parasparam | avinābhāvasambandhaṃ yo jānāti sa cakravit ||

113. Rāmabhadra Dīkṣita, *Patañjalicaritra* 8.71: govindadeśikam upāsya cirāya bhaktyā tasmin sthite nijamahimni videhamuktyā | advaitabhāṣyam upakalpya diśo vijitya kāñcīpure sthitim avāpa sa śankarāryaḥ ||

114. In fact, it is not uncommon for temple priests today to vehemently deny any connection between the Śrīcakra and any Śrīvidyā practice occurring in the temple. Personal communication, temple priest, Madurai Mīnākṣī-Sundareśvara Temple, July 2009.

115. Cidvilāsa, *Śankaravijayavilāsa* 30.21–31. sarvavicchankarācāryadeśikas tān alokata || papraccha rājasenaiva nirmatān iva tān asau | phāle tripuṇḍraṃ santyajya kuṅkumaṃ dhriyate katham || śucivāsaḥ samutsṛtya dhṛtaṃ raktāmbaraṃ kutaḥ | . . . duṣkarmaṇāṃ hi saṃsargo yuṣmākaṃ pāpahetave | ity ukte deśikendre 'smin śāktamārgasamuddhṛtāḥ || kiṃ yatin kathayasy adya manmatājñānato hi tat | . . . sākṣādbhagavatīyuktā śambhoḥ śaktiḥ parā nanu || kāraṇaṃ jagatām eṣā guṇātītasvarūpiṇī | tacchaktyā vaśataḥ sṛṣṭaṃ mahattatvam aśeṣataḥ || . . . atas tadpādapadmasya sevā muktipradāyinī || kuṃkumādīni cihnāni tasyāḥ prītyaiva dadhmahe | atas tadpdādukā bāhau kaṇṭhe 'pi dhriyate sadā || jīvanmuktā vayaṃ tasmāc chrīvidyopāsakāḥ sadā |

116. *Śankarābhyudaya* 7.71–74.

117. Evidently Rājacūḍāmaṇi follows the *kādi mata*, the branch of Śrīvidyā that begins the *vidyā* with the syllable *ka* (rather than *ha* or *sa* as is practiced in some traditions), a common feature of South Indian Śrīvidyā.

118. *Śankarābhyudaya* 7.86: itthaṃ pañcadaśākṣarīm anugatair varṇaiḥ kṛtopakramaiḥ kāmākṣīṃ bahirāhitasthitimatīṃ padyaiḥ samārādhayan | kampātīranivāsinīṃ paricitaṃ nantuṃ bilābhyantaraṃ gacchan dvāri kṛtāsikāṃ bhagavatīṃ tuṣṭāva sa śyāmalām ||

119. Some traditions have described these as the *tritārikā* and *bālā* mantras.

120. *Śaṅkarābhyudaya* 7.93: ittham tām abhivandya viśvajananīm īśām athāntarviśan kalpānokahakānanālisubhage kampānadīrodhasi | kāmākṣīpadapadmapūtaśikharam kañcit puraḥ kāñcanakṣoṇībhṛtkuladhūrvaham pramumude paśyan sapady añjasā || Ra-makrsna Sastri's edition reads "padapadmabhūta," while the Sahṛdaya edition and SSES manuscript read "padapadmapūta."

121. *Śaṅkarābhyudaya* 8.4: kāñcanakṣiranīpāmrakāñcanāradrumām iha | kāñcana śrīpurābhikhyām kāmākṣyāḥ kalaye purīm ||

122. *Śaṅkarābhyudaya* 8.6-7: dīvyadbindutripañcāradviraṣṭāṣṭadalāmbujam | diśyān me kālacakrākhyam dīrgham āyus tadāsanam ||

123. Brahmāṇḍa Purāṇa 3.32.6-8: mahākālīmahākālau lalitājñāpravarttakau | viśvam kalayataḥ kṛtsnam prathame 'dhvani vāsinau || kālacakram mataṅgasya tasyaivāsanatām gatām | caturāvaraṇopetam madhye bindumanoharam trikoṇam pañcakoṇam ca ṣoḍaśacchadapaṅkajam | aṣṭārapaṅkajam caivam mahākālas tu madhyagaḥ ||

124. *Śaṅkarābhyudaya* 8.58-59: trailokyamohanam cakram trikam tad adhitasthuṣī | trāyatām prakaṭākhyābhis tripurā śaktir āvṛtā || kanantyaḥ śaktayaś cordhvam kanakāsanapaṅktiṣu | kāmākarṣiṇikāmukhyāḥ kāmadogdhryo bhavantu naḥ ||

125. Brahmāṇḍa Purāṇa 3.36.64: antaram trayam etat tu cakram trailokyamohanam | etasmiñ chaktayo yāsu tā uktāḥ prakaṭābhidhāḥ ||

126. *Śaṅkarābhyudaya* 8.60-61: sarvāśāpūrakam cakram samayā tripureśvarī | sākṣamālā vasati sā sannamadguptayoginī || avasthitās tato py uccaiḥ hāṭakāsanapaṅktiṣu | arcayāmo vayam devīr anaṅgakusumādimāḥ ||

127. Brahmāṇḍa Purāṇa 3.36.72: etās tu guptayoginyas tripureśī tu cakriṇī | sarvāśāpūrikābhikhyā cakrādhiṣṭhānadevatā ||

128. *Śaṅkarābhyudaya* 8.111: itthaṅkāram abhaṅgurāṅgajamahāyantrāvakṛṣṭyānamat pā [. . . vi] nivahojjvalābdhivihṛtīlolair girām gumphanaiḥ | kampātīranivāsinīm anuditam kāmeśvarīm arcayan brahmānandam avindata trijagatām kṣemaṅkaraḥ śaṅkaraḥ ||

129. *Śaṅkarābhyudaya* 7.66: śṛṅgārasāndrakavitāsaraṇāv ajitvā mām aṅga sāhasam idam sahasā na kuryāḥ | ity ūciṣīm vidhivadhūm ca vijitya vidyābhadrāsanam vidhir iva svayam adhyarukṣat || This verse places Śaṅkara in the position of Brahmā, evoking, by implication, an erotic connection between Śaṅkara and Brahmā's wife, Sarasvatī, who represents the very wisdom that Śaṅkara "conquers" when ascending to the throne of wisdom.

130. Luhmann (1995, 21). By *meaning*, Luhmann does not simply appeal to the abstract oft-touted concept of religious "meaning," which is almost impossible to define. Rather, he argues that a process of communication within a social system generates concepts, or systems of value, that are themselves necessary for the system to decide what elements of its own constitution to maintain or transform over the course of time. Social institutions, according to this model, do not reproduce themselves in the absence of such meaning; here we can observe a crucial distinction between systems theory and a crude Marxist social theory that derives religious concepts as ideology, arising purely as a function of societal phenomena.

3. PUBLIC PHILOLOGY

1. To be clear, the textual practices typical of this period differ significantly from earlier Sanskritic traditions of interreligious debate—for instance, the disputes between the

Bauddhas, Mīmāṃsakas, and Naiyāyikas in early philosophical (*śāstric*) discourse. From the early centuries of the Common Era onward, debate had been mediated largely through shared standards of veridicality, such as *pramāṇa* theory—that is, key criteria such as perception and inference that transcended the divides of competing canons and doctrines. In contrast, in sixteenth- and seventeenth-century South India, even the analytic tools of text criticism became the property of distinct sectarian traditions. This, in turn, necessitated a serious reconsideration of what precisely constituted the standards of scriptural interpretation and of textual interpretation in general.

2. A particularly intriguing example of caste and linguistic diversity in this philological turn is a seventeenth-century work of the Tamil Śaiva Siddhānta school titled the *Varṇāśramacandrikā*. The only known work of the lineage to be written in Sanskrit, the *Varṇāśramacandrikā* takes on caste politics in south Indian religious institutions by defending the legitimacy of the Veḷāḷa pontiffs of the tradition's monasteries. Through scrutiny of a compendious assortment of Śaiva scriptural citations, the text also makes the case that the tradition's particular requirement for ascending to the preceptor's seat—namely, lifelong chastity—is required by Śaiva Siddhānta scripture. See also Koppedrayer (1991).

3. tad alam anena maśakamṛgayāsaṃrambheṇety uparamyate. *Śivatattvarahasya,* pg. 23.

4. tathāhi, kim ativistṛtatvaṃ nāma? kiṃ svata evādhikagranthatvam? kiṃ vā klptasaṃkhyā-pekṣayādhikasaṃkhyāvattvenopalabhyamānatvam? ādye sarvapurāṇasādhāraṇyān neṣṭa-siddhiḥ; dvitīye tv asiddhaḥ; yo hi klptagranthasaṃkhyā puṣkalā na labhyata iti naṣṭakośo 'bha-vad grantha ityupālabhyate, taṃ praty eva katham uktalakṣaṇam ativistṛtatvam āpādanīyam (Nīlakaṇṭha Dīkṣita, *Śivatattvarahasya,* pgs. 20–21). The issue of prolixity arises for Nīlakaṇṭha in response to an imagined opponent who claims that the Śaiva Purāṇas are invalid textual authorities because of their prolixity, which, he argues, is grounds for suspecting interpolation. See below for further discussion of Nīlakaṇṭha's response to this opponent, and the numerous reasons he adduces for discarding the canonicity of the Śaiva Purāṇas.

5. yac coktam, ativistṛtatyā prakṣepaśaṅkāspadatvād iti, tad dhi na vivicya praśnam api kṣamate; tathā hi, kim ativistṛtatvam nāma? kiṃ svata evādhikagranthatvam? kiṃ vā klptasa-ṃkhyāpekṣayādhikasaṃkhyāvattvenopalabhyamānatvam? ādye sarvapurāṇasādhāraṇyān neṣṭasiddhiḥ; dvitīye tv asiddhaḥ; yo hi klptagranthasaṃkhyā puṣkalā na labhyata iti naṣṭakośo 'bhavad grantha ity upālabhyate, taṃ praty eva katham uktalakṣaṇam ativistṛtatvam āpādanīyam; idam anyad vā kiṃcid astv ativistṛtatvam, sarvadhāpi tat tat kiṃ vaiṣṇavapurāṇeṣu nāsti? tat kiṃ vyarthaiḥ pañcamyantaiḥ parān bhramayasi? āstaṃ tāvad idam. *Śivatattvarahasya,* pgs. 20–21.

6. Manuscripts authored primarily to offer explanations of this retroflex *ṇ* in *Nārāyaṇa* are numerous. Specialized lexicons are often invoked for the purpose of explaining the syllable *ṇa* as a distinct word endowed with its own denotative capacity. For instance, Govinda Nāyaka (ca. eighteenth century) invokes a certain *Ratnamālā* to the effect that "the word 'ṇa' in the masculine gender is in the sense of a lover, Bhairava, thorn, or a sound," on which grounds the name *Nārāyaṇa* can be derived as signifying "the lover of the women of Vraja." See below for a discussion of this passage and of manuscripts concerned with the *ṇa-tva*, or retroflexion, appearing in the name *Nārāyaṇa*.

7. Pollock, "Future Philology," 934.

8. See *Tantravārttika* 1.3.1.

9. See John Keune (2011, 225) for details on the evidence for Eknāth's editorial project. Hagiographies that narrate this episode include Keśavsvāmī's *Eknāthcaritra* (1760 C.E.) and Mahipati's *Bhaktilīlāmṛta* (1774 C.E.)

10. For the conceptual and social implications of Sāyaṇa's work, see Galewicz (2010).

11. See for instance Minkowski (2004, 2005, 2008).

12. The verse in question is: śrīmatsiddhikaraṃ kāntaṃ ramomāraṇātmakam | dayāsindhuṃ cidānandaṃ sitāsitam upāsmahe ||

13. sitāsitam upāsmaha ity anvayaḥ. sitāsitapadena hariharātmakaṃ vastu pratipādyate. itihāsapurāṇeṣu bahuśo hare śuddhaspaṭikasaṅkāśatvasya harau nīlameghasaṅkāśatvasya ca varṇanāt. na ca hariharayor bhedasya bahupramāṇasiddhatayā 'bhedāsaṃbhavāt katham etad iti vācyam . . . śiva eva hariḥ sākṣād dharir eva śivaḥ svayam | yaḥ paśyaty anayor bhedaṃ sa yāti nirayaṃ naraḥ || ityādyanekapurāṇavacanair hariharayor abhedāvagamāt. Gīrvāṇendra Dīkṣita, *Padārthadīpikāvyākhyā*, GOML, Madras, Ms. No. R. 5133, fol. 1–2.

14. bheda aupādhika eva. na ca vaiparītyam aśaṅkyam. sattvaṃ rajas tama ity udāhṛta-vacanenaiva bhedasyaupādhikatvāvagamāt naivam abhedasyaupādhikatvavacanaṃ paśyāmaḥ. atas tāttvika eva hariharayor abhedaḥ. Gīrvāṇendra Dīkṣita, *Padārthadī-pikāvyākhyā*, GOML, Madras, Ms. No. R. 5133, fol. 2.

15. Kauṇḍa Bhaṭṭa (fl. 1650), best known for his grammatical work, the *Vaiyākaraṇabhūṣaṇa*, was also directly connected to the intellectual communities of south India. Son of Raṅgoji Bhaṭṭa (himself a prolific Advaitin theologian) and nephew of Bhaṭṭoji Dīkṣita, Kauṇḍa Bhaṭṭa may well have been influenced by the sectarian ideas prominent in the south, as Gīrvāṇendra leads us to infer. For more details on his grammatical work, see the entry under his name in Potter, *Encyclopedia of Indian Philosophy*, vol. 5: *The Philosophy of the Grammarians*.

16. atra kecid āhuḥ skāndapurāṇāntargatānāṃ nāmnāṃ prāmāṇyaṃ na saṃbhavati, skāndādīnāṃ tāmasapurāṇatvenāpramāṇatvāt. tathā hi purāṇānāṃ kartā caturmukhaḥ keṣucit kalpeṣu sattvenodrikto bhavati, keṣucid rajasā, keṣucit tamasā, sa yadā sattvenodriktaḥ, tadā vaiṣṇavāni purāṇāni praṇināya, yadā rajasodriktas tadā brāhmāṇi, yadā tamasodriktas tadā śaivāni. evaṃ ca tamoguṇāndhabrahmapraṇītāni śaivapurāṇāni bhrāntajalpitānīvāpramāṇy eva, vaiṣṇavapurāṇāni tu sattvodriktabrahmapraṇītāni prā-jñavākyānīva pramāṇāni. yathoktaṃ mātsye: saṃkīrṇāḥ sāttvikāś caiva rājasāś caiva tāmasāḥ | yasmin kalpe tu yat proktaṃ purāṇaṃ brahmaṇā purā || tasya tasya tu māhātmyaṃ tatsvarūpēṇa varṇyate | agneḥ śivasya māhātmyaṃ tāmaseṣu prakīrtitam || rājaseṣu tu māhātmyam adhikaṃ brahmaṇo viduḥ | saṃkīrṇeṣu sarasvatyāḥ pitṝṇāṃ ca nigadyate || sāttvikeṣu ca kalpeṣu māhātmyam adhikaṃ hareḥ | teṣv eva yogisaṃsiddhā gamiṣyanti parāṃ gatim || Nīlakaṇṭha Dīkṣita, *Śivatattvarahasya*, pgs. 2–3.

17. See Schwartz (2010, 54–58), for a discussion of Rāmānuja's commentary on this passage and its continuities with the interpretive practices of the early Dharmaśāstrins.

18. See below for further discussion.

19. tad evaṃ vaktus tāmasatvadoṣāt, śrutivirodhāt, svavyāghātāt, svoktārthasya pramāṇatvābhimatapurāṇāntarān anugṛhītatvāt, laiṅgasyādau. . . . viśeṣaniṣṭhapraśno-pakrameṇa pravṛtatayā liṅgamāhātmyavarṇanāgrahasya spaṣṭatvāt, kaurmādiṣu naṣṭakośa-tvaprasiddheḥ, ativistṛtatayā ca sarveṣāṃ prakṣepaśaṅkāsaṃbhavāc ca śiva purāṇānāṃ na prāmāṇyaṃ saṃbhavati. viṣṇupurāṇānāṃ tu sarvaprakāreṇāpy uktavaiparītyāt prāmāṇyam asti. *Śivatattvarahasya*, pg. 5.

20. The only previous occurrence I have located for this particular term, *naṣṭakośa*, appears in Vedānta Deśika's *Śatadūṣaṇī*: yāni cānyāni vākyāni saṃpratipannaśrutismṛtiṣv adṛśyamānāni svācārānurūpamataparicaryayā keṣucid aprasiddheṣu vā *naṣṭakośeṣu* vā anirūpitamūlāgreṣu vā purāṇeṣu prakṣipya paṭhanti pāpiṣṭhāḥ tāni pratyakṣaśrutyādipar iśīlanaśāliniṣu gariṣṭhagoṣṭhīṣunāvakāśaṃ labhante. I thank David Brick for drawing my attention to this citation. *Kośa*, as a term for "manuscript" or "copy," was in active use in the Śrīvaiṣṇava circles preceding Vedānta Deśika (Cox 2016).

21. yad apy uktaṃ kaurmādiṣu naṣṭakośatvaprasiddher iti, tad apy asāram; tathā hi—yeyaṃ ṣaṭsahasragranthātmikā brāhmī saṃhitā pracarati, sā na naṣṭaiva; mātsyavacanāvagatasaptadaśasahasrīmadhye brahmasaṃhitātirikto yo 'yam ekādaśasahasragranthātmako bhāgaḥ sa naṣṭa iti cet, astu, ko netyāha; na hi vayaṃ tatratyāni vacanāny udāharāmaḥ. śrūyamāṇā tu yā saṃhitā na tasyāṃ taditaranāśaprayuktaṃ kiṃcid atiśaṅkābījam asti. taditarabhāgasya naṣṭatayā anayāpi saṃhitayā tadvad eva naṣṭayā bhavitavyam, kasyacil lope kasyacid alope ca niyāmakābhāvāt; śrūyamāṇā tu kenacit kalpiteti syād anāśvāsa iti cet, na, aprayojakatvāt—na hi kenacil luptam iti sarveṇa loptavyam, kenacid vā sthitam iti sarveṇa sthātavyam, na khalu aindrādivyākaraṇanāśanimittas tilamātro 'py anāśvāsaḥ pāṇinīye tava vā mama vāsti. kiṃ ca, evaṃ sati viṣṇupurāṇe 'pi mātsyavacanāvagatatrayoviṃśatisahasrīmadhye saptadaśasahasrīnāśaprayukto vidyamānaṣaṭsahasryām anāśvāso dusparihara evāpatet. *Śivatattvarahasya*, pgs. 19–20.

22. As it so happens, Nīlakaṇṭha's opponent's instincts in this case are sound, as nearly half of the text that constitutes the published Liṅga Purāṇa is a direct adaptation of an eleventh-century *paddhati* of the Śaiva Siddhānta composed by the Śaiva Ācārya and Maṭhādhipati Somaśambhu, a work that sets out to systemize Śaiva ritual practices within a conceptual framework that differs substantively from what one typically finds in the Purāṇic sources.

23. *Śivatattvarahasya*, pgs. 17–19.

24. Casaubon's theological agenda, in fact, is spelled out explicitly in the title of this work (1630), presented in the form of historical philology: *The originall of popish idolatrie, or The birth of heresies Published under the name of Causabon [sic], and called-in the same yeare, upon misinformation*. See also Grafton (1994) for further discussion of Casaubon's philological and theological contributions.

25. yad apy uktam viṣṇupurāṇam prati śivapurāṇoktadoṣasaptakarāhityāt tat pramāṇam iti, tatra pratijñāṃśa ekaḥ sādhuḥ, hetvaṃśas tu na parīkṣākṣamaḥ. . . . yat tāvad uktam vaktus tāmasatvadoṣād iti, tad evāsiddham; tathā hi purāṇānāṃ ko vaktety abhimānaḥ. caturmukha ity uktam eveti cet, satyam uktam; tad eva tu tvaduktaṃ bhavadbhrāntikalpitam; sāttvikādidurvibhāgakathanābhijñena bhavataiva pramāṇatayābhyupagate mahābhārata eva śāntiparvaṇi rājadharme śiva eva sarvapurāṇānām ādivaktety uktatvāt. . . . ity anuktapurāṇasamuccayārthakacakāravatyā śrutyā sargādyakāle śivāl labdhānāṃ purāṇānāṃ pravaktā paraṃ caturmukha iti siddhatvena tasya purāṇapraṇetṛtvāsiddheḥ. na ca pravaktus tamobhibhāvo doṣāya; tasya praṇetṛdoṣavatprabandhāprāmāṇyānāpā dakatvāt, anyathāsmadādipaṭhitavedavākyāni aprāmāṇy āpatteś ca. . . . yac coktam—svavyāghātād aprāmāṇyam iti, tad apy etenaiva nirākṛtam, nārāyaṇād rudrotpattiḥ guṇirudraviṣayā, trimūrtīnām utpattis tu paramśivaviṣayeti vyavasthābhiprāyakatayā svavyāghātagandhasyāpy abhāvāt.

26. See below for more details on the *Īśavilāsa* and on the identity of its author.

27. yasyājñayā jagatsraṣṭā viriñcaḥ pālako hariḥ | saṃhartā kālarudrākhyo namas tasmai pinākine || *Īśavilāsa* of Appayya Dīkṣita, fol. 1.

28. triumūrtibhinnaṃ śivam advayaṃ ca śrutyantavedyaṃ nikhilaprapañce | sṛṣṭyādihetuṃ satataṃ namāmi vighnaughaśāntyai sakalaṃ śaraṇyam || *Madhvamukhacapeṭikā*, VORI 6922; *Madhvatantracapeṭikāvyākhyāna* of Tirumalācārya, GOML, Madras, Ms. No. R. 2263b, fol. 1.

29. *yuktiyuktam* upādeyaṃ vacanaṃ bālakād api | anyat tṛṇam iva tyājyam apy uktaṃ padmajanmanā || Quoted by Nārāyaṇācārya, *Advaitakālānala*, pg. 42. This aphoristic verse is best known from the *Yogavāsiṣṭha/Mokṣopāya* textual corpus. See for instance *Mokṣopāya* 2.18.3.

30. The *Nyāyādhvadīpikā*, for instance, is, remarkably, a treatise of the Mīmāṃsā school of Vedic hermeneutics, about which more will be said below. The fascination with the homonymy of the term *nyāya* as "logic" and *nyāya* as a "maxim" of Mīmāṃsā hermeneutics is perhaps no accident.

31. See Mesquita (2000, 2008) for the controversy on the authenticity of Madhva's scriptural citations.

32. ityādiṛgvedamantrasya svakalpitavāyvavatāratrayaparatayā pradarśanam ity ādiprāmāṇikamaryādollaṅghanaṃ bhūyaḥ saṃdṛśyate. Appayya Dīkṣita, *Madhvatantramukhamardana*, pg. 11.

33. athāpi yuktiyuktaṃ vaco grāhyaṃ na tu puruṣagauravam iti nyāyena tanmataṃ śraddadhīmahi yadi tatropapannaṃ kiṃcid ākalayema. na tv evaṃprāyeṇa hi tanmate svamātrahṛdayārūḍhāni vacanāny evopajīvyāni na tu nyāyāḥ. ye tu nyāyāḥ pradarśitās te 'py atyantaśithilā eva kvacit kvacid āśritāḥ. pūrvamīmāṃsāmaryādā 'py asāmañjasyenaiva nītā. prāyeṇāsādhubhir eva śabdair vyavahāraḥ. ślokaracanāyām anvayāsaṃbhavo vṛttāny athābhāvaś cādhikaḥ. Appayya Dīkṣita, *Madhvatantramukhamardana*, pg. 11.

34. See Pollock (2004) for a discussion and partial translation of the work in question, the *Pūrvottaramīmāṃsāvādanakṣatramālā*, or "The Milky Way of Discourses on Pūrva and Uttara Mīmāṃsā," in Pollock's translation.

35. Diaconescu (2012), for instance, has observed that Appayya's language shows remarkably little Navya Nyāya inflection, without, however, inquiring into why this might be the case.

36. See also McCrea (2008) on the extensive discourse, both critical and approbative, generated in response to Appayya's provocative theses.

37. pūrvamīmāṃsakamaryādāsāmañjasyenaiva nīyateti tad ayuktam. asmadācāryo dāhṛtavacanāni svamātrahṛdayārūḍhānīti vadan kūpamaṇḍūkāyate. asmadācāryapradarśitanyāyānām eva matidārḍhyaṃ na parasparadarśitānām. pūrvamīmāṃsakamaryādāsāmañjasyaṃ cāsmanmata eva. Vijayīndra Tīrtha, *Madhvatantramukhabhūṣaṇa*, GOML, Madras, Ms. No. 15446, fol. 6.

38. yathā dvādaśākṣarā jagatī nāma vṛttaṃ tasyāś ca gurulaghuprakriyāvyutpādanena parasparāsaṃspṛṣṭāś catvāri sahasrāṇi ṣaṇṇavatiś ca bhedā bhavanti. tadantaḥpraviṣṭānāṃ katipayānāṃ vaṃśasthadrutavilambitādayaḥ saṃjñāḥ kṛtāḥ. evam ekasya chandasa ete, yathā yathā chandokṣarāṇām adhikatvaṃ bhavati tathā tathā lakṣādhikaprastāram ekaikaṃ vṛttaṃ bhavati. yāny api śārdūlavikrīḍitasragdharādīni vṛttāni tāni ca ślokapādaparyāptāny eveti niyamaḥ. na tu tad eva vṛttaṃ ślokasya pādacatuṣṭaye 'py apekṣaṇīyam ity asti. tena—sarvair devaiś ca bhaktyaiḥ svanimiṣanayanaiḥ kautukādvīkṣyamāṇaḥ pāyāc

cheṣagarutmadādidivijaiḥ saṃsevitaḥ svaṃ padam. ity atra ādyapāde sragdharā dvitīyapāde ca śārdūlavikrīḍitam. *Advaitakālānala,* pg. 51.

39. śivaṃ viṣṇuṃ vā yady abhidadhati śāstrasya viṣayaṃ tad iṣṭaṃ grāhyaṃ naḥ sagunam api tad brahmabhajatām. virodho nātīva sphurati na hi nindā nayavidāṃ na sūtrāṇām arthāntaram api bhavadvāryam ucitam. *Madhvatantramukhamardana,* pg. 2, v. 1.

40. na hi nindā nindyaṃ ninditum prayujyate. kiṃ tarhi ninditāditarat praśaṃsitum. tatra na ninditasya pratiṣedho gamyate, kiṃtv itarasya vidhiḥ.

41. virodhaṃ vākyānāṃ śrutiśikharabhājāṃ śamayituṃ pravṛttā mīmāṃsā bhavati sakalāpīha viphalā. *Advaitakālānala* 2.13.

42. yad api pūrvamīmāṃsāmaryādāpy asāmañjasyena nītety uktaṃ, tad apy uktaṃ na hi vayaṃ pūrvamīmāṃsakānāṃ kiṃkarāḥ. yattanmaryādayaiva vartemahi. kiṃ tu—yuktiyuktam upādeyaṃ vacanaṃ bālakād api | anyat tṛṇam iva tyājyam apy uktaṃ padmajanmanā || iti nyāyād yad upapannaṃ tat svīkurmaḥ, yad anupapannam . . . tatparityajāmas, tad etad bhūṣaṇam eva na tu dūṣaṇaṃ svatantratantrapravartakānām. anyathā samavāyānaṅgīkārāt kāṇādādimaryādollaṅghanaṃ prakṛtiprādhānyānaṅgīkārāt sāṃkhyamaryādol-laṅghanam ity ādy api dūṣaṇaṃ kimiti nodbhāvayeḥ. pratyuta sakalavādyanabhimatam ātmaikatvam akhaṇḍaṃ brahma viśvamithyātvaṃ vedasyātattvāvedakatvam abhyupagatavatas tavaiva śūnyavādyatiriktasarvatāntrikamaryādollaṅghanaṃ śūnyavādimatapraveśasyeti kathaṃ na nibhālayase. *Advaitakālānala,* pg. 42.

43. See Stoker (2007) for more details on Madhva's use of Nirukta in his *Ṛgbhāṣya.*

44. See for instance Bronner (2010, 233).

45. kiṃ ca yo devānāṃ nāmadhā eka eva iti śrutiparyālocanayā nārāyaṇa eva sarvadevanāmamukhyārtha iti siddhyati. anyathā tatra "namadhā eka eva" ityavadhāraṇasya bādhitārthāpatteḥ.

46. The fact that the debate at hand was not restricted to a small handful of interlocutors can be gleaned from a reference in the anonymous *Nārāyaṇaśabdanirukti* (see below) to an additional group of imagined opponents, whom the author claims to have already dismissed: "Previously, we had a debate with Mallanārādhya and so forth, who are very well acquainted with the works of Appayya Dīkṣita." He writes: "appayadīkṣitagittantheṣu samyakparicayaśālibhiḥ mallanārādhyaprabhṛtibhiḥ sahāsmākaṃ pūrvaṃ vivāde prasakte tair nārāṇām ayanau yasmāt sa iti śivaparatayā vigrahe kathite viṣṇuviṣayakanārāyaṇapadavigrahāṇām ivaitadvigrahasya nirvacanamūlakatvābhāvād agrāhyatvam ity asmābhir dūṣaṇe datte tair aṅgīkṛtyaiva sthitatvāt dīkṣitagranthasandarbhena sarvathā viruddhatvāc ca. tasmāt tāni vacanāny agrāhyāṇy eva." (*Nārāyaṇaśabdanirukti,* fol. 36). That the opponent in question appears to have a Vīraśaiva name suggests that sectarian debate had thoroughly permeated the south Indian religious landscape by the eighteenth century.

47. We encounter, for instance, the *Natvakhaṇḍana* of Veṅkaṭācārya, the *Natvacandrikā* of Kṛṣṇa Sudhī, the *Natvatattvaparitrāṇa* of Śrīnivāsadāsa, the *Natvatattvavibhūṣaṇa,* and several works titled the *Natvadarpaṇa,* to name a few.

48. These manuscripts, the *Nārāyaṇaśabdasādhāraṇya* of Govinda Nāyaka and the *Nārāyaṇaśabdanirukti* (or *Nārāyaṇaśabdasādhāraṇyakhaṇḍana*) of unknown authorship, are preserved in the Adyar Library and Research Centre in the same bundle, no. DX 819. Citations in this chapter are taken directly from the Adyar manuscripts. After transcribing these Adyar manuscripts, I discovered that an English translation of the two works has been

published by Bahulikar and Hebbar (2011), under the title *Who Is the Supreme God, Visnu or Siva?: A Rendering of the 16th Century ce Theological Debates in South India between the Vaisnava and the Saiva Sects of Hinduism.* While the editors fail to provide attestation of the origin of the manuscripts used for their translation, presumably the same Adyar manuscripts have been used for this edition as well. All translations in the present chapter are my own. The published translation, at times out of touch with the larger world of early modern Sanskrit intellectual life, frequently obscures the particulars of śāstric debate and fails to capture the idiom and force of the arguments. For instance, a reference made by Govinda Nāyaka to the *na hi nindā* maxim (discussed above), a subject of controversy since the time of Appayya, is occluded by the editors as follows: "Therefore, we should understand that all these Purāṇas extol particular deities by reducing the importance of others."

49. narāṇāṃ jīvāṇāṃ samūho nāraṃ tasmai nārāyaṇaḥ. mokṣaḥ ṇaṃ jñānaṃ vā yasmād bhavatīti. ṇas tu nirvṛtivācakaḥ. ṇaṃ sarojadale jñānam iti ratnamālāyāṃ caturthyā aluk. *Nārāyaṇaśabdasādhāraṇya,* fol. 11.

50. Govinda Nāyaka's Śrīvaiṣṇava critic, in the *Nārāyaṇaśabdanirukti,* dismisses these etymologies by citing Pāṇini 2.1.36, which informs us that dative compounds occur only when a word is joined with *artha, bali, hita,* or *sukha,* or when it indicates a dative of purpose, such as *kuṇḍalahiraṇyam* (gold for the purpose of earrings). In these cases, however, classical Pāṇinian grammar requires that the dative termination be elided as expected in such compounds. The particular compound *ahalyāyaijāraḥ,* he informs us, is a Vedic (*chāndasa*) usage and, hence, inapplicable to Purāṇic exegesis.

51. vraje nāraya ārīsamudāyāya ṇaḥ jāro vā ahalyāyaijāra iti vat caturthyā aluk. ṇaśabdas tu pumāñjāre bhairave kaṇṭake dhvanau iti ratnamālāyām. *Nārāyaṇaśabdasādhāraṇya,* fol. 10.

52. nāraṃ gaṅgājalaṃ tadāśayatvād vā āpo nārā iti sukṛtir iti kaurme. tatra tatra purāṇeṣu śivaparatvena nārāyaṇśabdaḥ śrūyata [emended from śūyata] iti, *Nārāyaṇaśabdasādhāraṇya,* fol. 15–16.

53. nārāyaṇapadasya caturmukhaparatvam api nirūpyate . . . nābhikamalanālāni ayanāni gamanāgamanamārgarūpāṇi yasyeti vā. ayanaṃ nilaye mārge || nāle nāle gatas tatra varṣāṇāṃ śatakaṃ mune | ārurohāya kamalaṃ nālamārgeṇa vai mune || iti śivapurāṇe. *Nārāyaṇaśabdasādhāraṇya,* fol. 18–19. Here the *la-kāra* and *repha* in *nāla* and *nāra* are treated interchangeably, in fact a common morphological pattern. I have not been able to confirm a Purāṇic precedent for the verse Govinda Nāyaka has cited here; the grammar shows signs of corruption in the transcribed manuscript.

54. trayāṇām ekacitpratibimbatvena sarveṣāṃ sarvanāmāni sambhavantīti vā. *Nārāyaṇaśabdasādhāraṇya,* fol. 22.

55. akṣatair viṣṇupūjananiṣedhakasya akṣataiḥ śivapūjananiṣedhaparatvaṃ pradoṣe śivadarśanavidhāyakasya tadā viṣṇudarśanavidhāyakatvam ekādaśyāṃ viṣṇuvratavidhāyakasya tadā śivavratavidhāyakatvam ityādirūpeṇādi vaktuṃ śakyatvāt. purāṇādyuktasarvadharmāṇāṃ yatheṣṭam anuṣṭheyatvāpattyā sarvavaidikavyavasthā-bhaṅgāpatteḥ. yathecchānuṣṭhātṝṇāṃ pratyavāyavattvābhāvāpatteś ca. *Nārāyaṇaśabdanirukti,* fol. 5.

56. nanu viṣṇur nārāyaṇaḥ kṛṣṇa ityādikośeṣu viṣṇuparatvenaiva dṛṣṭavān na mūrtitrayasādhāraṇyam iti cen na. kośaprasiddhas tu bālabodhanamātraiva. no cet tatrānuktānāṃ śabdānāṃ viṣṇuparatvaṃ na syāt. evam eva brahmaśivaparyāyeṣv api. . . . tasmāt

devatātrayaparatvena nārāyaṇādiśabdānāṃ śrutatvād iti kośādiṣu nārāyaṇādiśabdānāṃ viṣṇvādiṣu śaktisaṃkocenaiva viniyoga ity avagantavyam. ata eva anekaśakteḥ śabdasya śaktyavacchedena saṃjñini viniyogād iti kaiyaṭoktiḥ. traivarṇyavācakadvijaśabdasya ajñaprasiddhyā brāhmaṇe viniyogavat brāhmaṇakṣatriyaviśaḥ dvijā iti hi viśrutāḥ. iti nāradīye. smārtavaiṣṇavamādhvaśaivādivācakabrāhmaṇasmārtaśabdayoḥ prayoge ajñaprasiddhyā smārtānām eva bodhaḥ, na tu vaiṣṇavādīnāṃ tadvac ca nārāyaṇapadam api. *Nārāyaṇaśabdasādhāraṇya*, fol. 20–22.

57. na hi kosaḥ anekārtheṣu pūrvaiḥ prāyaśaḥ prayuktasya śabdasya tadekadeśe śaktir iti svayaṃ nirdhārayati na vā alpārtheṣu pūrvaiḥ prāyaśaḥ prayujyamānasya śabdasya bahvartheṣu śaktir iti vā vadati kiṃtu yāvatsv artheṣu viduṣām anindaprathamo nānyathāsiddhaḥ pracuraprayogaḥ tāvatsv eva śaktir iti vadati vyākaraṇavatkośasyāpi prayogaśaraṇatvāt, anyathā tasya sarvajanaparigrahābhāvāpatteḥ. ato mahājanapracuraprayogasiddhāṃ rūḍhiṃ sugrahatvāyakośasvayaṃ susṭhaṃ nirūpayatīti. *Nārāyaṇaśabdanirukti*, fol. 28–30.

58. Our author's complete argument on this point runs as follows: na hi kosaḥ anekārtheṣu pūrvaiḥ prāyaśaḥ prayuktasya śabdasya tadekadeśe śaktir iti svayaṃ nirdhārayati na vā alpārtheṣu pūrvaiḥ prāyaśaḥ prayujyamānasya śabdasya bahvartheṣu śaktir iti vā vadati kiṃtu yāvatsv artheṣu viduṣām anindaprathamo nānyathāsiddhaḥ pracuraprayogaḥ tāvatsv eva śaktir iti vadati vyākaraṇavatkośasyāpi prayogaśaraṇatvāt, anyathā tasya sarvajanaparigrahābhāvāpatteḥ. ato mahājanapracuraprayogasiddhāṃ rūḍhiṃ sugrahatvāya kośasvayaṃ susṭhaṃ nirūpayatīti.…yat prāye śrūyate yac ca tat tādṛg avagamyata iti nyāyena niyataprayogaviṣayapratipāditaśaktikapadāntarasahapaṭhitasya nārāyaṇapadasyāpi niyataprayogaviṣayapratipāditaśaktikatvasyaiva vaktavyavattvāc ca śiveśāneśvaramaheśvarādiśabdānāṃ stutyādibhāgavyatiriktakathābhāgeṣu viśeṣaṇatayā viśeṣyatayā ca viṣṇvādau bhāratabhāgavatādiṣu paraḥsahasraprayogāṇāṃ sāmānyaśaktigrāhakakośānāṃ ca sattvāt teṣāṃ sādhāraṇye 'pi nārāyaṇādiśabdānāṃ kathābhāgeṣu viśeṣaṇatayā svatantratayā vā nārāyaṇavyatirikte sāmānyaśaktyā sampratipannaprayogābhāvena kośābhāvena cāsādhāraṇatayā tṛṇaghṛtasāmānyaśaktānāṃ barhirājyādiśabdānāṃ saṃskṛtatṛṇaghṛtādāv āryāṇāṃ śaktisaṃkocena viniyogavat kośe śivādiśabdānāṃ rudrādau śaktisaṃkocena viniyogavac ca nārāyaṇaśabdasya śaktisaṃkocena viniyogakalpanāyāṃ nyāyāviṣayabhūtāyā asambhavāc ca viśiṣyāpi tvadudāhṛtavacanavyatiriktasthale kvāpi nārāyaṇapadasya śivādau prayogādarśanāt. *Nārāyaṇaśabdanirukti*, fol. 30–32.

59. The *Nīlakaṇṭha Bhāṣya* refers to Śrīkaṇṭha's *Bhāṣya* on the Brahmasūtras. The *Śivārkamaṇidīpikā* is Appayya Dīkṣita's subcommentary on Śrīkaṇṭha's *Bhāṣya*; the *Śivatattvaviveka* is a sectarian polemical work composed by Appayya Dīkṣita, an autocommentary on the author's *Śikhariṇīmālā* (such titles became commonplace owing to the reputation of antecedent works such as Madhva's *Viṣṇutattvanirṇaya*—cf. Nīlakaṇṭha Dīkṣita's *Śivatattvarahasya*). The *Śaivakarṇāmṛta* presumably refers to the work of Appayya's typically cited as the *Śivakarṇāmṛta*.

60. bhavadudāhṛtanārāyaṇapadaśivaparatvapratipādakair vacanaprayogā nārāyaṇapadasya śivaparatvasādhane atyantāgrahavadbhiḥ śaivatanmatānusāribhiḥ nīlakaṇṭhabhāṣyaśivārkamaṇidīpikāśivastutiśūktimālikāśivatattvavivekaśaivakarṇāmṛtādiṣu   anudāhṛtatvāt. tattadgranthasthapaṅktilekhanapūrvakaṃ   tatkhaṇḍakair asmadīyaiś cānudāhṛtatvāt bhāratādiṣv api prakṣiptadarśanād ativistṛtaśaivaskāndādiṣu prakṣiptasadbhāvaśaṅkāyā durvāratvāt. teṣāṃ śaivaskāndādīnāṃ prāyaśaḥ śaivair eva sampadyamānatvāt.

ādhunikadevālayādiviṣayakakalpitakṣetramāhātmyādīnāṃ   śaivaskāndāditanniṣṭhatvenaiva kriyamāṇatvāc ca paurāṇikā eva na bhavanti. And our author continues: appayyadīkṣitena skāndavacanam udāhṛtam ity uktam. tad api daśasaṃvatsaramadhye kaiścid ādhuknikaiḥ kalpayitvā kvacit kośeṣu likhitam eva pūrvapustakeṣv adarśanāt. dīkṣitagranthakhaṇḍakair asmadīyair anudāhṛtatvāt. *Nārāyaṇaśabdanirukti,* fol. 34–36.

61. tapaḥprabhāvād devaprasādāc ca brahma ha śvetāśvataro 'tha vidvān | *atyāśramibhyaḥ* paramaṃ pavitraṃ provāca samyagṛṣisaṃghajuṣṭam || (*ŚvetUp* 6.21)

62. For instance, Patrick Olivelle (1996, 265) translates the verse in question as follows: "By the power of his austerities and by the grace of God, the wise Śvetāśvatara first came to know *brahman* and then proclaimed it to those who had passed beyond their order of life as the highest means to purification that brings delight to the company of seers."

63. See Olivelle (1993, 222–234), for a thorough discussion of the concept of transcending the *varṇāśrama* system in Advaita Vedānta. The term *atyāśramin* itself rarely occurs in these Advaita Vedānta sources, although a handful of intriguing usages occur in the work of Śaṅkarācārya himself, who does interpret the term as "one who has transcended the *āśramas*." Other theologians, whom Olivelle cites, often use alternative terms such as *ativarṇāśramin,* a word that itself reveals the exegetical work it has been poised to accomplish in its modification from the original. We can observe that, by the time of Vedānta Deśika, opponents of Smārta-Śaivas had begun to return to the original term *atyāśramin,* advancing the interpretation of Śaṅkarācārya, astonishingly, in order to counter his Śaiva interlocutors who had recovered an understanding of word's original meaning.

64. On the history of the terms *Atimārga* and *Mantramārga,* and on the attested usages of the term *atyāśramavrata,* see Alexis Sanderson (2006, 156–164). The Niśvāsamūla, as well as the Svacchanda Tantra, employ a model in which five principal streams of religious practice emerge from the five faces of Śiva: in graded hierarchy from lowest to highest, the Laukika, Vaidika, Ādhyātmika (i.e., Sāṃkhya and Yoga), Atimārga, and Mantramārga.

65. As is noted in the Sanskrit original below, Nīlakaṇṭha's treatment of this verse preserves a variant reading from the one cited above.

66. śvetāśvataropaniṣadi śrūyate—tapaḥprabhāvād devaprasādāc ca brahmavic chvetāśvataro 'tha vidvān | atyāśramibhyaḥ paramaṃ pavitraṃ provāca samyagṛṣisaṃghajuṣṭam || iti. tatra tripuṇḍravidhānānte śrūyamāṇe—ayam atyāśramo dharmo yaiḥ samācaritaḥ purā | eṣām eva paraṃ jñānaṃ saṃsārachedakāraṇam || iti brahmottarakhaṇḍavacanenātyāśr amaśabdavācyatayā siddhaṃ tripuṇḍradhāraṇam anūdya brahmavidyopadeśakīrtanena tad uktaṃ brahmavidyāṅgatvasiddhau—tiryak tisro rekhāḥ prakurvīta vratam etac chāmbhavaṃ sarvavedeṣu vedavādibhir uktam. tatsamācaren mumukṣur apunarbhavāya. yad etat tripuṇḍraṃ bhasmanā karoti yo vidvān brahmacārī gṛhī vānaprastho yatir vā samastamahāpātakopapātakebhyaḥ pūto bhavatīti.

67. kecit tu smṛtyuktarītyā atyāśramaśabdārtham aṅgīkṛtya tatsthasya prakaraṇādivaśād vidyāviśeṣe 'dhikāram āhuḥ. yathā ca bhasmoddhūlanatripuṇḍradhāraṇādīnāṃ na brahmavidyāmātrāṅgatvaṃ tathā 'tharvaśirovākyavicāre vakṣyāma ity alam. *Turīyaśivakhaṇḍana,* pg. 53.

68. kaivalyaśrutāv upakramopasaṃhāragatātyāśramiśabdo 'pi yatyāśramapara eva yukta iti na tadbalenāpi kaivalyaśruteḥ prasiddhaśivaparatvāśāyuktā. suḥ pūjāyām atir atikramaṇe ca iti hi pāṇinisūtram. *Turīyaśivakhaṇḍana,* pgs. 52–53.

69. This work (see *Īśavilāsa*, TR. No. 291) is traditionally ascribed to one "Appayya Dīkṣita" but is not generally accepted as one of the works of the sixteenth-century polymath. It is certainly possible that the text was composed by one of his descendants, many of whom adopted the same title as their nom de plume.

70. Sources cited include the Atharvaśiras, Śvetāśvatara Upaniṣad, Kālāgnirudropaniṣad, Muṇḍaka Upaniṣad, Kaivalya Upaniṣad, Kūrma Purāṇa, and numerous others.

71. evaṃ tripuṇḍroddhūlanavratena arthād eva puṇḍrāntaraniṣedhāt tanmūlakāni ca ūrdhvapuṇḍraniṣedhakavākyāni vāsiṣṭha-laiṅgaparāśaropapurāṇa-mānava-sūtasaṃhitā-sāmbapurāṇādiṣu bahutarāṇi vistarabhayān na likhitāni. *Īśavilāsa*, fol. 385.

72. The term *Mahāpāśupata* in early Śaiva often refers to practitioners of the Kāpālika lineage or, in this instance, may distinguish the Pāśupatas in question from the Lākuliśa Pāśupatas. Because of the Vedicized inflection in this passage, it is not likely that this is in fact a Kāpālika source. See for instance Sanderson (1991, 3). The term appears in Śaiva sources as early as the Niśvāsamūla.

73. athāsminn antare 'paśyan samāyāntaṃ mahāmunim | śvetāśvataranāmānam mahāpāśupatottamam || bhasmasandigdhasarvāṅgakaupīnāc chādanānvitam | tapasākarṣitātmānaṃ śuddhayajñopavītinam || śiṣyatve pratijagrāha tapasākṣīṇakalmaṣaṃ | so 'nugrhya ca rājānaṃ suśīlaṃ śīlasamyutam || [emended from śilaṃ samyutam] sānyāsikaṃ vidhiṃ kṛtsnaṃ kārayitvā vicakṣaṇaḥ | dadau tadaiśvaraṃ jñānaṃ svaśākhāvihitaṃ vratam || aśeṣavedasāraṃ tat paśupāśavimocanam | atyāśramam iti khyātaṃ brahmādibhir anuṣṭhitam || (*Īśavilāsa*, pg. 379). I cite here the readings of the author of the *Īśavilāsa*, rather than those of any published edition of the Kūrma Purāṇa. The passage in question is *KP* 1.13.31–38.

74. The passage in question is slightly corrupted, but the sense is clear: bhasmadhāraṇasya purāṇābhipretatvād atyāśramapāśupatavratayoḥ samānaprayogatvāvagamād ekaphalāvacchinnaikaprayogasambandhinobrahmavidyādhikārīphalayormuṇḍaka-kaivalyavākyābhyāṃ pratyabhijñānānānūṇḍakaivalyātharvaśiraḥśvetāśvatarakālāgnirudropaniṣadvihitānāṃ śirovratapāśupatavrata-atyāśramavratānām ekatvam avagamyate. I suggest emending it to: brahmavidyādhikāritvaphalayoḥ, and pratyabhijñānāṃ muṇḍakavailyātharvaśiraḥ-.

75. This Kūrma Purāṇa passage has been discussed by Mark Dyczkowski (1989, 24) as evidence for an early Vedic lineage of Pāśupatas who opposed themselves to more antinomian traditions.

76. nanu bhavet tv etat tripuṇḍradhāraṇam śivopāsakānām. ambikopāsakānāṃ tu nedaṃ bhasmadhāraṇam kartavyam. . . . iti ced ucyate kaivalyopaniṣadi. . . . iti sāmbavidyāṅgatvena bhasmatripuṇḍravidhānāt, śrīvidyopāsakānāṃ ca sāmbaśivopāsakatvasyāsmābhir eva caturthaparicchede 'py avasthāpayiṣyamāṇatvena teṣām apy āvaśyakam eva bhasmatripuṇḍradhāraṇam. . . . nanv evam api kim ambikopāsakānāṃ candanāṅgarāgādiniyama ādaraṇīyaḥ, neti brūmaḥ. tathā hi yo yaddevatopāsanas tena taddevatālāñchanavatā bhavitavyam iti hi tantrāṇāṃ hṛdayam yato vidadhaty etāni—vaiṣṇavānāṃ vanamālādidhāraṇam, śaivānāṃ rudrākṣadhāraṇam ca. rājabhṛtyādiṣu cāyaṃ nyāyo lokānām api vidita eva. tad iha śṛṅgāranāyiketisamākhyādivyāpitasakalaśṛṅgāramaṅgalāyā bhagavatyā upāsakair api śṛṅgāraveṣaprāyair bhavitavyam iti śāktatantrāṇāṃ hṛdayam. . . . sa ca veṣaḥ smartṛbhir aniṣiddha eva grāhyaḥ. kūrmapurāṇe—. . . ityādinā lokodvegakaraṃ veṣaṃ niṣedhantīti. yasmin deśe yasmin kāle yena veṣeṇa lokā udvijante tatra tatra taṃ parityajya lokasaṅgraho yāvatā bhavati tāvad eva

grāhyam. ataḥ pāmarabahule loke manasaiva sarvaṃ saṃbhāvanīyam. na kiñcid bahiḥ prakāśanīyam. idam evābhipretyoktaṃ lalitākhyāne—saṃkalpabhūṣaṇo vāpīti.

77. evaṃ ca vaidikābhāsamādhvādikalpitaśrutiviruddhanirmūlavākyāvalambanena pūrvopārjitamahāpāpajanitasaṃskārasammohitadhiyo mūḍhās taptamūdrādharaṇaṃ kurvantītyāhāntyajatvam upagamyate pralayānte sakalanarakabhogabhājino bhavanti. ata eva vedādyadhikāriṇāṃ taptamudrāniṣedhakaṃ taddharaṇe prāyaścittavidhāyakaṃ prāyascittānanuṣṭhāne narakādibodhakaṃ vacanasahasraṃ tatra tatropalabhyate tatra diṅmātraṃ pradarśayāmaḥ (*Pākhaṇḍacapeṭikā*, pg. 2). Devoted entirely to demolishing the practice of branding on the basis of scriptural precedent, the *Pākhaṇḍacapeṭikā*, although preserved today in manuscripts housed in Calcutta, shows enormous influence from southern strategies of sectarian debate. As the issue of *taptamudrā* concerned southern theologians as well, it must be concluded that the author was either a southerner himself or directly influenced by formative models of sectarian debate developed in south India

78. Giorgio Agamben, *The Highest Poverty*, 16.

4. THE LANGUAGE GAMES OF ŚIVA

1. On the history and performance of Madurai's Cittirai Festival, at which the marriage of Śiva and Mīnākṣī now takes place, see Hudson (1982, 1977) and Harman (1992, 1985).

2. No original literary work detailing the sixty-four "Sacred Games of Śiva" has yet been faithfully translated into English or any other modern language. Aside from numerous modern Tamil prose renderings, synopses of these sixty-four narrative legends can be found in English (1) as an appendix to the dissertation of Amy Ruth Holt (2007), who has translated a modern Tamil summary of the games (although, it must be noted, what she has translated is a simplified work of modern prose and in no way, as she claims, a "printing" or "edition" of Parañcōti's *Tiruviḷaiyāṭal Purāṇam*); and (2) in Taylor's *Oriental Historical Manuscripts*. Synopses can be found in French in Dessigane, Pattabiramin, and Filliozat's (1960) literary and art-historical study of the "Sacred Games" in Madurai.

3. The approximate floruit of Nampi is best estimated on the basis of an inscription appearing to date from the mid-fourteenth century (in the eighty-sixth year of the reign of Kulaśekhara Pāṇḍya—that is, ca. 1354—describing the appropriation of land in the vicinity of Cidambaram that had in previous generations been gifted to a certain Perumpaṟṟapuliyūr Nampi. The inscription in question is ARE 183 of 1908 (incorrectly specified by Jeyechandrun (1985) as 13 of 1908).

4. A number of these narratives were evidently circulating in some form during the early centuries of Tamil literary history based on passing references and the attestation of foreign observers. For instance, the Cilappatikāram refers to a legend in which a Pandian ruler famously hurled his javelin into the sea, which Jeyechandrun (1985) contends may prefigure the thirteenth Game in Parañcōti's *TVP*. In the fourth century C.E., the Greek ethnographer Megasthenes recorded hearing a legend in which a Pandian ruler married the goddess of Madurai, evidently prefiguring the sacred marriage, which has come to serve as the centerpiece of the legends for modern audiences. A full fourteen of the "Sacred Games" are referred to in passing by Ñānacampantar in his Tamil bhakti hymns (see Jeyechandrun for this list). The number sixty-four is first associated with the "Sacred Games" in the *Kallāṭam* (ca. twelfth–thirteenth century), although only thirty-one of the narratives are

actually recounted. See also Wilden (2014) and Zvelebil (1973) for a discussion of previous versions of the Tamil Caṅkam legend, which conform in various degrees to the now-familiar version found in Parañcōti's *Tiruviḷaiyāṭal Purāṇam*.

5. The following verse, concluding the episode in which Patañjali witnesses Śiva's divine dance, exemplifies the high literary style Nampi adopts periodically throughout his *TVP*, heavily ornamented with alliteration such as never appears in Parañcōti's work: matañcorikol kuñcaravi ruñcaruma kañcukava rañcayila vañci koḻunaṉ / vitañceṟipu rañcuṭane ṭuñcaramvi ṭuñcaturaṉ viñcaiyarvi rañcariṟaiva / ṉitañceykoṭu nañcavura kañcacimi laiñcacaṭai yeñcalila cañca laṉuḷam / patañcalini ṟaiñcaṭiyi ṟaiñciṭana ṭañceytapa rañcuṭarta ruñcorupamē. Nampi, *TVP* (1906, 5.7).

6. Nampi, *TVP*, pg. 8, v. 23): "I join my head to the feet of Paramañānacivaṉ, disciplined in the precepts of the Lord covered with matted locks who rules over me mercifully, abiding in the Māḷikai monastery in ancient Tillai [Cidambaram] that grants boons, with [my] mind on Vināyakan who graces the white forest of the sages of rare penance." varantarun tollait tillai māḷikai maṭattu maṉṉu / maruntava muṉiveṉ kāṭa ṉaruḷvinā yakaṉma ṉattāṟ / parinteṉai yāṇṭu koṇṭa paṭarcaṭaik kaṭavu ṇīti / tiruntiya parama ñāṉa civaṉaṭi ceṉṉi cōrppām.

7. It is not universally accepted that the sixteenth-century polymath Appayya Dīkṣita was in fact the author of the *Prākṛtamaṇidīpikā*; in fact, evidence exists that raises considerable doubt about the matter. Minkowski (2010), for instance, demonstrates that the author of the *Prākṛtamaṇidīpikā* seems to have been a devotee of a Śaṅkarācārya preceptor, which appears unlikely in light of the evidence discussed in chapter 2 of the present work. V. Raghavan (1941) prefers to date the *Prākṛtamaṇidīpikā* in the late seventeenth century. The issue in the present context, however, hinges upon the discursive context of the work and its benedictory verse and not the actual authorship of the work.

8. pāṇigrahe pāṇḍyakumārikāyāḥ pāyāt samīkaṃ parameśvareṇa | anyonyalābhāc chivayor vicitraṃ yasmiñ jayo 'bhūd ubhayoḥ samānaḥ ||

9. Bertrand, *La Mission du Maduré*, 1854, vol. 4, pg. 23), extrait d'une lettre du P. Pierre Martin, missionaire de la Compagnie de Jésus, au P. Le Gobien, de la même compagnie: "Sa mère âgée de soixante ans se distingue par son habileté à gagne les âmes à Jésus-Christ; je veux vous en citer un exemple. Avant sa conversion, elle était fort dévouée à sa secte et savait par cœur toutes les fables de ses idoles. Son plaisir était de les raconter et elle le faisait avec grâce; ses voisines n'avaient pas de plus douce récréation que de venir s'asseoir autour d'elle pour l'écouter. Dès qu'elle eut reçu le baptême, elle invita ses amies, qui s'empressèrent d'accourir et la prièrent de leur conter quelque *divertissement* de Siven. 'Oh! ce sont là de vieilles histoires, répondit notre bonne conteuse, mais je vais vous en donner une qui est bien autre chose! elle est toute fraîche; moi-même je ne la sais que depuis quelques jours. Si vous m'écoutez avec attention, je vous ferai connaître le lieu où l'on va après la mort, où sont allés nos amis et nos ancêtres, où nous irons à notre tour.'" Italics as in the French printed edition.

10. See below for a discussion of Tirumalai Nāyaka's restructuring of the Cittirai Festival, as well as discussion of the canonization of the narrative structure of the "Sacred Games" concurrent with their popular dissemination during his reign.

11. On the trajectory of the vernacularization of the Indian subcontinent, and the concept of the "Vernacular Millennium," see Pollock (1998a, 1998b, 2006).

12. The literature of Nāyaka-period South India, although substantially in need of further study, has been treated in a series of essays in Rao, Shulman, and Subrahmanyam's *Symbols of Substance* (1992), a study particularly noteworthy in terms of its facility at negotiating the multilingualism (Sanskrit, Tamil, Telugu) of the period.

13. The precise date of composition of the *Śivalīlārṇava* is unknown. Nīlakaṇṭha's oeuvre can be dated fairly accurately based on the exact date of composition he provides for his *Nīlakaṇṭhavijayacampū*: 1637–1638 C.E.

14. *ŚLA* 1.37: vidvatpriyaṃ vyaṅgyapathaṃ vyatītya śabdārthacitreṣu kaler vilāsāt | prāpto 'nurāgo nigamān upekṣya bhāṣāprabandheṣv iva pāmarāṇām ||

15. Bronner and Shulman (2006, 6).

16. Bronner and Shulman (2006, 8).

17. *ŚLA* 1.38–39, 43: kṛte yuge vyañjanayāvatīrṇaṃ tretāyuge saiva guṇībabhūva / āsīt tṛtīye tu yuge 'rthacitraṃ yuge turīye yamakaprapañcam // diṣṭyādhirūḍhāḥ kavitādhirājyaṃ dhīrā ramante na hi śabdacitre / svarge 'pi gatvāpsarasāṃ nivāśe kāṇaiva kiṃ kāpi gaveṣaṇīyā // āpūrya vakraṃ laśunair vidhātā kiṃ nimbasāraiḥ kudhiyām asiñcat / na cet kathaṃ vāci tataḥ kṣarantyāṃ sa pūtigandhaḥ sa ca tiktabhāvaḥ.

18. For instance, *Dhvanyāloka* 3.41–42: pradhānaguṇabhāvābhyāṃ vyaṅgyasyaivaṃ vyavasthite / kāvye ubhe tato 'nyad yat tac citram abhidhīyate // citraṃ śabdārthabhedena dvividhaṃ ca vyavasthitam / tatra kiṃcic chabdacitraṃ vācyacitram ataḥ param.

19. Bronner and Shulman (2006, 6).

20. Harman, "Two Versions of a Tamil Text," 1987b; Dessigane et al., *La Legende des Jeux de Çiva à Madurai*, 1960; Shulman, "First Grammarian, First Poet," 2001; Wilden, 2014.

21. See below for a more thorough discussion of the dating of these works.

22. Extant manuscripts in Grantha, Malayalam, Telugu, and Kannada script are numerous. Unfortunately I am aware of no dated manuscripts of the text, which is perhaps unsurprising as southern palm-leaf manuscripts are much less frequently dated than contemporary paper Devanagari manuscripts from North India. All of the manuscripts I have examined appear to be of recent origin (eighteenth- and nineteenth-century).

23. *Payaṉ mutaliyaṉa*, pg. 314, v. 5. There is always the possibility of interpolation with such textual addenda (the equivalent of a *phalaśruti* in Sanskrit), which would leave even scantier reference to the designation of the text at hand or its status as a Purāṇam.

24. *Nūrcirappuppāyiram:* ampatumat tārccalli yāṉṭāṉ kavuṇiyarkō / ṉamperumpaṟ ṟappuliyūr nampiviyaṉ temperumā / ṉātiviḷai yāṭa laṟupattu nāṉkiṉaiyu / mēti muṭittā ṉuvantu. kārvaḷaṅkoṉ maṇṭalattuk kappiñci nāṭṭuraittōṉ / cārparacu rāmac caturvētimaṅkalamāñ cīrtakuteṉ cellinaka rāṉṭāṉcoṟ ṟillainampi / yārpuṉaivāṉ viḷaiyāṭa laṟupattu nāṉkaṉṟē. No evidence for the date or authorship of this work is available. The text can be found appended to U. Ve. Caminataiyar's edition of Nampi's *Tiruviḷaiyāṭal Purāṇam*.

25. To my knowledge the only piece of secondary scholarship to document this work in any detail is the Telugu monograph of Vadhluri Anjaneya Raju (1993), *Cokkanātha Caritra: Samagra Pariśīlana*. While providing a much-needed introduction to this otherwise neglected work of literature (even within the domain of strictly Telugu literary studies), Raju's work leaves something to be desired in terms of a critical awareness of literary transmission across linguistic boundaries. Raju asserts repeatedly without citing any evidence that the *Cokkanātha Caritramu* is a direct translation of the Sanskrit Hālāsya Māhātmya, claiming

that the numerous and significant variations from the latter can be explained strictly on the grounds of artistic license and the desire to avoid prolixity.

26. While this is not the occasion for an in-depth engagement with contemporary translation theory and its implications for making sense of South Asian translation practices, it is important to note that "faithful translation" that adheres to preserving as much of the exact meaning and syntactical structure of the original source language in a new medium occurs rather rarely in South Asian discourses, a state of affairs that is often not apparent in the secondary literature. By *transcreation,* however, I mean to clarify that the new work of literature is a distinctive literary product with its own perspective and agenda that, while preserving something of the spirit and core narrative of the "original," differs substantively from it in both form and content. In this coinage, transcreations are, at the same time, to be distinguished from adaptations that present themselves as only vaguely inspired by some original source. As we shall see, transcreations demonstrably have a more explicit genealogical relationship with a prior source text.

27. See Shulman and Rao (2002) for an English translation of the portions of the *Dhurjaṭi Māhātmyamu* that concern the origin of the Tamil Caṅkam.

28. The *Cokkanātar Ulā* is another example of a text that only barely survived the vicissitudes of history. In his introduction to the edition, U. Ve. Caminataiyar informs us (p. x) that some forty years before its publication, a single manuscript of the *Cokkanātar Ulā* was located in the home of one Śrī Kālivāṭīcuvar Ōtuvār, and this manuscript copy itself was quite old at the time. No further manuscripts were known to the editor at the time of publication.

29. tiruntupukaḻp parañcōti māmuṉivaṉ civaṉaruḷār ceppu meṉṉeṉ / poruntivaḷar tiruviḷaiyā ṭaṟpurā ṇamumirukkap piṉṉum yāṉīr / taruntaraṇi pukaḻpatiṉō rattiyā yattorvakai cāṟṟap pukkēṉ / maruntaṉaiyāṉ viḷaiyāṭaṟ kataiyōti yavaiaiaruḷum vaḻakkāṉ maṉṉō.

30. ōtariya vuttaramā purāṇan taṉṉu ḷuṇmaitaru cāracamuc cayattu muṉṉa / mētakunaṉ kataiviriviṟ kaṇṭe ṉakku viyāta vāṉ mīkiyeccaṉ coṉṉa veṉṉeṉ / ṭītilviḷai yāṭalkaḷiṟ piṟaṅku mintat tiruviḷaiyā ṭaliṉ parappaic curukki yiṉṟu / pōtayuṟa numakkuraittēṉ yāṉuñ cokkaṉ pukaḻiṉaiyār karai kaṇṭu pukaḻu vārē (1.35).

31. One intriguing example is the Tamil *Vacucaritram* of Ambalattatum Ayyan, an adaptation of the Telugu *Vasucaritramu* of Rāmarāja Bhūṣaṇa. N. Venkata Rao (1978) offers some general discussion on the intersection of Tamil and Telugu literature during and after this period.

32. Examples of the latter include Kālahasti Kavi's Sanskrit *Vasucaritracampū*, adapted from the *Vasucaritramu* of Rāmarāja Bhūṣaṇa; the *Rāmāyaṇasāra* of Madhuravāṇī, a Sanskritization of Raghunātha Nāyaka's Telugu *Rāmāyaṇasāratilaka*; and, without question, the *Śivalīlārṇava* of Nīlakaṇṭha Dīkṣita. Within the domain of strictly Purāṇic as well as theological textual traditions, cross-linguistic transmission has a somewhat older history that remains to be studied in detail. For instance, the Tamil *Periya Purāṇam* had made significant multilingual inroads in Śaiva circles outside the Tamil country; take, for instance, the Sanskrit Basava Purāṇa of Śaṅkarārādhya, adapted from the Telugu *Basavapurāṇamu* of Palkuriki Somanātha. The Sanskrit rendering is an intriguing work of Ārādhya Vīraśaivism (see Fisher, 2017). In the context of more formal theological exposition, the Tamil Śaiva Siddhānta had begun to engage in a certain re-Sanskritization as well, such as the Sanskrit commentaries of Nigamajñāna II on works of the Tamil Śaiva tradition (Ganesan 2009).

33. maturai nāyakaṉ cuntara pāṇṭiya vaṭanūṟ / katiru lāmaṇi yāṟukāṟ pīṭattiṟ kallū / rati-pa ṉāntiru viruntava ṉavaiyiṉil vāyaṟ / patiyil vālaṉa tāricen tamiḻiṉiṟ pakarntāṉ.

34. aṟukāṟpī ṭattuyarmā lāḻikaṭain tamutaiyaraṅ kēṟṟu māpōl / aṟukāṟpē ṭicaipāṭuṅ kūṭaṉmāṉ miyattaiyarun tamiḻaṟ pāṭi / aṟukāṟpī ṭuyarmuṭiyār cōkkēcar caṉṉitiyi lamarar cūḻum / aṟukāṟpīṭattiruntu parañcōti muṉivaraṅ kēṟṟi ṉāṉē (cirappuppāyiram, 1).

35. Ebeling (2010).

36. Cutler (2003) further documents this phenomenon in the literary education of U. Ve. Caminataiyar, whose early studies at Tiruvavatuturai included transcribing *talapurāṇams* composed by his teacher, Minatciuntara Pillai, which were regularly debuted at formal *araṅkēṟṟams* for the benefit of his patrons.

37. See Wentworth (2011).

38. The University of Madras *Tamil Lexicon* defines *aṟukārpīṭam* simply as a "six-footed stool, used in Śiva temples."

39. Contemporary and historical references to an *aṟukārpīṭam* in the Madurai temple do exist, although limited information is available as to its past or present function. For instance, Devakunjari (1979) writes with respect to the same temple, speaking first of the Amman (Mīnākṣī) *caṉṉiti* and second of that of Sundareśvara: "Facing the *gopura* is the *aṟukāl pīṭha* of the shrine" (217); "on the eastern *prākāra* is the Swami Sannidhi *aṟukāl pīṭha* which leads to the *maha mandapa*" (218). The historical chronicle of the priests of the Mīnākṣī-Sundareśvara temple, the *Stāṉikarvaralāṟu*, includes brief mentions of an *aṟukārpīṭam* in both the Mīnākṣī and Sundareśvara shrine as follows: "paiyalāḻukkuc cuvāmikōvil āṟukārpīṭattil nampiyār poṭṭukkaṭṭukiṟatu. Pūjai paṇṇukiṟa pērkaḷ vālipattil vētam, ākamāstiraṅkaḷellām paṭittu kurukkaḷiṭattil parīkṣai koṭuttu vīvākamāṉatiṉ pēril kāṇikkārar ammaṉkōvil āṟukārpīṭattil ācāriyavapiṣēkam paṇṇikkoṇṭu pūjai paṇṇivarukiṟatu" (*Stāṉikarvaralāṟu*, pgs. 298–299).

The chronicles recording renovations and additions to the temple complex over the centuries also reveal a memory of the construction of an *aṟukārpīṭam* in the Mīnākṣī and Sundareśvara shrines. From the *Tiruppaṇivivaram*: "cuvāmikōvil arttamaṇṭapam maṇimaṇṭapam makāmaṇṭapam āṟukārpīṭam cannitikkōpuram . . . kulacēkarapāṇṭiyaṉ piratiṣṭai ceytavai"; "ammaṉkōvil mutaṟpirākārac cuṟṟa maṇṭapamum paḷḷiyaṟaiyum āṟukārpīṭamum nāyakarcannitimaṇṭapamum ceyvittatu caka 1374" (*Tiruppaṇivivaram*, pgs. 14–15). Although the date(s) of composition/redaction of the *Tiruppaṇivivaram* are not known, evidently the *aṟukārpīṭam* in the Sundareśvara shrine was believed to have been built by Kulaśekhara Pāṇḍiyan, and the *aṟukārpīṭam* in the Mīnākṣī shrine by a certain Māvali (Skt. Mahābali) in Śaka 1374, ca. 1452 C.E.

Note that the irregular spelling *āṟukārpīṭam*, while not conventionally accepted in Tamil grammar, is employed in common by Aṉatāri in the *Cuntara Pāṇṭiyam*, by the *Stāṉika-rvaralāṟu*, and by the *Tiruppaṇivivaram*, suggesting that this irregular orthography seems to have been conventionally accepted at the time.

40. cīrvaḷartaṉ katampavaṉa māṉmiyamām vaṭanūlait teruḷu maṉpā / lērvaḷarteṉ maturaiyilvā ḷicaṉaippū caṉaiceyvō riyainta celvap / pārvaḷarntōṅ kiyapukalcēr talattōrteṉ moḻiyākap pakareṉ ṟōta / nīrvaḷarpain toṭaivirutta yāppa taṉā lavararuḷā ṉikaḻtta luṟṟēṉ (pāyiram, 16).

41. It is also worth noting that the caste affiliation of Nāyaka subordinate officers may have played a significant role in their incentive to patronize works of Tamil literature (see discussion below on the relationship between caste and the Tamil Śaiva monasteries), as

those employed under the Nāyaka regime were nearly exclusively of Brahmin or Vēḷāḷa background (Ludden 1978, 139), the latter forming the constituency typically observed sponsoring these works.

42. aṉṉava ṉaracar cūḻaṅ kacci vīrappa ṉeṉru / maṉṉava ṉaruḷcēr maṉraic cevvanti tuṉaivaṉ vāymait / teṉṉavaṉ ṟiruvi runtāṉ cavuntaraṉ ṟēva pāṭait / tuṉṉiruṅ kataiteṉ ṉūlāṟ colleṉac colla luṟṟēṉ (nakarac carukkam, 47).

43. vētanūṟ ṟeṉmuḷaicai vīramā raṅkaṭalcūḷ / pūtalaṅka ḷaṉpāyp purakkunāḷ ātinerit / teyva maturait tiruvāla vāyuṟainta / aiyarulāk koṇṭaruḷi ṉār (nūṟ ciṟappup pāyiram, 2).

44. Substantial documentary information concerning the economic influence of the Tarumapuram and Tiruvavatuturai *ātīnam*s in the nineteenth century has been gathered by Oddie (1984); for instance, by the late nineteenth century, Tiruvavatuturai directly owned and maintained twenty-five thousand acres of land and managed the cultivation of thousands of additional acres of land and other endowments under the control of various local temples. In 1841, Tarumapuram controlled property amounting to nearly half of the temple lands in Tanjore district. Although such statistical information is not available for earlier periods, inscriptions dating back to the seventeenth century confirm that ascetics served as managers of endowments at this time as well (Koppedrayer 1990, 25).

45. By at least the early eighteenth century, the Tamil Śaiva *maṭam*s provided centralized repositories of literary manuscripts available for consultation. Jesuit missionaries appear to have attained access to these collections, as is testified by Bartholomäus Ziegenbalg in his *Bibliotheca Malabarica*. See Sweetman (2012) for further details.

46. It is important to note that the Tamil Śaiva Siddhānta tradition is both institutionally and theologically distinct from the earlier pan-Indian Sanskritic Śaiva Siddhānta, an influential school of tantric Śaivism (Mantramārga) dating at least as far back to its earliest known textual exemplar, the Niśvāsatattvasaṃhitā (ca. fourth or fifth century C.E.). On the history of the Tamil Śaiva Siddhānta lineage and its exclusively Tamil-language scriptures, see Pechilis Prentiss (1996). It must be noted that great strides have been made in the study of the Sanskrit Śaiva Siddhānta since the composition of her article. Although no publication to date lays out our current knowledge of the Śaiva Siddhānta for nonspecialists, one can begin by consulting the work of Dominic Goodall.

47. While the earliest writings of the Tamil Śaiva Siddhānta tradition date back to the thirteenth or fourteenth century, the monasteries themselves seem to have acquired their present institutional shape at a somewhat later date. Although precise historical documentation is lacking, Aroonan (1984) attempts to calculate the intervening generations of preceptorial rule preceding our earliest dated references to arrive at an estimate of the mid-fifteenth century for the founding of Tiruvavatuturai and the mid-sixteenth century for Tarumapuram.

48. The social prominence of the Vēḷāḷa caste groups as controllers of the region's agricultural production has perhaps been most convincingly explicated by Stein (1980), who refers to a certain "Brahmin-Vēḷāḷa alliance," arguing that the establishment and maintenance of Brahmadeyas in the Tamil region proceeded largely at the discretion of Vēḷāḷa landholders.

49. In respect to both caste and patronage, another exemplar of these trends is the Tamil poet Antakakkavi, a Vēḷāḷa by heritage. Antakakkavi's works appear to have been sponsored by a number of subordinate officers, including a certain Oppilāta Maḻavarāyaṉ of Ariyilur and Mātait Tiruveṅkaṭanātar of Kayattaru near Tirunelveli. See Wentworth (2011, 232).

50. poṉṉalarpūṅ kaṭampavaṉa purāṉaṉ teṉṉūṟ potiyamuṉiyakattiyaṉmuṉ pukaṉṟa vāṟē / paṉṉupaya kaviñarcevik kamutamākap paraṉaruḷiṉ celuntamiḻāl viḷaṅkac ceytāṉ / reṉṉavarā yaṉpukalmāk kaṉṉaṉeytaṟ celvaṉuyar tarumilampūr vīmaṉāta / naṉṉeṟitēr purāṇamuḻu tuṇarntōṉ kaṅkai natikulavēḷ peruntoṇṭai nāṭṭi ṉāṉē (ciṟappup pāyiram, 18).

51. Well-known works of Kumārakurupara include his *Mīnāṭcīyammai Piḷḷaittamiḻ* (the *piḷḷaittamiḻ* genre captures the childhood and youth of a particular deity over the course of several life stages; see Richman 1997 for details on this work), *Mīnāṭcīyammai Iraṭṭaimaṇimālai,* and *Maduraikkalampakam.*

52. U. Ve. Caminataiyar refers to this particular branch of the lineage as based in the Kāñcī Ñāṉappirakāca Maṭam (*Cokkanātar Ulā*, xiii.)

53. pūmaṉṉu poliḻveṉṉai meykaṇṭāṉ kaccip / pukalpuṉaitat tuvañāṉa prakācamāy vantu / pāmaṉṉa vurai yeṉṉa vavaṉaruḷā lavaṉṟaṉ / patamparavic citamparappāṭ ṭiyaleṉappōr vakuttāṉ (See *Cokkanātar Ulā*, xvi).

54. Seastrand (2013).

55. See above for local inscriptions referring to these figures.

56. *Cokkanātha Caritramu,* pg. 4: bhaṭavaṃśamuna meccu paccakappuramu / tipparājasutuṇḍu tiru vēṅgaḷuṇḍu / ceppaṃga nērcuṃ brasiddhambugāṅga / nani vinna vincina nā cinna rāma / manujēndruṃ ḍadhikasammadamutō navuḍu / nanu bilipinci mannana gāravinci / vinutinci karpūra vīḍyambu licci / yanaghuṇḍu mī lāta yagu timma rāju / tana tammu ḍayyalu dānu nimmahiniṃ / brauḍuṇḍai vidyalaṃ baraga meppinci / prauḍarāyalacētaṃ bacca kappurampu / rāju nāmbaḍeṃ dimma rājukuṃ dippa rājudayaṃce virājitammuganu / rājula meppiṃce rasikuṃ ḍātanita / nujuṃḍa vārya sannuta kavīndruṇḍavu / prāvīṇya mativi śōbhanakā vyalīlaṃ / gāvuna nīvokka kāvyambu māku / dvipada bhāvambuna delivondi migula / nupamagā satyavu lullambu lalara / madhura vākyammula madiṃ goniyāḍa / madhurāpurēśu nirmala puṇyacarita / cauṣaṣṭi līlā vilāsambu lāndhra / bhāṣanu bedarāma pārthivu pēra / sucaritra vaibhavasutrāmu pēra / raciyiṃci vikhyāti rāṃcēyu murvi.

57. This circa-twelfth-century Telugu poet is remembered by subsequent authors in the tradition, such as Śrīnātha and Appakavi, as one of the greatest poets in the language. While a number of *kāvyas* are attributed to him, which are said to have been written in a style that makes heavy use of *śleṣa*, as well as the first work of Telugu prosody, none of his works seem to have survived. In the popular social imaginary of the Telugu literati, Bhīmakavi lives on as a Durvāsas-like figure with supernatural powers who curses the unfortunate kings who failed to pay him homage. See Datta, *Encylopaedia of Indian Literature,* 2005, 502–503.

58. *Cokkanātha Caritramu,* pg. 3: vyāsu vālmīki mahākāvyuṃ gāḷi- / dāsuni bhavabhūti daṇḍi māghunini / birudu vēmulavāḍabhīmu nannayanu / narayaṃ dikkana neṟṟapāryu śrīnāthu / nilaṃgalgu kavulanu nella sadbhakti / vilasita sadvākya vinuti nutiṃci / yēkṛti raciyiṃpa niṣṭārtha siddhi / yākṛti raciyimpa natibhaktiṃ būni.

59. For further details on the works of literature produced at the Tanjavur and Madurai Nāyaka courts, see N. Venkata Rao (1978) and Kodandaramaiah (1975).

60. Raghunātha Nāyaka's Telugu compositions are said to have originally included one hundred works (a common rhetorical trope of the period, applied to a number of celebrated intellectuals, including Appayya Dīkṣita), although only two have come down to us today, the *Raghunātharāmāyaṇamu* and *Vālmikicaritramu.* Further attestations are available through the numerous works of royal encomium composed by his court poets

in both Telugu and Sanskrit. Further Telugu works attributed to the Nāyaka include a number of *yakṣagānas*—*Gajendramokṣa; Rukmiṇīkṛṣṇavivāha; Jānakīpariṇaya;* a certain *Pārijātāpaharaṇa,* said to have been composed in only two *yāmas* in his youth, prompting his father, Acyutappa Nāyaka, to reward him with a *kanakābhiṣeka;* a *Nalacaritra* in eight cantos; and the *Acyutābhyudayamu,* a work of royal *praśasti* dedicated to his father.

61. See for instance Satyanarayanaravu (1966) on the iconicity of the Śāradā Dhvajamu in the Tanjavur court.

62. The earliest citations of the Hālāsya Māhātmya of which I am aware (aside from Nīlakaṇṭha Dīkṣita's replication of one of its verses, discussed below), occur in the *Varṇāśramacandrikā,* a late seventeenth-century theological treatise in Sanskrit on the role of caste in the selection of preceptors in the Tamil Śaiva Siddhānta tradition. See below for a discussion of this work.

63. In the single preliminary Telugu-language study of the *Cokkanātha Caritramu* available today, Raju insists mechanically, providing no evidence or argument, that Tiruvēṅgaḷakavi has simply elided these episodes from his otherwise direct "translation" of the Hālāsya Māhātmya.

64. In Tamil grammatical theory, consonants (*mey*) are said to attain movement (*iyakkam*) through the vowels (*uyir,* from the same root as the verbal participle *uyttiṭum* used in this verse), particularly the first vowel, the short a: "*meyyiṉ iyakkam akaramoṭu civaṇum*" *Tolkāppiyam* 2.13. Hence, this verse homologizes Śiva's authority over the Caṅkam poets and the city of Madurai with the power of the vowels to enliven the consonants. *Ālavāy* is another name for Madurai.

65. Parañcōti, *TVP* 51.8–10: ūṉiṭa rakaṉṟō yuṉṉā ruyirttuṇai yāvē ṉinta / māṉiṭa yōṉip paṭṭu mayaṅkukō veṉṉa vaṇṭu / tēṉiṭai yaḻunti vētañ ceppumveṇ kamalac celvi / tāṉiṭa rakala nōkkic caturmukat talaivaṉ cāṟṟum. mukiḻtaru mulainiṉ meyyā mutaleḻut taimbat toṉṟir / ṟikaḻtaru mākā rāti hākāra mīṟāc ceppip / pukaḻtaru nāṟpat teṭṭu nāṟpatteṉ pulava rāki akaḻtaru kaṭalcūḻ ñālat tavatarit tiṭuva vāka. attaku varuṇa mellā mēṟiniṉ ṟavaṟṟa varriṉ / meyttaku taṉmai yeyti vēṟuvē ṟiyakkan tōṉṟa uyttiṭu makārattiṟku mutaṉmaiyā yoḻuku nātar / muttami ḻāla vāyema mutalvaram muṟaiyāṉ maṉṉō. tāmoru pulava rākit tiruvurut tarittuc caṅka / māmaṇip pīṭat tēṟi vaikiyē nāṟpat toṉpa / tāmava rāki yuṉṉiṉ ṟavaravark kaṟivu tōṟri / yēmuṟap pulamai kāppā reṉṟṟaṉaṉ kamalap puttēḷ.

66. HM 57.13–17: atha vāgvādinī bhītā bhartuḥ pādāmbujadvayam | natvā spṛṣṭvā ca pāṇibhyāṃ prārthayāmāsa taṃ tadā || mayā cājñānavaśataḥ kṛtaṃ sarvaṃ ca bhartsanam | kṣamasva karuṇāsindho kaṭākṣeṇa vilokya mām || punaḥ punar iti brāhmyā prārthito 'haṃ savāhanaḥ | pratiśāpaṃ dadau tasyai bhāratyai cānukampayā || tvadaṅgasambhavā varṇā ādisāntāś ca vāṅmayāḥ | janiṣyanti mitho bhinnair ākāraiḥ sudhiyo bhuvi || hakārarūpī bhagavān sarvavyāpī sadāśivaḥ | teṣāṃ ca sudhiyāṃ madhye 'bhavatv ekaḥ kaviśvaraḥ | āhatyaikonapancāśat saṅghinaḥ śatkaviśvarāḥ ||

67. If anything, the ambiguity regarding the total number of letters would suggest a later provenance for the HM. While the Tirumantiram (see below) unambiguously accepts a total of fifty-one letters, Parañcōti vacillates uncertainly between forty-nine and fifty-one, whereas the HM settles squarely on forty-nine.

68. Shulman localizes the term *vidyāpīṭha* within a "northern" or "north-west" Śaiva tradition on the basis of a brief allusion to Sanderson's (1988) "Śaivism and the Tantric Traditions." In fact, Sanderson's original point with regard to this term was to distinguish

two subsets of the scriptural corpus of the early Bhairava Tantras, the *mantrapīṭha* and *vidyāpīṭha*. (Note that the term *vidyāpīṭha* discussed by Sanderson does not refer to a "seat" or "plank" such as occurs in the HM. See Sanderson [1988, 668–670]). Nevertheless, were we to posit a line of influence from the early Bhairava Tantras extending through the HM, we would be left with an entire millennium of intervening textual history to account for, thus arriving at no useful information concerning the more proximate origins of the HM.

69. For instance, HM 57.69–70: vidyāpīṭham iti prāhus tat pīṭhaṃ munayo khilāḥ | kecid vyākhyāpīṭham iti jñānapīṭham itītare || sarasvatīpīṭham iti mātṛkāpīṭham ity api | sārthaiś ca nāmabhiś cānyair varṇayanti kaviśvarāḥ || The term *mātṛkā* typically refers to a particular esoteric sequence of the letters of the Sanskrit alphabet; hence, its appearance here is especially appropriate to the plot of the episode.

70. HM 1.16: navaratnamayaṃ pīṭhaṃ navaśaktidhruvaṃ mahat | tanmadhye rājate liṅgaṃ śivasya paramātmanaḥ ||

71. Tirumantiram, 4:1219.

72. Tirumantiram, 4:924.

73. The traditional dating of the Tirumantiram, extending back as far as the fifth to seventh century C.E., while accepted by Brooks and some others, is historically inconceivable and incoherent outside of a Tamil nationalist agenda. See Goodall (2004, xxix). A date of the twelfth or thirteenth century is far more plausible. On the transmission of Śaiva and Śākta traditions from Kashmir to the Tamil country in the early second millennium, especially with regard to the Kālī Krama, an allied Śākta school, see Cox (2006).

74. *Kuruntokai*, trans. M. Shanmugam Pillai and David E. Ludden, 2.

75. The Sanskrit translation runs as follows: jānāsi puṣpagandhān bhramara tvaṃ brūhi tattvato me 'dya | devyāḥ keśakalāpe tulyo gandhena kiṃ gandhaḥ || In fact, both versions do succeed in preserving a sense of the distinct texture of the Tamil verse, given that the surrounding chapter of the HM is written entirely in *anuṣṭubh*, and this is the sole *āryā* verse in the twentieth canto of the *Śivalīlārṇava*.

76. ŚLA 20.46; HM 58.32.

77. ŚLA 1.37: vidvatpriyaṃ vyaṅgyapathaṃ vyatītya śabdārthacitreṣu kaler vilāsāt | prāpto 'nurāgo nigamānupekṣya bhāṣāprabandheṣv iva pāmarāṇām ||

78. ŚLA 20.1–6, 8–9, 12, 15–16. kapilakīramukhāḥ kavayas tataḥ katicid āsata tāmranadītaṭe | druhiṇaśāpavaśāj jananī girām avatatāra purā hi yadātmanā || atha caturguṇitā dvyadhikā daśa tridaśadeśikadhikkaraṇakṣamāḥ | prati yayur madhurām abhivanditum pramathanātham amī kavipuṅgavāḥ || kaviśarīrabhṛtā kavayas tu te samadhigamya hareṇa puraskṛtāḥ | samavagāhya suvarṇāsarojinīṃ dadṛśur adrisutādayitaṃ mahaḥ || dṛḍhavinītadhiyaḥ sudhiyas tu te dramiḍasūtrarahasyavivecane | mṛdusugandhivacaḥkusumasrajā vividhayā madhureśam apūjayan || akavayaḥ katicid vibudhādhamaḥ kukavayaś ca pare kṛtasaṃvidaḥ | kavibhir apratimair bhuvaneṣu taiḥ kalaham ādadhire 'tha vitaṇḍayā || śabdārthau doṣanirmuktau sālaṅkārau guṇottarau | kāvyam ātiṣṭhamānebhyaḥ kavibhyo 'yaṃ kṛto 'ñjaliḥ || kāvyārthād api kiṃ duṣṭaṃ kāmiduścaritottarāt | ata eva hi kāvyānām ālāpaḥ sadbhir ujjhitaḥ || athānya eva kalpyante guṇadoṣā nijecchayā | kākadantāḥ parīkṣyantāṃ gṛhyantāṃ grāmyasūktayaḥ || ayogyānāṃ hi kāvyānām agnisekādivākyavat | mūkataiva hi durbhedā muhyanty eṣu kathaṃ janāḥ || arthān api vyāpnuvantī hatasarvaniyantraṇā | vyañjanā śabdavṛttiś ced veśyā patnī na kiṃ bhavet || dhūmena dhvanyatāṃ vahniś cakṣuṣā dhvanyatāṃ ghaṭaḥ | arthaś ced dhvanayed arthaṃ kā pramāṇavyavasthitiḥ ||

79. *ŚLA* 20.17–19: duḥkhato 'pi tu kāvyokteḥ sukhāyārtho bhaved yadi | sukhaṃ bhavantaḥ śṛnvantu svanindāṃ kavibhiḥ kṛtām || aho bhāvavyaktēḥ pariṇatir aho gūḍharasa ity alīkavyāmīlannayanavigaladbāṣpasalilaiḥ | udañcadromāñcair udaralulitāmair iva muhuḥ kathaṃ vyāptā bhūmiḥ kavibhir apaṭujñānapaśubhiḥ || iti nigaditam evābhīkṣṇam āvarttayadbhiḥ pratikathakavacāṃsi kvāpy anākarṇayadbhiḥ | apathaciravinītair bāliśair āttagandhāḥ śaraṇam abhisamīyuś candracūḍaṃ kavīndrāḥ ||

80. *ŚLA* 20.24: vijñāpitaḥ kavivarair iti sundareśaḥ smitvā dadau phalakam ekam adṛṣṭapūrvam | yatrāsate kavaya eva yathābhilāṣam anye tu nāṅghrim api vinyasituṃ kṣamante ||

81. A *muḻam* is the measurement from the tip of the fingers to the elbow.

82. Parañcōti, *TVP* 54.11–12: viṭaikoṭu pōvā ṉoṉrai vēṇṭiṉā ṉēkun tēyaṉ / toṭaiperu tamiḻnā teṉru collupa vanta nāṭṭiṉ / iṭaipayiṉ maṉitta rellā miṉrami ḻāyntu kēḷvi / uṭaiyava reṉpa kēṭṭārk kuttara muraittal vēṇṭum. cittamā cakala vantac centami ḻiyaṉū raṉṉai / attāṉē yaruḻic ceyti yeṉraṉa ṉaṉaiyāṉ rēra / vaittaṉai mutaṉū raṉṉai marratu teḷinta piṉṉum / nittāṉē yaṭiyē ṉeṉru niṉṉati kāṉpē ṉeṉrāṉ.

83. Parañcōti, *TVP* 54.20: iruva kaippura vuraitaḻī yeḻumata moṭunār / poruḷo ṭumpuṇarn taiyiru kurramum pōkki / oruvi laiyiraṉ ṭaḻakoṭu muttieṉ ṉāṅkum / maruvu mātinū liṉaittokai vakaiviri muraiyāl.

84. *ŚLA* 20.57, 59: bhakto 'pi kīraḥ paramādbhutaṃ tat paśyann api pratyuta durbabhāṣe | mauḍhyān niruḍhād api pāmarāṇāṃ mauḍhyaṃ cidābhāsagataṃ garīyaḥ || bhāvatkyaḥ kṛtayaḥ śrutiḥ śrutir iti prauḍhiṃ parāṃ prāpitā adhyāhāraviparyayaprakaraṇotkarṣānuṣa-ṅgādibhiḥ | tātparyāntaravarṇanena ca samarthyante yad asmādṛśair taj jānan kavitāsu naḥ paśupate doṣekṣikāṃ mā kṛthāḥ ||

85. These terms had become current in the Mīmāṃsā system of hermeneutics by the time of the Śābara Bhāṣya (ca. 350 C.E.).

86. *ŚLA* 22.17.

87. *ŚLA* 22.12. For the significance of the term *atyāśrama* to intersectarian debate in the sixteenth and seventeenth centuries, see chapter 3.

88. Interestingly, Nīlakaṇṭha's description of the Jains betrays a possibly deliberate confusion between religious traditions he would have considered heterodox, especially Jainism and Buddhism, as he refers to the Jina variously as Śākya and Tathāgata. On the other hand, the doctrine articulated here is indubitably Jain. It seems unlikely, of course, that Nīlakaṇṭha would have encountered any living examples of Buddhist doctrine in the seventeenth-century Tamil country.

89. *ŚLA* 22.18–20: utsṛjya sarvāṇy upabṛmhaṇāni mīmāṃsitanyāyadṛḍhīkṛtāni | ullaṅghya tarkān api pāmarās te sambhūya taṃ pratyayato 'jigīṣan || saṃsāratāpān akhilān nihantuṃ śaknoti ahiṃsaiva hi śākyadṛṣṭā | nārcyo maheśo na śivā vibhūtir ity ārhatāḥ svām alikhan pratijñām || vedāḥ pramāṇaṃ saha kāmikādyair viśvādhikaḥ śaṅkara eka eva | bhasmaiva dhāryaṃ bhuvi mokṣamāṇair ity ālikhan svāṃ sa guruḥ pratijñām ||

90. *ŚLA* 22.28, 30–33: pāṇḍyas tataḥ pratyayadarśanena sambandhanāthaṃ śaraṇaṃ prapannaḥ | aśeṣapāpacchidurām ayācad dīkṣāṃ śivajñānavidhānadakṣām || ṣaḍadhvanaḥ pañca kalāś ca tasya saṃśodhayan deśikasārvabhaumaḥ | durdīkṣayā dūṣitam apy ayatnāt sambhāvayāmāsa śarīrakośam || śarīram āviśya sa tasya nāḍīsandhānamārgeṇa guruḥ punānaḥ | jātiṃ samuddhṛtya dayāsamudraś cakre śivajñānanidhānam enam || vittaṃ śarīraṃ hṛdayaṃ ca tasya vinyasa pāṇḍyaś caraṇāravinde | abhyarthayann ardhaśaśāṅkacūḍaṃ śaivādhvapanthaḥ

prasaśāsa pṛthvīm || śivavratasthāḥ śivamantrasaktāḥ śivāgamajñānasudhārasajñāḥ | prajā babhūvuḥ sakalās tadānīṃ prajeśvare śaivapadādhirūḍhe ||

91. Take, for instance, the following initiation procedure from the *Somaśambhupaddhati* (3.111–114), a commonly circulating and highly influential Saiddhāntika ritual manual: śiṣyadehaviniṣkrāntāṃ suṣumnām iva cintayet | nijavigrahalīnāṃ ca darbhaṃ mūlena mantritam || darbhāgraṃ dakṣiṇe tasya nidhāya karapallave | tanmūlam ātmajaṅghāyām agraṃ veti matāntaram || śiṣyasya hṛdayaṃ gatvā recakena śivāṇunā | pūrakeṇa samāgatya svakīyaṃ hṛdayāmbujam || śivāgninā punaḥ kṛtvā nāḍīsandhānam īdṛśam | hṛdā tatsannidhānārthaṃ juhuyād āhutitrayam || David Gordon White (2009, 146) notes that, outside of the confines of the Saiddhāntika tradition, *nāḍīsandhāna* figures prominently in a number of accounts of *yogin*s of various sects entering into the bodies of their practitioners.

92. With a few exceptions, Tantric knowledge systems preserve normative South Asian attitudes concerning the value of internally differentiated social hierarchies, as well as the importance of ritual eligibility (*adhikāra*). The key distinction is that the genealogical criteria for social inclusion of the Brahminical tradition are replaced by an equally stringent hierarchization on the basis of levels of ritual attainment, each with its own elaborate requirements concerning acculturation into discourse, examination, and credentialization. On the question of eligibility, Tantric traditions typically offer two understandings. Dualistic traditions, like the classical Śaiva Siddhānta, define it in terms of the pupil demonstrating mastery of a body of doctrinal and ritual knowledge that he has received from his teacher. More radical Śākta Śaiva nondualists, by contrast, equate *adhikāra* solely with the adept's ability to achieve and maintain increasingly more intensive and potent states of ritual possession, a capacity that is again meditated through the guidance of a charismatic teacher.

93. For instance, the Kāraṇa Āgama (20.54) specifies *jātyuddharaṇa* as an integral feature of *viśeṣa dīkṣā*, rather than the most general form of initiation, *samaya dīkṣā*: jātyuddhāravihīno yas sāmānyasamayī bhavet | tadyuktas tu viśeṣaḥ syāt cākṣuṣyādyās tu yāḥ smṛtāḥ ||

94. What is under discussion here is a series of terms of art from within Śaiva discourse that specify different varieties of initiation and training given solely to those disciples who are expected to succeed their guru in his office, or who otherwise aspire to fulfill his social function, which carries with it particular responsibilities—of an esoteric as well as practical nature—towards future disciples.

95. For further details on the *Varṇāśramacandrikā* and Tiruvampaḷatēcikar, seventh preceptor of the Tarumapuram *maṭam*, see Koppedrayer (1991).

96. *Varṇāśramacandrikā*, citing from the Skandakālottara: jātyuddharaṇahomaṃ tu ekaikaṃ tu śataṃ śatam | dahed vai śūdrajātiṃ tu analena tu ṣaṇmukha ||

97. See *Cokkanātar Ulā*, xiii (*nūlāciriyar varalāṟu*). Unfortunately, U. Ve. Caminataiyar does not cite a source for this anecdote, but as his early employment—as well as that of his chief instructor in Tamil literature, Minatcicuntara Pillai—was carried out through the facilities of the Tamil Śaiva *maṭam*s, the narrative was likely passed down orally. See Cutler (2003) for the institutional context of Tamil literary education in the nineteenth century.

98. Cited in Shulman (1980, 37–38).

99. Branfoot (2000).

100. See Jeyechandrun (1985) for a thorough treatment of the phases of temple construction and approximate dates of all temple improvements from the second Pandian

empire onward. Although Jeyechandrun's analysis deserves critical scrutiny in places, his encyclopedic work is foundational to our understanding of the history of the Mīnākṣī-Sundareśvara temple and its role in the changing cultural and political landscape of Madurai over the centuries.

101. Jeyechandrun (1985) notes a sequence of stucco figures depicting forty-seven of the sixty-four sacred games, currently located around the outer compound wall of the Sundareśvara shrine. While he dates these figures rather boldly to the twelfth or thirteenth centuries purely on the basis of the date of the Sundareśvara shrine itself, he acknowledges that they appear to have undergone substantial renovation. Thus the physical characteristics of the figures can furnish no concrete evidence in support of such an early date, nor do we have any grounds for affirming that these figures were original to the Sundareśvara shrine.

102. Among the sixty-four games, one concerns the role of the saint Māṇikkavācakar in transforming foxes into horses, and another concerns the transformation of the horses back into foxes.

103. *Stāṉikarvaralāṟu*, pgs. 270–271: karttākkaḷ tirumalaiccavuriyayyar avarkaḷ mīṉāṭcī cuntarēcuvararkaḷiṭattil nirambavum paktiyuṇṭāki ammaṉ piracaṉṉam āki viḷaiyāṭukiṟa nāḷaiyil, ayyar tīṭcitar cāmācikattil purāṇa cittamāy irukkiṟa tiruviḷaiyāṭalai stāṉītarkaḷ mūlamāy naṭappivikkac collik kaṭṭaḷaiyiṭṭatāvatu: catācivappaṭṭarkku aṅkam veṭṭukiṟa līlaiyum, vaḷaiyal viṟpatum piṭṭukku maṉ cumappatum kulacēkarappaṭṭarkku poṟkiḻiyaṟuppatum, kutirai kayiṟu mārukiṟa tiruviḷaiyāṭalum yāṉaiyēṟṟamum, maṟṟa līlaikaḷ ciṟṟutu pērpātiyākavum; ciṟitu līlaikaḷ parijanaṅkaḷaikkoṇṭu ceytuvarac colliyum kaṭṭaḷaiyiṭṭum kaṅkāṭcikaḷ pārttuc cantōṣamāyintappaṭi naṭantuvarukiṟatu.

104. The most popular of the sacred games, depicted in both statuary and festival performance, include the following: Taṭātakaip pirāṭṭiyār (Incarnation of Taṭātakai), Tirumaṇam (Sacred marriage), Kallāṉaikkuk karumparuttiyatu (Feeding the stone elephant sugarcane), Aṅkam veṭṭiṉatu (Cutting the limbs [of Cittaṉ]), Karikkuruvikku upatēcam ceytatu (Teaching the blackbird), Naripariyākkiyatu (Foxes become horses), Maṇcumantatu (Carrying earth [in exchange for sweetmeats]), and Camaṇaraik kaḻuvēṟṟiyatu (Mounting the Jains on stakes), Parañcōti, nos. 4, 5, 21, 27, 47, 59, 61, and 63, respectively.

105. Starting in the late seventeenth century and gaining momentum throughout the eighteenth century, numerous major as well as minor temple complexes throughout the Tamil region begin to display individual and complete-sequence mural paintings and sculptural reliefs of the "Sacred Games." The dissertation research of Amy Ruth Holt (2007) documents a series of sculptural images of the *Tiruviḷaiyāṭal* legends at the Naṭarāja temple in Cidambaram, the construction style and iconography of which, she contends, would date to the mid-seventeenth century (see 151–155). A complete series of *Tiruviḷaiyāṭal* murals now adorns the outer wall of the Bṛhadīśvara temple in Tanjavur; local authorities speculate the series dated to the reign of Serfoji II. A study by Jean Deloche (2011) documents a number of *Tiruviḷaiyāṭal* mural panels at the Nārumpūnātacāmi temple in Tiruppudaimarudur, Tirunelveli district. Three Śaiva temples from the immediate vicinity of Madurai, in Tiruvappudaiyar, Tiruppuvanam, and Tiruvideham, which are typically thought to date from the Nāyaka period, contain *Tiruviḷaiyāṭal* mural paintings. In addition, dissertation work of Anna Seastrand (2013) also documents the appearance of *Tiruviḷaiyāṭal* imagery at a number of temple sites.

Further evidence for the widespread popularity of the *Tiruviḷaiyāṭal* theme outside of Madurai includes other surviving examples of material culture from the period, including manuscript illuminations and book covers such as those preserved at the Tanjavur Maharaja Serfoji's Sarasvati Mahal Library in Tanjavur (a similar series exists in the Government Museum in Chennai, although I have not been able to obtain photographs), temple chariot carvings dating to the eighteenth and nineteenth centuries across the Tamil region (Kalidos 1985, 1988a, 1988b), and chariot textiles with images of the *Tiruviḷaiyāṭal* episodes.

106. The agency of images is perhaps most productively treated in the theoretical literature of New Materialism (e.g., Braidotti 1994), which presumes a monistic ontology that declines to differentiate the human as agent and the inanimate as object.

CONCLUSION

1. Luhmann (1995, 17) anticipates such a circumstance, in which shared resources come to play a role in constituting a distinct system: "The concept of boundaries means, however, that processes which cross boundaries (e.g., the exchange of energy or information) have different conditions for their continuance (e.g., different conditions of utilization or of consensus) after they cross the boundaries."

2. Haradatta, author of the *Śrutisūktimālā*, also known as the *Caturvedatātparyasaṅgraha*, is cited as early as Śripati's *Śrīkarabhāṣya*, a Vīraśaiva (Śaktiviśiṣṭādvaita) commentary on the Brahmasūtras (circa thirteenth or fourteenth century), and Umāpati's commentary on the Pauṣkara (circa fourteenth century).

3. mlecchācāraparāḥ sarve daridrāś ca dvijātayaḥ | bhaviṣyanty alpamatayaḥ yatis tatra bhaviṣyati || śive madaṃśasaṃbhūtaḥ śaṅkaraḥ śāṅkarottamaḥ | caturbhiḥ saha śiṣyais tu kalāv avatariṣyati || tasmai copaniṣadvidyā mayā dattā maheśvari | bhūmau pāṣaṇḍaṣaṇḍānāṃ khaṇḍanaṃ sa kariṣyati || kalāv eva mahādevi haradattābhidho dvijaḥ | aśaivadaṇḍanārthāya bhaviṣyati mahītale || dīkṣito 'pi bhaved kaścin madaṃśo bhūsuro 'mbike | bhāsurācāranirataḥ śaivacchandogavaṃśajaḥ || anye 'pi bhaktā deveśi cere cole ca pāṇḍyake | bhaviṣyanti mahābhaktā mayi sarvāsu jātiṣu || sundaro jñānasambandhas tathā māṇikyavācakaḥ |

4. The term *aṃśāvatāra* typically implies not that the individual is only partially a divine incarnation, but rather that he or she is a full incarnation of a portion of the god in question.

5. Ramanathan (1966). These newsletters published short essays in Sanskrit, English, Tamil, Telugu, and Hindi celebrating the remembered life of Appayya Dīkṣita, both historical and hagiographical, and advertising the publication ventures of many of his previously unpublished works.

6. This Sivananda is not to be confused with the nineteenth-century biographer of Appayya of the same name, author of the Appayyadīkṣitendravijaya, although both are descendants of the Dīkṣita family. Swami Sivananda, in fact, was born in Palamadai, Nīlakaṇṭha's ancestral *agrahāra*.

7. Shulman (2014).

8. Mūkakavi, known only by the name "the Mute Poet," is reputed by legend to have been deaf and dumb until granted the blessings of the goddess Kāmākṣī, at which point he

spontaneously burst into poetry, composing the *Mūkapañcaśatī*. Unsurprisingly, the very same narratives about his divine gift of poetic virtuosity are often applied in south Indian Smārta circles of Kālidāsa as well (see chapter 2 for further discussion). As for his historical origins, the editor of the *Mūkapañcaśatī* (*Kāvyamālā*, vol. 5), writes, "It is not certain when this poet, originating in the Drāviḍa country, was born, but it appears that he was not very ancient." His verses are scattered with Śrīvidyā terminology and specific references to the deities of Kanchipuram; in short, he could not possibly have lived earlier than the seventeenth century, as his writings evoke a full-fledged south Indian Smārta-Śaiva religiosity. I have seen no evidence that Nīlakaṇṭha or any other scholars of his generation were aware of his existence.

9. idaṃ hi paraśivenādināthena prathamam upadiṣṭaṃ śrīdevyai. akhilapuruṣārthaikaghaṭanāsvatantre 'smiṃs tantre sudṛḍhe pakṣapāta āviṣkṛtaḥ śrīśaṅkarācāryabhagavatpādair mantraśāstrasarvasvabhūtāṃ saundaryalaharīṃ lalitātriśatībhāṣyaṃ ca praṇītavadbhiḥ. vaidikaśikhāmaṇayo mahākavayaḥ prācīnāḥ kālidāsamūkādyā arvācīnā nīlakaṇṭhadīkṣitādayaś ca devīcaraṇāmbujadvandve dṛḍhaṃ baddhabhāvā iti ghaṇṭāghoṣo jegīyatetarām. vidyāraṇyaprabhṛtayo 'dvaitavidyādeśikavaryā api vidyāṃ samupāsāṃcakrira iti nirdhārito 'yaṃ viṣayaḥ. vidyāraṇyamunibhir vidyārṇavākhyo mahāmantraśāstragrantho vyaracīti, tathaiva śrīmadappayyadīkṣitaiḥ parimalābhidhāno mantraśāstragranthaḥ praṇāyīti ca karṇākarṇikayā śrūyate. paraṃ tu granthāv imau sākṣān na dṛṣṭacarau. ādiśaṅkarabhagatpādopakramam avicchinnapāramparyeṇa tatra tatra śaṅkaramaṭheṣv ācaryamāṇā śrīcakrapūjā ca pañcadaśākṣarīvidyāsampradāyavaidikatvaṃ niḥsandigdhaṃ pratiṣṭhāpayati. parahsahasrair hi śrutismṛtisampradāyapravarair ārādhyate kāñcīmaṇḍalaṃ maṇḍayantī kāmākṣyabhidhānā rājarājeśvarī yaiva paradevatā śrīvidyā, tathā madhurāpurīṃ vidyotayantī mīnākṣī yā śrīvidyāyāṃ mantriṇīti prathitā, tathā jambukeśvarakṣetraṃ bhāsayantī akhilāṇḍeśvaryāhvayā devī yā kila mantraśāstre daṇḍinī daṇḍanāthetyādīn vyapadeśān bhajate, tathaiva kanyākumārīkṣetraṃ prakāśayantī śrīkanyākumārī ya hi śrīvidyāyāṃ tryakṣarī bāleti prathitābhidhānā. śrautasmārtakarmānuṣṭhānatatparā dvijāḥ sarve 'pi pratyahaṃ samupāsate sāvitrīṃ vedamātaram. ata eva 'antaḥśāktā bahiḥśaivā bhuvi sarve dvijātayaḥ' iti vādo 'pi saṃgacchate. tena śrīvidyāsampradāya eva smārtasampradāya iti suśliṣṭam. Sastri, *Śrīvidyāsaparyāpaddhati*, 1938, pg. 3.

10. Personal communication with various descendants of Nīlakaṇṭha, January 2011.

11. "Follow Vivekananda's Message to Avert Attacks Like 9/11: PM Narendra Modi," *Hindustan Times*, September 11, 2014, www.hindustantimes.com/india-news/follow-vivekananda-s-message-to-avoid-attacks-like-9–11-modi/article1–1262751.aspx.

12. Vivekananda, *The Complete Works of Swami Vivekananda*, 1970, 2.

13. *Śivamahimnaḥ Stotram*, v. 7: trayī sāṃkhyaṃ yogaḥ paśupatimataṃ vaiṣṇavam iti prabhinne prasthāne param idam adaḥ pathyam iti ca | rucīnāṃ vaicitryād ṛjukuṭilanānāpathajuṣāṃ nṛṇām eko gamyas tvam asi payasām arṇava iva ||

14. Halbfass (1988, 411), quoting Hacker (1978).

15. On the Indian case, see most notably Bilgrami (2014).

16. See for instance Thomas (2014) and Schonthal (2012).

17. Doniger and Nussbaum (2015, 16).

18. Doniger (2009, 533).

19. See for instance Hawley (2015); Richardson (2014); Horstmann (1999); Case (1996).

20. Nussbaum, *The Clash Within*, 2007, 8.

BIBLIOGRAPHY

MANUSCRIPT SOURCES

Ambāstavavyākhyā of Ardhanārīśvara Dīkṣita. Government Oriental Manuscripts Library, Madras, Ms. No. R. 4028b.

Īśavilāsa of Appayya Dīkṣita (attributed). Adyar Library and Research Centre, Chennai, TR. No. 291.

Lalitāvilāsacampū. Government Oriental Manuscripts Library, Madras, Ms. No. R. 3248.

Madhvamukhacapeṭikā. Tirupati Veṅkaṭeśvara Oriental Research Institute, Tirupati, Ms. No. 6922.

Madhvatantracapeṭikāvyākhyāna. Government Oriental Manuscripts Library, Madras, Ms. No. R. 2263b.

Madhvatantramukhabhūṣaṇa. Government Oriental Manuscripts Library, Madras, Ms. No. D. 15446.

Mahābhāṣyapradīpaprakāśa of Nīlakaṇṭha Dīkṣita. Government Oriental Manuscripts Library, Madras, Ms. No. D. 9015a.

Nārāyaṇaśabdanirukti of Anonymous. Adyar Library and Research Centre, Chennai, Ms. No. DX 819.

Nārāyaṇaśabdārthanirvacana of Vijayīndra Tīrtha. Mysore Oriental Manuscripts Library, Mysore, Ms. No. 4025.

Nārāyaṇaśabdasādhāraṇya of Govinda Nāyaka. Adyar Library and Research Centre, Chennai, Ms. No. DX 819.

Padārthadīpikāvyākhyā of Gīrvāṇendra Dīkṣita. Government Oriental Manuscripts Library, Madras, Ms. No. R. 5133.

Patañjalicaritravyākhyā of Veṅkaṭeśvara Kavi. Tanjavur Maharaja Serfoji's Sarasvati Mahal Library, Ms. No. 3827.

Ṛgbhāṣya. Tanjavur Maharaja Serfoji's Sarasvati Mahal Library, Tanjavur, Ms. No. B. 9112.

Śaṅkarābhyudaya of Rājacūḍāmaṇi Dīkṣita. Government Oriental Manuscripts Library, Madras, R. No. 7549.

Śaṅkarābhyudaya of Rājacūḍāmaṇi Dīkṣita. Śrī Śāradā Education Society, Chennai, Ms. No. No. 779.

Śaṅkarābhyudaya of Rājacūḍāmaṇi Dīkṣita, with the commentary of Rāmakṛṣṇasūri. Adyar Library and Research Centre, Ms. No. D. V. 891.

Śaṅkarābhyudaya of Rājacūḍāmaṇi Dīkṣita, with the commentary of Rāmakṛṣṇasūri. Government Oriental Manuscripts Library, Madras, Ms. No. R. 7561.

Śāstradīpikāvyākhyā of Dinakara Bhaṭṭa. Tanjavur Maharaja Serfoji's Sarasvati Mahal Library, Tanjavur, Ms. No. 6924./B 2076.

Śāstramālāvṛtti of Ananta Bhaṭṭa. Tanjavur Maharaja Serfoji's Sarasvati Mahal Library, Tanjavur, Ms. No. 6862.

Saubhāgyacandrātapa of Nīlakaṇṭha Dīkṣita. Government Oriental Manuscripts Library, Madras, Ms. No. R. 7615.

Saubhāgyacandrātapa of Nīlakaṇṭha Dīkṣita. Oriental Research Institute, Kariavattom, Kerala, Ms. No. 2941.

Saubhāgyapaddhati. Government Oriental Manuscripts Library, Madras, Ms. No. R. 1389.

Śivadharma. Institut Français de Pondichéry, Transcript No. 72.

Śivalīlārṇava of Nīlakaṇṭha Dīkṣita. Adyar Library and Research Centre, Chennai, Ms. No. D. V. 1207.

Śivastotra of Nīlakaṇṭha Dīkṣita (attributed). Adyar Library and Research Centre, Chennai, Ms. No. D. IV. 1199.

Śivatattvarahasya of Nīlakaṇṭha Dīkṣita. Government Oriental Manuscripts Library, Madras, Ms. No. R. 5016.

Śivatattvarahasya of Nīlakaṇṭha Dīkṣita. Government Oriental Manuscripts Library, Madras, Ms. No. R. 7988.

Tattvakaustubha of Bhaṭṭoji Dīkṣita. Government Oriental Manuscripts Library, Madras, Ms. No. R. 791.

PUBLISHED PRIMARY SOURCES

Ācāryastavarājabhūṣaṇa of Rāmabhadra Dīkṣita See S. Sastri, ed. *Stavamaṇimālā.*

Āccāndīkṣitavaṃśāvali of Vīrarāghavakavi. Edited by P. P. Subrahmanya Sastri. Udupi: Srikrsnamudralaya, 1923.

Advaitadīpikā of Nṛsiṃhāśramin. Edited by S. Subrahmanya Sastri. Varanasi: Sampurnanand Sanskrit University, 1984.

Advaitakālānala of Nārāyaṇācārya. Bangalore: Srisatyapramodatirtha Granthalaya, 1970.

Ambāstavavyākhyā of Ardhanārīśvara Dīkṣita. In *Brahmavidyā: The Journal of the Advaita Sabhā, Kumbakonam* 15(3–4) and 16(1–2), 1962–1963.

Ānandasāgarastava of Nīlakaṇṭha Dīkṣita. See Filliozat, 1967.

Anyāpadeśaśataka of Nīlakaṇṭha Dīkṣita. See Filliozat, 1967.

Bertrand, J., ed. 1854. *La Mission du Maduré d'après des Documents Inedits.* Vol. 4. Paris: Librairie de Poussielgue-Rusand.

Brahmāṇḍa Purāṇa. Edited by Jagadish Lal Shastri. Delhi: Motilal Banarsidass, 1973.

Brahmasūtrabhāṣya of Śrīkaṇṭha. Edited by Ra. Halasyanathasastri. Sringeri: Vani Vilas Press, 1908.

Brown, Norman, ed. and trans. 1958. *The Saundaryalaharī, or Flood of Beauty.* Cambridge, MA: Harvard University Press.

Brunner-Lachaux, Hélène. 1985. *Mṛgendrāgama: Section des rites et section du comportement / avec la vṛtti de Bhaṭṭanārāyaṇakaṇṭha; traduction, introduction, et notes par Hélène Brunner-Lachaux.* Pondicherry: Institut français d'indologie.

Chāndogya Upaniṣad. Edited by Patrick Olivelle. New York: Oxford University Press, 1998.

Cokkanātar Ulā of Purāṇattirumalai Nātar. Edited by U. Ve. Caminataiyar. Madras: Kesari Accukutam, 1931.

Cokkanātha Caritramu of Paccakappurapu Tiruvēṅgaḷakavi. Edited by T. Chandrashekharan. Madras: Government Press, 1954.

Cuntara Pāṇṭiyam of Anatāriyappan. Edited by T. Chandrasekaran. Madras: Government Oriental Manuscripts Library. 1955.

Davis, Richard, ed. and trans. 2010. *A Priest's Guide for the Great Festival: Aghoraśiva Mahotsavavidhi.* New York: Oxford University Press.

Dhvanyāloka of Ānanadavardhana. Edited by K. Krishnamoorty. Dharwar: Karnatak University, 1974.

Filliozat, Pierre-Sylvain. 1967. *Oeuvres Poétiques de Nīlakaṇṭha Dīkṣita.* Vol. 1. Pondicherry: Institut Français D'Indologie.

Gaṅgāvataraṇa of Nīlakaṇṭha Dīkṣita. Edited by Pandit Bhavadatta Sastri, Mahamahopadhyaya Pandit Sivadatta, and Kasinath Pandurang Parab. Bombay: Nirnaya Sagar Press, 1902.

Goodall, Dominic, ed. and trans. 1998. *Bhaṭṭarāmakaṇṭhaviracitā Kiraṇavṛttiḥ: Bhaṭṭa Rāmakaṇṭha's Commentary on the Kiraṇavṛtti,* vol. 1, chaps. 1–6, Critical Edition and Annotated Translation. Pondicherry: Institut Français de Pondichéry and École française d'Extrême-Orient.

Goodall, Dominic, and R. Sathyanarayanan, ed. and trans. 2014. *Śaiva Rites of Expiation: A First Edition and Translation of Trilocanaśiva's Twelfth-Century Prāyaścittasamuccaya (with a Transcription of a Manuscript Transmitting Hṛdayaśiva's Prāyaścittasamuccaya).* Pondicherry: Institut français de Pondichéry and École française d'Extrême-Orient.

Goodall, Dominic, et al., eds. 2005. *The Pañcāvaraṇastava of Aghoraśivācārya: A Twelfth-Century South Indian Prescription for the Visualisation of Sadāśiva and His Retinue.* Pondicherry: Institut Français de Pondichéry and École française d'Extrême-Orient.

Goodall, Dominic, et al., ed. and trans. 2015. *The Niśvāsatattvasaṃhitā: The Earliest Surviving Śaiva Tantra,* vol. 1. *A Critical Edition and Annotated Translation of the Mūlasūtra, Uttarasutra and Nayasūtra.* Pondicherry: Institut français de Pondichéry, École française d'Extrême-Orient, Asien-Afrika-Institut, Universität Hamburg.

Guruguṇastava of Vādīndra Tīrtha. Edited by A. R. Pancamukhi. Dharwad: Śrīraghavendratīrtha Pratiṣṭhānam, 2008.

Gurutattvamālikā of Nīlakaṇṭha Dīkṣita. See Filliozat, 1967.

Hālāsya Māhātmya. Edited by A. Ramanujacharya. Madras: Prabhakara Press.

Haribhaktivilāsa of Gopāla Bhaṭṭa. Edited by Haridasa Sastri. Mathura: Srigadadharagaurahari Press, 1986.

Hariharādvaitabhūṣaṇa of Bodhendra Sarasvatī. Edited by T. Chandraeskharan. Madras: Government Oriental Manuscripts Library, 1954.

Jayasree, S. 1983. "Contribution of Atirātrayajvan to Sanskrit Literature, with a Critical Edition of Atirātra Yajvan's Kuśakumudvatīya Nāṭaka." PhD diss., University of Madras.

Kaliviḍambana of Nīlakaṇṭha Dīkṣita. See Vasudeva, ed., *Three Satires.*

Kāraṇāgama (*Kriyāpāda*). Varanasi: Saiva Bharati Sodha Pratisthana, 1994.

Katampavaṉa Purāṇam of Vīmaṉāta Paṇṭitar. Edited by Citamparam Vāmatēva Murukapattarakar. Madras: Vidyavartini Press, 1880.

Kāvyadarpaṇa of Rājacūḍāmaṇi Dīkṣita. Vol. 1: Ullāsas 106. Edited by K. S. Ramaswami Sastri. Srirangam: Vani Vilas Press, 1910.

Kiraṇavṛtti of Bhaṭṭa Rāmakaṇṭha II. See Goodall, 1998.

Kuruntokai: An Anthology of Classical Tamil Love Poetry. Translated by M. Shanmugam Pillai and David E. Ludden. Madurai: Koodal Publishers, 1976.

Kuśakumudvatīya Nāṭaka of Atirātra Yajvan. See Jayasree.

Madhvatantramukhamardana of Appayya Dīkṣita. Edited by Ramachandra Sastri. Pune: Anandasrama, 1940.

Mahārthamañjarī of Maheśvarānanda. Edited by T. Ganapati Sastri. Trivandrum: Trivandrum Superintendent, Government Press, 1919.

Mahotsavavidhi of Aghoraśiva. See Davis, 2010.

Mṛgendrāgama. See Brunner-Lachaux, 1985.

Mūkapañcaśatī of Mūkakavi. Edited by Pandit Durgaprasad and Kasinath Pandurang Parab. In *Kāvyamālā,* 2nd ed., vol. 5. Bombay: Nirnaya Sagar Press, 1937.

Mukundavilāsa of Nīlakaṇṭha Dīkṣita. Edited by Radhavallabha Tripathi. Sagaram: Samskrta Parisad, 1980.

Nalacaritranāṭaka of Nīlakaṇṭha Dīkṣita. Edited by Sankararama Sastri. Madras: Sri Balamanorama Press, 1925.

Nara Hari Nath, Yogi, ed. and trans. 1979. *Śrīmatpaśupatipurāṇam: Nepālī Hindī Bhāṣā Sahita.* Nepal: Bhimaprasada Upadhyaya.

Olivelle, Patrick., ed. and trans. 1996. *Upaniṣads.* New York: Oxford University Press.

Padārthadīpikā of Kauṇḍa Bhaṭṭa. Benares: Raj. Rajeswari Press, 1900.

Pākhaṇḍacapeṭikā of Vijayarāmārya. Edited by B. Mondal. Kolkata: Balaram Prakasani, 2006.

Pañcastavī. See *Saundaryalaharī.*

Pañcāvaraṇastava of Aghoraśiva. See Goodall, 2005.

Patañjalicarita of Rāmabhadra Dīkṣita. Edited by Pandit Sivadatta and Kasinatha Pandurang Parab. Bombay: Nirnaya Sagar Press, 1895.

Payakaramālai of Vimaṉāta Paṇṭitar. See *Tiruvālavāyuṭaiyār Tiruviḷaiyāṭaṟpurāṇam* of Perumparrappuliyr Nampi.

Prākṛtamaṇdīpa of Appayya Dīkṣita, with the *Prākṛtamaṇidīpadīdhiti* of Śrīnivāsagopālācārya. Edited by T. T. Śrīnivāsagopālācārya. Mysore: Oriental Research Institute, 1953.

Prapañcasārasaṅgraha of Gīrvāṇendra Sarasvatī. Tanjore: Sarasvati Mahal Library, 1976–1980.

Prapannāmṛtam of Anantācārya. Edited by Swami Ramanarayanacarya. Varanasi: Somani Trust, 1966.

Raja, C. Kunhan, ed. 1938. *Unpublished Upanishads.* Madras: Adyar Library.

Ramanathan, Adayapalam. 1966. "Srimad Appayya Deekshithendrar and His Works." *Srimad Appayya Deekshithendrar Jayanthi Souvenir,* September 30, 39–42.

Rice, Benjamin Lewis, ed. *Epigraphical Carnatica.* 13 vols. Bangalore: Mysore Government Press, 1886–1958.

Sabhārañjana of Nīlakaṇṭha Dīkṣita. See Filliozat, 1967.

Śaṅkarābhyudaya of Rājacūḍāmaṇi Dīkṣita. Edited by Balasubrahmanya Sastri, Sahṛdaya, 17 (or 5), pp. 122–129, 153–160, 177–184, 201–208, 225–232, 257–264; 18 (or 6), pp. 17–24, 41–48, 64–67, 161–168, 185–192, 209–212, 231–240, 1914–1915.

Śaṅkarābhyudaya of Rājacūḍāmaṇi Dīkṣita. Edited by S. V. Radhakrishna Sastri. Srirangam: S. V. Radhakrishna Sastri, on behalf of Simili Venkatarama Sastri Trust, 1986.

Śaṅkaravijaya of Anantānandagiri. Edited by Jayanārāyaṇa Tarkapañcānana. Calcutta: Baptist Mission Press, 1868.

Śaṅkaravijaya of Anantānandagiri. Edited by N. Veezhinathan. Madras: Government Oriental Manuscripts Library, 1971.

Śaṅkaravijayavilāsa of Cidvilāsa, edited by W. R. Antarkar. *Bharatiya Vidya* 33: 1–92, 1973.

Śāntivilāsa of Nīlakaṇṭha Dīkṣita. See Filliozat, 1967.

Sastri, Sankara Rama, ed. 1938. *Śrīvidyāsaparyāpaddhati.* Madras: Madrapura Śrī-brahma-vidyā-vimarśinī-sabhā.

Sastri, Subrahmanya, ed. *Stavamaṇimālā Nāma Śrīrāmabhadradīkṣitaviracitānāṃ Rāma-karṇasrasāyanastavādīnāṃ Stutimanyānāṃ Samuccayaḥ.* Tanjavur: Sripurnacandroday-amudrayantralaya, 1932.

Śatadūṣaṇī of Vedānta Deśika, with the *Tattvaṭīkā.* Edited by Umattur Viraraghavacarya. Madras: Viraraghavacharya, 1974.

Saundaryalaharī, Śrīśaṅkarācāryaviracitā Śrīlakṣmīdharavyākhyāsamalaṅkṛtā, Bhāvano-paniṣat Śrībhāskararājabhāṣyasahitā, Devīpañcastavī ca, edited by N. N. Swami Ghanapati. 3rd ed. Mysore: Oriental Research Institute, 1953.

Siddhāntakalpavallī of Sadāśivendra Sarasvatī. Edited by Hathibhai Shastri. Varanasi: Acyu-tagranthamala Karyalaya, 1940.

Śivadharmottara (or Paśupātimataṃ Śivadharmamahāśāstram Paśupātināthadarśana). Edited by Yogī Naraharinātha. Kāṣṭhamaṇḍapa: Gorakṣanāthamandira Mṛgasthalī, 1979.

Śivalīlārṇava of Nīlakaṇṭha Dīkṣita. Edited by T. Ganapatisastri. Trivandrum: Travancore Government Press, 1909.

Śivalīlārṇava of Nīlakaṇṭha Dīkṣita. Srirangam: Vani Vilas Press, 1911.

Śivamahimnaḥ Stotram. Edited by W. Norman Brown. Poona: American Institute for Indian Studies, 1965.

Śivapādakamalareṇusahasram (or *Śivalīlārṇava*) of Nañjarāja Kaḷale. Edited by V. S. Sarma. *Journal of the Tanjore Sarasvati Mahal Library,* v. 7, 1949–1950.

Śivarahasya. Edited by Ve. Svaminatha Atreya. Tanjavur: Tanjavur Maharaja Serfoji's Sarasvati Mahal Library, 1971.

Śivārkamaṇidīpikā of Appayya Dīkṣita. See *Brahmasūtrabhāṣya* of Śrīkaṇṭha.

Śivatattvarahasya of Nīlakaṇṭha Dīkṣita, edited by T. K. Balasubrahmanyam, Vani Vilas Sanskrit Series, Srirangam: Vani Vilas, 1915.

Śivotkarṣamañjari. See Filliozat, 1967.

Slaje, Walter. 1993. *Bhāskarakaṇṭhas Mokṣopāya-Ṭīkā: ein Kommentar in der Tradition der kaschmirischen Yogavāsiṣṭha-Überlieferung: 2. Prakaraṇa (Mumukṣuvyavahāra).* Graz: Leykam.

Somaśambhupaddhati of Somaśambhu. Edited by Hélène Brunner-Lachaux. Pondicherry: Institut français d'indologie, 1963.

Śrīkarabhāṣya of Śrīpati. Edited by C. Hayavadana Rao. New Delhi: Akshaya Prakashan, 2003.

Śrīmadappayyadīkṣitendravijaya of Śivānanda Yogīndra. Edited by T. Ganapati Sastri. Chennai: Dixon Press, 1921.

Śrutisuktimālā of Haradatta, with the *Caturvedatātparyasaṅgraha* of Śivaliṅgabhūpāla. Edited by P. A. Ramasamy Sastri. Kumbakonam: Sri Vidya Press.

"Stāṇikarvaralāṟu." 1906. *Centamiḻ.* Madurai: vol. 5., pg. 87–95, 141–148, 220–222, 261–272, 294–300.

Svacchandatantra. Srinagar: Kashmir Series of Text and Studies, 1935.

Śvetāśvatara Upaniṣad. See Olivelle.

Tantravārttika of Kumārila Bhaṭṭa. Edited by Ganganatha Jha. Calcutta: Asiatic Society of Bengal, 1924.

Tattvaprakāśa of Bhojadeva. Edited by V. Dvivedī. Varanasi: Sampurnananda Sanskrit University, 1988.

Taylor, William, ed. and trans. 1835. *Oriental Historical Manuscripts in the Tamil Language.* Madras: J. C. Taylor.

Turīyaśivakhaṇḍana of Vijayīndra Tirtha. Edited by Vidvān Śrī E. Vi. Bhīmabhaṭṭamahodayāḥ. Mantralayam: Sri Gurusarvabhouma Samskrita Vidyapeetham, 1995.

Tirumantiram of Tirumūlar. Edited and translated by T. V. Venkataraman. 10 vols. Quebec: Babaji's Kriya Yoga and Publications, 2010.

Tiruvālavāyuṭaiyār Tiruppaṇimālai. Sthala Varalāru. Tiruppaṇi Vivaram. Edited by P. Pandithurai Thevar. Madurai: Madurai Tamil Sangam Publications, 1929.

Tiruvālavāyuṭaiyār Tiruviḷaiyāṭaṟpurāṇam of Perumparrappuliyūr Nampi. Edited by U. Ve. Caminataiyar. Chennai: Kapir Accukkutattir Patippikkapperratu, 1906.

Tiruviḷaiyāṭal Purāṇam of Parañcōti Muṉivar. Edited by Ikkatu Rathinavelu Muthaliar. Madras: Murukavelputtaka Salai, 1937.

Tiruviḷaiyāṭal Purāṇam of Parañcōti Muṉivar. Edited by and commentary by Na. Mu. Vekatacami Natar. 3 vols. Tirunelveli: Tirunelvelit Tennintiya Caivacittanta Nurpatippuk Kalakam, 1965.

Vairāgyaśataka of Nīlakaṇṭha Dīkṣita. See Filliozat, 1967.

Varṇāśramacandrikā of Tiruvampaḷatēcikar. Edited by Narayana Sastri. Mayuram: Dharmapuram Adhinam, 1930.

Vasucaritacampū of Kālahasti Kavi. Edited by B. Rama Raju. Hyderabad: Osmania University, 1965.

Vasudeva, Somadeva., ed. and trans. 2005. *Three Satires.* In *The Clay Sanskrit Library.* New York: New York University Press.

Vedārthasaṅgraha of Rāmānuja. Edited by J. Van Buitenen. Pune: Deccan College Post Graduate and Research Institute, 1956.

Watson, Alex, Dominic Goodall, and S. L. P. Anjaneya Sarma, ed. and trans. 2013. *An Enquiry into the Nature of Liberation: Bhaṭṭa Rāmakaṇṭha's Paramokṣanirāsakārikāvṛtti, a Commentary on Sadyojyotiḥ's Refutation of Twenty Conceptions of the Liberated State (Mokṣa).* Pondicherry: Institut Français de Pondichéry and École française d'Extrême-Orient.

Yātrāprabandha of Samarapuṅgava Dīkṣita. Edited by Pandita Kedaranatha. Bombay: Nirnaya Sagar Press, 1936.

SECONDARY SOURCES

Acharya, Diwakar. 2010. "The Antestividhi: A Manual on the Last Rite of the Lakulīśa Pāśupatas." *Journal Asiatique* 298(1): 133–156.

Adcock, C. S. 2014. *The Limits of Tolerance: Indian Secularism and the Politics of Religious Freedom*. New York: Oxford University Press.

Agamben, Giorgio. 2013. *The Highest Poverty: Monastic Rules and Forms-of-Life*. Palo Alto, CA: Stanford University Press.

Aiyar, K. Narayanaswami. 1963. *The Thirty-Two Vidyās*. Madras: Adyar Library and Research Centre.

Aiyer, R. Krishnaswami, and K. R. Venkataraman. 1965. *The Truth about the Kumbhakonam Mutt*. Madras: R. A. Sattanatham.

Appadurai, Arjun. 1990. "Disjuncture and Difference in the Global Cultural Economy." *Theory, Culture and Society* 7: 295–310.

Appadurai, Arjun, and Carol A. Breckenridge. 1995. "Public Modernity in India." In *Consuming Modernity: Public Culture in a South Asian World*. Edited by Carol A. Breckenridge. Minneapolis: University of Minnesota Press.

Aroonan, K. Nambi. 1984. "Three Saivite Mutts in Tanjavur." In *Changing South Asia: Religion and Society* Vol. 1. Edited by K. Ballhatchet and David Taylor. London: School of Oriental and African Studies.

Asad, Talal. 1993. *Genealogies of Religion: Discipline and Reasons of Power in Christianity and Islam*. Baltimore, MD: Johns Hopkins University Press.

Bader, Jonathan. 2000. *Conquest of the Four Quarters: Traditional Accounts of the Life of Śaṅkara*. New Delhi: Aditya Prakashan.

Baudrillard, Jean. 1995. *Simulacra and Simulation*. Translated by Sheila Faria Glaser. Ann Arbor, MI: University of Michigan Press.

Bilgrami, Akeel. 2014. *Secularism, Identity, and Enchantment*. Cambridge, MA: Harvard University Press.

Braidotti, Rosi. 1994. *Nomadic Subjects*. New York: Columbia University Press.

Branfoot, Crispin. 2011. "In a Land of Kings: Donors, Elites, and Temple Sculpture." In *South India under Vijayanagar: Art and Archaeology*, edited by Anila Verghese and Anna Dallapiccola. Oxford: Oxford University Press.

———. 2007. *Gods on the Move: Architecture and Ritual in the South Indian Temple*. London: Society for Asian Studies.

———. 2001. "Tirumala Nayaka's 'New Hall' and the European Study of the South Indian Temple." *Journal of the Royal Asiatic Society* 11(2): 191–217.

———. 2000. "Approaching the Temple in Nayaka-Period Madurai: The Kūṭ \ al Aḻakar Temple." *Artibus Asiae* 60(2): 197–221.

Bronner, Yigal. 2015. "South Meets North: Banaras from the Perspective of Appayya Dīkṣita." *South Asian History and Culture* 6(1): 10–31.

———. 2010. *Extreme Poetry: The South Asian Movement of Simultaneous Narration*. New York: Columbia University Press.

———. 2007. "Singing to God, Educating the People: Appayya Dīkṣita and the Function of Stotras." *Journal of the American Oriental Society* 127(2): 1–18.

Bronner, Yigal, and David Shulman. 2006. "'A Cloud Turned Goose': Sanskrit in the Vernacular Millennium." *Indian Economic and Social History Review* 43(1): 1–30.

Brooks, Douglas Renfrew. 1992a. *Auspicious Wisdom: The Texts and Traditions of Śrīvidyā Śākta Tantrism in South India.* Albany: State University of New York Press.

———. 1992b. "Encountering the Hindu 'Other': Tantrism and the Brahmans of South India." *Journal of the American Academy of Religion* 60(3): 405–436.

———. 1990. *The Secret of the Three Cities: An Introduction to Hindu Śākta Tantrism.* Chicago: University of Chicago Press.

Bühnemann, Gudrun. 2001. *The Iconography of Hindu Tantric Deities.* Vol. 2. *The Pantheons of the Prapañcasāra and the Śāradātilaka.* Groningen, Netherlands: Egbert Forsten.

Casaubon, Isaac. 1630. *The originall of popish idolatrie, or The birth of heresies. Published under the name of Causabon [sic], and called-in the same yeare, upon misinformation.* Amsterdam: Printed by the successors of Giles Thorpe.

Case, Margaret, ed. 1996. *Govindadeva: A Dialogue in Stone.* New Delhi: Indira Gandhi National Center for the Arts.

Clark, Matthew. 2006. *The Dasanami Samnyasis: The Integration of Ascetic Lineages into an Order.* Leiden, Netherlands: Brill.

Clémentin-Ojha, Catherine. 1999. *Le trident sur le palais: Une cabale anti-vishnouite dans un royaume hindou à l'époque coloniale.* Paris: École française d'Extrême-Orient.

Collins, Randall. 2003. "A Network-Location Theory of Culture." *Sociological Theory* 21(1): 69–73.

Cox, Whitney. 2016. *Modes of Philology in Late-Medieval South India.* Leiden, Netherlands: Brill.

———. 2006. "Making a Tantra in Medieval South India: The Mahārthamañjarī and the Textual Culture of Cōḻa Cidambaram." PhD diss., University of Chicago.

Cutler, Norman. 2003. "Three Moments in the Genealogy of Tamil Literary Culture." In *Literary Cultures in History: Reconstructions from South Asia,* ed. Sheldon Pollock. Berkeley: University of California Press.

Dalmia, Vasudha. 1995. "'The Only Real Religion of the Hindus': Vaisnava Self-Representation in the Late Nineteenth Century." In *Representing Hinduism: The Construction of Religious Traditions and National Identity,* edited by Vasudha Dalmia and Heinrich von Stietencron. New Delhi: Sage Publications.

Datta, Amaresh. 2005. *Encyclopaedia of Indian Literature.* 9 vols. New Delhi: Sahitya Akademi.

Davis, Richard. 2004. "A Muslim Princess in the Temples of Viṣṇu." *International Journal of Hindu Studies* 8(1): 137–156.

———. 1986–1992. "Aghora Śiva's Background." *Journal of Oriental Research, Madras,* no. 54–62: 367–378.

Deloche, Jean. 2011. *A Study in Nayaka-Period Social Life: Tiruppudaimarudur Paintings and Carvings.* Pondicherry: Institut Français de Pondichéry.

Dessigane, R., P. Z. Pattabiramin, and J. Filliozat. 1960. *La Légende des Jeux de Çiva à Madurai, d'après les Textes et les Peintures.* Vols. 1–2. Pondicherry: Institut Français d'Indologie.

Devakunjari, D. 1979. *Madurai through the Ages: From the Earliest Times to 1801 a.d.* Madras: Madras Society for Archaeological, Historical, and Epigraphical Research.

Diaconescu, Bodgan. 2012. "On the New Ways of the Late Vedic Hermeneutics: Mīmāṃsā and Navya-Nyāya." *Asiatische Studien* 66(2): 261–306.

Doniger, Wendy. 2009. *The Hindus: An Alternative History.* New York: Oxford University Press.

Doniger, Wendy, and Martha C. Nussbaum, ed. 2015. *Pluralism and Democracy in India: Debating the Hindu Right.* New York: Oxford University Press.

Dubois, Joel. 2014. *The Hidden Lives of Brahman: Shankara's Vedanta through His Upanishad Commentaries, in Light of Contemporary Practice.* Albany: State University of New York Press.

Dyczkowski, Mark. 2009. *Manthānabhairava Kumārikākhaṇḍa: The Section Concerning the Goddess of the Tantra of the Churning Bhairava.* New Delhi: Indira Gandhi National Centre for the Arts, 2009.

———. 1989. *The Canon of the Saivagama and the Kubjika Tantras of the Western Kaula Tradition.* Delhi: Motilal Banarsidass.

Ebeling, Sascha. 2010. *Colonizing the Realm of Words: The Transformation of Tamil Literature in Nineteenth-Century South India.* Albany: State University of New York Press.

Elison, William. 2014. "Sai Baba of Bombay: A Saint, His Icon, and the Urban Geography of Darshan." *History of Religions* 54(2): 151–187.

Filliozat, Pierre-Sylvain. 1967. *Oeuvres poétiques de Nīlakaṇṭha Dīkṣita.* Vol. 1. Pondicherry: Institut Français D'Indologie.

Fisher, Elaine. Forthcoming (2017). "Remaking South Indian Śaivism: The Confluence of Śaivism and Advaita Vedānta." *International Journal of Hindu Studies.*

Flood, Gavin. 2006. *The Tantric Body: The Secret Tradition of Hindu Religion.* London: I. B. Tauris.

Fraser, Nancy. 1991. "Rethinking the Public Sphere: A Contribution to the Critique of Actually Existing Democracies." *Social Text* 25–26: 56–80.

Fuller, C. J., and Haripriya Narasimhan. 2014. *Tamil Brahmins: The Making of a Middle Class.* Chicago: University of Chicago Press.

Galewicz, Cezary. 2010. *A Commentator in Service of the Empire: Sayana and the Royal Project of Commenting on the Whole of the Veda.* Vienna: Sammlung de Nobili.

Ganesan, T. 2009. *Two Saiva Teachers of the Sixteenth Century.* Pondicherry: Institut Français de Pondichéry.

Gode, P. K. 1944. "Godāvaramiśra, the Rājaguru and Mantri of Gajapati Pratāparudradeva of Orissa and His Works—between A.D. 1497–1539." *Poona Orientalist* 9(1): 11–19.

Gonda, Jan. 1980. "The Śatarudrīya." In *Sanskrit and Indian Studies: Essays in Honour of Daniel H. H. Ingalls (Studies of Classical India),* vol. 2, edited by M. Nagatomi. New York: Springer.

Goodall, Dominic. 2004. Introduction to *The Parākhyatantra: A Scripture of the Śaiva Siddhānta,* edited and translated by Dominic Goodall. Critical edition and annotated translation. Pondicherry: Institut français de Pondichéry, École française d'Extrême-Orient.

———. 2000. "Problems of Name and Lineage: Relationships between South Indian Authors of the Saiva Siddhanta." *Journal of the Royal Asiatic Society,* 3rd ser., 10(2): 205–216.

Goodall, Dominic, and Harunaga Isaacson. 2011. "Tantric Hinduism." In *The Continuum Companion to Hinduism,* ed. Jessica Frazier. Oxford: Continuum International.

———. 2007. "Workshop on the Niśvāsatattvasaṃhitā: The Earliest Surviving Śaiva Tantra?" *Newsletter of the Nepalese German Manuscript Cataloguing Project* 3: 4–6.

Grafton, Anthony. 2015. "Humanist Philologies: Texts, Antiquities, and Their Scholarly Transformations in the Early Modern West." In *World Philology,* edited by Sheldon

Pollock, Benjamin A. Elman, and Ku-ming Kevin Chang. Cambridge, MA: Harvard University Press.

———. 1994. *Defenders of the Text: The Traditions of Scholarship in an Age of Science.* Cambridge, MA: Harvard University Press.

Gregory, Brad S. 2012. *The Unintended Reformation: How a Religious Revolution Secularized Society.* Cambridge, MA: Harvard University Press.

Habermas, Jurgen. 1989. *The Structural Transformation of the Public Sphere: An Inquiry into a Category of Bourgeois Society.* Translated by Thomas Burger and Fredrick Lawrence. Cambridge, MA: MIT Press.

Hacker, Paul. 1978. *Kleine Schriften.* Edited by L. Schmithausen. Wiesbaden, Ger.: Franz Steiner.

Halbfass, Wilhelm. 1988. *India and Europe: An Essay in Understanding.* Albany: State University of New York Press.

Harman, William P. 1992. *The Sacred Marriage of a Hindu Goddess.* Delhi: Motilal Banarsidass.

———. 1987a. "The Authority of Sanskrit in Tamil Hinduism: A Case Study in Tracing a Text to Its Sources." *Mankind Quarterly* 27(3): 295–315.

———. 1987b. "Two Versions of a Tamil Text and the Contexts in Which They Were Written." *Journal of the Institute of Asian Studies* 5(1): 1–18.

———. 1985. "Kinship Metaphors in the Hindu Pantheon: Śiva as Brother-in-Law and Son-in-Law." *Journal of the American Academy of Religion* 53(3): 411–430.

Hatley, Shaman. 2007. "The Brahmayāmalatantra and Early Śaiva Cult of Yoginīs." PhD diss., University of Pennsylvania.

Hawley, John Stratton. 2015. *A Storm of Songs: India and the Idea of the Bhakti Movement.* Cambridge, MA: Harvard University Press.

———. 1991. "Naming Hinduism." *Wilson Quarterly* (Summer): 20–34.

Hazra, R. C., 1985. "The Śivadharmottara." *Purāṇa* 27: 181–209.

Holt, Amy Ruth. 2007. "Shiva's Divine Play: Art and Literature at a South Indian Temple." PhD diss., Ohio State University.

Horstmann, Monika. 2009. *Der Zusammenhalt der Welt: Religiöse Herrschaftslegitimation und Religionspolitik Mahārāja Savāī Jaisinghs (1700–1743).* Wiesbaden. Ger.: Otto Harrassowitz.

———. 2006. *Visions of Kingship in the Twilight of Mughal Rule.* Amsterdam: Royal Netherlands Academy of Arts and Sciences.

———. 1999. *In Favour of Govindadevji: Historical Documents Relating to a Deity of Vrindaban and Eastern Rajasthan.* New Delhi: Manohar.

Howes, Jennifer. 1999. "Kings and Things: The Courts of Pre-colonial South India." PhD diss., School of Oriental and African Studies, University of London.

Hudson, Dennis. 1982. "Two Chitra Festivals in Madurai." In *Religious Festivals in South India and Sri Lanka,* edited by G. Welbon and G. Yocum. New Delhi: Manohar.

———. 1977. "Siva, Minaksi, Visnu—Reflections on a Popular Myth in Madurai." *Indian Economic and Social History Review* 14(1) (January–March): 107–118.

Inamdar, N. R. 1983. *Political Thought and Leadership of Lokamanya Tilak.* New Delhi: Concept Publishing.

Ishimatsu, Ginette. 1994. "Ritual Texts, Authority and Practice in Contemporary Śiva Temples in Tamil Nadu." PhD diss., University of California, Berkeley.

Iyer, S. Veniktasubramonya. 1947. "The Saubhāgyacandrātapa of Nīlakaṇṭha Dīkṣita." *Journal of Oriental Research, Madras* 16(4): 183–188.

Jameson, Fredric. 1991. *Postmodernism, or, the Cultural Logic of Late Capitalism.* Durham, NC: Duke University Press.

Jayasree, S. 1983. "Contribution of Atirātrayajvan to Sanskrit Literature." PhD diss., University of Madras.

Jeyechandrun, A. V. 1985. *The Madurai Temple Complex, with Special Reference to Language and Literature.* Madurai: Madurai Kamaraj University.

Josi, Kesava Ramavara. 1977. *Nīlakaṇṭha Dīkṣita va tyāncā Kāvyasampad.* Nagpur: Nagpur Vidyapith.

Kachroo, Meera. 2015. "Professional Prayoga: Marketing Yantras in Contemporary Srividya." Paper presented to the American Academy of Religion Annual Meeting, Atlanta, GA.

Kahn, Victoria. 2014. *The Future of Illusion: Political Theology and Early Modern Texts.* Chicago: University of Chicago Press.

Kalidos, Raju. 1988a. *Temple Cars in Medieval Tamilaham.* Madurai: Vijay Publications.

———. 1988b. "The Wood Carvings of Tamil Nadu: An Iconographical Survey." *Journal of the Royal Asiatic Society of Great Britain and Ireland* 1: 98–125.

———. 1985. "Temple Cars of Madurai: A Study in Architectural Patterns." *Journal of Tamil Studies* 28: 5–13.

Keune, Jon Milton. 2011. "Eknāth Remembered and Reformed: Bhakti, Brahmans, and Untouchables in Marathi Historiography." PhD diss., Columbia University.

Khanna, Madhu. 1986. "The Concept and Liturgy of the Śrīcakra Based on Śivānanda's Trilogy." PhD diss., Oxford University.

Knott, Kim. 2005. *The Location of Religion: A Spatial Analysis.* London: Equinox Publishing.

Kodandaramaiah, T. 1975. *The Telugu Poets of Madurai and Tanjore.* Hyderabad: Andhra Pradesh Sahitya Akademi.

Koppedrayer, K. I. 1991. "The 'Varṇāśramacandrikā' and the 'Śūdra's' Right to Preceptorhood: The Social Background of a Philosophical Debate in Late Medieval South India." *Journal of Indian Philosophy* 19(3): 297–314.

———. 1990. "The Sacred Presence of the Guru: The Velala Lineage of Tiruvavatuturai, Dharmapuram, and Tiruppanantal." PhD diss., McMaster University.

Kruijtzer, Gijs. 2002. "Madanna, Akkanna and the Brahmin Revolution: A Study of Mentality, Group Behaviour and Personality in Seventeenth-Century India." *Journal of the Economic and Social History of the Orient* (45)2: 231–267.

Kulke, Hermann. 1993. "Mahārājas, Mahants, and Historians: Reflections on the Historiography of Early Vijayanagara and Sringeri." In *Kings and Cults: State Formation and Legitimation in India and Southeast Asia,* edited by Kulke. Delhi: Manohar.

———. 1985. "Mahārājas, Mahants and Historians: Reflections on the Historiography of Early Vijayanagara and Sringeri." In *Vijayanagara, City and Empire: New Currents of Research,* vol. 1, edited by Anna Dallapiccola. Stuttgart: Steiner Verlag.

LaRocque, Brendan. 2004. "Trade, State, and Religion in Early Modern India: Devotionalism and the Market Economy in the Mughal Empire." PhD diss., University of Wisconsin-Madison.

Leach, Robert. 2013. "Textual Traditions and Religious Identities in the Pāñcarātra." PhD diss., University of Edinburgh.

Lefebvre, Henri. 1992. *The Production of Space*. Oxford: Blackwell.

Long, Jeffrey. 2007. *A Vision for Hinduism: Beyond Hindu Nationalism*. New York: I. B. Tauris.

Lorenzen, David. 1999. "Who Invented Hinduism?" *Comparative Studies in Society and History* 41(4): 630–659.

———. 1995. "The Historical Vicissitudes of Bhakti Religion." In *Bhakti Religion in North India: Community Identity and Political Action*, edited by D. Lorenzen, pp. 1–32. Albany: State University of New York Press.

Ludden, David. 1978. "Agrarian Organization in the Tinnevelly District: 800 to 1900 A.D." PhD diss., University of Pennsylvania.

Luhmann, Niklas. 1995. *Social Systems*. Translated by John Bednarz Jr. Stanford, CA: Stanford University Press.

Lutgendorf, Philip. 2012. "Making Tea in India: Chai, Capitalism, Culture." *Thesis Eleven* 113(1): 11–31.

Magnone, Paolo. 2005. "Śivadharmottara Purāṇa: A Survey." In *Epics, Khilas, and Purāṇas: Continuities and Ruptures; Proceedings of the Third Dubrovnik International Conference on the Sanskrit Epics and Purāṇas, September 2002*, edited by Petteri Koskikallio and Mislav Jezic. Zagreb: Croatian Academy of Sciences and Arts.

Marty, Martin E. 1974. "Reinhold Niebuhr: Public Theology and the American Experience." *Journal of Religion* 54(4): 332–359.

Masuzawa, Tomoko. 2005. *The Invention of World Religions: Or, How European Universalism Was Preserved in the Language of Pluralism*. Chicago: University of Chicago Press.

McCrea, Lawrence. 2016. "Appayyadīkṣita's Invention of Śrīkaṇṭha's Vedānta." *Journal of Indian Philosophy* 44(1): 81–94.

———. 2009. *The Teleology of Poetics in Medieval Kashmir*. Cambridge, MA: Harvard Oriental Series.

———. 2008. "Playing with the System: Fragmentation and Individualization in Late Precolonial Mīmāṃsā." *Journal of Indian Philosophy* 36(5–6): 575–585.

Mesquita, Roque. 2008. *Madhva's Quotes from the Puranas and Mahabharata: An Analytic Compilation of Untraceable Source-Quotations in Madhva's Works, along with Footnotes*. Delhi: Aditya Prakashan.

———. 2000. *Madhva's Unknown Literary Sources: Some Observations*. New Delhi: Aditya Prakashan.

Minkowski, Christopher. 2011. "Advaita Vedānta in Early Modern History." *South Asian History and Culture* 2(2): 205–231.

———. 2010. "I'll Wash Out Your Mouth with My Boot: A Guide to Philological Argument in Early Modern Banaras." In *Epic and Argument in Sanskrit Literary History: Essays in Honor of Robert P. Goldman*, edited by Sheldon Pollock. Delhi: Manohar.

———. 2008. "Meanings Numerous and Numerical: Nīlakaṇṭha and Magic Squares in the *Ṛgveda*." In *Indologica T. Ya. Elizarenkova Memorial Volume*, edited by L. Kulikov and M. Rusanov. Moscow: Russian State University for the Humanities.

———. 2005. "Nīlakaṇṭha's Vedic Readings in the *Harivaṃśa* Commentary." In *Epics, Khilas, and Purāṇas: Continuities and Ruptures; Proceedings of the Third Dubrovnik International Conference on the Sanskrit Epics and Purāṇas, September 2002*, edited by Petteri Koskikallio and Mislav Jezic. Zagreb: Croatian Academy of Sciences and Arts.

———. 2004. "The Vedastuti and Vedic Studies: Nīlakaṇṭha on Bhāgavata Purāṇa X.87." In *The Vedas: Texts, Languages and Ritual: Proceedings of the Third International Vedic Studies Workshop*, edited by A. Griffiths and J. E. M. Houben. Groningen: Egbert Forsten.

Mirnig, Nina. 2009. "Liberating the Liberated: A History of the Development of Cremation and Ancestor Worship in the Early Śaiva Siddhānta." PhD diss., Oxford University.

Monier-Williams, Monier. 1891. *Brāhmanism and Hinduism, or, Religious Thought and Life in India*. New York: Macmillan.

Nicholson, Andrew. 2015. *Lord Śiva's Song: The Īśvara Gītā*. Albany: State University of New York Press.

———. 2010. *Unifying Hinduism: Philosophy and Identity in Indian Intellectual History*. New York: Columbia University Press.

———. 2005a. "Doctrine and Boundary-Formation: The Philosophy of Vijñānabhikṣu in Indian Intellectual History." PhD diss., University of Chicago.

———. 2005b. "Vijñānabhikṣu's Yoga: A Note on Doctrine and Identity in Late Medieval India." *Journal of Vaishnava Studies* 14(1): 43–63.

Novetzke, Christian. Forthcoming. *The Premodern Public Sphere in India: Religion, Caste, Gender, and Cultural Politics in Thirteenth-Century Maharashtra*.

Nussbaum, Martha. 2007. *The Clash Within: Democracy, Religious Violence, and India's Future*. Cambridge, MA: Harvard University Press.

Oddie, G. A. 1984. "The Character, Role, and Significance of Non-Brahman Saivite Maths in Tanjore District in the Nineteenth Century." In *Changing South Asia: Religion and Society*, edited by K. Ballhatchet and David Taylor. London: School of Oriental and African Studies.

O'Hanlon, Rosalind. 2011. "Speaking from Śiva's Temple: Banaras Scholar Households and the Brahman 'Ecumene' of Mughal India." *South Asia History and Culture* 2(2): 253–277.

———. 2010. "Letters Home: Banaras Pandits and the Maratha Regions in Early Modern India." *Modern Asian Studies* 44(2): 201–240.

Olivelle. 1993. *The Āśrama System: The History and Hermeneutic of a Religious Institution*. New York: Oxford University Press.

Orsi, Robert. 2006. *Between Heaven and Earth: The Religious Worlds People Make and the Scholars Who Study Them*. Princeton, NJ: Princeton University Press.

Pauwels, Heidi. 2009. "Imagining Religious Communities in the Sixteenth Century: Harirām Vyās and the Haritrayī." *International Journal of Hindu Studies* 13(2): 143–161.

Pechilis Prentiss, Karen. 1996. "A Tamil Lineage for Śaiva Siddhānta Philosophy." *History of Religions* 35(3): 231–257.

Pennington, Brian. 2005. *Was Hinduism Invented? Britons, Indians and the Colonial Construction of Religion*. New York: Oxford University Press.

Pinch, William. 2006. *Warrior Ascetics and Indian Empires*. New York: Cambridge University Press.

Pollock, Sheldon. 2009. "Future Philology? The Fate of a Soft Science in a Hard World." *Critical Inquiry* 35: 931–961.

———. 2006. *The Language of the Gods in the World of Men: Sanskrit, Culture and Power in Premodern India*. Berkeley: University of California Press.

———. 2005. *The Ends of Man at the End of Premodernity*. 2014 Gonda Lecture. Amsterdam: Royal Netherlands Academy of Arts and Sciences.

————. 2004. "The Meaning of *Dharma* and the Relationship of the Two Mīmāṃsās: Appayya Dīkṣita's Discourse on the Refutation of a Unified Knowledge System of Pūrvamīmāṃsā and Uttaramīmāṃsā." *Journal of Indian Philosophy* 32: 769–811.

————. 2001. "New Intellectuals in Seventeenth-Century India." *Indian Economic and Social History Review* 38(1): 3–31.

————. 1998a. "The Cosmopolitan Vernacular." *Journal of Asian Studies* 57(1): 6–37.

————. 1998b. "India in the Vernacular Millennium: Literary Culture and Polity, 1000–1500." *Daedalus* 127(3): 41–74.

Potter, Karl. 2001. *Encyclopedia of Indian Philosophy*, vol. 5: *The Philosophy of the Grammarians*. Delhi: Motilal Banarsidass.

Prasad, Leela. 2007. *The Poetics of Conduct: Narrative and Moral Being in a South Indian Town*. New York: Columbia University Press.

Raghavan, V. 1941. "Appayya Dīkṣitas II and III." *Proceedings of the All-India Oriental Conference* 10: 176–180.

Rahimi, Babak. 2011. *Theater State and the Formation of the Early Modern Public Sphere in Iran: Studies on Safavid Muharram Rituals, 1590–1641*. Leiden: Brill.

Raju, Anjaneya Vadhluri. 1993. *Cokkanātha Caritra: Samagra Pariśīlana*. Bhagyanagar: Prin Phas Printars.

Raman, Srilata. 2007. *Self-Surrender (Prapatti) to God in Srīvaiṣnavism: Tamil Cats and Sanskrit Monkeys*. New York: Routledge.

Ramesan, N. 1972. *Sri Appayya Dikshita*. Hyderabad: Srimad Appayya Dikshitendra Granthavali Prakasana Samithi.

Rao, Ajay K. 2014. *Re-figuring the Rāmāyaṇa as Theology: A History of Reception in Premodern India*. New York: Routledge.

Rao, K. Ramachandra. 1990. *The Tāntrik Practices in Śrī-Vidyā (with Śrī Śāradā-Chatuśśatī)*. Bangalore: Kalpatharu Research Academy.

Rao, N. Venkata. 1978. *The Southern School in Telugu Literature*. Madras: University of Madras.

Rao, Velcheru Narayana, David Shulman and S. Subrahmanyam. 2003. *Textures of Time: Writing History in South India 1600–1800*. New York: Other Press.

————. 1992. *Symbols of Substance: Court and State in Nyaka Period Tamilnadu*. Delhi: Oxford University Press.

Rastogi, Navjivan. 1979. *The Krama Tantricism of Kashmir*. Vol. 1. Delhi: Motilal Banarsidass.

Richardson, E. Allen. 2014. *Seeing Krishna in America: The Hindu Bhakti Tradition of Vallabhacarya in India and Its Movement to the West*. Jefferson, NC: McFarland.

Richman, Paula. 1997. *Extraordinary Child: Poems from a South Indian Devotional Genre*. Honolulu: University of Hawai'i Press.

Sanderson, Alexis. 2010. "The Influence of Shaivism on Pala Buddhism." Lecture delivered May 1, 2010, University of Chicago.

————. 2009. "The Śaiva Age." In *Genesis and Development of Tantrism*, edited by Shingo Einoo. Tokyo: Institute of Oriental Culture, University of Tokyo.

————. 2006. "The Lākulas: New Evidence of a System Intermediate between Pāñcārthika Pāśupatism and Āgamic Śaivism." *Indian Philosophical Annual* 24: 143–217.

————. 2003-2004. *The Śaiva Religion among the Khmers, Part I. Bulletin de l'École française d'Extrême-Orient* 90–91: 349–462.

———. 1995. "Meaning in Tantric Ritual." In *Essais sur le Rituel III: Colloque du Centenaire de la Section des Sciences religieuses de l'École Pratique des Hautes Études,* edited by A. M. Blondeau and K. Schipper. Bibliothèque de l'École des Hautes Études, Sciences Religieuses, vol. 102. Louvain-Paris: Peeters.

———. 1991. "Summary of Tantric Śaivism: 24 Lectures Delivered at the École Pratique des Hautes Études, Section 5, from April to June 1991." Unpublished ms.

———. 1988. "Śaivism and the Tantric Traditions." In *The World's Religions,* edited by S. Sutherland, L. Houlden, P. Clarke, and F. Hardy. London: Routledge and Kegan Paul.

Sarma, Varanasi Raj Gopal, ed. 1987. *Kanchi Kamakoti Math: A Myth.* Varanasi: Ganga-Tunga Prakashan.

Sastri, P. P. Subrahmanya. 1942. "Two Rare Treatises on Saktism." In *Book of Commemoration Presented to Sri Vaittamanidhi Mudumbai Gopalakrishnamacharya, on his 61th Birthday by His Pupils and Friends, October 20, 1942.* Madras: N.p.

Sastri, Y. Mahalinga. 1929. "More about the Age and Life of Śrīmad Appayya Dīkṣita." *Journal of Oriental Research, Madras* 2: 140–160.

Sathyanatha Aiyar. 1924. *History of the Nayaks of Madurai.* Oxford: Oxford University Press.

Satyanarayanaravu, Yandamuri. 1966. *Sarada dhvajamu: Tanjavuru rajula kalamuloni telugu sahitya caritra.* Vijayavada: Uttama Sahiti.

Schonthal, Benjamin. 2012. "Ruling Religion: Buddhism, Politics and Law in Contemporary Sri Lanka." PhD diss., University of Chicago.

Schwartz, Jason. Forthcoming. "Ending the Śaiva Age: The Rise of the Brahmin Legalist-Pastor and the Universalization of Hindu Dharma." PhD diss., University of California, Santa Barbara.

———. 2012. "Caught in the Net of *Śāstra:* Devotion and Its Limits in an Evolving Śaiva Corpus." *Journal of Hindu Studies* 5(2): 210–231.

———. 2010. "Devoted to the Texts: Bhakti in the Śāstric Imagination of Premodernity." MA thesis, Columbia University.

Seastrand, Anna. 2013. "Praise, Politics, and Language: South Indian Murals, 1500–1800." PhD diss., Columbia University.

Sharma, B. N. K. 2000. *History of the Dvaita School of Vedānta and its Literature.* 3rd rev. ed. Delhi: Motilal Banarsidass.

Shulman, David. 2014. *Muttusvāmi Dīkṣitar and the Invention of Modern Carnatic Music: The Abhayāmbā Vibhakti-kṛtis.* Amsterdam: Royal Netherlands Academy of Arts and Sciences.

———. 2001. "First Grammarian, First Poet: A South Indian Vision of Cultural Origins." *Indian Economic and Social History Review* 38: 353–373.

———. 1980. *Tamil Temple Myths: Sacrifice and Divine Marriage in the South Indian Śaiva Tradition.* Princeton, NJ: Princeton University Press.

———. 1976. "The Mythology of the Tamil Śaiva Talapurāṇam." PhD diss., School of Oriental and African Studies.

Shulman, David, and Velcheru Narayana Rao. 2002. *Classical Telugu Poetry: An Anthology.* Berkeley: University of California Press.

Sivananda, Swami. 1947. *Lives of Saints.* Risikesh: Sivananda Publication League.

Smith, Brian K. 1989. *Reflections on Resemblance, Ritual and Religion.* New York: Oxford University Press.

Smith, Jonathan Z. 1990. *Drudgery Divine: On the Comparison of Early Christianities and the Religions of Late Antiquity.* Chicago: University of Chicago Press.

Smith, Wilfred Cantwell. 1962. *The Meaning and End of Religion.* New York: Mentor Books.

Staal, Frits. 1965. "Euclid and Panini." *Philosophy East and West* 15(2): 99–116.

Stein, Burton. 1980. *Peasant, State and Society in Medieval South India.* Delhi: Oxford University Press.

Stietencron, Heinrich von. 1989. "Hinduism: On the Proper Use of a Deceptive Term." In *Hinduism Reconsidered,* edited by Günther-Dietz Sontheimer and Hermann Kulke. Delhi: Manohar.

Stoker, Valerie. 2011. "Polemics and Patronage in Sixteenth-Century Vijayanagara: Vyāsatīrtha and the Dynamics of Hindu Sectarian Relations." *History of Religions* 51(2): 129–155.

———. 2007. "Vedic Language and Vaiṣṇava Theology: Madhva's Use of *Nirukta* in his *Ṛgbhāṣya.*" *Journal of Indian Philosophy* 35: 169–199.

Subrahmaniam, T. N., ed. 1957. *South Indian Temple Inscriptions.* 4 vols. Madras: Government Oriental Manuscripts Library.

Subrahmanyam, Sanjay. 2001. *Penumbral Visions: Making Polities in Early Modern South India.* Ann Arbor: University of Michigan Press.

Sweetman, William, ed. and trans. 2012. *Bibliotheca Malabarica: Bartholomäus Ziegenbalg's Tamil Library.* With R. Ilakkuvan. Pondicherry: Institut Français D'Indologie.

———. 2003. *Mapping Hinduism: "Hinduism" and the Study of Indian Religions 1600–1776.* Halle: Verlag der Franckeschen Stiftugen zu Halle.

Taylor, Charles. 2007. *A Secular Age.* Cambridge, MA: Harvard University Press.

Thomas, Jolyon. 2014. "Japan's Preoccupation with Religious Freedom." PhD diss., Princeton University.

Troeltsch, Ernst. 1931. *The Social Teachings of the Christian Churches.* 2 vols. New York: Macmillan.

Tweed, Thomas. 2008. *Crossing and Dwelling: A Theory of Religion.* Cambridge, MA: Harvard University Press.

Unni, N. Parameshwaran. 1995. *Nilakantha Diksita.* New Delhi: Sahitya Akademi.

van der Veer, Peter. 1994. *Religious Nationalism: Hindus and Muslims in India.* Berkeley: University of California Press.

Vasquez, Manuel. 2010. *More Than Belief: A Materialist Theory of Religion.* New York: Oxford University Press.

Vasudeva, Somadeva. 2012. "Powers and Identities: Yoga Powers and the Tantric Śaiva Tradition." In *Yoga Powers: Extraordinary Capacities Attained through Meditation and Concentration,* edited by Knut Jacobsen. Leiden: Brill.

Venkatkrishnan, Anand. 2015. "Love in the Time of Scholarship: An Advaita Vedāntin Reads the *Bhakti Sūtras.*" *Journal of Hindu Studies* 8(1): 139–152.

Venkatraman, K. R. 1973. *Devī Kāmākṣī in Kāñchī: A Short Historical Study.* 2nd ed. Srirangam: Vani Vilas Press.

Viswanathan, S. 1982. *The Sivalilarnava of Nilakantha Diksita: A Critical Study.* Chennai: Ramakrishna Mission, Vivekananda College.

Vivekananda, Swami. 1970. *The Complete Works of Swami Vivekananda.* Mayavati ed., vol. 1. Calcutta: Advaita Ashrama.

Wallerstein, Immanuel. 1976. *The Modern World System: Capitalist Agriculture and the Origins of the European World Economy in the Sixteenth Century.* New York: Academic Press.

Wallis, Christopher. 2008. "The Descent of Power: Possession, Mysticism, and Initiation in the Śaiva Theology of Abhinavagupta." *Journal of Indian Philosophy* 36: 247–295.

Warner, Michael. 2002. *Publics and Counterpublics.* New York: Zone Books.

Watson, Alex. 2006. *The Self's Awareness of Itself: Bhaṭṭa Rāmakaṇṭha's Arguments against the Buddhist Doctrine of No-Self.* Vienna: Sammlung de Nobili Institut für Südasien-, Tibet- und Buddhismuskunde der Universität.

Wentworth, Blake. 2011. "Yearning for a Dreamed Real: The Procession of the Lord in the Tamil Ulās." PhD diss., University of Chicago.

White, David Gordon. 2009. *Sinister Yogis.* Chicago: University of Chicago Press.

White, Hayden. 1975. *Metahistory: The Historical Imagination in Nineteenth-Century Europe.* Baltimore, MD: Johns Hopkins University Press.

Wilden, Eva. 2014. *Manuscript, Print and Memory: Relics of the Caṅkam in Tamilnadu.* Berlin: De Gruyter.

Wilke, Annette. 2012. "Recoding the Natural and Animating the Imaginary: Kaula Body-Practices in the Paraśurāma-Kalpasūtra, Ritual Transfers, and the Politics of Representation." In *Transformations and Transfer of Tantra in Asia and Beyond,* edited by István Keul. Berlin: De Gruyter.

Yates, Frances Amelia. 1964. *Giordano Bruno and the Hermetic Tradition.* Chicago: University of Chicago Press.

Zvelebil, Kamil. 1973. "The Earliest Account of the Tamil Academies." *Indo-Iranian Journal* 15(2): 109–135.

INDEX

Abhinava-Kālidāsa, 58
Abhinava Vidyātīrtha, 189
Abhiṣekha Pāṇḍya, 197
Āccān Dīkṣita, 51, 71, 212n54
Āccāndīkṣitavaṃśāvali, 218n44
Ācāryastavarāja, 67–68, 217n29
Ācāryastavarājabhūṣaṇa, 67
Acharya, Diwakar, 206n6
Acyuta, 46
Acyutābhyudayamu, 244n60
Acyutadevarāya, 8–9
Acyutappa Nāyaka, 244n60
Adaiyappalam, 10, 217n27
Adcock, C. S., 192
adhikāra, 247n92
adhyāhāra, 171
Advaitadīpikā, 63, 215n15
Advaitakālānala, 114, 117–18, 231n29, 232n38,
    232n41, 232n42
advaitapīṭhasthita, 64
Advaitarasamañjarī, 68
Advaita Vedānta: of Appayya Dīkṣita, 209–
    10n28; early modern, 48, 63, 215n14; and
    Śaiva Siddhānta, 40, 42–45, 219n51, 219n52;
    and Śaṅkarācārya lineages, 27, 60; and
    Śrīvidyā, 74–76, 187
Adyar Library and Research Centre, 122,
    232–33n48
Āgamas, 74–75, 84

Agamben, Giorgio, 18, 134, 237n78
Āgamic Śaivism, 128; of Mantramārga, 203n5;
    See also Śaivism
Agastya, sage, 88, 155, 169–70, 200
Age of Vedānta, 45
Aghora *mantra*, 39, 208n18
Aghoraśiva, 40, 41, 42, 208n16, 209n22
Agnihotra oblation, 42
agrahāra, 10, 217n27; Nīlakaṇṭha Dīkṣita's
    agrahāra in Palamadai, 1, 10, 55, 188, 219n46,
    224n99, 249n6
Airāvata's curse, removing, 195
Aiśa, 207n10
Aiyar, Narayanaswami, 220n62
Aiyer, R. Krishnaswami, 225n104
Ākāśavāsīs, 55, 213n56
Akattiyam, 170
Akbar, Mughal emperor, 193
Akkanna, 213n55
Aḻakar Temple, 26, 179
Alaṅkārasarvasva, 82
Alaṅkāraśāstra, 104, 167
alchemy, 199; alchemical nectar, 62
Āmardaka Maṭha at Cidambaram, 40
Amareśvara Sarasvatī, 215n12
Amareśvara temple, 206n2
Ambāstava, 86, 217n33, 221n71, 223n94, 224n96,
    224n100
Ambāstavavyākhyā, 68–69, 79, 82, 84

Amṛtānandanātha, 221n81

aṃśāvatāra, 56, 249n4

Ānandasāgarastava, 49, 50, 71, 72

Ānandavardhana, 145

Ananta Bhaṭṭa, 52

Anantānandagiri, 91, 95, 225n110, 226n111;
　　Anantānandagiri's *Śaṅkaravijaya*, 88, 91

Anatāri, 148, 151, 153

Anderson, Benedict, 58

Antakakkavi, 152, 242n49

anugraha (grace), 42

anuṣaṅga, 171

apauruṣeyatva, 40

Apollinaire, Guillaume, 145

Appa Dīkṣita, 54, 55, 213n54

Appadurai, Arjun, 24, 26

Appakavi, 243n57

Appa-tidshadar, 54

Appayya Deekshithendrar Granthavali
　　Prakasana Samithi, 185

Appayya Dīkṣita, 9–11; author of *Īśavilāsa*,
　　113, 130–32, 236n69; authorship of
　　Prākṛtamaṇidīpikā, 141–42, 238n7; dialogue
　　with Mādhva theologians, 12, 112, 114–119;
　　hagiography of, 55, 185–89, 214n59, 249n6;
　　indebtedness to Vīraśaiva philosophy, 45, 73,
　　205n26, 210n29; and Mīmāṃsā, 115–119; and
　　Navya Nyāya, 231n25; and Śāktism, 49, 71–72,
　　218–19n45; and Śivādvaita, 9–11, 44–45, 73,
　　75, 204–05n20, 209–10n28, 210n29, 217n27

Appayya Dīkṣita, works of:
　　Durgacandrakalāstuti, 218–19n45;
　　Kalpataruparimala, 10; *Kuvalayānanda*,
　　10; *Madhvatantramukhamardana*,
　　12, 114–119; *Nyāyarakṣāmaṇi*, 10;
　　Siddhāntaleśasaṅgraha, 68; *Śikhariṇīmālā*,
　　234n59; *Śivādvaitanirṇaya*, 220n65;
　　Śivakarṇāmṛta, 234n59; *Śivārcanacandrikā*,
　　11, 71, 76; *Śivārkamaṇidīpikā*, 10–11, 44–45;
　　Śivatattvaviveka, 234n59

Appayyadīkṣitendravijaya, 218n44

araṅkēṟṟam, 152, 176, 241n36

Archaeological Survey of India (Mysore), 213n56

Ardhanārīśvara, 63

Ardhanārīśvara Dīkṣita, 68–69; and the birth of
　　Samayin Śrīvidyā, 77–87, 218n36; comparison
　　to Lakṣmīdhara, 80, 222n84; works of:
　　221n72

Aroonan, K. Nambi, 242n47

aṟukāṟpīṭam, 151–52, 241n38, 241n39

Asad, Talal, 205n28

Ascetic *(cittar)*, becoming all-powerful, 197

āstika (believers), 1, 4–5, 32, 38

Atharvaṇas, 84

Atimārga, 128, 235n64; Atimārgic Pāśupatas, 128

Atirātra Yajvan, 55, 57–59, 62, 71, 85–86, 213n57

ativistṛtatva, 101

Ātmabodhaṭīkā, 64

ātman, 7, 42, 44

Ātmārpaṇastuti, 218n45

ātmaśuddhi and *bhūtaśuddhi*, 37

atyāśrama, 130, 246n87; *atyāśramavrata*, 128–29,
　　130, 235n64; *atyāśramin*, 128, 129, 235n63

Aurangzeb, Mughal emperor, 193

avyāhata, 11, 223n93

Ayya Dīkṣita, 53, 54, 212n54

Ayyan, Ambalattatum, 240n31

Ayya-tidshader-ayyen, 54

Bader, Jonathan, 217n34, 224–25n102

Bagalamukhī, 85

Balagangadhar "Lokamanya" Tilak: Hinduism
　　defined by, 3–4

Bāṇabhadra, musician devotee, 199

Bangles, selling, 198

Basavapurāṇamu, 240n32

Baudrillard, Jean, 26

beatitude *[apavarga]*, 42

Benares, 12, 21, 107, 205, 218

Bengali Renaissance, 190, 191

Berger, Peter, 17

Bhāgavata Purāṇa, 36, 111, 205n20, 207n12

Bhairava, 37, 123; Bhairava Tantras, 207n9,
　　245n68

Bhairavī, 85

bhakti, 7, 15, 36, 74–75, 207n12; bhakti movement,
　　12, 203n7; North Indian bhakti, 12, 18, 48,
　　193, 205n29; Tamil bhakti saints, 87, 145, 167,
　　1717–3, 185

Bhaktilīlāmṛta, 229n9

Bhānuji Dīkṣita, 205n20, 229n15

Bharadvāja, 55–56

Bhāskararāya, 60, 72, 219n49; on Kālidāsa,
　　218n36l and Kaula Śrīvidyā, 79; lineage,
　　214n6; commentary on Lalitāsahasranāma, 91

bhasmoddhūlana, 129

Bhaṭṭa Mīmāṃsā, 53, 55

Bhaṭṭa Rāmakaṇṭha II, 43

Bhaṭṭoji Dīkṣita, 205n20

Bhavabhūti, 157

Bhedadhikkāra, 215n15

Bhedadhikkāravivṛti, 68

Bhīma of Vemulavāda, 157

Bhoja of Dhārā, 209n20

Bibliotheca Malabarica: Bartholomäus Ziegenbalg's Tamil Library, 242n45
bigotry, 190
Bilgrami, Akeel, 205n28, 250n15
birudas, 11
Bishop of Exeter, 8
Bisschop, Peter, 206–7n7
Blackbird, teaching, 200
Bodhendra Sarasvatī, 63–64
Brahmā, 113–14, 123, 227n129
Brahmānanda Sarasvatī, 67
Brahmāṇḍa Purāṇa, 88, 91, 225n103, 227n123, 227n125, 227n127
Brahmanism, 7–8
Brahmanism and Hinduism, 7
Brahmasūtrabhāṣya, 215n8, 220n63
Brahmasūtras, 5–6; and sectarian theology, 5–6, 104, 118; commentaries on, 9, 11, 43–46, 60, 205n26, 215n8, 220n63, 234n59, 249n2
Brahmavidyās, 75, 220n62
Brahmayāmala, 223n93
Brahminism, 8, 23, 34–38, 140; Brahminical darśanas, 43; Brahminical Dharmaśāstra, 39; Brahminical Śaivism, 48, 113
Brahminicide, sin of, 195, 199
Brāhmanism and Hinduism, 203n9
Brahmins, 23, 36, 42, 54, 58, 195, 197, 198, 199, 200, 205n36, 213n56; Śaiva Brahmins, 24, 30; Tamil Brahmins, 205n36, 205n37; Vaidika Brahmins, 53
Braidotti, Rosi, 249n106
Branfoot, Crispin, 211n43, 247n99
Brāhma Purāṇas, 108
Brāhmī Saṃhitā, 110
Breckenridge, Carol, 24
Brick, David, 230n20
Bṛhadīśvara temple (Tanjavur), 179, 248n105
Bronner, Yigal, 203n12, 214n59, 217n27, 232n44, 239n15, 239n16, 239n19
Brooks, Douglas Renfrew, 49, 205n37, 214n5, 219n49, 221n78, 245n73
Brown, Norman, 78, 206n2
Brunner-Lachaux, Hélène, 206n6, 208n16
Buddhism, 34, 194
Bühnemann, Gudrun, 215n13

Caminataiyar, U. Ve., 175, 241n36, 243n52, 247n97
Campaka Pāṇḍya, 164, 170
Campantar. *See* Ñāṇacampantar.
Caṇḍamāruta, 11
Candrāloka, 82

Candraśekhara Bhāratī, 215n9
Caṅkam. *See* Tamil Caṅkam.
Caṅkam plank, 168–69; giving, 200
Caṅkam Poets' Quarrel, resolving, 200
Canonization: of *Tiruviḷaiyāṭal Purāṇam,* 159–65
Carcā Stotra, 61, 215n10
Carvāka, 17
Casaubon, Isaac, 112, 230n24
Case, Margaret, 250n19
Caste, 21, 26, 54, 135, 178–9, 192, 228n2, 241n41; caste-blindness, 36; caste consciousness, conservatism in, 174; mixing of, 36; removal of caste (*jātyuddharaṇa*), 173; Śaivism and caste, 36–7, 39; Vēḷāḷa castes, 154–55, 242n48, 242n49, 244n62
Caturvedatātparyasaṅgraha, 249n2
Cenna Keśava Temple, 32
Cēra king, 196, 199
Cervaikkārar, Nociyūr Palaniyappan, 148
Cevvanti, 153–54
Chāndogya Upaniṣad, 46, 210n30
Cicchakti, 74, 220n65
Cidambaram, 105, 138; Golden Hall in, 196; Śaiva community, 175
Cidgaganacandrikā, 218n36
Cidvilāsa, 226n111, 226n115; Cidvilāsa's *Śaṅkaravijayavilāsa,* 88, 91, 92
Cilappatikāram, 237n4
Ciñciṇīmatasārasamuccaya, 214n4
Cinnabomma Nāyaka (king), 10–11, 204n17
Cinna Rāma, 148, 156
Cintāmaṇigṛha, 95
Citamparappāṭiyal, 155
Citampara Purāṇam, 175
Citrabhānu year, 10
citra kāvya, 145
Citrā sacrifice, 42
Cittirai Festival, Madurai, 26, 237n1, 238n10; performance of Sanskrit dramas, 57, 62–63; and sectarianism, 26; and public space, 138; Tirumalai Nāyaka, restructured by, 142, 178–79
Civakurunātapiḷḷai, 175–76
Clark, Matthew, 205n38, 215n7
The Clash Within, 250n20
Clémentin-Ojha, Catherine, 205n30
Cokkanātar Ulā, 154, 155, 175, 240n28, 243n52, 247n97
Cokkanātha Caritramu, 148, 156, 157, 159, 160, 163, 239–40n25, 243n56, 243n58, 244n63
Cokkanātha Caritra: Samagra Pariśīlana, 239–40n25

Cokkanātha Makhin, 51
Cōḻa empire, 9, 150 ,196, 197, 198, 199, 200; Cōḻa
    period literary culture, 138, 150
communalism, 7, 191–93
Community. *See specific* entries
The Complete Works of Swami Vivekananda,
    250n12
consciousness, 41, 74
conservatism, in caste consciousness, 174
contemplation [*manana*], 42
Cox, Whitney, 214n5, 230n20, 245n73
Crane bathing, 200
Cuntaracamantar, 198
Cuntara Pāṇṭiyam, 148, 151, 153, 159, 163, 241n39
Cutler, Norman, 241n36, 247n97

daharākāśavidyā, 44, 75, 76
Dakṣa forest, 198
Dakṣiṇāmūrti, 197
Dalmia, Vasudha, 203n2
dantadhāvana, 206n6
darśana, 5, 43, 48, 104
darśana of Śiva, 124
Daśanāmī, 60
Datta, Amaresh, 243n57
Davis, Richard, 205n35, 209n22, 219n50
Deloche, Jean, 248n105
de Nobili, Roberto, 8
de Simini, Florinda, 206n7
Dessigane, R., 237n2, 239n20
Devakunjari, D., 241n39
Devanāgarī, 89; paper transcript, 211n41, 218n42
Devīmāhātmya, 49, 222n88
devotion. *See bhakti.*
Dhanañjaya, 195
Dhanapati, merchant, 200
Dhārā, King Bhoja of, 209n20
dhāraṇās, 75
Dharmaśāstras, 77, 206n6, 220n68; Śaiva
    Dharmaśāstras, 5, 35, 39, 206n6
Dhurjaṭi Māhātmyamu, 240n27
Dhvanyāloka, 145, 239n18
Diaconescu, Bodgan, 231n35
Die Wirtschaftethik der Weltreligionen, 203n6
Dinakarabhaṭṭīya, 52, 212n48
Divine Life Society, 185
Divyāgamas, 76
Doniger, Wendy, 192, 193, 205n34, 250n17, 250n18
doxography, 48
dṛk and *kriyā śakti*, 42
Drudgery Divine, 16
Dumont, Louis, 203n6

Durgācandrakalāstuti, 219n45
Durjanamukhacapeṭikā, 12
Durvāsas, sage, 195, 222n84, 243n57
Dvaita, 45, 46; Dvaita theology, 116; *See also*
    Mādhva
Dyczkowski, Mark, 214n4, 236n75

early modernity: and Hindu sectarianism,
    5–9, 13, 22, 31, 44–45, 98, 191; and modern
    pluralism, 189–94; non-Western, 4, 15–19;
    and philology, 103–04, 112; and public space,
    27; and the religious public, 101, 136–137,
    140–41; and satire, 14, 70; and secularism, 15,
    17–18; and textual culture, 28, 150–51, 155–56;
    and theologization of public discourse, 20
Ebeling, Sascha, 241n35
Eight great siddhis, 198
Ekādaśī, 124
Ekāmranātha Śaiva temple in Kanchipuram, 9,
    91–92, 225n103
Ekavīrā, 213n56
Eknāth, 104; *Eknāthcaritra*, 229n9
Elison, William, 25–26
Encyclopedia of Indian Philosophy, 229n15
Encylopaedia of Indian Literature, 243n57
Enlightenment, European, 17, 134, 135, 192;
    rationality, 18
entextualization, of public space, 182
Epigraphical Carnatica, 206n1
etymology and lexicography in intersectarian
    debate, 120–28
"Euclid and Panini," 104
Euro-American secularism, 193
Eurocentrism, 192
European imperialism, 192

fanaticism, 190
Filliozat, J., 237n2, 239n20
Filliozat, Pierre-Sylvain, 212n52, 216n20, 216n21,
    218n37
Fisher, Elaine, 205n26, 210n29, 219n52, 220n65
Fishing net, throwing, 201
Flood, Gavin, 208n14
Franciscan community, 134
Fraser, Nancy, 23, 140
Fuller, C. J., 49, 205n36, 205n37

Gajapati Pratāparudra (Orissa), 221n75
Galewicz, Cezary, 229n10
Ganapathi, 54
Gandhian secularism, 192
Ganesan, T., 240n32

Gaṅgādhara, 123
Gauḍapāda, 221n81
Gaurī, 197
Gāyatrī *mantra*, 37
Gīrvāṇendra Dīkṣita, 107, 108, 112, 229n13,
    229n14
Gīrvāṇendra Sarasvatī, 63; as guru of Nīlakaṇṭha
    Dīkṣita, 49, 99, 135; lineage, 63, 216n19, and
    Smārta-Śaiva community, 63–71, 215–16n17;
    works of: *Prapañcasārasaṅgraha*, 63, 65–66
goddess: Akhilāṇḍeśvarī, 188, 223n91; Ekavīrā,
    213n56; Kālī, 61; Kāmākṣī, 61, 69, 87, 88,
    89, 93–95, 249n8; Lalitā Tripurasundarī,
    59, 70, 72, 135; Maṅgalanāyakī, 1; Mīnākṣī,
    49, 57, 71–72; Pārvatī, 63; Rājarājeśvarī, 188;
    Sarasvatī, 164
Gode, P. K., 221n75
Golden Hall in Cidambaram, 196
Golden Lotus Tank, 177, 179
Golkonda, 213n55
Golovkova, Anya, 214n4
Gonda, Jan, 210n32
Goodall, Dominic, 207n9, 208n16, 208n17,
    208n18, 209n26, 214n5, 219n50, 219n51,
    219n52, 242n46, 245n73
Gopālabhaṭṭa, 207n12
Government Oriental Manuscripts Library
    (Chennai), 212n49, 225n105
Govinda Nāyaka, 122–28, 228n6, 232–33n48,
    233n50, 233n53
Govindapāda, 80
grace, 41
Grafton, Anthony, 103, 230n24
grammatical theory (Tamil), 169–70
Grantha script, 51–52, 70, 89, 239n22
Gregory, Brad S., 205n27
guṇas, 47, 112
Guṇḍodara, 196
Gupta and Vākāṭaka courts, 58
Guruguṇastava, 53, 212n52
Gurutattvamālikā (GTM), 64, 67, 216n17, 216n22,
    216n23

Habermas's "public sphere," 21–23, 140
Hacker, Paul, 191, 250n14
hagiography, 11, 13, 58, 59, 61, 79, 90, 185
Hālāsya Māhātmya (*HM*), 146–47, 156; citations
    of, 164, 174–75; origins, 163–64; and
    Parañcōti's *TVP*, similarity, 159–65, 178;
    Śāktism in, 162–63, 244–45n68; and the
    Telugu *Cokkanātha Caritramu*, 160
Halbfass, Wilhelm, 191, 250n14

Haradatta, 185, 249n2
Haradatta's *Śrutisūktimālā*, 43
Haribhaktivilāsa, 207n12
Hariharādvaitabhūṣaṇa, 64, 192, 216n18
Harman, William P., 237n1, 239n20
Hatley, Shaman, 207n9
Hawley, John Stratton, 12, 203n2, 203n7, 250n19
Hazra, R. C., 206n7
Hermes Trismegistus, 69
Hermetic tradition, 69
"heterodox" (*nāstika*) sects, 5
The Highest Poverty, 237n78
Hinduism, 3–4, 28, 194. *See also specific* entries;
    defined, 33, 189; defined by Balagangadhar
    "Lokamanya" Tilak, 3–4, 31; defined by Brian
    K. Smith, 33; defined by V. D. Savarkar, 3;
    invention of, 183; neo-Hinduism, 189–191;
    and publicity, 24, 140; and pluralism, 48,
    194–193; Hinduism and Śaivism, 33; 38;
    sectarianism and, 5, 6–14, 45–48, 98, 136;
    Hindu Universalism, 189–90; Hindu Right,
    192; and *Unifying Hinduism*, 5, 38, 47–48
Hindustan Times, 250n11
Hindutva, 3, 31
Holt, Amy Ruth, 237n2, 248n105
Horstmann, Monika, 205n23, 250n19
Howes, Jennifer, 214n58
Hudson, Dennis, 205n35, 237n1

icchā, 42
Inamdar, N. R., 203n4
inclusivism, 191–93
Indra, 195, 196
-Indra Sarasvatī, 64
intersectarian debate, 9, 69; lexicography
    and etymology in, 120–28; intersectarian
    philology, 101, 105
The Invention of World Religions, 203n10
Isaacson, Harunaga, 207n9
Īśavilāsa, 113, 130, 231n26, 236n69, 236n71, 236n73
Ishimatsu, Ginette, 219n50
Īśvara Gītā, 47, 48, 211n38
Iṭaikkāṭar, poet, 201
Iyer, S. Veniktasubramonya, 218n38

Jagadguru Bhāratī Tīrtha, 2, 3, 188, 189
Jagannāthāśramin, 215n17
Jainism, 137, 172–3, 197, 198, 201, 205n22, 246n88,
    248n104
Jambukeśvara temple, 213n56, 223n91
Jameson, Fredric, 26
jātyuddharaṇa, 173

Jayalaksmi Indological Bookhouse, 187
Jesuits, 142, 242n45
Jeyechandrun, A. V., 53, 237n3, 237n4,
    247–48n100, 248n101
jīvanmuktas, 128
Jñānaśambhu of Varanasi, 208n16
Jñāneśvarī, 104
Josi, Kesava Ramavara, 212n54, 218n37
Journal of Hindu Studies, 210n34

Kabir, 18, 205n29
Kacci Vīrappa Nāyaka, 153, 154
Kadambavanapurāṇam, 149
Kahn, Victoria, 205n27
Kailāsa, mount, 196
Kaivalya Upaniṣad, 130
Kaivalyopaniṣad, 131–32
Kaiyaṭa, 125
Kālahasti Kavi, 68, 240n32
Kālahasti Māhātmyamu, 148
Kālāmukhas, 43, 128
Kālarudra, 114
Kālakaṇṭheśvara temple, 10, 217n27
Kālidāsa, Mahākavi, 57–98, 157, 187, 188
Kalidos, Raju, 249n105
Kālī Krama, 214n5, 245n73
Kaliviḍambana, 14, 70
Kali Yuga, 144
Kalpataruparimala, 10
Kāmādhikaraṇa, 44, 55, 76
Kāmakoṭi Pīṭha, Kāñcī, 63, 88, 216n19; Kāmakoṭi
    Pīṭha Śaṅkarācāryas, 64
Kāmākṣīdāsa, 68
Kāmākṣī, 61, 69, 87, 88, 89, 93–95, 249n8
Kāmākṣī Temple of Kanchipuram, 97, 183–84,
    222n84, 225n103
Kamalākarabhaṭṭa, 52, 220n68
Kāmeśvara, 73; and Kāmeśvarī, 61, 89,
    95–97
Kāmika Āgama, 173
Kampā River, 94
kanakābhiṣeka, 11
Kāñcanamālā, queen, 196
Kāñcī Kāmakoṭi Pīṭha, 63, 88, 216n19
Kāpālika, 84, 128, 223n93
Kāraṇa Āgama, 55, 247n93
Karṇāvataṃsastuti, 83, 223n92
karṣaṇa rituals, 224n95
Kārttikeya Yakṣīs, 198
Kashmiri Śaiva traditions, 219n48
Kashmiri Śrīvidyā tradition, 82, 219n48
Katampa forest, 195

Katampavaṇapurāṇam (The *purāṇa* of the
    Kadamba Forest), 149, 152, 154–55
Kauṇḍa Bhaṭṭa, 107, 229n15
Kauṇḍinya, 206n4
Kauṇḍinya Gotra, 213n56
Kaulas, 35; Kaula Śrīvidyā, 77–79, 83–85, 220n70
kavi praśaṃsā, 157
Kavitārkikasiṃha, 105
Kāvyadarpaṇa, 66, 217n25
Kāvyādarśa, 82
Kāvyaprakāśa, 82
Keśava Dīkṣita, 221n72
Keśavsvāmī, 229n9
Keune, John, 229n9
Khanna, Madhu, 219n48
Knott, Kim, 180
knowledge [*jñāna*], 42
Kodandaramaiah, T., 243n59
Koppedrayer, K. I., 228n2, 242n44, 247n95
Krama, Kālī, 214n5, 245n73
Krama Stotra, 218n36
kriyā, 42
Kriyāsāra, 218n41
Kṛṣṇa bhakti, 48
Kṛṣṇānanda Sarasvatī, 67
Kṛṣṇa Yajurveda, 37, 82
Kṛta Yuga, 145
Kruijtzer, Gijs, 213n55
Kulabhūṣaṇa Pāṇḍya, 198
kuladevatā (family deity), 72
kulaguru, 65
Kulasāra, 35, 207n10
Kulaśekhara Pāṇḍya, 195, 237n3
Kulke, Hermann, 215n7
Kulottuṅga Pāṇḍya, 197
Kumārakurupara, 155
Kumārasvāmin, 40, 42, 43, 44
Kumpakonam *purāṇa*, 175–76
Kuṇḍalinī yoga, 62, 223n93
Kuppuswami Sastri Research Institute, 56
Kūrma Purāṇa, 109, 123, 131, 132, 236n70, 236n73,
    236n75
Kuruntokai, 164, 245n74
Kuśakumudvatīyanāṭaka, 59
Kuvalayānanda, 10
K. V. Sharma Research Institute, 89

Laghu Stotra, 61
Lakṣmīdhara: 221n75; on external worship,
    85; and Kālidāsa, 61, 215n10; and Samayin
    Śrīvidyā, 78–85, 221n78, 223–24n95
La Legende des Jeux de Çiva à Madurai, 239n20

Lalitāsahasranāma, 1–2, 91, 222n88

Lalitopākhyāna, 88, 91, 94, 95–96, 132

Language games of Śiva, 137–94

LaRocque, Brendan, 205n22

Leach, Robert, 210n35

Lefebvre, Henri, 181

lexicography and etymology in intersectarian debate, 120–28

liberation [*mokṣa*], 42; Liberation to crane, giving, 200

liṅga, 35, 109, 111, 195, 197, 201

Liṅgamāhātmya, 109, 111

liṅgapratiṣṭhānavidhi, 35

Liṅga Purāṇa, 109, 111, 131, 230n22

Lives of Indian Saints, 55

Lives of Saints, 185

Long, Jeffrey, 191

longue durée, 24

Lorenzen, David, 203n3

Ludden, David, 242n41, 245n74

Luhmann, Niklas, 13, 97–98, 184, 205n24, 227n130, 249n1

Lutgendorf, Philip, 205n32

Madanna, 213n55

Mādhavīya *Saṅkara Vijaya*, 88, 225n102, 225n104

Madhuravāṇī, 240n32

Madhusūdana Sarasvatī, 48, 206n2

Madhva, 46, 115, 231n31, 232n43, 234n59; critique by Appayya Dīkṣita, 12, 115; scriptural exegesis, 46, 120, 232n43; scriptural passages, fabrication of, 115–16

Madhvamukhacapeṭikā, 113, 231n28

Madhvatantracapeṭikāvyākhyāna, 231n28

Madhvatantramukhabhūṣaṇa, 231n37

Madhvatantramukhamardana, 12, 114, 115, 117, 118, 231n32, 231n33, 232n39

Mādhva Vaiṣṇavism, 45–46, 114–115; Appayya Dīkṣita, debate with, 114–20; and branding (*taptamudrādharaṇa*), 132; and Dvaita Vedānta, 45–46; Mādhva theologians, 53, 114, 121; Mīmāṃsā hermeneutics, views on, 116–19; and Navya Nyāya, 106, 114–116; scriptural exegesis, 120–21, 124–25, 130; *upakrama* vs *upasaṃhāra* debate, 112

Madurai, 195, 196, 197, 198, 199, 200, 201, 219n46. *See also* specific entries; Cittirai Festival, 26, 57, 62–63, 71, 138, 179–80, 238n10; Nāyaka kingdoms of, 29, 144; public religious culture in seventeenth-century, 175–82; Sthalapurāṇa of, invention of, 143–49; *Tiruviḷaiyāṭal Purāṇam* in seventeenth-century, 175–82

Maduraic Cokkanātar Ulā, 148

Maduraikkalampakam, 243n51

Māghu, 157

Magnone, Paolo, 206n7

Mahābhārata, 117, 220n60

Mahābhāṣyapradīpa, 49

Mahābhāṣyapradīpaprakāśa, 211n41

Mahādeva Dīkṣita, 213n56

Mahāpāśupata, 131, 236n72

mahāpāśupatavrata, 128–29

Mahārthamañjarī, 221n71

Mahārthamañjarīparimala, 221n81

Maheśvara, 42

Maheśvarānanda, 221n71

Mahātripurasundarī, 76

mahāvākya, 46

Mahīdhara, 215n16

Mahipati, 229n9

Mahotsavavidhi, 209n22

Mālatīmādhava, 82

Malayadhvaja, 195, 196

Malayalam, 63

Mālinīvijayottara, 207n9

Mānavadharmaśāstra, 131

maṅgala verses, 113

Māṇikkavācakar, 145, 171, 201, 248n102

Maṇipravāḷam, 10, 204n14

Mantramahodadhi, 215n16

Mantramārga, 36, 37, 38, 73, 128, 235n64, 242, 203n5

mantriṇī (chief minister) of Lalitā, 94

Maratha court of Tanjavur, 60

Marriage of Kuśa and Kumudvatī, 57–58

Martin, P. Pierre, 142

Marty, Martin E., 20

Masuzawa, Tomoko, 203n10

Mataṅgapārameśvara, 41

Mātaṅgī, 85

maṭha, See monastery

maṭhādhipatya, 53

mātṛkāpīṭha, 162

Matsya Purāṇa, 111, 211n36

māyāvādins, 48

McCrea, Lawrence, 45, 104, 210n29, 210n34, 231n36

Megasthenes, 237n4

Meru, mount, 196–97

Mesquita, Roque, 231n31

metrics: Sanskrit, 41, 89, 94, 115, 117, 164; Tamil, 153, 155

Meykaṇṭar, 155

Mīmāṃsā, 17, 40, 43, 104; Appayya Dīkṣita, defended by, 114–120; early modern, 52–53, 55; and philology, 104–05; hermeneutics, 74, 118–19, 170–71; and sectarianism, 17, 106, 119, 130, 228n1; and Vedas, authorlessness of, 40

Mīmāṃsāsūtrabhāṣya, 118

Mīnākṣī, 49–50, 137–39, 141, 155, 166, 177; as *kuladevatā*, 71–72, 189; as *mantriṇī*, 188; sacred marriage of, 26, 50, 57, 178–9

Mīnākṣī-Sundareśvara Temple, 26 138–39; festivals, 26, 178, 180; historical chronicles, 178, 241n39; honors, distribution of, 154; management of, 53–54; performance of literary works, 138, 152; and public space, 178–82; *putu maṇṭapam*, 50; rennovation, 165, 177, 247–48n100; and Śrīvidyā, 226n114; *See also* Cittirai festival

Minatcicuntara Pillai, 175, 176, 241n36, 245n74, 247n97

Mīṉāṭcīyammai Piḷḷaittamiḻ, 243n51

Ministers, changing piglets into, 200

Minkowski, Christopher, 204n20, 215n14, 215n16, 229n11, 238n7

Mirnig, Nina, 206n6

Modi, Narendra, 190

mokṣa, 42–43

Mokṣadharma, 42

Mokṣopāya, 231n29

monastery (*maṭha, maṭam*): Kāñcī Kāmakoṭi Pīṭha, 63, 88, 189, 216n19; Mādhva, 212n51; and the religious public, 20, 22, 68, 183; Śaiva Siddhānta, 40; Śākta, 213n56; Śaṅkarācārya, 2–3, 27, 29, 64, 188, 205n38, 215n7, 225n109; Sringeri, 2, 88; 188, 215n7, 215n8; Tamil Śaiva, 138, 155–156, 238n6, 242n45, 247n95, 247n97

Monier-Williams, Monier, Sir, 7–8, 13, 31, 190, 203n9

Mount Kailāsa, 142

Mount Meru, 94; with mace, hitting, 196–97

Mṛgendra Āgama, 41

Mūkakavi, 87, 187, 224n101, 249n8

Mūkapañcaśatī, 224n101, 250n8

Muktabodha Indological Research Institute, 207n7

Mukti Maṇḍapa, 21

Mulaicai, 154

Multilingual literary: production in Nāyaka-period South India, sites of, 149–59; sphere, 146

Murukaṉ, incarnation of, 196, 200

Mutaliyar caste, 54

Nagojī Bhaṭṭa, 228n88

na hi nindā 118–19

Nairuktika etymology, 120

Naiṣadhīyacarita, 82, 157

Naiyāyika, 116

Nakkīrar, 170, 171, 200

nakṣatramālā, 64

Nalacaritranāṭaka, 204n17

Nallaṉ, farmer, 199

Nalla Adhvarin, 68

Nampi, Perumparrapuliyūr, 138–39, 146–150, 237n3, 238n5, 238n6, 239n24

Nampi's *TVP. See Tiruvilaiyāṭal Purāṇam (TVPs)*

Ñānacampantar, 87, 145, 171, 172–74, 201, 224n101

Nandi, 198, 201

Nannaya, 157

Nāradīya, 125

Narasimhan, Haripriya, 49, 205n36, 205n37

Nārāyaṇa, 107, 228n6; many meanings of, 120–28

Nārāyaṇācārya, 114–15, 117–20, 130, 212n51, 231n29

Nārāyaṇaśabdanirukti, 124, 127, 232n46, 232n48, 233n50, 233n55, 234n57, 234n58, 235n60

Nārāyaṇaśabdārthanirvacana, 121

Nārāyaṇaśabdasādhāraṇya, 122–23, 232n48, 233n49, 233n51, 233n52, 233n53, 233n54, 234n56

Nārāyaṇaśabdasādhāraṇyakhaṇḍana, 232n48

Nareśvaraparīkṣāprakāśa, 209n27

Nārumpūnātacāmi temple (Tiruppudaimarudur), 248n105

naṣṭakośa, 109, 110

nāstikas, 5, 32, 35

Naṭarāja temple (Cidambaram), 179, 248n105

Nāth Maṭhādhipati of Mṛgasthalī (Nepal), 207n7

Naṭavacandrikā, 232n47

Naṭavadarpaṇa, 232n47

Naṭavakhaṇḍana, 232n47

Naṭavatattvaparitrāṇa, 232n47

Naṭavatattvavibhūṣaṇa, 232n47

Navya Nyāya, 106, 114–16

Nāyaka kingdoms, 26–27, 29, 144. *See also* Madurai, Tanjavur; Nāyaka portrait sculptures, 211n43

Nāyaka-period South India, 144, 146; *kavi praśaṃsā*, 157; sites of multilingual literary production in, 149–59; vernacular of, 150

neo-Hinduism, 190; neo-Hindu universalism, 25

New Catalogus Catalogorum, 122, 225n106

Nicholson, Andrew, 5, 38, 47–48, 203n3, 211n37, 211n38

nididhyāsana, 75, 76

Nīlakaṇṭha Bhāṣya, 127, 234n59; *See also*
  Śrīkaṇṭha Bhāṣya
Nīlakaṇṭha Caturdhara, 104
Nīlakaṇṭha Dīkṣita, 49–56; *agrahāra* in
  Palamadai, 1–2, 188–9; and Appayya Dīkṣita,
  11, 49, 71, 218–19n45; disciple of Gīrvāṇendra
  Sarasvatī, 63–68, 215–16n17; hagiography of,
  55, 185–87; interlocutors in north India, 52;
  on poetics, 14, 144–45, 166–168; and public
  philology, 101–02, 108–117; and public
  religious embodiment, 128–135; as public
  theologian, 16–18, 20, 184; and the "Sacred
  Games" in Madurai, 24, 26, 164–75; and Śaiva
  Siddhānta, 73, 173–75; and sectarian polemic,
  15, 108–117; as Śrīvidyā practitioner, 15, 29,
  68, 70–77, 86; on the vernacular, 144–46,
  170–175.
Nīlakaṇṭha Dīkṣita, works of:
  211n40; *Ānandasāgarastava*, 50,
  71–72; *Gurutattvamālikā*, 64, 67,
  215–16n17; *Kaliviḍambana*, 14, 70;
  Mahābhāṣyapradīpaprakāśa, 49,
  211n41; *Nīlakaṇṭhavijayacampū*,
  239n13; *Saubhāgyacandrātapa*,
  70–77; *Śivalīlārṇava*, 144–46, 164–75;
  Śivatattvarahasya, 73 ,76, 100–02, 108–113;
  Śivotkarṣamañjarī, 31, 56
Nīlakaṇṭhavijayacampū, 239n13
Nīpāraṇyapurāṇam, 149
nirguṇa bhakti, 205n29
nirguṇa brahman, 118
Niśvāsatattvasaṃhitā, 207n9, 219n50;
  Niśvāsaguhyasūtra, 35, 207n9;
  Niśvāsamūlasūtra, 128, 235n64
Nityā goddesses, 214n4
Nityākaula, 214n4
Nityāṣoḍaśikārṇava, 221n81
Novetzke, Christian, 24, 203n8
Nṛsiṃhāśramin, 63, 215–16n17, 215n15, 215n16
Nūṟcirappuppāyiram, 239n24
Nussbaum, Martha C., 192, 193, 194, 205n34,
  250n17, 250n20
Nyāyādhvadipikā, 115, 231n30
Nyāyamauktikamālā, 115
Nyāyāmṛta, 114
Nyāyarakṣāmaṇi, 10
Nyāyasaṅgraha, 115

Oddie, G. A., 242n44
O'Hanlon, Rosalind, 205n33, 211n44
Olivelle, Patrick, 235n62, 235n63
Omakareshwara (Madhya Pradhesh), 206n2

Oriental Historical Manuscripts, 54, 212n53,
  237n2
Orientalist philology, 7–8
Oriental Research Institute (Mysore), 70,
  225n105
orthodox *(āstika)*, 4–5, 32, 38, 43

Padārthadīpikā, 107, 112
Padārthadīpikāvyākhyā, 229n13, 229n14
paddhatis, 49, 68, 206n6
Pākhaṇḍacapeṭikā, 132–33, 237n77
pākhaṇḍas, 48
Palamadai, 1–2, 4, 188, 214n60, 219n46, 224n99
Palkuriki Somanātha, 240n32
Palm leaf manuscript, 211n41, 218n42
pañcamakāras, 78, 221n77
Pañcamatabhañjana Tātācārya, 11
Pañcarārtra; 34, 210n35, Pañcarātra Āgama,
  222n85
Pañcastavī, 77, 215n10, 217n33; *See also*
  Ambāstava (Hymn to the mother)
Pandian King's fever, curing, 201
Pandian rulers, 158; 195–201, 237n4
Pāṇinian grammar, 120–21, 124, 130
Paramañānacivan, 138, 238n6
Paramaśiva, 10, 41, 112–13, 121, 124, 191
Paramokṣanirāsakārikā, 43, 209n27
Paramokṣanirāsakārikāvṛtti, 219n51
Parañcōti Muṉivar, 27, 138, 143, 145–46; dating,
  138, 162–64; citations of, 149; sequence
  of "Sacred Games" of, 195; *Tiruviḷaiyāṭal
  Purāṇam*, 138–39, 147–48, 151–52, 159–64; *See*
  also *Tiruviḷayāṭal Purāṇam*
Parāśara Upapurāṇa, 131
Paraśurāmakalpasutra, 221n70
Pārijātaharaṇa, 221n72
Pārvatī, 224n101
"the passion of hicks for vernacular texts,"
  165–75
Pāśupatas, 43, 47, 131, 206n2, 206n4, 206n6,
  208n15; Pāśupata ascetics, 133–34;
  pāśupatavrata, 130; Pāñcārthika Pāśupatas,
  128, 206n2
Patañjali, 139, 196, 238n5
Patañjalicaritra, 51, 91, 226n113
Patañjalicaritravyākhyā, 211n45
Pattabiramin, P. Z., 237n2, 239n20
Pauwels, Heidi, 205n21
Payakaramālai, 147
Pedda Rāma, 148, 156
Pennington, Brian, 203n3
Periyapurāṇam, 167, 172, 240n32

Perumpaṟṟapuliyūr Nampi. *See* Nampi,
    Perumpaṟṟapuliyūr.
philology, 103–05, public philology, 101, 106; and
    public religious culture, 102–7, 125; in the
    public sphere, 128–36; and sectarian polemic,
    112, Orientalist philology, 8
Picumatabrahmayāmala, 223n93
Piglets: changing, into ministers, 200; giving
    breast to, 200
Pināka bow, 114
Pinch, William, 205n30
Plank, Caṅkam, 162, 168–69, 200; giving the, 199;
pluralism: and caste, 192; emic, 25, 48, 193–4;
    and inclusivism, 107, 191–92, linguistic, 140;
    modern, 189–94; and public space, 24–27,
    194; religious, 193–94; and sectarianism, 1–6,
    14, 31; Western, 192–3; *See also specific* entries
Pluralism and Democracy in India, 192
Pollock, Sheldon, 15, 211n44, 229n7, 231n34,
    238n11; and Sanskrit Cosmopolis, 48;
    Pollock's model of Vernacular Millennium,
    150–151; definition of philology, 103
Ponnanaiyāḷ, 199
Potter, Karl, 229n15
prakaraṇa, 171
Prakāśa, 49
Prākṛtamaṇidīpikā, 141, 238n7
prakṛti, 119
pramāṇa theory, 17, 228n1
Prapañcasāra, 63, 215n12
Prapañcasārasaṅgraha, 63, 65–66, 215n16
Prapannāmṛta, 204n18, 204n19
Prasad, Leela, 205n37
praśasti, 10, 32
Prasthānabheda, 48
Pratyabhijñā school of Kashmiri Śaivism, 72, 74
prāyaścitta, 208n18
Prāyaścittasamuccaya, 39, 208n17, 208n18
Prentiss, Pechilis, 242n46
Protestant Reformation, 205n27
Pūrva Mīmāṃsā, See Mīmāṃsā
pūrvapakṣin, 108
Pūrvottaramīmāṃsāvādanakṣatramālā, 231n34
publicity: and caste, 19, 135, 140–41, 181;
    circulation, 106, 137; and civil society,
    17, 19–22, 25, 192–94; counterpublics,
    22–23, 140; and definition of Hinduism, 5–6;
    embodiment, 128–136; and esotericism, 183,
    188, 224n99; and festivals, 27, 30, 140–42,
    178–81; and literacy, 24, 178; literary publics,
    57, 141, 152; mulitple publics, 6, 22–23,
    193–94, 140; orthopraxy, 131; and private

identity, 27, 100, 134–35; public canon, 176;
    public culture, 21, 24, 140–41, 181–82; public
    discourse, theolgoization of, 17–20; public
    memory, 70, 139, 167, 184, 186; public sphere,
    bourgeois (Habermas) 21–24, 140; public
    spheres, parallel, 22–23, 27, 182; reception,
    143; religious publics, 6, 12–13, 19–22 , 29,
    70, 141, 184; and secularism, 15–18, 181, 192;
    space, *See* public space; and temple worship,
    34, 37, 180–81
public philology, 100; constitutive of sectarian
    community boundaries, 101; etymology
    and lexicography, in, 120–128; and
    public space, 106, 133–36; and Sanskrit
    knowledge systems, 114–120; and sectarian
    polemic, 102, 105–08, 112
public religious culture: 12, 62; and philology,
    100, 102; in seventeenth-century Madurai,
    140–42, 175–82;
public space: 19–27, 133–36, 176, 178, 180 , 192–4;
    and pluralism, 194; and sectarian identities,
    22, 193; *See also* publicity
public theology, 6, 19–24; definition, of Martin
    Marty, 20; and embodiment, 128–136;
    making of a sectarian community, 27–30, 183;
    as public philology, 100; and public space,
    134; in Smārta-Śaivism, 49–56, and social
    systems, 189
Punjab University Library (Lahore), 89, 215n12
Purāṇas, 46–47, 149, 162; authoritativeness of, 47,
    108, 129; Śaiva, 102, 106–14; Vaiṣṇava, 46–7,
    100–101, 107–14, 123; *See also specific Purāṇas*
Purāṇa Tirumalainātar, 148, 154, 155, 175
Puṣpadanta, 32–33
Putu Maṇṭapam, 50, 177, 178

Raghavan, V., 220n62, 238n7
Rāghavendra Tīrtha, 53, 55, 212n51
Rāghavendra Vijaya, 212n51
Raghunātha Nāyaka, 157, 240n32, 243–44n60
Raghunātharāmāyaṇamu, 243n60
Raghunāthavilāsa, 165
rajas, 47, 108
Raju, Vadhluri Anjaneya, 239–40n25
Ramakrishna Paramahamsa, 189
Ramanathan, Adayapalam, 249n5
Raman, Srilata, 203n6
Ramesan, N., 204n13, 204n17
Ramnad, 214n58
Raṅgoji Bhaṭṭa, 229n15
Rao, Ajay K., 45, 210n34, 214n3, 215n9
Rao, N. Venkata, 240n31, 243n59

Rao, Velcheru Narayana, 239n12, 240n27

Rastogi, Navjivan, 218n36

Ratnamālā, 123

Reflections on Resemblance, Ritual and Religion, 33

reformation, 7; Protestant Reformation, 18, 205n27

Religion: church and sect, 7; comparison of, 16; in early modern South India, 14–19; and materialism, 102–03; and modernity, 17–21; and public space, 21–22, 25, 135, 180–81, 193–94; religious identity, 2, 6, 25, 183; religious pluralism, 193–94; and "sacred space," 180; and secularism, 16–19, 135; and violence, 19–20; world religions, concept of, 8

Religious publics, 5–6, 22–23, 140–4; construction of, 70; and Hindu sectarianism, 23, 101; as multiple, 135–36, 181, 194; *See also* publicity

"representational space," 181

Ṛgbhāṣya, 232n43

Ṛgveda, 35, 82, 104

Rice, Benjamin Lewis, 206n1

Richardson, E. Allen, 250n19

Richman, Paula, 243n51

Rājacūḍāmaṇi Dīkṣita, 66–69; as court poet of Tanjavur, 89, 165; disciple of Gīrvāṇendra Sarasvatī, 66–67; poetics of, 89–90, 93 ,97; and Śrīvidyā, 87–97, 222n85, 226n117

Rājacūḍāmaṇi Dīkṣita, works of: *Kāvyadarpaṇa,* 66; *Raghunāthavilāsa,* 165; *Śaṅkarābhyudaya,* 69, 87–97; *Śaṅkarācāryatārāvali,* 217n25

rājaguru, 54, 218n41

Rājaśekhara Pāṇḍya, 197

Rāmabāṇastava, 51, 211n47

Rāmabhadra Dīkṣita, 51, 67–68, 91, 211n47, 217n28, 217n29, 226n113

Rāmacandrendra Sarasvatī, 64

Rāmakaṇṭha II, 43, 209n26, 209n27, 219n51

Rāmakṛṣṇa Sūri, 89, 225n107

Rāmānanda, 221n78

Rāmānuja, 46, 47, 108–9, 209n28, 210n36, 220n62, 229n17

Rāmarāja Bhūṣaṇa, 240n31, 240n32

Rāmāśrama Dīkṣita, 205n20

Rāmāyaṇasāra, 240n32

Rāmāyaṇasāratilaka, 240n32

Rudra, 112–13, 121, 191

rūḍhir yogam apaharati, 124

rudrākṣa, 132

Śabara, 118

Śābara Bhāṣya, 246n85

sabhāpati, 57

Saccidānanda Śivābhinava Bhāratī, 215n9

Sacred city, establishing, 195

"Sacred Games of Siva," 26, 29–30, 137–43; canonization of, 148, 159–65, 178, 182; early history of, 237n4; performance of, 53, 178–80; and public culture, 30, 140, 182; multilingual variants, 143–149; representation in painting and sculpture, 177–78, 81, 237n2, 248n101, 248n104, 248n105; translations of, 237n2; *See also* Sacred Marriage, *Tiruviḷaiyāṭal Purāṇam*

Sacred Marriage, of Mīnākṣī, 26, 50, 57, 178–9, 196, 237n4

"sacred space," 180–81; *See also* space

Sadāśiva, 216n21

Sadāśiva Brahmendra, 68

Sadāśiva Dīkṣita, 213n56

ṣaḍdarśanas, 48

Sadyojyotis, 219n51

saguṇa, 73, 112–13, 118

Sāhityasarvasva, 221n72

Sahṛdaya, 89, 225n104

Sai Baba, 26

Saiddhāntika, *See* Śaiva Siddhānta

Śaiva, 2–3; *adhvan*s, 64; Atimārga, 128, 235n64; Āgamas, 40– 43, 45, 55, 72– 76, 173, 207n9, 219n53; Brahmins, 24, 30, 42, 132, 197; initiation (*dīkṣā*), 36; *Mantramārga,* 36, 38, 73; Purāṇas, 102, 106, 107–14; Saiddhāntikas, 43; scriptures, 76, 105, 128; *tattva* systems, 34; theology, 10, 11, 28, 42, 204; *tilaka,* 134–35; *tripuṇḍra,* 92. See also *tripuṇḍra*; and Vaidika, 31– 38; *See also* Śaivism

Śaiva Advaita: *See* Śivādvaita

"The Śaiva Age", 34

Śaiva Dharmaśāstra literature, 35; *See also* Śivadharma, Śivadharmottara

Śaiva Viśiṣṭādvaita, 209n28; *See also* Śrīkaṇṭha, *Śrīkaṇṭhabhāṣya*

Śaivakarṇāmṛta, 127, 234n59

Śaivaparibhāṣā of Śivāgrayogin, 73

Śaiva Siddhānta 35, 38–41; and caste, 39, 172–73; initiation (*dīkṣā*), 173–74, 221n76; and non-dualism, 40, 73, 208n15, 219n51, 219n52; ritual, 55, 224n95, 230n22, 247n92; Saiddhāntika scriptures (Āgamas), 35, 40–43, 45, 55, 72–6, 173 207n9, 219n50, 219n53, 220n67, 240n93; Saiddhāntika temples, 55; and Śrīvidyā, 72–73, 76–77; Tamil Śaiva Siddhānta, 9, 154, 171–175, 228n2, 240n32, 242n46, 242n47, 244n62; theologians, 43, 208n19; theology, 216n21

Śaivism, 33; Āgamic, of Mantramārga, 203n5; and brahminical orthodoxy, 38–44; as a distinct religion, 5; transformation of, 203n5; *See also* Śaiva Siddhānta
Śaivism and Vaiṣṇavism, 7–9, 31, 46; *See also* specific entries.
sakalīkaraṇa, nyāsa, 37
Śāktism, 15, 59, 86; and Appayya Dīkṣita, 49, 218–19n45; of ferocious Goddesses, 85, 213n45; and Kālidāsa, 61–63, 217–18n26; in Kashmir, 72, 82; and Śaṅkarācārya, 77, 79–81, 87, 92–97; sectarian marks, 92–93; scriptures, 76; and Tamil Śaivism, 60, 162–63, 214n5; *See also* Śrīvidyā
śaktipāta, 65
Sāḷuva Nāyaka, 9
samādhi shrines, 55
Samarapuṅgava Yajvan, 204n17
samaya, 78, 82
Samaya Śrīvidyā, 79, 82–85; *See also* Śrīvidyā
Samayimatajīvana, 79; *See also* Ambāstavavyākhyā
Sāmbapurāṇa, 131
saṃhāra (destruction), 42
Sāṃkhya *guṇas,* 112
sampradāya, 5, 12, 209n28; *See also* specific entries
Sanaka, 84
Sanatkumārasaṃhitā, 222n85
Sanderson, Alexis, 5, 36, 206n6, 206n7, 207n9, 214n4, 215n9, 235n64, 236n72, 244–45n68; and the Śaiva Age, 34
saṅghaphalaka, 162; *See also* Caṅkam plank
Śaṅkarābhyudaya, 66, 69, 87–97, 222n86, 224–25n102, 225n104, 225n109
Śaṅkarācārya, 60; chronicles (*digvijaya*), 88–89, 92–93, 217n34, 224–25n102; and goddess worship (Śrīvidyā), 80–81, 87–97, 189; Jagadgurus, 4, 27, 60; and Kālidāsa, 58–62; and Kanchipuram, 29, 64, 69, 216n19; and the making of sectarian community, 62, 97–98; monasteries (*maṭhas*), 2, 60; philosophy (Advaita Vedānta), 61, 76, 128, 220n62, 220n66, 235n63; and Smarta Brahmins, 62–70; Śaṅkarācārya monastic lineages, 29, 60–61, 70, 79, 187–89, 215n7, 215n8; works, attributed, 77–78, 80–81, 217n33
Śaṅkarācāryapuram, 216n19
Śaṅkarācāryatārāvali, 217n25
Śaṅkaradigvijaya, 87–88, 93
Śaṅkaravijaya, 225n102, 225n110, 226n111
Śaṅkaravijayavilāsa, 226n111, 226n115
Sāṅkhya, 43, 47, 108
Saṅkṣepaśārīraka, 215n15
Sanskrit: aesthetics, *See* Alaṅkāraśāstra; metrics, 41, 89, 94, 115, 117, 164; Sanskritic Śaiva Siddhānta, 38–39; Sanskrit Smārta culture, 187; and vernacular, relationship between, 150
Sanskrit Cosmopolis, 58
Sanskrit knowlege systems, 115–16, 125, 128, 142; classical, 228n1
Sanskrit Knowledge Systems Project, 15
Śāntivilāsa, 75, 220n64
Śāradā Dhvajamu, 158, 244n61
Śāradā Pīṭha, 89
Sārasamuccaya, 150
Sarasvatī, 200, 227n129
Sarasvati Bhavan Library (Varanasi), 211n41
Sarasvatīkaṇṭhābharaṇa, 209n20
Śārīrādhikaraṇa, 44
Sarma, S. L. P. Anjaneya, 219n51
Sarma, Varanasi Raj Gopal, 216n19
Sarvajñānottara, 208n19, 219n52
Sarvajñapīṭha, 66, 88
sarvaśabdavācyatva, 120, 124
sarvatantrasvatantra, 10, 115
śāstra, 23, 36, 48–49, 51, 170; *śāstric* discipline, 104; *See also* specific entries
Śāstradīpikāvyākhyā, 52
Śāstramālāvyākhyāna, 52, 212n48
Sastri, Mahalinga, 213n54
Sastri, P. P. S., 71, 187, 218n38, 218n42
Sastri, Ramakrsna, 227n120
Sastri, Sankara Rama, 187, 188, 250n9
Sastri, Suryanarayana, 220n65
Sastri, Y. M., 204n13
śāśvataṃ śivam acyutam, 109
Śatarudrīya, 37
Sathyanarayanan, R., 208n17
sattva, 108
Satyanarayanaravu, Yandamuri, 244n61
Satyānandanātha, 215n9
Satyāprīṇana, 221n72
Saubhāgyacandrātapa, 11, 15, 49, 55, 66, 68, 129, 131, 187, 204n15, 211n42, 217n32, 218n38, 218n41, 219n53, 220n68; authorship, 71; manuscripts, 70; Śrīvidyā and society in, 70–77
Saubhāgyacintāmaṇi, 80, 222n84
Saubhāgyapaddhati, 71
Saubhāgyavidyā, 80–82, 87, 221n81
Saundaryalaharī, 61, 80, 82, 84, 85, 86, 97, 222n83, 223n97

Savarkar, V. D.: envisioning of Hindutva, 2
Sawai Jai Singh II, 12
Sāyaṇa, 229n10
Schonthal, Benjamin, 250n16
Schwartz, Jason, 206n7, 207n12, 220n68, 229n17
scripture: exegesis, 109, 116–20, 130, 170–71; Kaula, 35; and philology, 105, 107–14; Śaiva (Āgama), 37, 40, 55, 73–74, 128, 172–73; Śākta, 76, 81, 83; and sectarianism, 5, 17, 29, 100–01, 105, 127, 130–32; Tamil language, 73; Vedic, 38, 41–44, 46, 60, 74; See also specific entries
Seastrand, Anna, 243n54, 248n105
sectarianism, 5–6, 190; and communalism, 7; defined by Ernst Troeltsch (sect), 7; defined by Monier Monier-Williams, 8, 190; and definition of Hinduism, 5–6, 190; Hindu sectarian community, making of, 189–94; and Orientalism, 13; origin of, 45–48; parallel, 22; and pluralism, 1–6, 24, 192–94; sectarian communities, 6, 13, 27–30; sectarian identity, embodiment of, 128–136; sectarianization of classical knowledge systems, 114–20; sectarian publics, construction of India's, 19–24; sectarian scripture, 105; sectarian social systems, 98; and violence, 6–7
secularism, 14, 17–18, 205n27, 205n28; global, 192–93
secularization, 17–18, 20, 22, 135
self [ātman], 42
Sen, Keshab Chandar, 8
Setupati king, 214n58
Sharma, B. N. K., 212n51
Shulman, David, 160, 162, 176, 239n12, 239n15, 239n16, 239n19, 239n20, 240n27, 244n68, 247n98, 249n7
Siddhāntakalpavallī, 68
Siddhāntaleśasaṅgraha, 68
Siddhis, eight great, 198
Sidney, Philip, Sir, 69
Śikhariṇīmālā, 234n59
Silver Hall, of Madurai temple, 196
śirovrata, 130
Śiva, sixty-four games, 195–201
Śiva and Mīnākṣī: sacred marriage, 26, 57
Śivadharma, 35, 206–7n7, 207n8, 207n9, 207n12
Śivadharmottara, 36, 206–7n7
Śivādvaita: philosophy, 9–11, 45, 67, 112, 209–10n28, 210n29; of Śrīkaṇṭha, 75, 209–10n28; of Appayya Dīkṣita, 9–11, 44–45, 75–76, 205n26, 209–10n28, 234n59; and Sanskritic Vīraśaivism, 43, 45, 73, 205n26

Śivādvaitanirṇaya, 220n65
Śivalīlārṇava (ŚLA), 53, 63, 87, 144–46, 164–175, 239n13; poetics in, 167–68; Śaivism in, 171–74; and the vernacular, 144–46, 165–66
śivaliṅga, 35, 111, 195, 197
Śivamahimnaḥ Stotram, 32, 33, 190, 206n2, 206n3, 250n13
Sivananda, Swami, 185
Śivapurāṇa, 123, 127
Śivarahasya, 184
Śivārcanacandrikā, 11, 71, 76
Śivārkamaṇidīpikā, 10, 11, 44, 45, 127, 204n17, 220n63, 234n59
Śivāṣṭottarasahasranāmastotra, 49, 73
Śivastutisūktimālikā, 127
Śivatattvarahasya, 15, 49, 55, 73, 76, 100, 101, 108, 117, 127, 219n53, 228n4
Śivatattvaviveka, 127, 234n59
Śivopaniṣad, 207n7
Śivotkarṣamañjarī, 56
Skanda Purāṇa, 108, 127
śleṣa, 120
Smārta Brahmins, 28, 86–87, 95, 205n36, 205n37, 212n52; and Śaṅkarācāryas, 62–70
Smārta-Śaivism, 49; and Advaita Vedānta, 43–44; early modern, 49–55; and hermeneutics (Mīmāṃsā), 106, 116; origins of, 28–29, 62, 97–98; and Kālidāsa, 58–59, 61–62; modern, 183–89, 205n36, 205n37; public embodiment, 128–29, 131–33; public orthodoxy, 77–79, 134, 166, 172; public theology, 28, 100; Śaiva Purāṇas, defense of, 108; as a sectarian community, 6, 27, 62, 189; and Śaṅkarācārya lineages, 4, 27, 60–69, 183–84, 188, 211n47; Śivādvaita, influence of, 209–10n28; and Śrīvidyā, 59–60, 70–77, 187–88; theologians, 9–11, 14–15, 49, 70, 100;
Smith, B. K., 33, 203n2, 206n15
Smith, Jonathan Z., 16
Smith, W. C., 203n2
Somaśambhu, 230n22
Somaśambhupaddhati, 208n16, 247n91
South Indian Temple Inscriptions, 203n11
space: entextualization of, 182; festivals, and, 179; Lefebvre, Henri, 181; polarization of, 25, 133, 193; public, 19–27, 133–36, 176, 178, 180, 192–4; and religious pluralism, 194; "sacred space," 176, 180; and sectarian communities, 27, 106; urban, 6, 23; and visual culture, 26, 181
Śrāddha, 34
Śrauta ritual, 35

Śrīcakra, 66, 87, 88, 90–91, 223n91, 224n99, 226n114

Śrīkaṇṭha, 9–11, 43–45, 67, 75, 205n25, 209–10n28, 210n29, 217n27, 220n63, 234n59

Śrīkaṇṭhabhāṣya, 9–11, 42–45, 205n26, 209n28, 220n63, 234n59, 249n2

Śrīkaṇṭhamatapratiṣṭhāpanācārya, 11, 204n15

Śrīkarabhāṣya, 43, 249n2

Śrīnātha, 157

Sringeri: Sringeri Śaṅkarācāryas, 3–4, 29, 60, 86, 88–89, 188–89, 205n38, 215n7, 215n8, 215n9, 224n99, 224–25n102

Śrīnivāsa Bhaṭṭa, 218n41

Śrīnivāsadāsa, 232n47

Śrīpadārthadīpikā or *Śrīpadārthavyavasthā,* 71

Śrīpati's *Śrīkarabhāṣya,* 43, 249n2

Śrīrudram, 210n32

Śrīvaiṣṇavism, 9, 13, 45, 214n3; Śaiva Purāṇas, interpretation of, 108–09; theologians, 11, 46, 105, 230n20; and Viśiṣṭādvaita Vedānta, 45

Śrīvidyā, 55, 59–60; and Carnatic music, 183, 187; deities, 59, 61, 69, 73, 94–97, 188; history, 60, 214n4, 214n6, 219n48, 219n49; *kādi mata,* 226n117; and Kālidāsa, 59, 61–62, 217n36; Kaula, 77–79, 83–86, 220–21n70, ; and the making of sectarian community, 97–98; mantra, root *(mūlamantra),* 87, 93–94; in Nepal, 222n88; and public esotericism, 183; public philology, contrast with, 102; ritual manuals (paddhati), 70–77; ritual practice *(upāsanā),* ; Samaya (orthodox), 77–87; and Śaṅkarācārya, hagiography of, 87–97; and Śaṅkarācārya lineages, 60, 70, 215n9; scriptures, 68–69; sectarian insignia *(tilaka),* 92–93, 131–32; and Smārta-Śaivism, 62–70, 218–29n45; and worship of images *(yantra),* 83–84, 86

Śrīvidyāsaparyāpaddhati, 187–88, 250n9

Śrīvidyā, scriptures of: Lalitāsahasranāma, 1, 91, 189, 222n88; Lalitopākhyāna, 88, 91, 94–96, 131; Nityākaula, 214n4; Nityāṣoḍaśikārṇava, 221n81; Saubhāgyavidyā and Subhagodaya, 80–81, 83–84, 87, 221n81, 223n95; Śubhāgamapañcaka, 81–82, 84; Vāmakeśvarīmata, 76, 82–83

Śrīvidyā, Society of Mylapore, 187

Śrī Vijayendra Maṭha (Kumbakonam), 212n51

śṛṅgāra rasa, 97

sṛṣṭi (creation), 42

śruti and *smṛti,* 42

Śrutisūktimālā, 249n2

Staal, Frits, 104

Stāṇikarvaralāṟu, 53, 178, 212n49, 213–14n54, 241n39

Stein, Burton, 242n48

Sthalapurāṇa, of Madurai, invention of, 143–49; See also Talapurāṇams

Stietencron, Heinrich von, 203n2

Stoker, Valerie, 210n33, 214n3, 232n43

The Structural Transformation of the Public Sphere, 140

Śubhāgamapañcaka, 81, 82

Subhagodaya, 82, 83, 87, 223n95

Subhagodayastuti, 221n81

Subrahmanyam, P., 55–56

Subrahmanyam, Sanjay, 16, 239n12

Śūdrakamalākara, 220n68

Śūdras, 36, 39, 77, 82, 140, 154, 174, 220n68

Sūtasaṃhitā, 105, 131

Svacchanda Tantra, 36, 207n9, 208n13, 235n64

svakapolakalpita, 115

Svayamprakāśayati, 63

Śvetāśvatara Upaniṣad, 109, 128, 131, 219n54

Sweetman, William, 8, 242n45

Śyāmalā, 94

Śyāmalādaṇḍaka, 218n36

Symbols of Substance, 239n12

systems theory, 13–15, 97–98, 184, 227n130

Taittirīya Śākhā, 82

Taittirīya Saṃhitā, 37

Taittirīya Upaniṣad, 44

Talapurāṇams, 127 139; composition of, 175–76, 241n36, genre, 147, 149–50; of Madurai, 143, 149; performance of, 152

Talavaralāṟu, 212n49

tamas, 47, 108; *tāmasa* Purāṇas, 112–13; *tāmasa śāstra,* 47

Tamil, 28–30, 40, 63, 138–64, 166–7; bhakti saints, 145, 171–74, 185, 201; Brahminism, 27, 49, 58, 205n36, 205n37; Caṅkam, 145, 160–64, 167–69, 200, 237–38n4, 240n27; grammatical theory, 169–71, 244n64; *Tamil Lexicon,* 241n38; literary culture, Cōḷa period, 136; literature, patronage of, 144, 146, 153–56, 241n41; 247n97; Śaiva Siddhānta, 9, 154, 171–175, 228n2, 240n32, 242n46, 242n47, 244n62; Sanskrit and Telugu, relation to, 149–59

Tamil Brahmins: The Making of a Middle Class, 205n36

Tamil Śaivism: bhakti saints, 145, 171–74, 185, 201; canon, 162, 172; monastic centers *(maṭams),* 138, 154–56, 238n6, 242n44, 242n45, 247n97; theology, 163

Tanjavur, 153; Nāyaka kingdoms of, 144, 157. *See also* Nāyaka-period South India

Tanjavur Maharaja Serfoji's Sarasvati Mahal Library, 211n45, 212n48, 249n105

Tantra, 34, 36, 38: and Dharmaśāstra, 35–36, 206n7, 220n68; philosophy, 208n15; ritual manual (*paddhati*), 49, 66, 69–77, 187; ritual practice, 38, 135, 206n6, 208n14, 247n92; tantric Śaivism, 35, 36, 72, 242n46; tantric *saṃskāras*, 77; tantric Vaiṣṇavism, 210n35; transgressive, 77, 82, 85, 92, 184, 221n77; and Vedic Brahminism, 74, 76–87; *See also* Mantramārga, Śaiva Siddhānta, Śrīvidyā

Tantravārttika, 229n8

taptamudrādharaṇa, 132, 237n77

Tarkatāṇḍava, 114

Tarumapuram, 242n44, 242n47

Tarumi, 164, 170; giving prize to, 200

Taṭātakai, incarnation of, 141–42, 195–196

Tattvacintāmaṇi (Crest jewel of principles) of Gaṅgeśa, *114*

Tattvañānaprakācar, 155

Tattvaprakāśa, 40, 209n20

Tattvaviveka, 215n15

Taylor, Charles, 17, 135

Taylor, William, 54, 212n53, 237n2

Telugu: classical literature, 243n57; in multilingual literary sphere, 146; Nāyaka-period literature, 144, 150–51, 239n12, 243n60; and political aesthetics, 156–58; relation to Tamil and Sankrit, 28, 30, 240n31, 240n32; in the "Sacred Games," 139, 143, 148–9, 151, 239n24

Tēvāram, 172

textual criticism, practical applications of, 128–36

theology: 5; beyond the text, 99–107; Dvaita (dualist), 116, 118; public, and sectarian communities 6, 19–20, 24, 27–30, 135, 183, 189; and public philology, 100; Śaiva, 10–11, 34, 40–42; sectarian, 12, 45, 104; Tamil Śaiva, 163; Vedic, 34; of Western modernity, 18

Thomas, Jolyon, 250n16

Tikkana, 157

Tilak, Balagangadhar "Lokamanya": definition of Hinduism by, 31

tilaka, 75, 77, 129–34

tirobhāva (concealment), 42

Tirumalai Nāyaka, 142; Ākāśavāsīs as *rajagurus* of, 55, 213n56; granting Palamadai agrahāra, 219n46; improvement of Mīṇākṣī-Sundareśvara temple, 177–78, 211n43;

patronage of Nīlakaṇṭha Dīkṣita, 49–50, 53–55; Śākta worship of Rājarājeśvarī, 214n58; sponsorship of "Sacred Games," 53, 138, 158, 178–79

Tirumaṅkalakkuṭi Ceṣaiyaṅkār, 176

Tirumantiram, 60, 162, 163, 244n67, 245n71, 245n72; dating, 245n73

Tiruppaṇivivaram, 212n49, 241n39

Tiruvampaḷatēcikar, 174

Tiruvavatuturai, 242n44, 242n47

Tiruvēṅgaḷakavi, 148, 156, 244n63

Tiruviḷaiyāṭal Purāṇam (TVP), of Parañcōti Muṉivar, 138, 146; canonization of, 139, 159–66; citation of, 149; dating, 146, 164–65; and performance of "Sacred Games," 27, 180–81; premiere (*araṅkēṟṟam*), 151–52; Sacred Marriage, treatment of, 137–38; style, 138, 167; as *talapurāṇam* of Madurai, 143, 152, 176; Tamil Caṅkam myths, treatment of, 169–70; *See also* "Sacred Games of Śiva"

Tiruviḷaiyāṭal Purāṇam (TVP), of Perumpaṟṟapuliyūr Nampi: 146, 150; dating, 146; patronage, 238n6; Sacred Marriage, treatment of, 139; style, 138–39, 238n5; title of, 147; See also "Sacred Games of Śiva"

Tiruvuccāttānar Nāṉmaṇimālai, 148

tolerance, 191–92

Tolkāppiyam, 170, 171

transcreation, 148, 156

Treta Yuga, 145

Trika, 72, 207n9;

Trilocanaśiva, 39–40, 208n16, 208n17, 208n18

Trimūrti—Brahmā, Viṣṇu, and Rudra-Śiva, 112–13, 121–23

tripuṇḍra, 128, 130; practice of applying, 129–32

Tripurā Upaniṣad, 221n78

Troeltsch, Ernst, 7, 194, 203n6

The Truth about the Kumbhakonam Mutt, 225n104

Turīyaśivakhaṇḍana, 116–17, 121, 130, 235n67, 235n68

twin texts, 159–65

Ugravarman Pāṇḍya, 196–97

Uṇādimaṇidīpikā, 217n28

Unifying Hinduism, 5, 38, 203n3

unmediated (*aparokṣabhūta*), 42

Unni, N. Parameshwaran, 218n37

Unpublished Upaniṣads, 207n7

upakrama and *upasaṃhāra*, 112

Upaniṣad Brahmendra, 64

Upaniṣads, 82; Upaniṣadic meditation (*brahmavidyā*), 44; *See also* specific entries
upāsana, 75–77
upāsanā, 69, 82, 88, 93, 223n95; *See also* Śrīvidyā
ūrdhvapuṇḍra, 131
utkarṣa, 171
Uttaramahāpurāṇa, 150
Uttara Mīmāṃsā, 115; *See also* Vedānta

Vacucaritram, 240n31
Vādīndra Tīrtha, 53, 212n52
Vaidika, 1, 5, 124; Brahminism, 34; Brahmins, 53, 54; Dharmaśāstras, 77; Hindus, 121; and Śaiva, 31– 38; observances, 35; Śrīvidyā, 80; religions, 206n7, 207n8; ritual technology, 35; *saṃskāras*, 77
Vaikai River, 26, 196, 201
Vaiśeṣika, 119
Vaśiṣṭha Purāṇa, 131
Vaiṣṇavism, 4–5; and Cittirai festival, 26, 179; devotion (bhakti), 12, 205n22, 297n12; and orthodoxy, 12, 102; polemics, 108, 117–120, 126–127; Purāṇas, 46–7, 100–101, 107–14, 123; scripture, 102, 111, 204–5n20, 207n12; and sectarianism, 4–9, 45–48, 105, 193, 197, 210n35; tantric (Pañcarātra), 34, 61, 210n35; temple worship, 19, 32, 54, 100, 140, 193; theologians, 11, 61, 109, 130; and Vedānta, 45–46; *See also*, Mādhva Vaiṣṇavism, Śrīvaiṣṇavism
Vaiyākaraṇabhūṣaṇa, 229n15
Vālmīki, 157
Vālmikicaritramu, 243n60
Vāmakeśvarīmata, 76, 82, 83
van der Veer, Peter, 203n3
Vanikar caste, 198
Varadārāja, 9, 92
Varadārāja temple (Kanchipuram), 203n11
Varaguṇa Pāṇḍya, 199
Vārāhī, 85
Varṇāśramacandrikā, 174, 228n2, 244n62, 247n95, 247n96
varṇāśramadharma, 36, 38, 39, 235n63
Vasanta Maṇṭapam, 54
Vasiṣṭha, 84
Vasiṣṭhasaṃhitā, 222n85
Vasucaritracampū, 240n32
Vasucaritramu, 240n31, 240n32
Vasudeva, Somadeva, 205n25, 207n9
Vātulaśuddhottara Āgama, 55
Vāyu, 115

Vedas, 32, 82, 185, 188, 197, 201, 210n32, 210n35; commentary, 104; and definition of Hinduism, 3, 5, 33; hermeneutics, *See* Mīmāṃsā; and Mādhva Vaiṣṇavism, 46, 124; and Śaivism, 33–37, 129, 133, 140, 144, 172–73, 190, 206n4, 207n8; and Śrīvidyā, 73–76; Vedic sages, 81
Vedānta, 13, 35, 48, 61, 115, 230n20; Age of, 45; and Mīmāṃsā, 43; Vedāntic ontology, 45–46; Vedānta-inflected Śaivism, 43; Vedānta Sūtras, 208n15
Vedānta Deśika, 105, 230n20, 235n63
Vedāntasāra, 215n15
Vedārthasaṅgraha, 47, 108–9, 210n36
Vēḷāḷas, 23, 140, 154–55, 174, 241–42n41, 242n48, 242n49
Veṅkaṭācārya, 232n47
Venkataraman, K. R., 216n19, 225n104
Veṅkaṭeśvara Kavi, 51, 211n45
Venkatkrishnan, Anand, 205n31
Vernacularization, 144–46; Nāyaka-period, 150; re-Sanskritization, 166; Sanskrit and, relationship between, 150–51
Vernacular Millennium, 143, 144, 150; Pollock's model, 151
Vidhirasāyana, 116
vidyābhadrāsana, 93
vidyāpīṭha, 162
Vidyāraṇya, 185
Vijayanagara Empire, 100, 144, 150, 153, 165; Vijayanagara and Nāyaka rule, 9
Vijayarāmārya, 132
Vijayīndra Tīrtha, 116, 121, 123, 130, 231n37
Vijñānabhikṣu, 47–48, 211n37, 211n38
Vīmanāta Paṇṭitar, 149, 152, 154–55
Vināyaka Subrahmaniya, 212n54
violence, 6–7, 19, 20, 22, 190
Vīrarāghava Nāyaka, 158
Vīraśaivism, 232n46; in Andhra Pradesh, 73, 210n29; and Śivādvaita philosophy, 205n26, 210n29, 249n2, 42, 43, 45–46, 73, 218n41; in Vijayanagara region, 43
A Vision for Hinduism: Beyond Hindu Nationalism, 191
Viśiṣṭādvaita, 45
Viṣṇu, 112–13, 207n12, 210n35; as supreme deity, 31
Viṣṇutattvanirṇaya, 234n59
Viśvanātha Nāyaka, 165, 177
Viśveśvara Temple, 21
Viswanathan, S., 218n37

Vivaraṇasāra, 221n72
Vivekananda, Swami, 189, 190–91,
    192, 250n12
Vṛtra, demon, 195
Vyāghrapada, sage, 196
Vyāsa, 157
Vyāsa Tīrtha, 114–15

Wallerstein, Immanuel, 16
Wallis, Christopher, 217n24
Warner, Michael, 23, 140
Wars of Religion, 19–20
Watson, Alex, 209n26, 209n27, 219n51
Weber, Max, 7, 17, 203n6, 205n22
Wentworth, Blake, 241n37, 243n49
White, David Gordon, 247n91
White, Hayden, 18–19

Wilden, Eva, 238n4, 239n20
Wilke, Annette, 219n49, 221n70
Wittgenstein, Ludwig, 143

Yajur Veda, 210n32
Yama, 197
yamaka (paronomasia), 90, 145
Yānaimalai mountain, 137, 197
Yāska's Nirukta, 120
Yātrāprabandha, 204n17
Yoga, school (*darśana*) of Brahminical
    philosophy, 34
Yogavāsiṣṭha, 231n29
Yogi Nara Hari Nath, 207n7

Ziegenbalg, Bartholomäus, 8
Zvelebil, Kamil, 238n4

CPSIA information can be obtained
at www.ICGtesting.com
Printed in the USA
LVOW01s0958010317

525658LV00004B/9/P